C++ Data Structures and Algorithm Design Principles

Leverage the power of modern C++ to build robust and scalable applications

John Carey

Shreyans Doshi

Payas Rajan

C++ Data Structures and Algorithm Design Principles

Authors: John Carey, Shreyans Doshi, and Payas Rajan

Technical Reviewer: Shubham Srivastava

Managing Editor: Aniket Shedge

Acquisitions Editors: Kunal Sawant and Sneha Shinde

Production Editor: Shantanu Zagade

Editorial Board: Shubhopriya Banerjee, Bharat Botle, Ewan Buckingham, Mahesh Dhyani, Manasa Kumar, Alex Mazonowicz, Bridget Neale, Dominic Pereira, Shiny Poojary, Abhisekh Rane, Erol Staveley, Ankita Thakur, Nitesh Thakur, and Jonathan Wray.

First Published: October 2019

Production Reference: 1311019

ISBN: 978-1-83882-884-4

Published by Packt Publishing Ltd.

Livery Place, 35 Livery Street

Birmingham B3 2PB, UK

Table of Contents

Chapter 2: Trees, Heaps, and Graphs   55

Chapter 3: Hash Tables and Bloom Filters   101

Chapter 4: Divide and Conquer   143

Chapter 5: Greedy Algorithms　　　　195

Chapter 6: Graph Algorithms I　　　　243

Chapter 7: Graph Algorithms II — 293

Preface

About

This section briefly introduces the authors, the coverage of this book, the technical skills you'll need to get started, and the hardware and software requirements required to complete all of the included activities and exercises.

About the Book

C++ is a mature multi-paradigm programming language that enables you to write high-level code with a high degree of control over the hardware. Today, significant parts of software infrastructure, including databases, browsers, multimedia frameworks, and GUI toolkits, are written in C++.

This book starts by introducing C++ data structures and how to store data using linked lists, arrays, stacks, and queues. In later chapters, the book explains the basic algorithm design paradigms, such as the greedy approach and the divide-and-conquer approach, which are used to solve a large variety of computational problems. Finally, you will learn the advanced technique of dynamic programming to develop optimized implementations of several algorithms discussed in the book.

By the end of this book, you will have learned how to implement standard data structures and algorithms in efficient and scalable C++ 14 code.

About the Authors

John Carey

A composer and pianist, John Carey's formal education is almost exclusively based within the musical realm. Having used computers and other forms of technology extensively in his artistic endeavors, he invested years of self-study in the subjects of programming and mathematics and now works professionally as a software engineer. He believes his unusual background provides him with a unique and relatively non-academic perspective on the topic of software development. He currently works for Hydratec Industries, a company that primarily develops CAD software for fire sprinkler system designers that is used to perform hydraulic calculations on proposed designs so as to determine their efficacy and legality.

Shreyans Doshi

Shreyans graduated with a Bachelor of Technology degree in Computer Engineering from Nirma University, Ahmedabad. After graduation, he joined the finance industry to work on ultra-low latency trading systems using cutting-edge C++ applications. For the past three years, he has been designing trading infrastructure in C++.

Payas Rajan

Payas graduated with a Bachelor of Technology degree in Computer Science from NIT Allahabad. Later, he joined Samsung Research India, where he helped develop the multimedia framework for Tizen devices. Currently working as a teaching and research assistant while pursuing a PhD specializing in geospatial databases and route planning algorithms at the University of California Riverside, he has been creating applications using C++ for a decade.

Learning Objectives

By the end of this book, you will be able to:

- Build applications using hash tables, dictionaries, and sets
- Implement a URL shortening service using a bloom filter
- Apply common algorithms such as heapsort and merge-sort for string data types
- Use C++ template metaprogramming to write code libraries
- Explore how modern hardware affects the actual runtime performance of programs
- Use appropriate modern C++ idioms such as **std::array**, instead of C-style arrays

Audience

This book is intended for developers or students who want to revisit basic data structures and algorithm design techniques. Although no mathematical background is required, some basic knowledge of complexity classes and Big O notation, along with a qualification in an algorithms course, will help you get the most out of this book. Familiarity with the C++ 14 standard is assumed.

Approach

This book uses a practical and hands-on approach to explain various concepts. Through exercises, the book shows that different data structures that theoretically should perform similarly actually perform quite differently on modern computers. The book does not delve into any theoretical analyses and instead focuses on benchmarking and practical results.

Hardware Requirements

For the optimal student experience, we recommend the following hardware configuration:

- Any entry-level PC/Mac with Windows, Linux, or macOS is sufficient
- Processor: Intel Core 2 Duo, Athlon X2, or better
- Memory: 4 GB RAM
- Storage: 10 GB available space

Software Requirements

You'll also need the following software installed in advance:

- Operating system: Windows 7 SP1 32/64-bit, Windows 8.1 32/64-bit, or Windows 10 32/64-bit, Ubuntu 14.04 or later, or macOS Sierra or later

- Browser: Google Chrome or Mozilla Firefox

- Any modern compiler and IDE (optional) that supports the C++ 14 standard.

Installation and Setup

Before you embark on this book, install the following libraries used in this book. You will find the steps to install these here:

Installing Boost libraries:

Some exercises and activities in the book require the Boost C++ libraries. You can find the libraries, as well as the installation instructions, on the following links:

Windows: https://www.boost.org/doc/libs/1_71_0/more/getting_started/windows.html

Linux/macOS: https://www.boost.org/doc/libs/1_71_0/more/getting_started/unix-variants.html

Installing the Code Bundle

Copy the code bundle for the class to the `C:/Code` folder.

Additional Resources

The code bundle for this book is also hosted on GitHub at https://github.com/TrainingByPackt/CPP-Data-Structures-and-Algorithm-Design-Principles.

We also have other code bundles from our rich catalog of books and videos available at https://github.com/PacktPublishing/. Check them out!

Lists, Stacks, and Queues

Learning Objectives

By the end of this chapter, you will be able to:

- Describe the importance of using the right data structure in any application

- Implement various built-in data structures, depending on the problem, to make application development easier

- Implement a custom linear data structure suited for given situations if the ones provided by C++ are not good enough for the use case

- Analyze real-life problems where different types of linear data structures are helpful and decide which one will be the most suitable for a given use case

This chapter describes the importance of using the right data structures in any application. We will learn how to use some of the most common data structures in C++, as well as built-in and custom containers, using these structures.

Introduction

The management of data is one of the most important considerations to bear in mind while designing any application. The purpose of any application is to get some data as input, process or operate on it, and then provide suitable data as output. For example, let's consider a hospital management system. Here, we could have data about different doctors, patients, and archival records, among other things. The hospital management system should allow us to perform various operations, such as admit patients, and update the joining and leaving of doctors of different specialties. While the user-facing interface would present information in a format that is relevant to the hospital administrators, internally, the system would manage different records and lists of items.

A programmer has at their disposal several structures to hold any data in the memory. The choice of the right structure for holding data, also known as a **data structure**, is crucial for ensuring reliability, performance, and enabling the required functionalities in the application. Besides the right data structures, the right choice of algorithms to access and manipulate the data is also necessary for the optimal behavior of the application. This book shall equip you with the ability to implement the right data structures and algorithms for your application design, in order to enable you to develop well-optimized and scalable applications.

This chapter introduces basic and commonly used linear data structures provided in C++. We will look at their individual designs, pros, and cons. We will also implement said structures with the help of exercises. Understanding these data structures will help you to manage data in any application in a more performant, standardized, readable, and maintainable way.

Linear data structures can be broadly categorized as contiguous or linked structures. Let's understand the differences between the two.

Contiguous Versus Linked Data Structures

Before processing the data in any application, we must decide how we want to store data. The answer to that question depends on what kind of operations we want to perform on the data and the frequency of the operations. We should choose the implementation that gives us the best performance in terms of latency, memory, or any other parameter, without affecting the correctness of the application.

A useful metric for determining the type of data structure to be used is algorithmic complexity, also called **time complexity**. Time complexity indicates the relative amount of time required, in proportion to the size of the data, to perform a certain operation. Thus, time complexity shows how the time will vary if we change the size of the dataset. The time complexity of different operations on any data type is dependent on how the data is stored inside it.

Data structures can be divided into two types: contiguous and linked data structures. We shall take a closer look at both of them in the following sections.

Contiguous Data Structures

As mentioned earlier, **contiguous data structures** store all the elements in a single chunk of memory. The following diagram shows how data is stored in contiguous data structures:

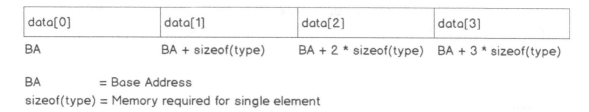

data[0]	data[1]	data[2]	data[3]
BA	BA + sizeof(type)	BA + 2 * sizeof(type)	BA + 3 * sizeof(type)

BA   = Base Address
sizeof(type) = Memory required for single element

Figure 1.1: Diagrammatic representation of contiguous data structures

In the preceding diagram, consider the larger rectangle to be the single memory chunk in which all the elements are stored, while the smaller rectangles represent the memory allocated for each element. An important thing to note here is that all the elements are of the same type. Hence, all of them require the same amount of memory, which is indicated by `sizeof(type)`. The address of the first element is also known as the **Base Address (BA)**. Since all of them are of the same type, the next element is present in the `BA + sizeof(type)` location, and the one after that is present in `BA + 2 * sizeof(type)`, and so on. Therefore, to access any element at index `i`, we can get it with the generic formula: `BA + i * sizeof(type)`.

In this case, we can always access any element using the formula instantly, regardless of the size of the array. Hence, the access time is always constant. This is indicated by O(1) in the Big-O notation.

The two main types of arrays are static and dynamic. A static array has a lifetime only inside its declaration block, but a dynamic array provides better flexibility since the programmer can determine when it should be allocated and when it should be deallocated. We can choose either of them depending on the requirement. Both have the same performance for different operations. Since this array was introduced in C, it is also known as a C-style array. Here is how these arrays are declared:

- A static array is declared as `int arr[size];`.

- A dynamic array in C is declared as `int* arr = (int*)malloc(size * sizeof(int));`.

- A dynamic array is declared in C++ as `int* arr = new int[size];`.

A static array is aggregated, which means that it is allocated on the stack, and hence gets deallocated when the flow goes out of the function. On the other hand, a dynamic array is allocated on a heap and stays there until the memory is freed manually.

Since all the elements are present next to each other, when one of the elements is accessed, a few elements next to it are also brought into the cache. Hence, if you want to access those elements, it is a very fast operation as the data is already present in the cache. This property is also known as cache locality. Although it doesn't affect the asymptotic time complexity of any operations, while traversing an array, it can give an impressive advantage for contiguous data in practice. Since traversing requires going through all the elements sequentially, after fetching the first element, the next few elements can be retrieved directly from the cache. Hence, the array is said to have good cache locality.

Linked Data Structures

Linked data structures hold the data in multiple chunks of memory, also known as nodes, which may be placed at different places in the memory. The following diagram shows how data is stored in linked data structures:

Figure 1.2: Linked data structures

In the basic structure of a linked list, each node contains the data to be stored in that node and a pointer to the next node. The last node contains a **NULL** pointer to indicate the end of the list. To reach any element, we must start from the beginning of the linked list, that is, the head, and then follow the next pointer until we reach the intended element. So, to reach the element present at index **i**, we need to traverse through the linked list and iterate **i** times. Hence, we can say that the complexity of accessing elements is $O(n)$; that is, the time varies proportionally with the number of nodes.

If we want to insert or delete any element, and if we have a pointer to that element, the operation is really small and quite fast for a linked list compared to arrays. Let's take a look at how the insertion of an element works in a linked list. The following diagram illustrates a case where we are inserting an element between two elements in a linked list:

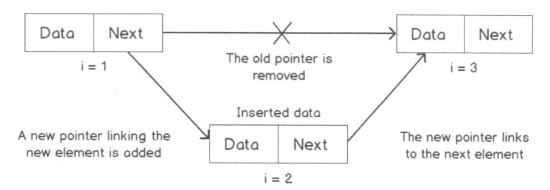

Figure 1.3: Inserting an element into a linked list

For insertion, once we've constructed the new node to be inserted, we just need to rearrange the links so that the next pointer of the preceding element ($i = 1$) points to the new element ($i = 2$) instead of its current element ($i = 3$), and the next pointer of the new element ($i = 2$) points to the current element's next element ($i = 3$). In this way, the new node becomes part of the linked list.

Similarly, if we want to remove any element, we just need to rearrange the links so that the element to be deleted is no longer connected to any of the list elements. Then, we can deallocate that element or take any other appropriate action on it.

A linked list can't provide cache locality at all since the elements are not stored contiguously in memory. Hence, there's no way to bring the next element into the cache without actually visiting it with the pointer stored in the current element. So, although, in theory, it has the same time complexity for traversal as an array, in practice, it gives poor performance.

The following section provides a summary of the comparison of contiguous and linked data structures.

Comparison

The following table briefly summarizes the important differences between linked and contiguous data structures in general:

Contiguous Data Structures	Linked Data Structures
All the data is stored next to one another in memory.	Data is stored in nodes, which may be scattered across the memory.
Accessing random element is immediate due to contiguous data.	Accessing random elements is linear and, hence, slower.
Since data is stored contiguously, traversal is faster due to cache locality.	Traversal is a bit slower as there is no cache locality.
No memory overhead on top of the memory required for storing the elements themselves.	Extra memory is required to store pointers in each node.

Figure 1.4: Table comparing contiguous and linked data structures

The following table contains a summary of the performance of arrays and linked lists regarding various parameters:

Parameter	Array	Linked List
Random access	O(1)	O(n)
Insertion at end	O(1)	O(1)
Insertion in the middle	O(n)	O(1)
Cache locality	Yes	No

Figure 1.5: Table showing time complexities of some operations for arrays and linked lists

For any application, we can choose either data structure or a combination of both, based on the requirements and the frequencies of the different operations.

Arrays and linked lists are very common and are extensively used in any application to store data. Hence, the implementation of these data structures must be as bug-free and as efficient as possible. To avoid reinventing the code, C++ provides various structures, such as **std::array**, **std::vector**, and **std::list**. We will see some of them in more detail in upcoming sections.

Limitations of C-style Arrays

Though C-style arrays do the job, they are not commonly used. There are a number of limitations that indicate the necessity of better solutions. Some of the major limitations among those are as follows:

- Memory allocation and deallocation have to be handled manually. A failure to deallocate can cause a memory leak, which is when a memory address becomes inaccessible.

- The **operator[]** function does not check whether the argument is larger than the size of an array. This may lead to segmentation faults or memory corruption if used incorrectly.

- The syntax for nested arrays gets very complicated and leads to unreadable code.

- Deep copying is not available as a default function. It has to be implemented manually.

To avoid these issues, C++ provides a very thin wrapper over a C-style array called **std::array**.

std::array

std::array automates the allocation and deallocation of memory. **std::array** is a templatized class that takes two parameters – the type of the elements and the size of the array.

In the following example, we will declare **std::array** of **int** of size **10**, set the value of any of the elements, and then print that value to make sure it works:

```cpp
std::array<int, 10> arr;        // array of int of size 10


arr[0] = 1;                     // Sets the first element as 1
std::cout << "First element: " << arr[0] << std::endl;


std::array<int, 4> arr2 = {1, 2, 3, 4};
std::cout << "Elements in second array: ";
  for(int i = 0; i < arr.size(); i++)
    std::cout << arr2[i] << " ";
```

This example would produce the following output:

```
First element: 1

Elements in second array: 1 2 3 4
```

As we can see, **std::array** provides **operator[]**, which is same as the C-style array, to avoid the cost of checking whether the index is less than the size of the array. Additionally, it also provides a function called **at(index)**, which throws an exception if the argument is not valid. In this way, we can handle the exception in an appropriate manner. So, if we have a piece of code where we will be accessing an element with a bit of uncertainty, such as an array index being dependent on user input, we can always catch the error using exception handling, as demonstrated in the following example.

```
try
{
    std::cout << arr.at(4);     // No error
    std::cout << arr.at(5);     // Throws exception std::out_of_range
}
catch (const std::out_of_range& ex)
{
    std::cerr << ex.what();
}
```

Apart from that, passing **std::array** to another function is similar to passing any built-in data type. We can pass it by value or reference, with or without **const**. Additionally, the syntax doesn't involve any pointer-related operations or referencing and de-referencing operations. Hence, the readability is much better compared to C-style arrays, even for multidimensional arrays. The following example demonstrates how to pass an array by value:

```
void print(std::array<int, 5> arr)
{
    for(auto ele: arr)
    {
        std::cout << ele << ", ";
    }
}
std::array<int, 5> arr = {1, 2, 3, 4, 5};
print(arr);
```

This example would produce the following output:

```
1, 2, 3, 4, 5
```

We can't pass an array of any other size for this function, because the size of the array is a part of the data type of the function parameter. So, for example, if we pass **std::array<int, 10>**, the compiler will return an error saying that it can't match the function parameter, nor can it convert from one to the other. However, if we want to have a generic function that can work with **std::array** of any size, we can make the size of the array templatized for that function, and it will generate code for all the required sizes of the array. So, the signature will look like the following:

```
template <size_t N>

void print(const std::array<int, N>& arr)
```

Apart from readability, while passing **std::array**, it copies all the elements into a new array by default. Hence, an automatic deep copy is performed. If we don't want that feature, we can always use other types, such as reference and **const** reference. Thus, it provides greater flexibility for programmers.

In practice, for most operations, **std::array** provides similar performance as a C-style array, since it is just a thin wrapper to reduce the effort of programmers and make the code safer. **std::array** provides two different functions to access array elements – **operator[]** and **at()**. **operator[]**, is similar to C-style arrays, and doesn't perform any check on the index. However, the **at()** function provides a check on the index, and throws an exception if the index is out of range. Due to this, it is a bit slower in practice.

As mentioned earlier, iterating over an array is a very common operation. **std::array** provides a really nice interface with the help of a range for loops and iterators. So, the code for printing all the elements in an array looks like this:

```
std::array<int, 5> arr = {1, 2, 3, 4, 5};

for(auto element: arr)

{

    std::cout << element << ' ';

}
```

This example would show the following output:

```
1 2 3 4 5
```

In the preceding example, when we demonstrated printing out all of the elements, we iterated using an index variable, where we had to make sure that it was correctly used according to the size of the array. Hence, it is more prone to human error compared to this example.

The reason we can iterate over **std::array** using a range-based loop is due to iterators. **std::array** has member functions called **begin()** and **end()**, returning a way to access the first and last elements. To move from one element to the next element, it also provides arithmetic operators, such as the increment operator (**++**) and the addition operator (**+**). Hence, a range-based **for** loop starts at **begin()** and ends at **end()**, advancing step by step using the increment operator (**++**). The iterators provide a unified interface across all of the dynamically iterable STL containers, such as **std::array**, **std::vector**, **std::map**, **std::set**, and **std::list**.

Apart from iterating, all the functions for which we need to specify a position inside the container are based on iterators; for example, insertion at a specific position, deletion of elements in a range or at a specific position, and other similar functions. This makes the code more reusable, maintainable, and readable.

> **Note**
>
> For all functions in C++ that specify a range with the help of iterators, the **start()** iterator is usually inclusive, and the **end()** iterator is usually exclusive, unless specified otherwise.

Hence, the **array::begin()** function returns an iterator that points to the first element, but **array::end()** returns an iterator just after the last element. So, a range-based loop can be written as follows:

```
for(auto it = arr.begin(); it != arr.end(); it++)
{
    auto element = (*it);
    std::cout << element << ' ';
}
```

There are some other forms of iterators, such as **const_iterator** and **reverse_iterator**, which are also quite useful. **const_iterator** is a **const** version of the normal iterator. If the array is declared to be a **const**, its functions that are related to iterators, such as **begin()** and **end()**, return **const_iterator**.

reverse_iterator allows us to traverse the array in the reverse direction. So, its functions, such as the increment operator (**++**) and **advance**, are inverses of such operations for normal iterators.

Besides the **operator[]** and **at()** functions, **std::array** also provides other accessors, as shown in the following table:

Function	Description
front()	It returns the first element of the array.
back()	It returns the last element of the array.
data()	It returns a pointer to the actual buffer stored inside the object. This allows us to do pointer arithmetic or any similar operations. This function is specifically helpful when dealing with old/legacy code that only accepts a raw pointer as a function parameter.

Figure 1.6: Table showing some accessors for std::array

The following snippet demonstrates how these functions are used:

```
std::array<int, 5> arr = {1, 2, 3, 4, 5};

std::cout << arr.front() << std::endl;        // Prints 1

std::cout << arr.back() << std::endl;         // Prints 5

std::cout << *(arr.data() + 1) << std::endl; // Prints 2
```

Another useful functionality provided by **std::array** is the relational operator for deep comparison and the copy-assignment operator for deep copy. All size operators (**<, >, <=, >=, ==, !=**) are defined for **std::array** to compare two arrays, provided the same operators are also provided for the underlying type of **std::array**.

C-style arrays also support all the relational operators, but these operators don't actually compare the elements inside the array; in fact, they just compare the pointers. Therefore, just the address of the elements is compared as integers instead of a deep comparison of the arrays. This is also known as a **shallow comparison**, and it is not of much practical use. Similarly, assignment also doesn't create a copy of the assigned data. Instead, it just makes a new pointer that points to the same data.

> **Note**
>
> Relational operators work for **std::array** of the same size only. This is because the size of the array is a part of the data type itself, and it doesn't allow values of two different data types to be compared.

In the following example, we shall see how to wrap a C-style array, whose size is defined by the user.

Exercise 1: Implementing a Dynamic Sized Array

Let's write a small application to manage the student records in a school. The number of students in a class and their details will be given as an input. Write an array-like container to manage the data, which can also support dynamic sizing. We'll also implement some utility functions to merge different classes.

Perform the following steps to complete the exercise:

1. First, include the required headers:

    ```
    #include <iostream>
    #include <sstream>
    #include <algorithm>
    ```

2. Now, let's write a basic templated structure called **dynamic_array**, as well as primary data members:

    ```
    template <typename T>
    class dynamic_array
    {
        T* data;
        size_t n;
    ```

3. Now, let's add a constructor that takes the size of the array and copies it:

    ```
    public:
    dynamic_array(int n)
    {
        this->n = n;
        data = new T[n];
    }

        dynamic_array(const dynamic_array<T>& other)
      {
        n = other.n;
        data = new T[n];

        for(int i = 0; i < n; i++)
        data[i] = other[i];
      }
    ```

4. Now, let's add **operator[]** and **function()** in the **public** accessor to support the access of data directly, in a similar way to **std::array**:

```cpp
T& operator[](int index)
{
    return data[index];
}

const T& operator[](int index) const
{
    return data[index];
}

T& at(int index)
{
    if(index < n)
    return data[index];
    throw "Index out of range";
}
```

5. Now, let's add a function called **size()** to return the size of the array, as well as a destructor to avoid memory leaks:

```cpp
size_t size() const
{
    return n;
}

~dynamic_array()
{
    delete[] data;    // A destructor to prevent memory leak
}
```

6. Now, let's add iterator functions to support range-based loops to iterate over **dynamic_array**:

```cpp
T* begin()
{
    return data;
}

const T* begin() const
{
    return data;
```

```cpp
}

T* end()
{
    return data + n;
}
const T* end() const
{
    return data + n;
}
```

7. Now, let's add a function to append one array to another using the + operator. Let's keep it as a **friend** function for better usability:

```cpp
friend dynamic_array<T> operator+(const dynamic_array<T>& arr1, dynamic_
array<T>& arr2)
{
    dynamic_array<T> result(arr1.size() + arr2.size());
    std::copy(arr1.begin(), arr1.end(), result.begin());
    std::copy(arr2.begin(), arr2.end(), result.begin() + arr1.size());

    return result;
}
```

8. Now, let's add a **to_string** function that takes a separator as a parameter with the default value as ",":

```cpp
std::string to_string(const std::string& sep = ", ")
{
  if(n == 0)
    return "";
  std::ostringstream os;
  os << data[0];

  for(int i = 1; i < n; i++)
    os << sep << data[i];

  return os.str();
}
};
```

9. Now, let's add a **struct** for students. We'll just keep the name and the standard (that is, the grade/class in which the student is studying) for simplicity, and also add **operator<<** to print it properly:

```
struct student
{
    std::string name;
    int standard;
};

std::ostream& operator<<(std::ostream& os, const student& s)
{
    return (os << "[Name: " << s.name << ", Standard: " << s.standard <<
    "]");
}
```

10. Now, let's add a **main** function to use this array:

```
int main()
{
    int nStudents;
    std::cout << "Enter number of students in class 1: ";
    std::cin >> nStudents;

dynamic_array<student> class1(nStudents);
for(int i = 0; i < nStudents; i++)
{
    std::cout << "Enter name and class of student " << i + 1 << ": ";
    std::string name;
    int standard;
    std::cin >> name >> standard;
    class1[i] = student{name, standard};
}

// Now, let's try to access the student out of range in the array
try
{
    class1[nStudents] = student{"John", 8};  // No exception, undefined
behavior
    std::cout << "class1 student set out of range without exception" <<
std::endl;
```

```
        class1.at(nStudents) = student{"John", 8};   // Will throw exception
    }
    catch(...)
    {
    std::cout << "Exception caught" << std::endl;
    }

    auto class2 = class1;   // Deep copy

        std::cout << "Second class after initialized using first array: " <<
    class2.to_string() << std::endl;

        auto class3 = class1 + class2;
        // Combines both classes and creates a bigger one

        std::cout << "Combined class: ";
        std::cout << class3.to_string() << std::endl;

        return 0;
    }
```

11. Execute the preceding code with three students – **Raj(8)**, **Rahul(10)**, and **Viraj(6)** as input. The output looks like the following in the console:

```
Enter number of students in class 1 : 3
Enter name and class of student 1: Raj 8
Enter name and class of student 2: Rahul 10
Enter name and class of student 3: Viraj 6
class1 student set out of range without exception
Exception caught
Second class after initialized using first array : [Name: Raj, Standard:
8], [Name: Rahul, Standard: 10], [Name: Viraj, Standard: 6]
Combined class : [Name: Raj, Standard: 8], [Name: Rahul, Standard: 10],
[Name: Viraj, Standard: 6], [Name: Raj, Standard: 8], [Name: Rahul,
Standard: 10], [Name: Viraj, Standard: 6]
```

Most of the functions mentioned here have a similar implementation to that of **std::array**.

Now that we have seen various containers, we shall learn how to implement a container that can accept any kind of data and store it in a common form in the following exercise.

Exercise 2: A General-Purpose and Fast Data Storage Container Builder

In this exercise, we will write a function that takes any number of elements of any type, which can, in turn, be converted into a common type. The function should also return a container having all the elements converted into that common type, and it should also be fast to traverse:

1. Let's begin by including the required libraries:

   ```
   #include <iostream>
   #include <array>
   #include <type_traits>
   ```

2. First, we'll try to build the signature of the function. Since the return type is a container that is fast to traverse, we'll go ahead with **std::array**. To allow any number of parameters, we'll use variadic templates:

   ```
   template<typename ... Args>
   std::array<?,?> build_array(Args&&... args)
   ```

   Considering the requirement that the container should be fast to traverse for the return type, we can choose an array or a vector. Since the number of elements is known at the compile time based on the number of parameters to the function, we can go ahead with **std::array**.

3. Now, we must provide the type of the elements and the number of elements for **std::array**. We can use the **std::common_type** template to find out what the type of elements inside **std::array** will be. Since this is dependent on arguments, we'll provide the return type of the function as a trailing type:

   ```
   template<typename ... Args>
   auto build_array(Args&&... args) -> std::array<typename std::common_
   type<Args...>::type, ?>
   {
       using commonType = typename std::common_type<Args...>::type;
       // Create array
   }
   ```

4. As shown in the preceding code, we now need to figure out two things – the number of elements, and how to create the array with `commonType`:

```
template< typename ... Args>
auto build_array(Args&&... args) -> std::array<typename std::common_
type<Args...>::type, sizeof...(args)>
{
    using commonType = typename std::common_type<Args...>::type;
    return {std::forward<commonType>(args)...};
}
```

5. Now, let's write the `main` function to see how our function works:

```
int main()
{
    auto data = build_array(1, 0u, 'a', 3.2f, false);
    for(auto i: data)
        std::cout << i << " ";
    std::cout << std::endl;
}
```

6. Running the code should give the following output:

```
1 0 97 3.2 0
```

As we can see, all final output is in the form of float, since everything can be converted to float.

7. To test this further, we can add the following inside the `main` function and test the output:

```
auto data2 = build_array(1, "Packt", 2.0);
```

With this modification, we should get an error saying that all the types can't be converted to a common type. The exact error message should mention that template deduction has failed. This is because there is no single type in which we can convert both the string and number.

Builder functions, such as the one we have created in this exercise, can be used when you are not sure about the type of data, yet you need to optimize efficiency.

There are a lot of useful features and utility functions that `std::array` doesn't provide. One major reason for this is to maintain similar or better performance and memory requirements compared to C-style arrays.

For more advanced features and flexibility, C++ provides another structure called `std::vector`. We will examine how this works in the next section.

std::vector

As we saw earlier, **std::array** is a really good improvement over C-style arrays. But there are some limitations of **std::array**, where it lacks functions for some frequent use cases while writing applications. Here are some of the major drawbacks of **std::array**:

- The size of **std::array** must be constant and provided at compile time, and fixed. So, we can't change it at runtime.

- Due to size limitations, we can't insert or remove elements from the array.

- No custom allocation is possible for **std::array**. It always uses stack memory.

In the majority of real-life applications, data is quite dynamic and not a fixed size. For instance, in our earlier example of a hospital management system, we can have more doctors joining the hospital, we can have more patients in emergencies, and so on. Hence, knowing the size of the data in advance is not always possible. So, **std::array** is not always the best choice and we need something with dynamic size.

Now, we'll take a look at how **std::vector** provides a solution to these problems.

std::vector – Variable Length Array

As the title suggests, **std::vector** solves one of the most prominent problems of arrays – fixed size. **std::vector** does not require us to provide its length during initialization.

Here are some of the ways in which we can initialize a vector:

```
std::vector<int> vec;
// Declares vector of size 0


std::vector<int> vec = {1, 2, 3, 4, 5};
// Declares vector of size 5 with provided elements


std::vector<int> vec(10);
// Declares vector of size 10


std::vector<int> vec(10, 5);
// Declares vector of size 10 with each element's value = 5
```

As we can see from the first initialization, providing the size is not mandatory. If we don't specify the size explicitly, and if we don't infer it by specifying its elements, the vector is initialized with the capacity of elements depending on the compiler implementation. The term "size" refers to the number of elements actually present in the vector, which may differ from its capacity. So, for the first initialization, the size will be zero, but the capacity could be some small number or zero.

We can insert elements inside the vector using the **push_back** or **insert** functions. **push_back** will insert elements at the end. **insert** takes the iterator as the first parameter for the position, and it can be used to insert the element in any location. **push_back** is a very frequently used function for vectors because of its performance. The pseudocode of the algorithm for **push_back** would be as follows:

```
push_back(val):

    if size < capacity

    // If vector has enough space to accommodate this element

    - Set element after the current last element = val

    - Increment size

    - return;


    if vector is already full

    - Allocate memory of size 2*size

    - Copy/Move elements to newly allocated memory

    - Make original data point to new memory

    - Insert the element at the end
```

The actual implementation might differ a bit, but the logic remains the same. As we can see, if there's enough space, it only takes O(1) time to insert something at the back. However, if there's not enough space, it will have to copy/move all the elements, which will take O(n) time. Most of the implementations double the size of the vector every time we run out of capacity. Hence, the O(n) time operation is done after n elements. So, on average, it just takes one extra step, making its average time complexity closer to O(1). This, in practice, provides pretty good performance, and, hence, it is a highly used container.

For the **insert** function, you don't have any option other than to shift the elements that come after the given iterator to the right. The **insert** function does that for us. It also takes care of reallocation whenever it is required. Due to the need to shift the elements, it takes O(n) time. The following examples demonstrate how to implement vector insertion functions.

Consider a vector with the first five natural numbers:

```
std::vector<int> vec = {1, 2, 3, 4, 5};
```

> **Note**
>
> Vector doesn't have a **push_front** function. It has the generic **insert** function, which takes the iterator as an argument for the position.

The generic **insert** function can be used to insert an element at the front, as follows:

```
vec.insert(int.begin(), 0);
```

Let's take a look a few more examples of the **push_back** and **insert** functions:

```
std::vector<int> vec;
// Empty vector {}

vec.push_back(1);
// Vector has one element {1}

vec.push_back(2);
// Vector has 2 elements {1, 2}

vec.insert(vec.begin(), 0);
// Vector has 3 elements {0, 1, 2}

vec.insert(find(vec.begin(), vec.end(), 1), 4);
// Vector has 4 elements {0, 4, 1, 2}
```

As shown in the preceding code, **push_back** inserts an element at the end. Additionally, the **insert** function takes the insertion position as a parameter. It takes it in the form of an iterator. So, the **begin()** function allows us to insert an element at the beginning.

Now that we have learned about the normal insertion functions, let's take a look at some better alternatives, available for vectors, compared to the **push_back** and **insert** functions. One of the drawbacks of **push_back** and **insert** is that they first construct the element, and then either copy or move the element to its new location inside the vector's buffer. This operation can be optimized by calling a constructor for the new element at the new location itself, which can be done by the **emplace_back** and **emplace** functions. It is recommended that you use these functions instead of normal insertion functions for better performance. Since we are constructing the element in place, we just need to pass the constructor parameters, instead of the constructed value itself. Then, the function will take care of forwarding the arguments to the constructor at the appropriate location.

std::vector also provides **pop_back** and **erase** functions to remove elements from it. **pop_back** removes the last element from the vector, effectively reducing the size by one. **erase** has two overloads – to remove the single element provided by the iterator pointing to it, and to remove a range of elements provided by the iterator, where the range is defined by defining the first element to be removed (inclusive) and the last element to be removed (exclusive). The C++ standard doesn't require these functions to reduce the capacity of the vector. It depends entirely on the compiler implementation. **pop_back** doesn't require any rearranging of elements, and hence can be completed very quickly. Its complexity is $O(1)$. However, **erase** requires the shifting of the elements, and hence takes $O(n)$ time. In the following exercise, we shall see how these functions are implemented.

Now, let's take a look at the example about removing elements from a vector in different ways:

Consider a vector with 10 elements – **{0, 1, 2, 3, 4, 5, 6, 7, 8, 9}**:

```
vec.pop_back();
// Vector has now 9 elements {0, 1, 2, 3, 4, 5, 6, 7, 8}


vec.erase(vec.begin());
// vector has now 7 elements {1, 2, 3, 4, 5, 6, 7, 8}


vec.erase(vec.begin() + 1, vec.begin() + 4);
// Now, vector has 4 elements {1, 5, 6, 7, 8}
```

Now, let's take a look at some other useful functions:

- **clear()**: This function simply empties the vector by removing all of the elements.

- **reserve(capacity)**: This function is used to specify the capacity of the vector. If the value specified as the parameter is greater than the current capacity, it reallocates memory and the new capacity will be equal to the parameter. However, for all other cases, it will not affect the vector's capacity. This function doesn't modify the size of the vector.

- **shrink_to_fit()**: This function can be used to free up the extra space. After calling this function, size and capacity become equal. This function can be used when we are not expecting a further increase in the size of the vector.

Allocators for std::vector

std::vector resolves the drawback of **std::array** regarding custom allocators by allowing us to pass an allocator as a template parameter after the type of data.

To use custom allocators, we follow certain concepts and interfaces. Since a vector uses allocator functions for most of its behaviors related to memory access, we need to provide those functions as part of the allocator – **allocate**, **deallocate**, **construct**, and **destroy**. This allocator will have to take care of memory allocation, deallocation, and handling so as not to corrupt any data. For advanced applications, where relying on automatic memory management, mechanisms can be too costly, and where the application has got its own memory pool or similar resource that must be used instead of default heap memory, a customer allocator is very handy.

Therefore, **std::vector** is a really good alternative to **std::array** and provides a lot more flexibility in terms of its size, growth, and other aspects. Asymptotically, all the similar functions of an array have the same time complexity as a vector. We usually pay extra performance cost only for the extra features, which is quite reasonable. For an average case, the performance of a vector is not very far from an array. Hence, in practice, **std::vector** is one of the most commonly used STL containers in C++ because of its flexibility and performance.

std::forward_list

So far, we've only seen array-like structures, but, as we saw, insertion and deletion in the middle of the data structures are very inefficient operations for contiguous data structures. And that's where linked-list-like structures come into the picture. A lot of applications require frequent insertion and deletion in the middle of a data structure. For example, any browser with multiple tabs can have an extra tab added at any point in time and at any location. Similarly, any music player will have a list of songs that you can play in a loop, and you can also insert any songs in the middle. In such cases, we can use a linked-list structure for good performance. We'll see the use case of a music player in *Activity 1*, *Implementing a Song Playlist*. Now, let's explore what kind of containers C++ provides us with.

The basic structure of a linked list requires us to have a pointer and to manage memory allocation and deallocation manually using the `new` and `delete` operators. Although it is not difficult, it can lead to bugs that are difficult to trace. Hence, just like `std::array` provides a thin wrapper over C-style arrays, `std::forward_list` provides a thin wrapper over a basic linked list.

The purpose of `std::forward_list` is to provide some additional functionality without compromising performance compared to a basic linked list. To maintain performance, it doesn't provide functions to get the size of the list or to get any element but the first one directly. Hence, it has a function called `front()` to get the reference to the first element, but nothing like `back()` to access the last element. It does provide functions for common operations, such as insertion, deletion, reverse, and splice. These functions don't affect the memory requirements or performance over basic linked lists.

Additionally, just like `std::vector`, `std::forward_list` can also take a custom allocator as the second template parameter if required. Hence, we can easily use it for advanced applications that benefit from custom memory management.

Inserting and Deleting Elements in forward_list

`std:: forward_list` provides the `push_front` and `insert_after` functions, which can be used to insert an element in a linked list. Both of these are slightly different compared to insertion functions for vectors. `push_front` is useful for inserting an element at the front. Since `forward_list` doesn't have direct access to the last element, it doesn't provide a `push_back` function. For insertion at a specific location, we use `insert_after` instead of `insert`. This is because inserting an element in a linked list requires updating the next pointer of the element, after which we want to insert a new element. If we provide just the iterator, where we want to insert a new element, we can't get access to the previous element quickly, since traversing backward is not allowed in `forward_list`.

Since this is a pointer-based mechanism, we don't really need to shift the elements during insertion. Hence, both of the insertion functions are quite a bit faster compared to any array-based structures. Both the functions just modify the pointers to insert a new element at the intended position. This operation is not dependent on the size of the list and therefore has a time complexity of O(1). We shall take a look at the implementation of these functions in the following exercise.

Now, let's see how we can insert elements in a linked list:

```
std::forward_list<int> fwd_list = {1, 2, 3};


fwd_list.push_front(0);
// list becomes {0, 1, 2, 3}


auto it = fwd_list.begin();


fwd_list.insert_after(it, 5);
// list becomes {0, 5, 1, 2, 3}


fwd_list.insert_after(it, 6);
// list becomes {0, 6, 5, 1, 2, 3}
```

forward_list also provides **emplace_front** and **emplace_after**, which is similar to **emplace** for a vector. Both of these functions do the same thing as insertion functions, but more efficiently by avoiding extra copying and moving.

forward_list also has **pop_front** and **erase_after** functions for the deletion of elements. **pop_front**, as the name suggests, removes the first element. Since it doesn't require any shifting, the operation is quite fast in practice and has a time complexity of O(1). **erase_after** has two overloads – to remove a single element (by taking an iterator to its previous element), and to remove multiple elements in a range (by taking an iterator to the element before the first element of the range and another iterator to the last element).

The time complexity of the **erase_after** function is linear to the number of elements that are erased because the deletion of elements can't be done via deallocating just a single chunk of memory. Since all the nodes are scattered across random locations in memory, the function needs to deallocate each of them separately.

Now, let's see how we can remove the elements from the list:

```cpp
std::forward_list<int> fwd_list = {1, 2, 3, 4, 5};


fwd_list.pop_front();
// list becomes {2, 3, 4, 5}


auto it = fwd_list.begin();


fwd_list.erase_after(it);
// list becomes {2, 4, 5}


fwd_list.erase_after(it, fwd_list.end());
// list becomes {2}
```

Let's explore what other operations we can do with **forward_list** in the following section.

Other Operations on forward_list

Apart from the **erase** functions to delete elements based on its position determined by iterators, **forward_list** also provides the **remove** and **remove_if** functions to remove elements based on their values. The **remove** function takes a single parameter – the value of the elements to be removed. It removes all the elements that match the given element based on the equality operator defined for the type of the value. Without the equality operator, the compiler doesn't allow us to call that function and throws a compilation error. Since **remove** only deletes the elements based on the equality operator, it is not possible to use it for deletion based on other conditions, since we can't change the equality operator after defining it once. For a conditional removal, **forward_list** provides the **remove_if** function. It takes a predicate as a parameter, which is a function taking an element of the value type as a parameter, and a Boolean as the return value. So, all the elements for which the predicate returns true are removed from the list. With the latest C++ versions, we can easily specify the predicate with lambdas as well. The following exercise should help you to understand how to implement these functions.

Exercise 3: Conditional Removal of Elements from a Linked List Using remove_if

In this exercise, we'll use the sample information of a few Indian citizens during the elections and remove ineligible citizens, based on their age, from the electoral roll. For simplicity, we'll just store the names and ages of the citizens.

We shall store the data in a linked list and remove the required elements using **remove_if**, which provides a way to remove elements that meet a certain condition, instead of defining the positions of the elements to be removed:

1. Let's first include the required headers and add the **struct citizen**:

```cpp
#include <iostream>
#include <forward_list>

struct citizen
{
    std::string name;
    int age;
};

std::ostream& operator<<(std::ostream& os, const citizen& c)
{
    return (os << "[Name: " << c.name << ", Age: " << c.age << "]");
}
```

2. Now, let's write a **main** function and initialize a few citizens in a **std::forward_list**. We'll also make a copy of it to avoid having to initialize it again:

```cpp
int main()
{
    std::forward_list<citizen> citizens = {{"Raj", 22}, {"Rohit", 25},
    {"Rohan", 17}, {"Sachin", 16}};

    auto citizens_copy = citizens;

    std::cout << "All the citizens: ";
    for (const auto &c : citizens)
        std::cout << c << " ";
    std::cout << std::endl;
```

3. Now, let's remove all of the ineligible citizens from the list:

```
citizens.remove_if(
    [](const citizen& c)
    {
        return (c.age < 18);
    });

std::cout << "Eligible citizens for voting: ";
for(const auto& c: citizens)
    std::cout << c << " ";
std::cout << std::endl;
```

The **remove_if** function removes all the elements for which the given predicate is true. Here, we've provided a lambda since the condition is very simple. If it were a complicated condition, we could also write a normal function that takes one parameter of the underlying type of list and returns a Boolean value.

4. Now, let's find out who'll be eligible for voting next year:

```
citizens_copy.remove_if(
    [](const citizen& c)
    {
    // Returns true if age is less than 18
        return (c.age != 17);
    });

std::cout << "Citizens that will be eligible for voting next year: ";
for(const auto& c: citizens_copy)
    std::cout << c << " ";
std::cout << std::endl;
}
```

As you can see, we are only keeping those citizens with an age of 17.

5. Run the exercise. You should get an output like this:

```
All the citizens: [Name: Raj, Age: 22] [Name: Rohit, Age: 25] [Name:
Rohan, Age: 17] [Name: Sachin, Age: 16]
Eligible citizens for voting: [Name: Raj, Age: 22] [Name: Rohit, Age: 25]
Citizens that will be eligible for voting next year: [Name: Rohan, Age:
17]
```

The **remove_if** function has a time complexity of O(*n*) since it simply traverses the list once while removing all the elements as required. If we want to remove the elements with specific values, we can use another version of **remove**, which simply takes one parameter of the object and removes all the objects from the list matching the given value. It also requires us to implement the == operator for the given type.

forward_list also provides a **sort** function to sort the data. All the array-related structures can be sorted by a generic function, **std::sort(first iterator, last iterator)**. However, it can't be used by linked list-based structures because we can't access any data randomly. This also makes the iterators provided by **forward_list** different from the ones for an array or a vector. We'll take a look at this in more detail in the next section. The **sort** function that is provided as part of **forward_list** has two overloads – **sort** based on the less than operator (<), and **sort** based on a comparator provided as a parameter. The default **sort** function uses **std::less<value_type>** for comparison. It simply returns **true** if the first parameter is less than the second one, and hence, requires us to define the less than operator (<) for custom-defined types.

In addition to this, if we want to compare it based on some other parameters, we can use the parametric overload, which takes a binary predicate. Both the overloads have a linearathmic time complexity – O(*n* × *log n*). The following example demonstrates both overloads of **sort**:

```
std::forward_list<int> list1 = {23, 0, 1, -3, 34, 32};


list1.sort();
// list becomes {-3, 0, 1, 23, 32, 34}


list1.sort(std::greater<int>());
// list becomes {34, 32, 23, 1, 0, -3}
```

Here, **greater<int>** is a predicate provided in the standard itself, which is a wrapper over the greater than operator (>) to sort the elements into descending order, as we can see from the values of the list..

Other functions provided in **forward_list** are **reverse** and **unique**. The **reverse** function simply reverses the order of the elements, in a time duration that is linear to the number of elements present in the list, that is, with a time complexity of O(n). The **unique** function keeps only the unique elements in the list and removes all the repetitive valued functions except the first one. Since it is dependent on the equality of the elements, it has two overloads – the first takes no parameters and uses the equality operator for the value type, while the second takes a binary predicate with two parameters of the value type. The **unique** function was built to be linear in time complexity. Hence, it doesn't compare each element with every other element. Instead, it only compares consecutive elements for equality and removes the latter one if it is the same as the former one based on the default or custom binary predicate. Hence, to remove all of the unique elements from the list using the **unique** function, we need to sort the elements before calling the function. With the help of a given predicate, **unique** will compare all the elements with their neighboring elements and remove the latter elements if the predicate returns **true**.

Let's now see how we can use the **reverse**, **sort**, and **unique** functions for lists:

```
std::forward_list<int> list1 = {2, 53, 1, 0, 4, 10};


list1.reverse();
// list becomes {2, 53, 1, 0, 4, 10}


list1 = {0, 1, 0, 1, -1, 10, 5, 10, 5, 0};


list1.sort();
// list becomes {-1, 0, 0, 0, 1, 1, 5, 5, 10, 10}


list1.unique();
// list becomes {-1, 0, 1, 5, 10}


list1 = {0, 1, 0, 1, -1, 10, 5, 10, 5, 0};


list1.sort();
// list becomes {-1, 0, 0, 0, 1, 1, 5, 5, 10, 10}
```

The following example will remove elements if they are not greater than the previously valid element by at least 2:

```
list1.unique([](int a, int b) { return (b - a) < 2; });
// list becomes {-1, 1, 5, 10}
```

> **Note**
>
> Before calling the **unique** function, the programmer must make sure that the data is already sorted. Hence, we are calling the **sort** function right before it. The **unique** function compares the element with the previous element that has already met the condition. Additionally, it always keeps the first element of the original list. Hence, there's always an element to compare with.

In the next section, we will take a look at how the **forward_list** iterator is different from the vector/array iterators.

Iterators

As you may have noticed in some of the examples for arrays and vectors, we add numbers to the iterators. Iterators are like pointers, but they also provide a common interface for STL containers. The operations on these iterators are strictly based on the type of iterators, which is dependent on the container. Iterators for vectors and arrays are the most flexible in terms of functionality. We can access any element from the container directly, based on its position, using **operator[]** because of the contiguous nature of the data. This iterator is also known as a random access iterator. However, for **forward_list**, there is no direct way to traverse back, or even go from one node to its preceding node, without starting from the beginning. Hence, the only arithmetic operator allowed for this is increment. This iterator is also known as a forward iterator.

There are other utility functions that we can use, such as **advance**, **next**, and **prev**, depending on the type of iterators. **next** and **prev** take an iterator and a distance value, and then return the iterator pointing to the element that is at the given distance from the given iterator. This works as expected provided that the given iterator supports the operation. For example, if we try to use the **prev** function with a **forward** iterator, it will throw a compilation error, since this iterator is a forward iterator and can only move forward. The time taken by these functions depends on the type of iterators used. All of them are constant time functions for random access iterators, since addition and subtraction are constant-time operations. For the rest of the iterators, all of them are linear to the distance that needs to be traversed forward or backward. We shall use these iterators in the following exercise.

Exercise 4: Exploring Different Types of Iterators

Let's say that we have a list of the winners of the Singapore F1 Grand Prix from the last few years. With the help of vector iterators, we'll discover how we can retrieve useful information from this data. After that, we'll try to do the same thing with **forward_list**, and see how it differs from vector iterators:

1. Let's first include the headers:

```
#include <iostream>
#include <forward_list>
#include <vector>

int main()
{
```

2. Let's write a vector with a list of winners:

```
std::vector<std::string> vec = {"Lewis Hamilton", "Lewis Hamilton", "Nico
Roseberg", "Sebastian Vettel", "Lewis Hamilton", "Sebastian Vettel",
"Sebastian Vettel", "Sebastian Vettel", "Fernando Alonso"};

auto it = vec.begin();        // Constant time
std::cout << "Latest winner is: " << *it << std::endl;

it += 8;                      // Constant time
std::cout << "Winner before 8 years was: " << *it << std::endl;

advance(it, -3);              // Constant time
std::cout << "Winner before 3 years of that was: " << *it << std::endl;
```

3. Let's try the same with the **forward_list** iterators and see how they differ from vector iterators:

```
std::forward_list<std::string> fwd(vec.begin(), vec.end());

auto it1 = fwd.begin();
std::cout << "Latest winner is: " << *it << std::endl;

advance(it1, 5);   // Time taken is proportional to the number of elements

std::cout << "Winner before 5 years was: " << *it << std::endl;
```

```
// Going back will result in compile time error as forward_list only
allows us to move towards the end.

// advance(it1, -2);      // Compiler error
}
```

4. Running this exercise should produce the following output:

```
Latest winner is : Lewis Hamilton
Winner before 8 years was : Fernando Alonso
Winner before 3 years of that was : Sebastian Vettel
Latest winner is : Sebastian Vettel
Winner before 5 years was : Sebastian Vettel
```

5. Now, let's see what happens if we add a number to this iterator by putting the following line inside the **main** function at the end:

```
it1 += 2;
```

We'll get an error message similar to this:

```
no match for 'operator+=' (operand types are std::_Fwd_list_iterator<int>'
and 'int')
```

The various iterators we have explored in this exercise are quite useful for easily fetching any data from your dataset.

As we have seen, **std::array** is a thin wrapper over a C-style array, and **std::forward_list** is nothing but a thin wrapper over a singly linked list. It provides a simple and less error-prone interface without compromising on performance or memory.

Apart from that, since we can access any element immediately in the vector, the addition and subtraction operations on the vector iterator are O(1). On the other hand, **forward_list** only supports access to an element by traversing to it. Hence, its iterators' addition operation is O(n), where n is the number of steps we are advancing.

In the following exercise, we shall make a custom container that works in a similar way to **std::forward_list**, but with some improvements. We shall define many functions that are equivalent to **forward_list** functions. It should also help you understand how these functions work under the hood.

Exercise 5: Building a Basic Custom Container

In this exercise, we're going to implement an **std::forward_list** equivalent container with some improvements. We'll start with a basic implementation called **singly_ll**, and gradually keep on improving:

1. Let's add the required headers and then start with the basic implementation of **singly_ll** with a single node:

```cpp
#include <iostream>
#include <algorithm>

struct singly_ll_node
{
    int data;
    singly_ll_node* next;
};
```

2. Now, we'll implement the actual **singly_ll** class, which wraps the node around for better interfacing:

```cpp
class singly_ll
{
public:
    using node = singly_ll_node;
    using node_ptr = node*;

private:
    node_ptr head;
```

3. Now, let's add **push_front** and **pop_front**, just like in **forward_list**:

```cpp
public:
void push_front(int val)
{
    auto new_node = new node{val, NULL};
    if(head != NULL)
        new_node->next = head;
    head = new_node;
}

void pop_front()
{
    auto first = head;
    if(head)
```

```
        {
            head = head->next;
            delete first;
        }
        else
            throw "Empty ";
    }
```

4. Let's now implement a basic iterator for our **singly_ll** class, with constructors and accessors:

```
struct singly_ll_iterator
{
private:
    node_ptr ptr;
public:
    singly_ll_iterator(node_ptr p) : ptr(p)
    {
}

int& operator*()
{
    return ptr->data;
}

node_ptr get()
{
    return ptr;
}
```

5. Let's add the **operator++** functions for pre- and post-increments:

```
singly_ll_iterator& operator++()      // pre-increment
{
        ptr = ptr->next;
        return *this;
}

singly_ll_iterator operator++(int)     // post-increment
{
    singly_ll_iterator result = *this;
++(*this);
return result;
}
```

6. Let's add equality operations as **friend** functions:

```cpp
      friend bool operator==(const singly_ll_iterator& left, const singly_
ll_iterator& right)
        {
            return left.ptr == right.ptr;
        }

      friend bool operator!=(const singly_ll_iterator& left, const singly_
ll_iterator& right)
        {
            return left.ptr != right.ptr;
        }
};
```

7. Let's jump back to our linked list class. Now that we've got our iterator class, let's implement the **begin** and **end** functions to ease the traversal. We'll also add **const** versions for both:

```cpp
singly_ll_iterator begin()
{
    return singly_ll_iterator(head);
}

singly_ll_iterator end()
{
    return singly_ll_iterator(NULL);
}

singly_ll_iterator begin() const
{
    return singly_ll_iterator(head);
}

singly_ll_iterator end() const
{
    return singly_ll_iterator(NULL);
}
```

8. Let's implement a default constructor, a copy constructor for deep copying, and a constructor with **initializer_list**:

```cpp
singly_ll() = default;

singly_ll(const singly_ll& other) : head(NULL)
{
    if(other.head)
        {
            head = new node;
            auto cur = head;
            auto it = other.begin();
            while(true)
            {
                cur->data = *it;

                auto tmp = it;
                ++tmp;
                if(tmp == other.end())
                    break;

                cur->next = new node;
                cur = cur->next;
                it = tmp;
            }
        }
}

singly_ll(const std::initializer_list<int>& ilist) : head(NULL)
{
    for(auto it = std::rbegin(ilist); it != std::rend(ilist); it++)
            push_front(*it);
}
};
```

9. Let's write a **main** function to use the preceding functions:

```cpp
int main()
{
    singly_ll sll = {1, 2, 3};
    sll.push_front(0);

    std::cout << "First list: ";
    for(auto i: sll)
        std::cout << i << " ";
    std::cout << std::endl;

    auto sll2 = sll;
    sll2.push_front(-1);
    std::cout << "Second list after copying from first list and inserting
-1 in front: ";
    for(auto i: sll2)
        std::cout << i << ' ';   // Prints -1 0 1 2 3
    std::cout << std::endl;

    std::cout << "First list after copying - deep copy: ";
for(auto i: sll)
        std::cout << i << ' ';   // Prints 0 1 2 3
    std::cout << std::endl;
}
```

10. Running this exercise should produce the following output:

```
First list: 0 1 2 3
Second list after copying from first list and inserting -1 in front: -1 0 1
2 3
First list after copying - deep copy: 0 1 2 3
```

As we can see in the preceding example, we are able to initialize our list using **std::initializer_list**. We can call the **push**, **pop_front**, and **back** functions. As we can see, **sll2.pop_back** only removed the element from **sll2**, and not **sll**. **sll** is still intact with all five elements. Hence, we can perform a deep copy as well.

Activity 1: Implementing a Song Playlist

In this activity, we'll look at some applications for which a doubly-linked list is not enough or not convenient. We will build a tweaked version that fits the application. We often encounter cases where we have to customize default implementations, such as when looping songs in a music player or in games where multiple players take a turn one by one in a circle.

These applications have one common property – we traverse the elements of the sequence in a circular fashion. Thus, the node after the last node will be the first node while traversing the list. This is called a circular linked list.

We'll take the use case of a music player. It should have following functions supported:

1. Create a playlist using multiple songs.

2. Add songs to the playlist.

3. Remove a song from the playlist.

4. Play songs in a loop (for this activity, we will print all the songs once).

> **Note**
>
> You can refer to *Exercise 5, Building a Basic Custom Container* where we built a container from scratch supporting similar functions.

Here are the steps to solve the problem:

1. First, design a basic structure that supports circular data representation.

2. After that, implement the **insert** and **erase** functions in the structure to support various operations.

3. We have to write a custom iterator. This is a bit tricky. The important thing is to make sure that we are able to traverse the container using a range-based approach for a loop. Hence, **begin()** and **end()** should return different addresses, although the structure is circular.

4. After building the container, build a wrapper over it, which will store different songs in the playlist and perform relevant operations, such as **next**, **previous**, **print all**, **insert**, and **remove**.

> **Note**
>
> The solution to this activity can be found on page 476.

std::forward_list has several limitations. **std::list** presents a much more flexible implementation of lists and helps overcome some of the shortcomings of **forward_list**.

std::list

As seen in the previous section, **std::forward_list** is just a nice and thin wrapper over the basic linked list. It doesn't provide functions to insert elements at the end, traverse backward, or get the size of the list, among other useful operations. The functionality is limited to save memory and to retain fast performance. Apart from that, the iterators of **forward_list** can support very few operations. In most practical situations in any application, functions such as those for inserting something at the end and getting the size of the container are very useful and frequently used. Hence, **std::forward_list** is not always the desired container, where fast insertion is required. To overcome these limitations of **std::forward_list**, C++ provides **std::list**, which has several additional features owing to the fact that it is a bidirectional linked list, also known as a doubly-linked list. However, note that this comes at the cost of additional memory requirements.

The plain version of a doubly-linked list looks something like this:

```
struct doubly_linked_list
{
    int data;
    doubly_linked_list *next, *prev;
};
```

As you can see, it has one extra pointer to point to the previous element. Thus, it provides us with a way in which to traverse backward, and we can also store the size and the last element to support fast **push_back** and **size** operations. Also, just like **forward_list**, it can also support customer allocator as a template parameter.

Common Functions for std::list

Most of the functions for **std::list** are either the same or similar to the functions of **std::forward_list**, with a few tweaks. One of the tweaks is that function names ending with **_after** have their equivalents without **_after**. Therefore, **insert_after** and **emplace_after** become simply **insert** and **emplace**. This is because, with the **std::list** iterator, we can also traverse backward, and hence there's no need to provide the iterator of the previous element. Instead, we can provide the iterator of the exact element at which we want to perform the operation. Apart from that, **std::list** also provides fast operations for **push_back**, **emplace_back**, and **pop_back**. The following exercise demonstrates the use of insertion and deletion functions for **std::list**.

Exercise 6: Insertion and Deletion Functions for std::list

In this exercise, we shall create a simple list of integers using **std::list** and explore various ways in which we can insert and delete elements from it:

1. First of all, let's include the required headers:

```
#include <iostream>
#include <list>

int main()
{
```

2. Then, initialize a list with a few elements and experiment on it with various insertion functions:

```
std::list<int> list1 = {1, 2, 3, 4, 5};

list1.push_back(6);
// list becomes {1, 2, 3, 4, 5, 6}

list1.insert(next(list1.begin()), 0);
// list becomes {1, 0, 2, 3, 4, 5, 6}

list1.insert(list1.end(), 7);
// list becomes {1, 0, 2, 3, 4, 5, 6, 7}
```

As you can see, the **push_back** function inserts an element at the end. The **insert** function inserts **0** after the first element, which is indicated by **next(list1. begin())**. After that, we are inserting **7** after the last element, which is indicated by **list1.end()**.

3. Now, let's take a look at the remove function, **pop_back**, which was not present in **forward_list**:

```
list1.pop_back();
// list becomes {1, 0, 2, 3, 4, 5, 6}

std::cout << "List after insertion & deletion functions: ";
for(auto i: list1)
    std::cout << i << " ";
}
```

4. Running this exercise should give the following output:

   `List after insertion & deletion functions: 1 0 2 3 4 5 6`

   Here, we are removing the last element that we just inserted.

> **Note**
>
> Although **push_front**, **insert**, **pop_front**, and **erase** have the same time complexity as equivalent functions for **forward_list**, these are slightly more expensive for **std::list**. The reason for this is that there are two pointers in each node of a list instead of just one, as in the case of **forward_list**. So, we have to maintain the validity of the value of both the pointers. Hence, when we are repointing these variables, we need to make almost double the effort compared to singly linked lists.

Earlier, we saw an insertion for a singly-linked list. Let's now demonstrate what pointer manipulation looks like for a doubly-linked list in the following diagram:

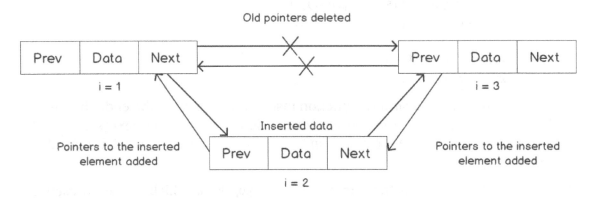

Figure 1.7: Inserting an element in a doubly linked list

As you can see, the number of operations is constant even in the case of **std::list**; however, compared to **forward_list**, we have to fix both the **prev** and **next** pointers in order to maintain a doubly-linked list, and this costs us almost double in terms of memory and performance compared to **forward_list**. A similar idea applies to other functions as well.

Other functions such as **remove**, **remove_if**, **sort**, **unique**, and **reverse** provide similar functionalities as compared to their equivalent functions for **std::forward_list**.

Bidirectional Iterators

In the *Iterators* section, we saw the difference between the flexibility of array-based random access iterators and `forward_list`-based forward iterators. The flexibility of `std::list::iterator` lies between both of them. It is more flexible compared to forward iterators, since it can allow us to traverse backward. Hence, `std::list` also supports functions for reverse traversal by exposing reverse iterators where the operations are inverted. Having said that, it is not as flexible as random access iterators. Although we can advance in either direction by any number of moves, since these moves have to be done by traversing the elements one by one instead of jumping directly to the desired element, the time complexity is still linear, and not a constant, as in the case of random access iterators. Since these iterators can move in either direction, they are known as bidirectional iterators.

Iterator Invalidation for Different Containers

So far, we've seen that iterators provide us with a uniform way of accessing, traversing, inserting, and deleting elements from any container. But there are some cases when iterators become invalid after modifying the container, because the iterators are implemented based on pointers, which are bound to memory addresses. So, if the memory address of any node or element changes because of modification in the container, it invalidates the iterator, and using it regardless can lead to undefined behavior.

For example, a very basic example would be `vector::push_back`, which simply adds a new element at the end. However, as we saw earlier, in some cases, it also requires the movement of all the elements to a new buffer. Hence, all iterators, pointers, and even the references to any of the existing elements will be invalidated. Similarly, if the `vector::insert` function leads to reallocation, all the elements will need to be moved. Hence, all the iterators, pointers, and references are invalidated. If not, the function will invalidate all the iterators pointing to the element that is on the right side of the insertion position, since these elements will be shifted during the process.

Unlike vectors, linked list-based iterators are safer for insertion and deletion operations because the elements will not be shifted or moved. Hence, none of the insertion functions for `std::list` or `forward_list` affect the validity of the iterators. An exception is that deletion-related operations invalidate iterators of the elements that are deleted, which is obvious and reasonable. It doesn't affect the validity of the iterators of the rest of the elements. The following example shows iterator invalidation for different iterators:

```
std::vector<int> vec = {1, 2, 3, 4, 5};


auto it4 = vec.begin() + 4;
```

```
// it4 now points to vec[4]
```

```
vec.insert(vec.begin() + 2, 0);
// vec becomes {1, 2, 0, 3, 4, 5}
```

it4 is invalid now, since it comes after the insertion position. Accessing it will lead to undefined behavior:

```
std::list<int> lst = {1, 2, 3, 4, 5};
```

```
auto l_it4 = next(lst.begin(), 4);
```

```
lst.insert(next(lst.begin(), 2), 0);
// l_it4 remains valid
```

As we saw, **std::list** is much more flexible compared to **std::forward_list**. A lot of operations, such as **size**, **push_back**, and **pop_back**, are provided, which operate with a time complexity of O(1). Hence, **std::list** is used more frequently compared to **std::forward_list**. **forward_list** is a better alternative if we have very strict constraints of memory and performance, and if we are sure that we don't want to traverse backward. So, in most cases, **std::list** is a safer choice.

Activity 2: Simulating a Card Game

In this activity, we'll analyze a given situation and try to come up with the most suitable data structure to achieve the best performance.

We'll try to simulate a card game. There are 4 players in the game, and each starts with 13 random cards. Then, we'll try to pick one card from each player's hand randomly. That way, we'll have 4 cards for comparison. After that, we'll remove the matching cards from those 4 cards. The remaining cards, if any, will be drawn back by the players who put them out. If there are multiple matching pairs out of which only one can be removed, we can choose either one. If there are no matching pairs, players can shuffle their own set of cards.

Now, we need to continue this process over and over until at least one of them is out of cards. The first one to get rid of all their cards wins the game. Then, we shall print the winner at the end.

Perform the following steps to solve the activity:

1. First, determine which container would be the most suitable to store the cards of each player. We should have four containers that have a set of cards – one for each player.

2. Write a function to initialize and shuffle the cards.

3. Write a function to randomly deal all the cards among the four players.

4. Write a matching function. This function will pick a card from each player and compare it as required by the rules of the game. Then, it will remove the necessary cards. We have to choose the card wisely so that removing it would be faster. This parameter should also be considered while deciding on the container.

5. Now, let's write a function, to see whether we have a winner.

6. Finally, we'll write the core logic of the game. This will simply call the matching function until we have a winner based on the function written in the previous step.

> **Note**
>
> The solution to this activity can be found on page 482.

std::deque – Special Version of std::vector

So far, we have seen array-based and linked list-based containers. **std::deque** mixes both of them and combines each of their advantages to a certain extent. As we have seen, although vector is a variable-length array, some of its functions, such as **push_front** and **pop_front**, are very costly operations. **std::deque** can help us overcome that. Deque is short for double-ended queue.

The Structure of Deque

The C++ standard only defines the behavior of the containers and not the implementation. The containers we have seen so far are simple enough for us to predict their implementation. However, deque is slightly more complicated than that. Therefore, we'll first take a look at its requirements, and then we will try to dive into a little bit of implementation.

The C++ standard guarantees the following time complexities for different operations of deque:

- O(1) for **push_front**, **pop_front**, **push_back**, and **pop_back**
- O(1) for random access to all the elements
- Maximum of N/2 steps in the case of insertion or deletion in the middle, where N = the size of the deque

Looking at the requirements, we can say that the container should be able to grow in either direction very fast, and still be able to provide random access to all the elements. Thus, the structure has to be somewhat like a vector, but still expandable from the front as well as the back. The requirement for insertion and deletion gives a slight hint that we will be shifting the elements because we are only allowed to take up to N/2 steps. And that also validates our previous assumption regarding behavior that is similar to vector. Since the container can grow in either direction quickly, we don't necessarily have to shift the elements toward the right every time. Instead, we can shift the elements toward the nearest end. That will give us a time complexity of a maximum of N/2 steps, since the nearest end can't be more than N/2 nodes away from any insertion point inside the container.

Now, let's focus on random access and insertion at the front. The structure can't be stored in a single chunk of memory. Rather, we can have multiple chunks of memory of the same size. In this way, based on the index and size of the chunks (or the number of elements per chunk), we can decide which chunk's indexed element we want. That helps us to achieve random access in O(1) time only if we store pointers to all the memory chunks in a contiguous location. Hence, the structure can be assumed to be similar to a vector of arrays.

When we want to insert something at the front, and we don't have enough space in the first memory chunk, we have to allocate another chunk and insert its address in the vector of pointers at the front. That might require reallocation of the vector of pointers, but the actual data will not be moved. To optimize that reallocation, instead of starting from the first chunk, we can start the insertion from the middle chunk of the vector. In that way, we are safe up to a certain number of front insertions. We can follow the same while reallocating the vector of pointers.

> **Note**
>
> Since the deque is not as simple as the other containers discussed in this chapter, the actual implementation might differ or might have a lot more optimizations than we discussed, but the basic idea remains the same. And that is, we need multiple chunks of contiguous memory to implement such a container.

The functions and operations supported by deque are more of a combination of functions supported by vectors and lists; hence, we have **push_front**, **push_back**, **insert**, **emplace_front**, **emplace_back**, **emplace**, **pop_front**, **pop_back**, and **erase**, among others. We also have the vector's functions, such as **shrink_to_fit**, to optimize the capacity, but we don't have a function called **capacity** since this is highly dependent on the implementation, and is, therefore, not expected to be exposed. And, as you might expect, it provides random access iterators just like a vector.

Let's take a look at how we can use different insertion and deletion operations on deque:

```
std::deque<int> deq = {1, 2, 3, 4, 5};


deq.push_front(0);

// deque becomes {0, 1, 2, 3, 4, 5}


deq.push_back(6);

// deque becomes {0, 1, 2, 3, 4, 5, 6}


deq.insert(deq.begin() + 2, 10);

// deque becomes {0, 1, 10, 2, 3, 4, 5, 6}


deq.pop_back();

// deque becomes {0, 1, 10, 2, 3, 4, 5}


deq.pop_front();

// deque becomes {1, 10, 2, 3, 4, 5}


deq.erase(deq.begin() + 1);

// deque becomes {1, 2, 3, 4, 5}


deq.erase(deq.begin() + 3, deq.end());

// deque becomes {1, 2, 3}
```

Such a structure may be used in cases such as boarding queues for flights.

The only thing that differs among the containers is the performance and memory requirements. Deque will provide very good performance for both insertion and deletion at the front as well as the end. Insertion and deletion in the middle is also a bit faster than for a vector on average, although, asymptotically, it is the same as that of a vector.

Apart from that, deque also allows us to have customer allocators just like a vector. We can specify it as a second template parameter while initializing it. One thing to note here is that the allocator is part of the type and not part of the object. This means we can't compare two objects of two deques or two vectors where each has a different kind of allocator. Similarly, we can't have other operations, such as an assignment or copy constructor, with objects of different types of allocators.

As we saw, **std::deque** has a slightly more complex structure compared to other containers we examined before that. It is, in fact, the only container that provides efficient random access along with fast **push_front** and **push_back** functions. Deque is used as an underlying container for others, as we'll see in the upcoming section.

Container Adaptors

The containers that we've seen until now are built from scratch. In this section, we'll look at the containers that are built on top of other containers. There are multiple reasons to provide a wrapper over existing containers, such as providing more semantic meaning to the code, restricting someone from accidentally using unintended functions just because they are available, and to provide specific interfaces.

One such specific use case is the **stack** data structure. The stack follows the **LIFO** (**Last In First Out**) structure for accessing and processing data. In terms of functions, it can insert and delete only at one end of the container and can't update or even access any element except at the mutating end. This end is called the top of the stack. We can easily use any other container, such as a vector or deque too, since it can meet these requirements by default. However, there are some fundamental problems in doing that.

The following example shows two implementations of the stack:

```
std::deque<int> stk;


stk.push_back(1);   // Pushes 1 on the stack = {1}


stk.push_back(2);   // Pushes 2 on the stack = {1, 2}
```

```
stk.pop_back();     // Pops the top element off the stack = {1}

stk.push_front(0); // This operation should not be allowed for a stack

std::stack<int> stk;

stk.push(1);        // Pushes 1 on the stack = {1}

stk.push(2);        // Pushes 2 on the stack = {1, 2}

stk.pop();          // Pops the top element off the stack = {1}

stk.push_front(0); // Compilation error
```

As we can see in this example, the first block of the stack using deque provides a semantic meaning only by the name of the variable. The functions operating on the data still don't force the programmer to add code that shouldn't be allowed, such as **push_front**. Also, the **push_back** and **pop_back** functions expose unnecessary details, which should be known by default since it is a stack.

In comparison to this, if we look at the second version, it looks much more accurate in indicating what it does. And, most importantly, it doesn't allow anyone to do anything that was unintended, even accidentally.

The second version of the stack is nothing but a wrapper over the previous container, deque, by providing a nice and restricted interface to the user. This is called a container adaptor. There are three container adaptors provided by C++: **std::stack**, **std::queue**, and **std::priority_queue**. Let's now take a brief look at each of them.

std::stack

As explained earlier, adaptors simply reuse other containers, such as deque, vector, or any other container for that matter. **std::stack**, by default, adapts **std::deque** as its underlying container. It provides an interface that is only relevant to the stack – **empty**, **size**, **top**, **push**, **pop**, and **emplace**. Here, **push** simply calls the **push_back** function for the underlying container, and **pop** simply calls the **pop_back** function. **top** calls the **back** function from the underlying container to get the last element, which is the top of the stack. Thus, it restricts the user operations to LIFO since it only allows us to update values at one end of the underlying container.

Here, we are using deque as an underlying container, and not a vector. The reason behind it is that deque doesn't require you to shift all the elements during reallocation, unlike vector. Hence, it is more efficient to use deque compared to vector. However, if, for some scenario, any other container is more likely to give better performance, stack gives us the facility to provide a container as a template parameter. So, we can build a stack using a vector or list as well, as shown here:

```
std::stack<int, std::vector<int>> stk;

std::stack<int, std::list<int>> stk;
```

All the operations of a stack have a time complexity of O(1). There is usually no overhead of forwarding the call to the underlying container as everything can be inlined by the compiler with optimizations.

std::queue

Just like `std::stack`, we have another container adapter to deal with the frequent scenario of **FIFO** (**First In First Out**) in many applications, and this structure is provided by an adaptor called `std::queue`. It almost has the same set of functions as a stack, but the meaning and behavior are different in order to follow FIFO instead of LIFO. For **std::queue**, **push** means **push_back**, just like a stack, but **pop** is **pop_front**. Instead of **pop**, since queue should be exposing both the ends for reading, it has **front** and **back** functions.

Here's a small example of the usage of **std::queue**:

```
std::queue<int> q;

q.push(1);   // queue becomes {1}

q.push(2);   // queue becomes {1, 2}

q.push(3);   // queue becomes {1, 2, 3}

q.pop();     // queue becomes {2, 3}

q.push(4);   // queue becomes {2, 3, 4}
```

As shown in this example, first, we are inserting 1, 2, and 3 in that order. After that, we are popping one element off the queue. Since 1 was pushed first, it is removed from the queue first. Then, the next push inserts 4 at the back of the queue.

`std::queue` also uses `std::deque` as an underlying container for the same reason as stack, and it also has a time complexity of O(1) for all the methods shown here.

std::priority_queue

Priority queue provides a very useful structure called **heap** via its interface. A heap data structure is known for fast access to the minimum (or maximum) element from the container. Getting the min/max element is an operation with a time complexity of O(1). Insertion has O(*log n*) time complexity, while deletion can only be performed for the min/max element, which always stays on the top.

An important thing to note here is that we can only have either the min or max function made available quickly, and not both of them. This is decided by the comparator provided to the container. Unlike stack and queue, a priority queue is based on a vector by default, but we can change it if required. Also, by default, the comparator is `std::less`. Since this is a heap, the resultant container is a max heap. This means that the maximum element will be on top by default.

Here, since insertion needs to make sure that we can access the top element (min or max depending on the comparator) instantly, it is not simply forwarding the call to the underlying container. Instead, it is implementing the algorithm for heapifying the data by bubbling it up to the top as required using the comparator. This operation takes a time duration that is logarithmic in proportion to the size of the container, hence the time complexity of O(*log n*). The invariant also needs to be maintained while initializing it with multiple elements. Here, however, the `priority_queue` constructor does not simply call the insertion function for each element; instead, it applies different heapification algorithms to do it faster in O(*n*).

Iterators for Adaptors

All the adaptors that we have seen so far expose functionality only as required to fulfill its semantic meaning. Logically thinking, traversing through stack, queue, and priority queue doesn't make sense. At any point, we should only be able to see the front element. Hence, STL doesn't provide iterators for that.

Benchmarking

As we have seen that different containers have a variety of pros and cons, no one container is the perfect choice for every situation. Sometimes, multiple containers may give a similar performance on average for the given scenario. In such cases, benchmarking is our friend. This is a process of determining the better approach based on statistical data.

Consider a scenario where we want to store data in contiguous memory, access it, and operate on it using various functions. We can say that we should either use **std::vector** or **std::deque**. But we are not sure which among these will be the best. At first glance, both of them seem to give good performance for the situation. Among different operations, such as access, insertion, **push_back**, and modifying a specific element, some are in favor of **std::vector** and some of are in favor of **std::deque**. So, how should we proceed?

The idea is to create a small prototype of the actual model and implement it using both **std::vector** and **std::deque**. And then, measure the performance of both over the prototype. Based on the result of the performance testing, we can choose the one that gives better results overall.

The simplest way to do that is to measure the time required to perform different operations for both and compare them. However, the same operation may take different amounts of time during different runs, since there are other factors that come into the picture, such as OS scheduling, cache, and interrupts, among others. These parameters can cause our results to deviate quite heavily, because, to perform any operation once, is a matter of a few hundred nanoseconds. To overcome that, we can perform the operation multiple times (by that, we mean a few million times) until we get a considerable time difference between both the measurements.

There are some benchmarking tools that we can use, such as quick-bench.com, which provide us with an easy way to run benchmarks. You can try running the operations mentioned earlier on vector and deque to quickly compare the performance differences.

Activity 3: Simulating a Queue for a Shared Printer in an Office

In this activity, we'll simulate a queue for a shared printer in an office. In any corporate office, usually, the printer is shared across the whole floor in the printer room. All the computers in this room are connected to the same printer. But a printer can do only one printing job at any point in time, and it also takes some time to complete any job. In the meantime, some other user can send another print request. In such a case, a printer needs to store all the pending jobs somewhere so that it can take them up once its current task is done.

Perform the following steps to solve the activity:

1. Create a class called **Job** (comprising an ID for the job, the name of the user who submitted it, and the number of pages).

2. Create a class called **Printer**. This will provide an interface to add new jobs and process all the jobs added so far.

3. To implement the **printer** class, it will need to store all the pending jobs. We'll implement a very basic strategy – first come, first served. Whoever submits the job first will be the first to get the job done.

4. Finally, simulate a scenario where multiple people are adding jobs to the printer, and the printer is processing them one by one.

> **Note**
>
> The solution to this activity can be found on page 487.

Summary

In this chapter, we learned how we should go about designing an application based on its requirements by choosing the way we want to store the data. We explained different types of operations that we can perform on data, which can be used as parameters for comparison between multiple data structures, based on the frequency of those operations. We learned that container adaptors provide a very useful way to indicate our intentions in the code. We saw that using more restrictive containers provided as adaptors, instead of using primary containers providing more functionality, is more effective in terms of maintainability, and also reduces human errors. We explained various data structures – **std::array**, **std::vector**, **std::list**, and **std::forward_list**, which are very frequent in any application development process, in detail and their interfaces provided by C++ by default. This helps us to write efficient code without reinventing the whole cycle and making the process a lot faster.

In this chapter, all the structures we saw are linear in a logical manner, that is, we can either go forward or backward from any element. In the next chapter, we'll explore problems that can't be solved easily with these structures and implement new types of structures to solve those problems.

Trees, Heaps, and Graphs

Learning Objectives

By the end of this chapter, you will be able to:

- Analyze and identify where non-linear data structures can be used

- Implement and manipulate tree structures to represent data and solve problems

- Traverse a tree using various methods

- Implement a graph structure to represent data and solve problems

- Represent a graph using different methods based on a given scenario

In this chapter, we will look at two non-linear data structures, namely trees and graphs, and how they can be used to represent real-world scenarios and solve various problems.

Introduction

In the previous chapter, we implemented different types of linear data structures to store and manage data in a linear fashion. In linear structures, we can traverse in, at most, two directions – forward or backward. However, the scope of these structures is very limited, and they can't be used to solve advanced problems. In this chapter, we'll explore a more advanced class of problems. We will see that the solutions we implemented previously are not good enough to be used directly. Due to this, we'll expand upon those data structures to make more complex structures that can be used to represent non-linear data.

After looking at these problems, we'll discuss basic solutions using the **tree** data structure. We'll implement different types of trees to solve different kinds of problems. After that, we'll have a look at a special type of tree called a **heap**, as well as its possible implementation and applications. Following that, we'll look at another complex structure – **graphs**. We'll implement two different representations of a graph. These structures help translate real-world scenarios into a mathematical form. Then, we will apply our programming skills and techniques to solve problems related to those scenarios.

A strong understanding of trees and graphs serves as the basis for understanding even more advanced problems. Databases (B-trees), data encoding/compression (Huffman tree), graph coloring, assignment problems, minimum distance problems, and many more problems are solved using certain variants of trees and graphs.

Now, let's look at some examples of problems that cannot be represented by linear data structures.

Non-Linear Problems

Two main categories of situations that cannot be represented with the help of linear data structures are hierarchical problems and cyclic dependencies. Let's take a closer look at these cases.

Hierarchical Problems

Let's look at a couple of examples that inherently have hierarchical properties. The following is the structure of an organization:

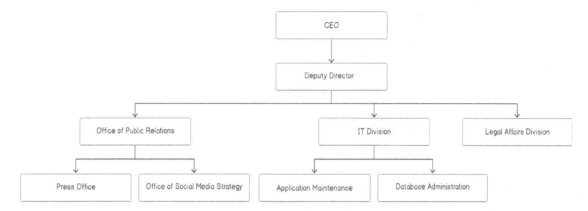

Figure 2.1: Organization structure

As we can see, the CEO is the head of the company and manages the Deputy Director. The Deputy Director leads three other officers, and so on.

The data is inherently hierarchical in nature. This type of data is difficult to manage using simple arrays, vectors, or linked lists. To solidify our understanding, let's look at another use case; that is, a university course's structure, as shown in the following figure:

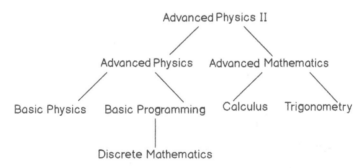

Figure 2.2: Course hierarchy in a university course structure

The preceding figure shows the course dependencies for some courses in a hypothetical university. As we can see, to learn Advanced Physics II, the student must have successfully completed the following courses: Advanced Physics and Advanced Mathematics. Similarly, many other courses have their own prerequisites.

Given such data, we can have different types of queries. For example, we may want to find out which courses need to be completed successfully so that we can learn Advanced Mathematics.

These kinds of problems can be solved using a data structure called a tree. All of the objects are known as the nodes of a tree, while the paths leading from one node to another are known as edges. We'll take a deeper look at this in the *Graphs* section, later in this chapter.

Cyclic Dependencies

Let's look at another complex real-world scenario that can be represented better with a non-linear structure. The following figure represents the friendship between a few people:

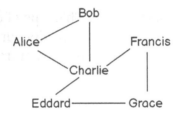

Figure 2.3: A network of friends

This structure is called a graph. The names of people, or the elements, are called nodes, and the relations between them are represented as edges. Such structures are commonly used by various social networks to represent their users and the connections between them. We can observe that Alice is friends with Charlie, who is friends with Eddard, who is friends with Grace, and so on. We can also infer that Alice, Bob, and Charlie know each other. We may also infer that Eddard is a first-level connection for Grace, Charlie is a second-level connection, and Alice and Bob are third-level connections.

Another area where graphs are useful is when we want to represent networks of roads between cities, as you will see in the *Graphs* section later in this chapter.

Tree – It's Upside Down!

As we discussed in the previous section, a tree is nothing but some objects or nodes connected to other nodes via a relationship that results in some sort of hierarchy. If we were to show this hierarchy in a graphical way, it would look like a tree, while the different edges would look like its branches. The main node, which is not dependent on any other node, is also known as a root node and is usually represented at the top. So, unlike an actual tree, this tree is upside down, with the root at its top!

Let's try to construct a structure for a very basic version of an organizational hierarchy.

Exercise 7: Creating an Organizational Structure

In this exercise, we will implement a basic version of the organizational tree we saw in the introduction to this chapter. Let's get started:

1. First, let's include the required headers:

```
#include <iostream>
#include <queue>
```

2. For simplicity, we'll assume that any person can have, at most, two subordinates. We'll see that this is not difficult to extend to resemble real-life situations. This kind of tree is also known as a **binary tree**. Let's write a basic structure for that:

```
struct node
{
    std::string position;
    node *first, *second;
};
```

As we can see, any node will have two links to other nodes – both of their subordinates. By doing this, we can show the recursive structure of the data. We are only storing the position at the moment, but we can easily extend this to include a name at that position or even a whole struct comprising all the information about the person in that position.

3. We don't want end users to deal with this kind of raw data structure. So, let's wrap this in a nice interface called **org_tree**:

```
struct org_tree
{
    node *root;
```

4. Now, let's add a function to create the root, starting with the highest commanding officer of the company:

```
static org_tree create_org_structure(const std::string& pos)
{
    org_tree tree;
    tree.root = new node{pos, NULL, NULL};
    return tree;
}
```

This is a static function just to create the tree. Now, let's see how we can extend the tree.

5. Now, we want to add a subordinate of an employee. The function should take two parameters – the name of the already existing employee in the tree and the name of the new employee to be added as a subordinate. But before that, let's write another function that will help us find a particular node based on a value to make our insertion function easier:

```
static node* find(node* root, const std::string& value)
{
    if(root == NULL)
        return NULL;
    if(root->position == value)
        return root;
    auto firstFound = org_tree::find(root->first, value);
    if(firstFound != NULL)
        return firstFound;
    return org_tree::find(root->second, value);
}
```

While we are traversing the tree in search of an element, either the element will be the node we are at, or it will be in either of the right or left subtrees.

Hence, we need to check the root node first. If it is not the desired node, we'll try to find it in the left subtree. Finally, if we haven't succeeded in doing that, we'll look at the right subtree.

6. Now, let's implement the insertion function. We'll make use of the **find** function in order to reuse the code:

```
bool addSubordinate(const std::string& manager, const std::string&
subordinate)
{
    auto managerNode = org_tree::find(root, manager);
    if(!managerNode)
```

```
    {
        std::cout << "No position named " << manager << std::endl;
        return false;
    }
    if(managerNode->first && managerNode->second)
    {
        std::cout << manager << " already has 2 subordinates." <<
std::endl;
        return false;
    }
    if(!managerNode->first)
        managerNode->first = new node{subordinate, NULL, NULL};
    else
        managerNode->second = new node{subordinate, NULL, NULL};
    return true;
}
};
```

As we can see, the function returns a Boolean, indicating whether we can insert the node successfully or not.

7. Now, let's use this code to create a tree in the **main** function:

```
int main()
{
    auto tree = org_tree::create_org_structure("CEO");
    if(tree.addSubordinate("CEO", "Deputy Director"))
        std::cout << "Added Deputy Director in the tree." << std::endl;
    else
        std::cout << "Couldn't add Deputy Director in the tree" <<
std::endl;

    if(tree.addSubordinate("Deputy Director", "IT Head"))
        std::cout << "Added IT Head in the tree." << std::endl;
    else
        std::cout << "Couldn't add IT Head in the tree" << std::endl;
    if(tree.addSubordinate("Deputy Director", "Marketing Head"))
        std::cout << "Added Marketing Head in the tree." << std::endl;
    else
        std::cout << "Couldn't add Marketing Head in the tree" <<
std::endl;

    if(tree.addSubordinate("IT Head", "Security Head"))
```

```
            std::cout << "Added Security Head in the tree." << std::endl;
        else
            std::cout << "Couldn't add Security Head in the tree" <<
    std::endl;

        if(tree.addSubordinate("IT Head", "App Development Head"))
            std::cout << "Added App Development Head in the tree." <<
    std::endl;
        else
            std::cout << "Couldn't add App Development Head in the tree" <<
    std::endl;

    if(tree.addSubordinate("Marketing Head", "Logistics Head"))
            std::cout << "Added Logistics Head in the tree." << std::endl;
        else
            std::cout << "Couldn't add Logistics Head in the tree" <<
    std::endl;

        if(tree.addSubordinate("Marketing Head", "Public Relations Head"))
            std::cout << "Added Public Relations Head in the tree." <<
    std::endl;
        else
            std::cout << "Couldn't add Public Relations Head in the tree" <<
    std::endl;

        if(tree.addSubordinate("Deputy Director", "Finance Head"))
            std::cout << "Added Finance Head in the tree." << std::endl;
        else
            std::cout << "Couldn't add Finance Head in the tree" << std::endl;
    }
```

You should get the following output upon executing the preceding code:

```
Added Deputy Director in the tree.
Added IT Head in the tree.
Added Marketing Head in the tree.
Added Security Head in the tree.
Added App Development Head in the tree.
Added Logistics Head in the tree.
Added Public Relations Head in the tree.
Deputy Director already has 2 subordinates.
Couldn't add Finance Head in the tree
```

This output is illustrated in the following diagram:

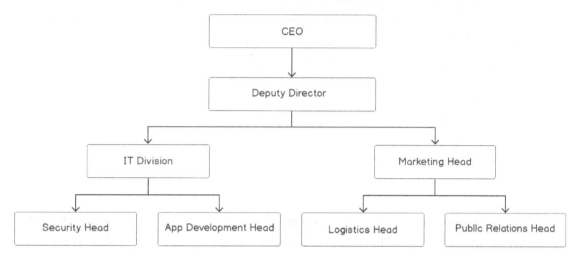

Figure 2.4: Binary tree based on an organization's hierarchy

Up until now, we've just inserted elements. Now, we'll look at how we can traverse the tree. Although we've already seen how to traverse using the **find** function, that's just one of the ways we can do it. We can traverse a tree in many other ways, all of which we'll look at in the following section.

Traversing Trees

Once we have a tree, there are various ways we can traverse it and get to the node that we require. Let's take a brief look at the various traversal methods:

- **Preorder traversal**: In this method, we visit the current node first, followed by the left child of the current node, and then the right child of the current node in a recursive fashion. Here, the prefix "pre" indicates that the parent node is visited before its children. Traversing the tree shown in *figure 2.4* using the preorder method goes like this:

    CEO, Deputy Director, IT Head, Security Head, App Development Head, Marketing Head, Logistics Head, Public Relations Head,

As we can see, we are always visiting the parent node, followed by the left child node, followed by the right child node. We do this not just for the root, but for any node with respect to its subtree. We implement preorder traversal using a function like this:

```cpp
static void preOrder(node* start)
{
    if(!start)
        return;
    std::cout << start->position << ", ";
    preOrder(start->first);
    preOrder(start->second);
}
```

- **In-order traversal**: In this type of traversal, first we'll visit the left node, then the parent node, and finally the right node. Traversing the tree that's shown in *figure 2.4* goes like this:

  Security Head, IT Head, App Development Head, Deputy Director, Logistics Head, Marketing Head, Public Relations Head, CEO,

  We can implement this in a function like so:

```cpp
static void inOrder(node* start)
{
    if(!start)
        return;
    inOrder(start->first);
    std::cout << start->position << ", ";
    inOrder(start->second);
}
```

- **Post-order traversal**: In this traversal, we first visit both the children, followed by the parent node. Traversing the tree that's shown in *figure 2.4* goes like this:

  Security Head, App Development Head, IT Head, Logistics Head, Public Relations Head, Marketing Head, Deputy Director, CEO,

We can implement this in a function like so:

```cpp
static void postOrder(node* start)
{
    if(!start)
        return;
    postOrder(start->first);
    postOrder(start->second);
    std::cout << start->position << ", ";
}
```

- **Level order traversal**: This requires us to traverse the tree level by level, from top to bottom, and from left to right. This is similar to listing the elements at each level of the tree, starting from the root level. The results of such a traversal are usually represented as per the levels, as shown here:

```
CEO,
Deputy Director,
IT Head, Marketing Head,
Security Head, App Development Head, Logistics Head, Public Relations
Head,
```

The implementation of this method of traversal is demonstrated in the following exercise.

Exercise 8: Demonstrating Level Order Traversal

In this exercise, we'll implement level order traversal in the organizational structure we created in *Exercise 7, Creating an Organizational Structure*. Unlike the previous traversal methods, here, we are not traversing to the nodes that are directly connected to the current node. This means that traversing is easier to achieve without recursion. We will extend the code that was shown in *Exercise 7* to demonstrate this traversal. Let's get started:

1. First, we'll add the following function inside the **org_tree** structure from *Exercise 7*:

```cpp
static void levelOrder(node* start)
{
    if(!start)
        return;
    std::queue<node*> q;
    q.push(start);
    while(!q.empty())
    {
        int size = q.size();
```

```
        for(int i = 0; i < size; i++)
        {
            auto current = q.front();
            q.pop();
            std::cout << current->position << ", ";
            if(current->first)
                q.push(current->first);
            if(current->second)
                q.push(current->second);
        }
        std::cout << std::endl;
    }
}
```

As shown in the preceding code, first, we're traversing the root node, followed by its children. While visiting the children, we push their children in the queue to be processed after the current level is completed. The idea is to start the queue from the first level and add the nodes of the next level to the queue. We will continue doing this until the queue is empty – indicating there are no more nodes in the next level.

2. This is what our output should look like:

```
CEO,
Deputy Director,
IT Head, Marketing Head,
Security Head, App Development Head, Logistics Head, Public Relations
Head,
```

Variants of Trees

In the previous exercises, we've mainly looked at the **binary tree**, which is one of the most common kinds of trees. In a binary tree, each node can have two child nodes at most. However, a plain binary tree doesn't always serve this purpose. Next, we'll look at a more specialized version of the binary tree, called a binary search tree.

Binary Search Tree

A **binary search tree** (**BST**) is a popular version of the binary tree. BST is nothing but a binary tree with the following properties:

- Value of the parent node ≥ value of the left child

- Value of the parent node ≤ value of the right child

In short, left child ≤ parent ≤ right child.

This leads us to an interesting feature. At any point in time, we can always say that all the elements that are less than or equal to the parent node will be on the left side, while those greater than or equal to the parent node will be on the right side. So, the problem of searching an element keeps on reducing by half, in terms of search space, at each step.

If the BST is constructed in a way that all the elements except those at the last level have both children, the height of the tree will be *log n*, where *n* is the number of elements. Due to this, the searching and insertion will have a time complexity of O(*log n*). This type of binary tree is also known as a **complete binary tree**.

Searching in a BST

Let's look at how we can search, insert, and delete elements in a binary search tree. Consider a BST with unique positive integers, as shown in the following figure:

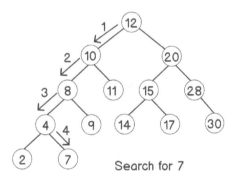

Figure 2.5: Searching for an element in a binary search tree

Let's say that we have to search for 7. As we can see from the steps represented by arrows in the preceding figure, we choose the side after comparing the value with the current node's data. As we've already mentioned, all the nodes on the left will always be less than the current node, and all the nodes on the right will always be greater than the current node.

Thus, we start by comparing the root node with 7. If it is greater than 7, we move to the left subtree, since all the elements there are smaller than the parent node, and vice versa. We compare each child node until we stumble upon 7, or a node less than 7 with no right node. In this case, coming to node 4 leads to our target, 7.

As we can see, we're not traversing the whole tree. Instead, we are reducing our scope by half every time the current node is not the desired one, which we do by choosing either the left or the right side. This works similar to a binary search for linear structures, which we will learn about in *Chapter 4, Divide and Conquer*.

Inserting a New Element into a BST

Now, let's look at how insertion works. The steps are shown in the following figure:

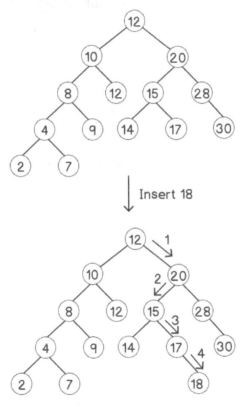

Figure 2.6: Inserting an element into a binary search tree

As you can see, first, we have to find the parent node where we want to insert the new value. Thus, we have to take a similar approach to the one we took for searching; that is, by going in the direction based on comparing each node with our new element, starting with the root node. At the last step, 18 is greater than 17, but 17 doesn't have a right child. Therefore, we insert 18 in that position.

Deleting an Element from a BST

Now, let's look at how deletion works. Consider the following BST:

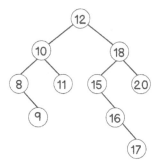

Figure 2.7: Binary search tree rooted at 12

We will delete the root node, 12, in the tree. Let's look at how we can delete any value. It's a bit trickier than insertion since we need to find the replacement of the deleted node so that the properties of the BST remain true.

The first step is to find the node to be deleted. After that, there are three possibilities:

- The node has no children: simply delete the node.
- The node has only one child: point the parent node's corresponding pointer to the only existing child.
- The node has two children: in this case, we replace the current node with its successor.

The successor is the next biggest number after the current node. Or, in other words, the successor is the smallest element among all the elements greater than the current one. Therefore, we'll first go to the right subtree, which contains all the elements greater than the current one, and find the smallest among them. Finding the smallest node means going to the left side of the subtree as much as we can because the left child node is always less than its parent. In the tree shown in *figure* 2.7, the right subtree of 12 starts at 18. So, we start looking from there, and then try to move down to the left child of 15. But 15 does not have a left child, and the other child, 16, is larger than 15. Hence, 15 should be the successor here.

To replace 12 with 15, first, we will copy the value of the successor at the root while deleting 12, as shown in the following figure:

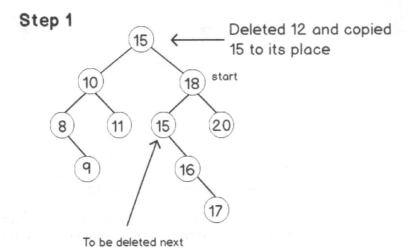

Figure 2.8: Successor copied to the root node

Next, we need to delete the successor, 15, from its old place in the right subtree, as shown in the following figure:

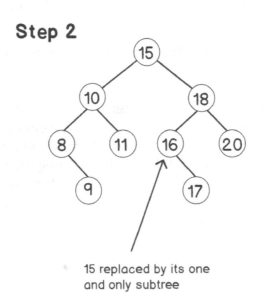

Figure 2.9: Successor deleted from its old place

In the last step, we're deleting node 15. We use the same process for this deletion as well. Since 15 had just one child, we replace the left child of 18 with the child of 15. So, the whole subtree rooted at 16 becomes the left child of 18.

> **Note**
>
> The successor node can only have one child at most. If it had a left child, we would have picked that child and not the current node as the successor.

Time Complexities of Operations on a Tree

Now, let's look at the time complexity of these functions. Theoretically, we can say that we reduce the scope of the search by half each time. Hence, the time that's required to search for the BST with n nodes is $T(n) = T(n / 2) + 1$. This equation results in a time complexity of $T(n) = O(log\ n)$.

But there's a catch to this. If we look at the insertion function closely, the order of insertion actually determines the shape of the tree. And it is not necessarily true that we'll always reduce the scope of the search by half, as described by $T(n/2)$ in the previous formula. Therefore, the complexity $O(log\ n)$ is not always accurate. We'll look at this problem and its solution in more depth in the *Balanced Tree* section, where we will see how we can calculate time complexity more accurately.

For now, let's implement the operations we just saw in C++.

Exercise 9: Implementing a Binary Search Tree

In this exercise, we will implement the BST shown in *figure 2.7* and add a **find** function to search for elements. We will also try our hand at the insertion and deletion of elements, as explained in the previous subsections. Let's get started:

1. First, let's include the required headers:

    ```cpp
    #include <iostream>
    ```

2. Now, let's write a node. This will be similar to our previous exercise, except we'll have an integer instead of a string:

    ```cpp
    struct node
    {
        int data;
        node *left, *right;
    };
    ```

3. Now, let's add a wrapper over the node to provide a clean interface:

```
struct bst
{
    node* root = nullptr;
```

4. Before writing the insertion function, we'll need to write the **find** function:

```
node* find(int value)
{
    return find_impl(root, value);
}

    private:
node* find_impl(node* current, int value)
{
    if(!current)
    {
        std::cout << std::endl;
        return NULL;
    }
    if(current->data == value)
    {
        std::cout << "Found " << value << std::endl;
        return current;
    }
    if(value < current->data)  // Value will be in the left subtree
    {
        std::cout << "Going left from " << current->data << ", ";
        return find_impl(current->left, value);
    }
    if(value > current->data) // Value will be in the right subtree
    {
        std::cout << "Going right from " << current->data << ", ";
        return find_impl(current->right, value);
    }
}
```

Since this is recursive, we have kept the implementation in a separate function and made it private so as to prevent someone from using it directly.

5. Now, let's write an **insert** function. It will be similar to the **find** function, but with small tweaks. First, let's find the parent node, which is where we want to insert the new value:

```
public:
void insert(int value)
{
    if(!root)
        root = new node{value, NULL, NULL};
    else
        insert_impl(root, value);
}

private:
void insert_impl(node* current, int value)
{
    if(value < current->data)
    {
        if(!current->left)
            current->left = new node{value, NULL, NULL};
        else
            insert_impl(current->left, value);
    }
    else
    {
        if(!current->right)
            current->right = new node{value, NULL, NULL};
        else
            insert_impl(current->right, value);
    }
}
```

As we can see, we are checking whether the value should be inserted in the left or right subtree. If there's nothing on the desired side, we directly insert the node there; otherwise, we call the **insert** function for that side recursively.

6. Now, let's write an **inorder** traversal function. In-order traversal provides an important advantage when applied to BST, as we will see in the output:

```cpp
public:
void inorder()
{
    inorder_impl(root);
}

private:
void inorder_impl(node* start)
{
    if(!start)
        return;
    inorder_impl(start->left);        // Visit the left sub-tree
    std::cout << start->data << " ";  // Print out the current node
    inorder_impl(start->right);       // Visit the right sub-tree
}
```

7. Now, let's implement a utility function to get the successor:

```cpp
public:
node* successor(node* start)
{
    auto current = start->right;
    while(current && current->left)
        current = current->left;
    return current;
}
```

This follows the logic we discussed in the *Deleting an Element in BST* subsection.

8. Now, let's look at the actual implementation of **delete**. Since deletion requires repointing the parent node, we'll do that by returning the new node every time. We'll hide this complexity by putting a better interface over it. We'll name the interface **deleteValue** since **delete** is a reserved keyword, as per the C++ standard:

```cpp
void deleteValue(int value)
{
    root = delete_impl(root, value);
}

private:
node* delete_impl(node* start, int value)
{
```

```
        if(!start)
            return NULL;
        if(value < start->data)
            start->left = delete_impl(start->left, value);
        else if(value > start->data)
            start->right = delete_impl(start->right, value);
        else
        {
            if(!start->left)  // Either both children are absent or only left
child is absent
            {
                auto tmp = start->right;
                delete start;
                return tmp;
            }
            if(!start->right)  // Only right child is absent
            {
                auto tmp = start->left;
                delete start;
                return tmp;
            }

            auto succNode = successor(start);
            start->data = succNode->data;
            // Delete the successor from right subtree, since it will always
be in the right subtree
            start->right = delete_impl(start->right, succNode->data);
        }
        return start;
    }
};
```

9. Let's write the **main** function so that we can use the BST:

```
int main()
{
    bst tree;
    tree.insert(12);
    tree.insert(10);
    tree.insert(20);
    tree.insert(8);
    tree.insert(11);
    tree.insert(15);
```

```
        tree.insert(28);
        tree.insert(4);
        tree.insert(2);

        std::cout << "Inorder: ";
        tree.inorder();  // This will print all the elements in ascending
    order
        std::cout << std::endl;

        tree.deleteValue(12);
        std::cout << "Inorder after deleting 12: ";
        tree.inorder();  // This will print all the elements in ascending
    order
        std::cout << std::endl;

        if(tree.find(12))
            std::cout << "Element 12 is present in the tree" << std::endl;
        else
            std::cout << "Element 12 is NOT present in the tree" << std::endl;
    }
```

The output upon executing the preceding code should be as follows:

```
Inorder: 2 4 8 10 11 12 15 20 28
Inorder after deleting 12: 2 4 8 10 11 15 20 28
Going left from 15, Going right from 10, Going right from 11,
Element 12 is NOT present in the tree
```

Observe the preceding results of in-order traversal for a BST. In-order will visit the left subtree first, then the current node, and then the right subtree, recursively, as shown in the comments in the code snippet. So, as per BST properties, we'll visit all the values smaller than the current one first, then the current one, and after that, we'll visit all the values greater than the current one. And since this happens recursively, we'll get our data sorted in ascending order.

Balanced Tree

Before we understand a balanced tree, let's start with an example of a BST for the following insertion order:

```
bst tree;

tree.insert(10);

tree.insert(9);

tree.insert(11);
```

```
tree.insert(8);

tree.insert(7);

tree.insert(6);

tree.insert(5);

tree.insert(4);
```

This BST can be visualized with the help of the following figure:

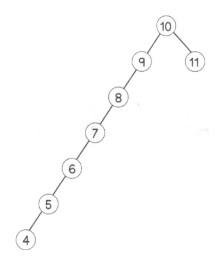

Figure 2.10: Skewed binary search tree

As shown in the preceding figure, almost the whole tree is skewed to the left side. If we call the **find** function, that is, **bst.find(4)**, the steps will look as follows:

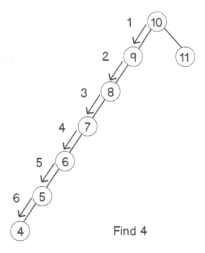

Figure 2.11: Finding an element in a skewed binary search tree

As we can see, the number of steps is almost equal to the number of elements. Now, let's try the same thing again with a different insertion order, as shown here:

```
bst tree;
tree.insert(7);
tree.insert(5);
tree.insert(9);
tree.insert(4);
tree.insert(6);
tree.insert(10);
tree.insert(11);
tree.insert(8);
```

The BST and the steps required to find element 4 will now look as follows:

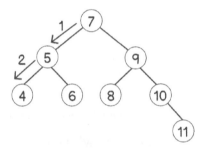

Figure 2.12: Finding an element in a balanced tree

As we can see, the tree is not skewed anymore. Or, in other words, the tree is balanced. The steps to find 4 have been considerably reduced with this configuration. Thus, the time complexity of **find** is not just dependent on the number of elements, but also on their configuration in the tree. If we look at the steps closely, we are always going one step toward the bottom of the tree while searching for something. And at the end, we end up at the leaf nodes (nodes without any children). Here, we return either the desired node or NULL based on the availability of the element. So, we can say that the number of steps is always less than the maximum number of levels in the BST, also known as the height of the BST. So, the actual time complexity for finding an element is O(height).

In order to optimize the time complexity, we need to optimize the height of the tree. This is also called *balancing a tree*. The idea is to reorganize the nodes after insertion/deletion to reduce the skewness of the tree. The resultant tree is called a height-balanced BST.

There are various ways in which we can do this and get different types of trees, such as an AVL tree, a Red-Black tree, and so on. The idea behind an AVL tree is to perform some rotations to balance the height of the tree, while still maintaining the BST properties. Consider the example that's shown in the following figure:

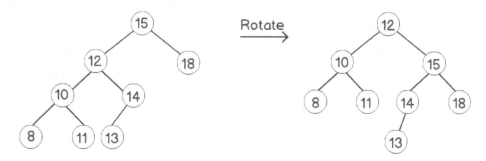

Figure 2.13: Rotating a tree

As we can see, the tree on the right is more balanced compared to the one on the left. Rotation is out of the scope of this book and so we will not venture into the details of this example.

N-ary Tree

Up until now, we've mainly seen binary trees or their variants. For an N-ary tree, each node can have N children. Since N is arbitrary here, we are going to store it in a vector. So, the final structure looks something like this:

```
struct nTree
{
    int data;
    std::vector<nTree*> children;
};
```

As we can see, there can be any number of children for each node. Hence, the whole tree is completely arbitrary. However, just like a plain binary tree, a plain N-ary tree also isn't very useful. Therefore, we have to build a different tree for different kinds of applications, where the hierarchy is of a higher degree than a binary tree. The example shown in *figure 2.1*, which represents an organization's hierarchy, is an N-ary tree.

In the computer world, there are two really good, well-known implementations of N-ary trees, as follows:

- Filesystem structures in computers: Starting from **root** (/) in Linux or drives in Windows, we can have any number of files (terminal nodes) and any number of folders inside any folder. We'll look at this in greater detail in *Activity 1, Creating a Data Structure for a Filesystem*.

- Compilers: Most compilers build an Abstract Syntax Tree (AST) based on syntax defined by the standard that's used for the source code. Compilers generate lower-level code by parsing the AST.

Activity 4: Create a Data Structure for a Filesystem

Create a data structure using an N-ary tree for a filesystem that supports the following operations: go to directory, find file/directory, add file/directory, and list file/directory. Our tree will hold the information and folder hierarchy (path) of all the elements (files and folders) in the filesystem.

Perform the following steps to solve this activity:

1. Create an N-ary tree with two data elements in a node – the name of the directory/file and a flag indicating whether it's a directory or a file.

2. Add a data member to store the current directory.

3. Initialize the tree with a single directory root (/).

4. Add the find directory/file function, which takes a single parameter – **path**. The **path** can be either absolute (starting with /) or relative.

5. Add functions to add a file/directory and list files/directories located at a given path.

6. Similarly, add a function to change the current directory.

> **Note**
>
> The solution to this activity can be found on page 490.

We've printed directories with **d** in front to distinguish them from files, which are printed with a "-" (hyphen) in front. You can experiment by creating more directories and files with absolute or relative paths.

So far, we haven't supported certain Linux conventions, such as addressing any directory with a single dot and addressing a parent directory with double dots. This can be done by extending our node to also hold a pointer to its parent node. This way, we can traverse in both directions very easily. There are various other extensions possible, such as the addition of symlinks, as well as globing operators to expand the names of the various files/directories using "*". This exercise provides us with a base so that we can build something on our own based on our requirements.

Heaps

In the previous chapter, we had a brief look at heaps and how C++ provides heaps via STL. In this chapter, we'll take a deeper look at heaps. Just to recap, the following are the intended time complexities:

- $O(1)$: Immediate access to the max element

- $O(\log n)$: Insertion of any element

- $O(\log n)$: Deletion of the max element

To achieve $O(\log n)$ insertion/deletion, we'll use a tree to store data. But in this case, we'll 'use a complete tree. A **complete tree** is defined as a tree where nodes at all the levels except the last one have two children, and the last level has as many of the elements on the left side as possible. For example, consider the two trees shown in the following figure:

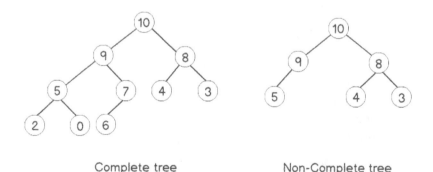

Complete tree   Non-Complete tree

Figure 2.14: Complete versus non-complete tree

Thus, a complete tree can be constructed by inserting elements in the last level, as long as there's enough space there. If not, we will insert them at the leftmost position on the new level. This gives us a very good opportunity to store this tree using an array, level by level. So, the root of the tree will be the first element of the array/vector, followed by its left child and then the right child, and so on. Unlike other trees, this is a very efficient memory structure because there is no extra memory required to store pointers. To go from a parent to its child node, we can easily use the index of the array. If the parent is the ith node, its children will always be $2*i + 1$ and $2*i + 2$ indices. And similarly, we can get the parent node for the ith child node by using $(i - 1) / 2$. We can also confirm this from the preceding figure.

Now, let's have a look at the invariants (or conditions) we need to maintain upon every insertion/deletion. The first requirement is instant access to the max element. For that, we need to fix its position so that it is accessible immediately every time. We'll always keep our max element at the top – the root position. Now, to maintain this, we also need to maintain another invariant – the parent node must be greater than both of its children. Such a heap is also known as a **max heap**.

As you can probably guess, the properties that are required for fast access to the maximum element can be easily inverted for fast access to the minimum element. All we need to do is invert our comparison function while performing heap operations. This kind of heap is known as a **min heap**.

Heap Operations

In this section, we will see how we can perform different operations on a heap.

Inserting an Element into a Heap

As the first step of insertion, we will preserve the most important invariant, which provides us with a way to represent this structure as an array – a complete tree. This can easily be done by inserting the new element at the end since it will represent the element in the last level, right after all the existing elements, or as the first element in a new level if the current last level is full.

Now, we need to preserve the other invariant – all the nodes must have a value greater than both of their children, if available. Assuming that our current tree is already following this invariant, after the insertion of the new element in the last position, the only element where the invariant may fail would be the last element. To resolve this, we swap the element with its parent if the parent is smaller than the element. Even if the parent already has another element, it will be smaller than the new element (new element > parent > child).

Thus, the subtree that's created by considering the new element as the root satisfies all the invariants. However, the new element may still be greater than its new parent. Therefore, we need to keep on swapping the nodes until the invariant is satisfied for the whole tree. Since the height of a complete tree is $O(log\ n)$ at most, the entire operation will take a maximum of $O(log\ n)$ time. The following figure illustrates the operation of inserting elements into a tree:

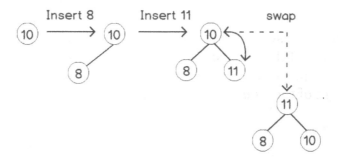

Figure 2.15: Inserting an element into a heap with one node

As shown in the preceding figure, after inserting 11, the tree doesn't have the heap property anymore. Therefore, we'll swap 10 and 11 to make it a heap again. This concept is clearer with the following example, which has more levels:

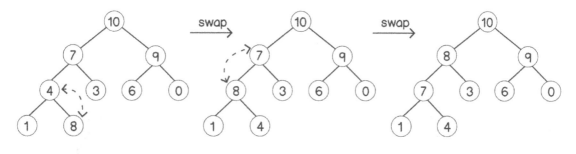

Insert 8

Figure 2.16: Inserting an element into a heap with several nodes

Deleting an Element from a Heap

The first thing to notice is that we can only delete the max element. We can't directly touch any other element. The max element is always present at the root. Hence, we'll remove the root element. But we also need to decide who'll take its position. For that, we first need to swap the root with the last element, and then remove the last element. That way, our root will be deleted, but it will break the invariant of having each parent node greater than its children. To resolve this, we'll compare the root with its two children and swap it with the greater one. Now, the invariant is broken at one of the subtrees. We continue the swapping process recursively throughout the subtree. That way, the breaking point of the invariant is bubbled down the tree. Just like insertion, we follow this until we meet the invariant. The maximum number of steps required will be equal to the height of the tree, which is O(log n). The following figure illustrates this process:

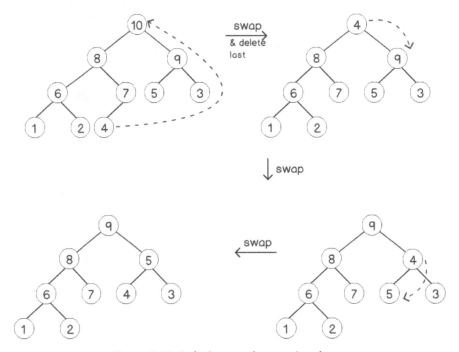

Figure 2.17: Deleting an element in a heap

Initialization of a Heap

Now, let's look at one of the most important steps – the initialization of a heap. Unlike vectors, lists, deques, and so on, a heap is not simple to initialize because we need to maintain the invariants of the heap. One easy solution would be to insert all the elements starting from an empty heap, one by one. But the time required for this would be O(n * log(n)), which is not efficient.

However, there's a **heapification** algorithm that can do this in $O(n)$ time. The idea behind this is very simple: we keep on updating the tree to match the heap properties for smaller subtrees in a bottom-up manner. For starters, the last level already has the properties of a heap. Followed by that, we go level by level toward the root, making each subtree follow the heap properties one by one. This process only has a time complexity of $O(n)$. And fortunately, the C++ standard already provides a function for this called `std::make_heap`, which can take any array or vector iterators and convert them into a heap.

Exercise 10: Streaming Median

In this exercise, we'll solve an interesting problem that frequently occurs in data analysis-related applications, including machine learning. Imagine that some source is giving us data one element at a time continuously (a stream of data). We need to find the median of the elements that have been received up until now after receiving each and every element. One simple way of doing this would be to sort the data every time a new element comes in and return the middle element. But this would have an $O(n \log n)$ time complexity because of sorting. Depending on the rate of incoming elements, this can be very resource-intensive. However, we'll optimize this with the help of heaps. Let's get started:

1. Let's include the required headers first:

   ```
   #include <iostream>
   #include <queue>
   #include <vector>
   ```

2. Now, let's write a container to store the data we've received up until now. We'll store the data among two heaps – one min heap and one max heap. We'll store the smaller, first half of the elements in a max heap, and the larger, or the other half, in a min heap. So, at any point, the median can be calculated using only the top elements of the heaps, which are easily accessible:

   ```
   struct median
   {
       std::priority_queue<int> maxHeap;
       std::priority_queue<int, std::vector<int>, std::greater<int>> minHeap;
   ```

3. Now, let's write an **insert** function so that we can insert the newly arrived data:

```
void insert(int data)
{
    // First element
    if(maxHeap.size() == 0)
    {
        maxHeap.push(data);
        return;
    }

    if(maxHeap.size() == minHeap.size())
    {
        if(data <= get())
            maxHeap.push(data);
        else
            minHeap.push(data);
        return;
    }
    if(maxHeap.size() < minHeap.size())
    {
        if(data > get())
        {
            maxHeap.push(minHeap.top());
            minHeap.pop();
            minHeap.push(data);
        }
        else
            maxHeap.push(data);
        return;
    }
    if(data < get())
    {
        minHeap.push(maxHeap.top());
        maxHeap.pop();
        maxHeap.push(data);
    }
    else
        minHeap.push(data);
}
```

4. Now, let's write a **get** function so that we can get the median from the containers:

```
double get()
{
    if(maxHeap.size() == minHeap.size())
        return (maxHeap.top() + minHeap.top()) / 2.0;
    if(maxHeap.size() < minHeap.size())
        return minHeap.top();
    return maxHeap.top();
}
};
```

5. Now, let's write a **main** function so that we can use this class:

```
int main()
{
    median med;
    med.insert(1);
    std::cout << "Median after insert 1: " << med.get() << std::endl;

    med.insert(5);
    std::cout << "Median after insert 5: " << med.get() << std::endl;

    med.insert(2);
    std::cout << "Median after insert 2: " << med.get() << std::endl;

    med.insert(10);
    std::cout << "Median after insert 10: " << med.get() << std::endl;

    med.insert(40);
    std::cout << "Median after insert 40: " << med.get() << std::endl;

    return 0;
}
```

The output of the preceding program is as follows:

```
Median after insert 1: 1
Median after insert 5: 3
Median after insert 2: 2
Median after insert 10: 3.5
Median after insert 40: 5
```

This way, we only need to insert any newly arriving elements, which only has a time complexity of $O(log\ n)$, compared to the time complexity of $O(n\ log\ n)$ if we were to sort the elements with each new element.

Activity 5: K-Way Merge Using Heaps

Consider a biomedical application related to genetics being used for processing large datasets. It requires ranks of DNA in a sorted manner to calculate similarity. But since the dataset is huge, it can't fit on a single machine. Therefore, it processes and stores data in a distributed cluster, and each node has a set of sorted values. The main processing engine requires all of the data to be in a sorted fashion and in a single stream. So, basically, we need to merge multiple sorted arrays into a single sorted array. Simulate this situation with the help of vectors.

Perform the following steps to solve this activity:

1. The smallest number will be present in the first element of all the lists since all the lists have already been sorted individually. To get that minimum faster, we'll build a heap of those elements.

2. After getting the minimum element from the heap, we need to remove it and replace it with the next element from the same list it belongs to.

3. The heap node must contain information about the list so that it can find the next number from that list.

> **Note**
>
> The solution to this activity can be found on page 495.

Now, let's calculate the time complexity of the preceding algorithm. If there are *k* lists available, our heap size will be k, and all of our heap operations will be $O(log\ k)$. Building heap will be $O(k\ log\ k)$. After that, we'll have to perform a heap operation for each element in the result. The total elements are $n \times k$. Therefore, the total complexity will be $O(nk\ log\ k)$.

The wonderful thing about this algorithm is that, considering the real-life scenario we described earlier, it doesn't actually need to store all the $n \times k$ elements at the same time; it only needs to store k elements at any point in time, where k is the number of lists or nodes in the cluster. Due to this, the value of k will never be too large. With the help of a heap, we can generate one number at a time and either process the number immediately or stream it elsewhere for processing without actually storing it.

Graphs

Although a tree is a pretty good way to represent hierarchical data, we can't represent circular or cyclic dependencies in a tree because we always have a single and unique path to go from one node to another. However, there are more complex scenarios that have a cyclic structure inherently. For example, consider a road network. There can be multiple ways to go from one place (places can be represented as nodes) to another. Such a set of scenarios can be better represented using graphs.

Unlike a tree, a graph has to store data for the nodes, as well as for the edges between the nodes. For example, in any road network, for each node (place), we have to store the information about which other nodes (places) it connects to. This way, we can form a graph with all the required nodes and edges. This is called an **unweighted graph**. We can add *weights*, or more information, to each of the edges. For our road network example, we can add the distance of each edge (path) from one node (place) to another. This representation, called a **weighted graph**, has all the information about a road network that's required to solve problems such as finding the path that has the minimum distance between one place and another.

There are two types of graphs – undirected and directed. An **undirected graph** indicates that the edges are bidirectional. Bidirectional indicates a bilateral or commutative property. For the road network example, a bidirectional edge between points A and B implies that we can go from A to B, as well as from B to A. But let's say we have some roads with a one-way restriction – we need to use a **directed graph** to represent that. In a direct graph, whenever we need to indicate that we can go in either direction, we use two edges – from point A to B, and B to A. We'll mainly focus on bidirectional graphs, but the things we'll learn here about structure and traversing methods hold true for directed graphs as well. The only change will be how we add edges to the graph.

Since a graph can have cyclic edges and more than one way to go from one node to another, we need to identify each node uniquely. For that, we can assign an identifier to each node. To represent the graph's data, we don't really need to build a node–like structure programmatically, as we did in trees. In fact, we can store the whole graph by combining **std** containers.

Representing a Graph as an Adjacency Matrix

Here is one of the simplest ways to understand a graph – consider a set of nodes, where any node can connect to any other node among the set directly. This means that we can represent this using a 2D array that's N × N in size for a graph with N nodes. The value in each cell will indicate the weight of the edge between the corresponding nodes based on the indices of the cell. So, **data[1][2]** will indicate the weight of the edge between node 1 and node 2. This method is known as an **adjacency matrix**. We can indicate the absence of an edge using a weight of -1.

Consider the weighted graph shown in the following figure, which represents an aviation network between a few major international cities, with hypothetical distances:

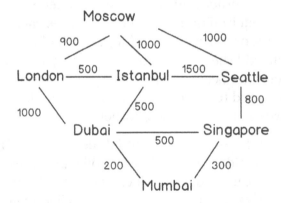

Figure 2.18: Aviation network between some cities

As shown in the preceding figure, we can go from London to Dubai via Istanbul or directly. There are multiple ways to go from one place to another, which was not the case with trees. Also, we can traverse from one node to another and come back to the original node via some different edges, which was also not possible in a tree.

Let's implement the matrix representation method for the graph shown in the preceding figure.

Exercise 11: Implementing a Graph and Representing it as an Adjacency Matrix

In this exercise, we will implement a graph representing the network of cities shown in the preceding figure, and demonstrate how it can be stored as an adjacency matrix. Let's get started:

1. First, let's include the required headers:

    ```cpp
    #include <iostream>
    #include <vector>
    ```

2. Now, let's add an **enum** class so that we can store the names of the cities:

    ```cpp
    enum class city: int
    {
        LONDON,
        MOSCOW,
        ISTANBUL,
        DUBAI,
        MUMBAI,
        SEATTLE,
        SINGAPORE
    };
    ```

3. Let's also add a **<<** operator for the **city** enum:

    ```cpp
    std::ostream& operator<<(std::ostream& os, const city c)
    {
        switch(c)
        {
            case city::LONDON:
                os << "LONDON";
                return os;
            case city::MOSCOW:
                os << "MOSCOW";
                return os;
            case city::ISTANBUL:
                os << "ISTANBUL";
                return os;
            case city::DUBAI:
                os << "DUBAI";
                return os;
            case city::MUMBAI:
                os << "MUMBAI";
    ```

```
                    return os;
               case city::SEATTLE:
                    os << "SEATTLE";
                    return os;
               case city::SINGAPORE:
                    os << "SINGAPORE";
                    return os;
               default:
                    return os;
          }
     }
```

4. Let's write the **struct graph**, which will encapsulate our data:

```
struct graph
{
     std::vector<std::vector<int>> data;
```

5. Now, let's add a constructor that will create an empty graph (a graph without any edges) with a given number of nodes:

```
graph(int n)
{
     data.reserve(n);
     std::vector<int> row(n);
     std::fill(row.begin(), row.end(), -1);
     for(int i = 0; i < n; i++)
     {
          data.push_back(row);
     }
}
```

6. Now, let's add the most important function – **addEdge**. It will take three parameters – the two cities to be connected and the weight (distance) of the edge:

```
void addEdge(const city c1, const city c2, int dis)
{
     std::cout << "ADD: " << c1 << "-" << c2 << "=" << dis << std::endl;

     auto n1 = static_cast<int>(c1);
     auto n2 = static_cast<int>(c2);
     data[n1][n2] = dis;
     data[n2][n1] = dis;
}
```

7. Now, let's add a function so that we can remove an edge from the graph:

```cpp
void removeEdge(const city c1, const city c2)
{
    std::cout << "REMOVE: " << c1 << "-" << c2 << std::endl;

    auto n1 = static_cast<int>(c1);
    auto n2 = static_cast<int>(c2);
    data[n1][n2] = -1;
    data[n2][n1] = -1;
}
};
```

8. Now, let's write the **main** function so that we can use these functions:

```cpp
int main()
{
    graph g(7);
    g.addEdge(city::LONDON, city::MOSCOW, 900);
    g.addEdge(city::LONDON, city::ISTANBUL, 500);
    g.addEdge(city::LONDON, city::DUBAI, 1000);
    g.addEdge(city::ISTANBUL, city::MOSCOW, 1000);
    g.addEdge(city::ISTANBUL, city::DUBAI, 500);
    g.addEdge(city::DUBAI, city::MUMBAI, 200);
    g.addEdge(city::ISTANBUL, city::SEATTLE, 1500);
    g.addEdge(city::DUBAI, city::SINGAPORE, 500);
    g.addEdge(city::MOSCOW, city::SEATTLE, 1000);
    g.addEdge(city::MUMBAI, city::SINGAPORE, 300);
    g.addEdge(city::SEATTLE, city::SINGAPORE, 700);

    g.addEdge(city::SEATTLE, city::LONDON, 1800);
    g.removeEdge(city::SEATTLE, city::LONDON);

    return 0;
}
```

9. Upon executing this program, we should get the following output:

```
ADD: LONDON-MOSCOW=900
ADD: LONDON-ISTANBUL=500
ADD: LONDON-DUBAI=1000
ADD: ISTANBUL-MOSCOW=1000
ADD: ISTANBUL-DUBAI=500
ADD: DUBAI-MUMBAI=200
```

```
ADD: ISTANBUL-SEATTLE=1500
ADD: DUBAI-SINGAPORE=500
ADD: MOSCOW-SEATTLE=1000
ADD: MUMBAI-SINGAPORE=300
ADD: SEATTLE-SINGAPORE=700
ADD: SEATTLE-LONDON=1800
REMOVE: SEATTLE-LONDON
```

As we can see, we are storing the data in a vector of a vector, with both dimensions equal to the number of nodes. Hence, the total space required for this representation is proportional to V2, where V is the number of nodes.

Representing a Graph as an Adjacency List

A major problem with a matrix representation of a graph is that the amount of memory required is directly proportional to the number of nodes squared. As you might imagine, this adds up quickly with the number of nodes. Let's see how we can improve this so that we use less memory.

In any graph, we'll have a fixed number of nodes, and each node will have a fixed maximum number of connected nodes, which is equal to the total nodes. In a matrix, we have to store all the edges for all the nodes, even if two nodes are not directly connected to each other. Instead, we'll only store the IDs of the nodes in each row, indicating which nodes are directly connected to the current one. This representation is also called an **adjacency list**.

Let's see how the implementation differs compared to the previous exercise.

Exercise 12: Implementing a Graph and Representing it as an Adjacency List

In this exercise, we will implement a graph representing the network of cities shown in *figure* 2.18, and demonstrate how it can be stored as an adjacency list. Let's get started:

1. We'll implement an adjacency list representation in this exercise. Let's start with headers, as usual:

   ```
   #include <iostream>
   #include <vector>
   #include <algorithm>
   ```

2. Now, let's add an **enum** class so that we can store the names of the cities:

   ```
   enum class city: int
   {
       MOSCOW,
       LONDON,
   ```

```
    ISTANBUL,
    SEATTLE,
    DUBAI,
    MUMBAI,
    SINGAPORE
};
```

3. Let's also add the **<<** operator for the **city** enum:

```cpp
std::ostream& operator<<(std::ostream& os, const city c)
{
    switch(c)
    {
        case city::MOSCOW:
            os << "MOSCOW";
            return os;
        case city::LONDON:
            os << "LONDON";
            return os;
        case city::ISTANBUL:
            os << "ISTANBUL";
            return os;
        case city::SEATTLE:
            os << "SEATTLE";
            return os;
        case city::DUBAI:
            os << "DUBAI";
            return os;
        case city::MUMBAI:
            os << "MUMBAI";
            return os;
        case city::SINGAPORE:
            os << "SINGAPORE";
            return os;
        default:
            return os;
    }
}
```

4. Let's write the **struct graph**, which will encapsulate our data:

```cpp
struct graph
{
    std::vector<std::vector<std::pair<int, int>>> data;
```

5. Let's see how our constructor defers from a matrix representation:

```
graph(int n)
{
    data = std::vector<std::vector<std::pair<int, int>>>(n,
std::vector<std::pair<int, int>>());
}
```

As we can see, we are initializing the data with a 2D vector, but all the rows are initially empty because there are no edges present at the start.

6. Let's implement the **addEdge** function for this:

```
void addEdge(const city c1, const city c2, int dis)
{
    std::cout << "ADD: " << c1 << "-" << c2 << "=" << dis << std::endl;

    auto n1 = static_cast<int>(c1);
    auto n2 = static_cast<int>(c2);
    data[n1].push_back({n2, dis});
    data[n2].push_back({n1, dis});
}
```

7. Now, let's write **removeEdge** so that we can remove an edge from the graph:

```
void removeEdge(const city c1, const city c2)
{
    std::cout << "REMOVE: " << c1 << "-" << c2 << std::endl;

    auto n1 = static_cast<int>(c1);
    auto n2 = static_cast<int>(c2);
    std::remove_if(data[n1].begin(), data[n1].end(), [n2](const auto&
pair)
        {
            return pair.first == n2;
        });
    std::remove_if(data[n2].begin(), data[n2].end(), [n1](const auto&
pair)
        {
            return pair.first == n1;
        });

}
};
```

8. Now, let's write the **main** function so that we can use these functions:

```
int main()
{
    graph g(7);
    g.addEdge(city::LONDON, city::MOSCOW, 900);
    g.addEdge(city::LONDON, city::ISTANBUL, 500);
    g.addEdge(city::LONDON, city::DUBAI, 1000);
    g.addEdge(city::ISTANBUL, city::MOSCOW, 1000);
    g.addEdge(city::ISTANBUL, city::DUBAI, 500);
    g.addEdge(city::DUBAI, city::MUMBAI, 200);
    g.addEdge(city::ISTANBUL, city::SEATTLE, 1500);
    g.addEdge(city::DUBAI, city::SINGAPORE, 500);
    g.addEdge(city::MOSCOW, city::SEATTLE, 1000);
    g.addEdge(city::MUMBAI, city::SINGAPORE, 300);
    g.addEdge(city::SEATTLE, city::SINGAPORE, 700);

    g.addEdge(city::SEATTLE, city::LONDON, 1800);
    g.removeEdge(city::SEATTLE, city::LONDON);

    return 0;
}
```

Upon executing this program, we should get the following output:

```
ADD: LONDON-MOSCOW=900
ADD: LONDON-ISTANBUL=500
ADD: LONDON-DUBAI=1000
ADD: ISTANBUL-MOSCOW=1000
ADD: ISTANBUL-DUBAI=500
ADD: DUBAI-MUMBAI=200
ADD: ISTANBUL-SEATTLE=1500
ADD: DUBAI-SINGAPORE=500
ADD: MOSCOW-SEATTLE=1000
ADD: MUMBAI-SINGAPORE=300
ADD: SEATTLE-SINGAPORE=700
ADD: SEATTLE-LONDON=1800
REMOVE: SEATTLE-LONDON
```

Since we are storing a list of adjacent nodes for each node, this method is called an adjacency list. This method also uses a vector of a vector to store the data, just like the former method. But the dimension of the inner vector is not equal to the number of nodes; instead, it depends on the number of edges. For each edge in the graph, we'll have two entries, as per our **addEdge** function. The memory that's required for this type of representation would be proportional to E, where E is the number of edges.

Up until now, we've only seen how to build a graph. We need to traverse a graph to be able to perform any operations while using it. There are two widely used methods available – Breadth-First Search (BFS) and Depth-First Search (DFS), both of which we'll look at in *Chapter 6, Graph Algorithms I*.

Summary

In this chapter, we looked at a more advanced class of problems compared to the previous chapter, which helped us to describe a wider range of real-world scenarios. We looked at and implemented two major data structures – trees and graphs. We also looked at various types of trees that we can use in different situations. Then, we looked at different ways of representing data programmatically for these structures. With the help of this chapter, you should be able to apply these techniques to solve real-world problems of similar kinds.

Now that we've looked at linear and non-linear data structures, in the next chapter, we'll look at a very specific but widely used concept called lookup, where the goal is to store values in a container so that searching is super fast. We will also look at the fundamental idea behind hashing and how can we implement such a container.

3

Hash Tables and Bloom Filters

Learning Objectives

By the end of this chapter, you will be able to:

- Identify lookup-related problems easily in any large-scale application

- Evaluate whether a problem is suited for a deterministic or non-deterministic lookup solution

- Implement an efficient lookup solution based on a scenario

- Implement generic solutions provided as part of C++ STL in large applications

In this chapter, we'll look at the problem of fast lookup. We will learn about the various approaches to solving this problem and understand which one can be used for a given situation.

Introduction

Lookup is nothing but checking whether an element is present in a container or finding the corresponding value for a key in the container. In the student database system and the hospital management system examples that we mentioned in the previous chapters, a common operation is to fetch a particular record from the vast amount of data stored in the system. A similar problem also presents itself while getting the meaning of a word from a dictionary, checking whether a person is allowed to enter a certain facility based on a set of records (access control), and many more applications.

For most of these scenarios, just going through all the elements linearly and matching the values would be extremely time-consuming, especially considering the vast amount of records that are stored. Let's take a simple example of looking up a word in a dictionary. There are roughly 170,000 words in the English dictionary. One of the simplest ways to do this is to traverse the dictionary linearly and compare the given word with all the words in the dictionary until we've found the word, or we reach the end of the dictionary. But this is too slow, and it will have a time complexity of $O(n)$, where n is the number of words in the dictionary, which is not only huge but is also increasing day by day.

Hence, we need more efficient algorithms to allow for lookup that works much faster. We'll look at a couple of efficient structures in this chapter, that is, hash tables and bloom filters. We'll implement both of them and compare their pros and cons.

Hash Tables

Let's look at the very basic problem of searching in a dictionary. There are about 170,000 words in the Oxford English Dictionary. As we mentioned in the Introduction, a linear search will take $O(n)$ time, where n is the number of words. A better way to store the data is to store it in a height-balanced tree that has similar properties to a BST. This makes it much faster than linear search as it has a time complexity of only $O(log\ n)$. But for applications that require tons of such queries, this is still not a good enough improvement. Think about the time it will take for data containing millions or billions of records, such as neuroscientific data or genetic data. It would take days to find something in the data. For these situations, we need something much faster, such as a **hash table**.

One of the integral parts of hash tables is **hashing**. The idea behind this is to represent each value with a possibly unique key and, later on, use the same key to check for the presence of the key or to retrieve a corresponding value, depending on the use case. The function that derives a unique key from the given data is called a hash function. Let's look at how we can store and retrieve data by looking at some examples, and let's learn why we need such a function.

Hashing

Let's take one simple example before jumping into hashing. Let's say we have a container storing integers, and we want to know if a particular integer is part of the container or not as quickly as possible. The simplest way is to have a Boolean array with each bit representing a value that's the same as its index. When we want to insert an element, we'll set the Boolean value corresponding to that element to 0. To insert x, we simply set $data[x] = true$. Checking whether a particular integer, x, is inside the container is just as simple – we simply check whether $data[x]$ is $true$. Thus, our insertion, deletion, and search functions become O(1). A simple hash table for storing integers numbered from 0 to 9 would look as follows:

0	0
1	0
2	1
3	0
4	1
5	1
6	0
7	1
8	0
9	0

Figure 3.1: A simple hash table

However, there are some problems with this approach:

- What if the data is floating-point numbers?

- What if the data is not just a number?

- What if the range of the data is too high? That is, if we have a billion numbers, then we need a Boolean array that's one billion in size, and that is not always feasible.

To resolve this problem, we can implement a function that will map any value of any data type to an integer in the desired range. We can choose the range so that its Boolean array will have a feasible size. This function is called a **hash function**, as we mentioned in the previous section. It will take one data element as input and provide a corresponding output integer within the provided range.

The simplest hashing function for integers in a large range is the modulo function (denoted by %), which divides the element by a specified integer (n) and returns the remainder. So, we'll simply have an array of size n.

If we want to insert a given value, x, we can apply the modulo function on it (x % n), and we will always get a value between 0 and ($n - 1$), both inclusive. Now, x can be inserted at position (x % n). Here, the number that's obtained by applying the hash function is called the **hash value**.

A major problem we may encounter with this is that two elements may have the same output from the modulo function. An example is (9 % 7) and (16 % 7), which both result in a hash value of 2. Thus, if the slot corresponding to 2 is TRUE (or 1 for Boolean), we would have no idea which of 2, 9, 16, or any other integer that returns x % 7 = 2 is present in our container. This problem is known as collision, because multiple keys have the same values instead of unique values after applying the hash function.

If we store the actual value instead of a Boolean integer in our hash table, we will know which value we have, but we still cannot store multiple values with the same hash value. We will look at how to deal with this in the following section. But first, let's look at the implementation of a basic dictionary for a bunch of integers in the following exercise.

Exercise 13: Basic Dictionary for Integers

In this exercise, we shall implement a basic version of a hash map for unsigned integers. Let's get started:

1. First, let's include the required headers:

   ```
   #include <iostream>
   #include <vector>
   ```

2. Now, let's add the **hash_map** class. We'll alias **unsigned int** to avoid writing a long name:

   ```
   using uint = unsigned int;
   class hash_map
   {
       std::vector<int> data;
   ```

3. Now, let's add a constructor for this, which will take the size of the data or hash map:

   ```
   public:
   hash_map(size_t n)
   {
       data = std::vector<int>(n, -1);
   }
   ```

   As shown here, we're using **-1** to indicate the absence of an element. This is the only negative value we'll use as data.

4. Let's add the **insert** function:

```
void insert(uint value)
{
    int n = data.size();
    data[value % n] = value;
    std::cout << "Inserted " << value << std::endl;
}
```

As we can see, we are not really checking whether there was a value already present with the same hash value. We're simply overwriting if any value is already present. So, for a given hash value, only the latest inserted value will be stored.

5. Let's write a lookup function to see whether an element is present in the map or not:

```
bool find(uint value)
{
    int n = data.size();
    return (data[value % n] == value);
}
```

We'll simply check whether the value is present at the index calculated based on the hash value.

6. Let's implement a **remove** function:

```
void erase(uint value)
{
    int n = data.size();
    if(data[value % n] == value)
    {
data[value % n] = -1;
        std::cout << "Removed " << value << std::endl;
    }
}
};
```

7. Let's write a small lambda function in **main** to print the status of the lookup:

```
int main()
{
    hash_map map(7);

    auto print = [&](int value)
        {
```

```
        if(map.find(value))
            std::cout << value << " found in the hash map";
        else
            std::cout << value << " NOT found in the hash map";
        std::cout << std::endl;
    };
```

8. Let's use the **insert** and **erase** functions on the map:

```
map.insert(2);
map.insert(25);
map.insert(290);

print(25);
print(100);

map.insert(100);
print(100);
map.erase(25);


}
```

9. Here's the output of the program:

```
Inserted 2
Inserted 25
Inserted 290
25 found in the hash map
100 NOT found in the hash map
Inserted 100
100 found in the hash map
Removed 25
```

As we can see, we are able to find most of the values we inserted earlier, as expected, except for the last case, where **100** is overwritten by **0** because they have the same hash value. This is called a collision, as we described previously. In the upcoming sections, we'll see how we can avoid this kind of problem to make our results more accurate.

The following figures, which demonstrate the different functions from the previous exercise, should make this clearer:

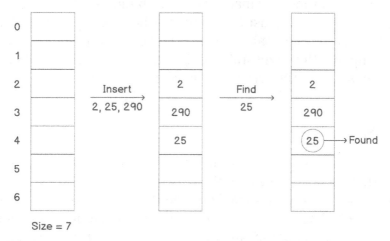

Figure 3.2: Basic operations in a hash table

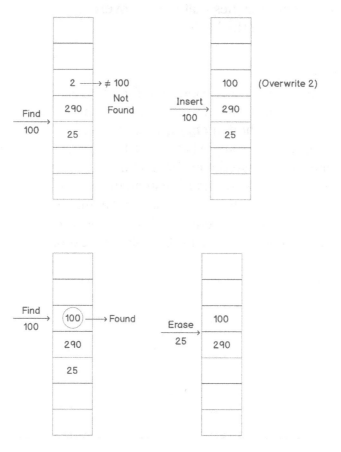

Figure 3.3: Basic operations in a hash table (continued)

As shown in the preceding figures, we can't insert two elements with the same hash value; we have to drop one of them.

Now, as we mentioned earlier, one major use of hash tables is to find a value corresponding to a key, and not just checking whether the key exists. This can be simply achieved by storing a key-value pair instead of just the key in the data. So, our insertion, deletion, and lookup functions will still calculate the hash value based on our key, but once we find the position in the array, we'll have our value as the second parameter of the pair.

Collisions in Hash Tables

In the previous sections, we took a look at how hash tables can help us store a lot of keys in a way that makes it easy to look up any required key. However, we also encountered a problem where multiple keys had the same hash value, also known as a **collision**. In *Exercise 13*, *Basic Dictionary for Integers*, we handled this issue by simply rewriting the key and retaining the latest key corresponding to a given hash value. However, this does not allow us to store all the keys. In the following subtopics, we shall take a look at a couple of approaches that help us overcome this problem and allow us to retain all of our key values in the hash table.

Close Addressing – Chaining

So far, we've only been storing a single element for any hash value. If we already have an element for a particular hash value, we have no option but to discard either the new value or the old value. The method of **chaining** is one way we can retain both values. In this method, instead of storing a single key in the hash table, we'll store a linked list for each index. So, whenever we have the problem of a collision, we'll simply insert the new key at the end of the list. Thus, essentially, instead of a single element, we can store as many elements as we want. The reason for choosing a linked list for each index instead of a vector (with **push_back** for new elements) is to enable the fast removal of elements from any position. Let's implement this in the following exercise.

Exercise 14: Hash Table with Chaining

In this exercise, we shall implement a hash table and use chaining to handle collisions. Let's get started:

1. First, let's include the required headers:

    ```
    #include <iostream>
    #include <vector>
    #include <list>
    #include <algorithm>
    ```

2. Now, let's add the **hash_map** class. We'll alias **unsigned int** to avoid writing a long name:

    ```
    using uint = unsigned int;
    class hash_map
    {
        std::vector<std::list<int>> data;
    ```

3. Now, let's add a constructor for **hash_map** that will take the size of the data or hash map:

    ```
    public:
    hash_map(size_t n)
    {
        data.resize(n);
    }
    ```

4. Let's add an **insert** function:

    ```
    void insert(uint value)
    {
        int n = data.size();
        data[value % n].push_back(value);
        std::cout << "Inserted " << value << std::endl;
    }
    ```

    As we can see, we are always inserting the value in the data. One alternative could be to search for the value and insert it only if the value is not present.

5. Let's write the lookup function to see whether an element is present in the map:

```
bool find(uint value)
{
    int n = data.size();
    auto& entries = data[value % n];
    return std::find(entries.begin(), entries.end(), value) != entries.end();
}
```

As we can see, our lookup seems faster than conventional methods, but not as fast as it was earlier. This is because now, it is also dependent on the data, as well as the value of **n**. We'll come back to this point again after this exercise.

6. Let's implement a function to remove elements:

```
void erase(uint value)
{
    int n = data.size();
    auto& entries = data[value % n];
    auto iter = std::find(entries.begin(), entries.end(), value);

    if(iter != entries.end())
    {
        entries.erase(iter);
        std::cout << "Removed " << value << std::endl;
    }
}
};
```

7. Let's write the same **main** function as in the previous exercise and look at the difference:

```
int main()
{
    hash_map map(7);

    auto print = [&](int value)
        {
```

```
        if(map.find(value))
            std::cout << value << " found in the hash map";
        else
            std::cout << value << " NOT found in the hash map";
        std::cout << std::endl;
    };
```

8. Let's use the **insert** and **erase** functions on **map**:

```
map.insert(2);
map.insert(25);
map.insert(290);

map.insert(100);
map.insert(55);

print(100);
map.erase(2);


}
```

Here's the output of our program:

```
Inserted 2
Inserted 25
Inserted 290
Inserted 100
Inserted 55
100 found in the hash map
Removed 2
```

As we can see, the values are not overwritten because we can store any number of values in the list. Hence, our output is completely accurate and reliable.

The following images illustrate how different operations are performed on a dataset:

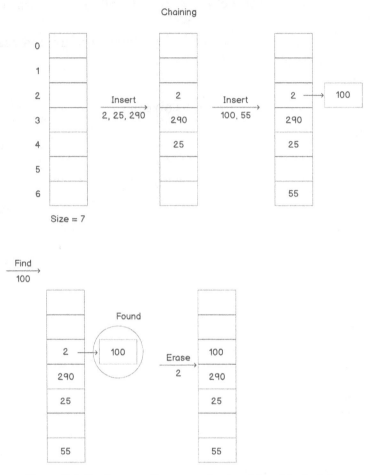

Figure 3.4: Basic operations on a hash table with chaining

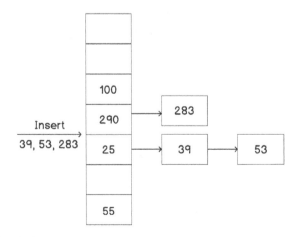

Figure 3.5: Basic operations on a hash table with chaining (continued)

As we can see, we are appending elements with the same hash value in a list placed in the node instead of a single element.

Now, let's consider the time complexity of these operations. As we saw, the insertion function is still O(1). Although **push_back** may be a bit slower than just setting a value, it is not significantly slower. Considering the problem that this approach solves, it is a small price to pay. But lookup and deletion may be significantly slower, depending on our hash table's size and dataset. For example, if all the keys have the same hash value, the time required for the search will be O(n), as it will simply become a linear search in a linked list.

If the hash table is very small compared to the number of keys to be stored, there will be a lot of collisions, and the lists will be longer on average. On the other hand, if we keep a very big hash table, we may end up having very sparse data and end up wasting memory. So, the hash table's size should be optimized based on the application's context and scenario. We can define these things mathematically as well.

The **load factor** indicates the average number of keys present per list in our hash table. It can be computed using the following formula:

$$load\ factor = \frac{number\ of\ keys}{size\ of\ hash\ table}$$

Figure 3.6: Load factor

If the number of keys is equal to our hash table size, the load factor will be 1. This is an ideal scenario; we'll get close to O(1) for all the operations, and all the space will be utilized properly.

If the value is less than 1, this means that we are not storing even one key per list (assuming we want a list at every index) and essentially wasting some space.

If the value is more than 1, this implies that the average length of our lists is more than 1, and hence our find and removal functions will be a bit slower on average.

The value of the load factor can be computed in O(1) at any time. Some advanced hash table implementations make use of this value to modify the hash function (also known as rehashing) if the value crosses certain thresholds on either side of 1. The hash function is modified so that the load factor is moved closer to 1. Then, the size of the hash table can be updated according to our load factor and the values redistributed based on the updated hash function. Rehashing is an expensive operation, and hence should not be performed too frequently. But if it is applied with a proper strategy, we can achieve really good results in terms of average time complexity.

However, the load factor is not the only factor determining the performance of this technique. Consider the following scenario: We have a hash table of size 7 and it has seven elements. However, all of them have the same hash value, and hence all of them are present in a single bucket. So, the search will always take $O(n)$ instead of $O(1)$ time. However, the load factor will be 1, which is an absolutely ideal value. Here, the actual problem is the hash function. The hash function should be designed in such a way that different keys are distributed as evenly as possible across all the possible indexes. Basically, the difference between the minimum bucket size and the maximum bucket size should not be very high (which is seven in this case). If the hash function is designed in a way that all seven elements get different hash values, then all the search function calls will result in $O(1)$ complexity and instant results. This is because the difference between the min and max bucket size will be 0. However, this is usually not done in hash table implementation. It is supposed to be taken care of by the hash function itself because the hash table is not dependent on the implementation of the hash function.

Open Addressing

Another method for resolving collisions is **open addressing**. In this method, we store all the elements inside the hash table instead of chaining the elements to the hash table. Hence, to accommodate all the elements, the size of the hash table must be greater than the number of elements. The idea is to probe if a cell corresponding to a particular hash value is already occupied. There are multiple ways we can probe the value, as we shall see in the following subtopics.

Linear probing

This is a simple probing technique. If there is a collision at a particular hash value, we can simply look at the subsequent hash value for an empty cell and insert our element once we find room for it. If the cell at $hash(x)$ is full, then we need to check whether the cell at $hash(x + 1)$ is empty. If it is also full, look at $hash(x + 2)$, and so on.

The following figure illustrates how linear probing works:

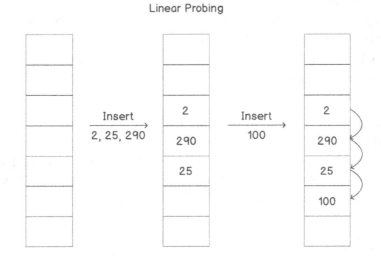

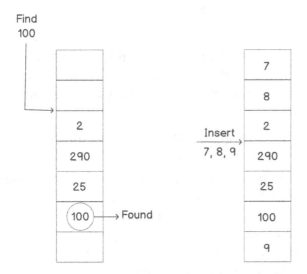

Figure 3.7: Basic operations on a hash table with linear probing

Insert
————→   Hash table full.
  20   Can't insert anymore without reshashing.

Figure 3.8: Unable to insert elements after hash table fills up

As we can see, we are inserting an element in the next available slot if the position corresponding to its hash value is already occupied. After inserting the first three elements, we can see that they are clustered together. If more elements are inserted in the same range, all of them will go at the end of the cluster consecutively, thus making the cluster grow. Now, when we try to search for a value that is not present at the location first calculated by the hash function, but is present at the end of a big cluster, we have to search through all the keys in the cluster linearly. And therefore, the search becomes drastically slow.

Thus, we have a major problem if the data is densely clustered. We can say that the data is densely clustered if the data is distributed in such a way that there are some groups around which the frequency of values is very high. For example, let's say that if there are a lot of keys with a hash value of 3 to 7 in a hash table of 100. All the keys will be probed to some values consecutively after that, and it will slow down our searching drastically.

Quadratic probing

As we saw, the major problem with linear probing was clustering. The reason behind this was that we were going linearly in the case of collisions. This problem can be resolved to a large extent by using a quadratic equation instead of a linear one. And that's what quadratic probing provides.

First, we try to insert the value x at the position $hash(x)$. If that position is already occupied, we go to the position $hash(x + 1^2)$, and then $hash(x + 2^2)$, and so on. So, we increase the offset in a quadratic fashion and thus decrease the probability of creating small clusters of data.

There is one more advantage of both probing techniques – the position of an element can be affected by other elements that don't have the same hash value. So, basically, even if there's just one key with a certain hash value, it can collide because of some other element is present in that location, which was not the case with chaining. For example, in linear probing, if we have two keys with a hash value of 4, one of them will be inserted at position 4 and the other will be inserted at position 5. Next, if we need to insert a key with a hash value of 5, it will need to be inserted at 6. This key was affected even though it did not have the same hash value as any other key.

Perfect Hashing – Cuckoo Hashing

As the heading suggests, **cuckoo hashing** is one of the perfect hashing techniques. The methods we mentioned previously don't provide a guarantee of O(1) time complexity in the worst case, but cuckoo hashing can achieve that if implemented properly.

In cuckoo hashing, we keep two hash tables of the same size, each with their own unique hash function. Any element can be present in either of the hash tables, and its position is based on the corresponding hash function.

There are two main ways in which cuckoo hashing differs from our previous hashing techniques:

- Any element can be present in any of the two hash tables.

- Any element can be moved to another location in the future, even after insertion.

Earlier hashing techniques did not allow elements to be moved after insertion unless we did a complete rehashing, but this is not the case with cuckoo hashing because any element can have two possible locations. We can still increase the degree by increasing the number of possible locations for any element so that we gain better results and have less frequent rehashing. However, in this chapter, we'll only look at the version with two possible locations (hash tables) because it's easier to understand.

For lookup, we only need to look at two positions to determine whether the element is present or not. Hence, a lookup always requires O(1) time.

However, an insertion function can take a longer time. An insertion function, in this case, first checks whether it is possible to insert the new element, let's say A, in the first hash table. If so, it inserts the element there, and we are done. But if that position is occupied by a preexisting element, let's say B, we still go ahead with inserting A and move B to the second hash table. If this new position in the second hash table is also occupied, let's say by element C, we again insert B there and move C to the first table. We can carry this on recursively until we are able to find empty slots for all the elements. This process is illustrated in the following figure:

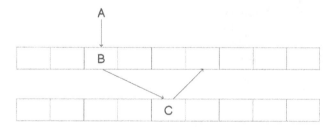

Figure 3.9: Cuckoo hashing

One major problem is that we could end up in a cycle and the recursion may lead to an infinite loop. For the example in the previous paragraph, consider that there is an element, D, where we wish to insert C, but if we try to move D, it goes to the location of A. Thus, we are in an infinite cycle. The following figure should help you visualize this:

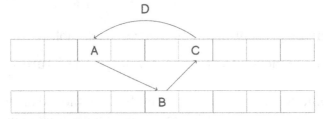

Figure 3.10: A cycle formed during cuckoo hashing

To address this, once we've identified the cycle, we need to rehash everything with new hash functions. The hash tables that were created with new hash functions may still have the same problems, so we may have to rehash and try out different hash functions. However, with smart strategies and wisely chosen hash functions, we can achieve a performance of amortized O(1) with high probability.

Just like open addressing, we can't store more elements than the combined size of the hash tables. To ensure good performance, we should make sure that our load factor is less than 50%, that is, the number of elements should be less than half of the available capacity.

We'll take a look at the implementation of cuckoo hashing in the following exercise.

Exercise 15: Cuckoo Hashing

In this exercise, we'll implement cuckoo hashing to create a hash table and insert various elements in it. We shall also get a trace of how the operation proceeds, which will allow us to take a look at how insertion works. Let's get started:

1. Let's start by including the required headers, as usual:

```
#include <iostream>
#include <vector>
```

2. Let's add a class for the hash map. We'll also store size separately this time:

```
class hash_map
{
    std::vector<int> data1;
    std::vector<int> data2;
    int size;
```

   As we can see, we use two tables.

3. Now, let's add the corresponding hash functions:

```
int hash1(int key) const
{
    return key % size;
}

int hash2(int key) const
{
    return (key / size) % size;
}
```

Here, we have kept both functions very simple, but these functions can be adapted as per the requirements.

4. Now, let's add a constructor that will set our data for initialization:

```
public:
hash_map(int n) : size(n)
{
    data1 = std::vector<int>(size, -1);
    data2 = std::vector<int>(size, -1);
}
```

As we can see, we are simply initializing both the data tables as empty (indicated by **-1**).

5. Let's write a **lookup** function first:

```
std::vector<int>::iterator lookup(int key)
{
    auto hash_value1 = hash1(key);
    if(data1[hash_value1] == key)
    {
        std::cout << "Found " << key << " in first table" << std::endl;
        return data1.begin() + hash_value1;
    }

    auto hash_value2 = hash2(key);
    if(data2[hash_value2] == key)
    {
```

```
        std::cout << "Found " << key << " in second table" << std::endl;
        return data2.begin() + hash_value2;
    }


    return data2.end();
}
```

We are trying to find the key in both tables and return the relevant iterator if one is found. We don't always need the iterator, but we'll use it in the deletion function to make things easier. We are returning the end of the **data2** table if the element is not found. As we can see, the lookup will have a time complexity of O(1) and will be performed pretty quickly.

6. Let's implement a delete function:

```
void erase(int key)
{
    auto position = lookup(key);
    if(position != data2.end())
    {
        *position = -1;
        std::cout << "Removed the element " << key << std::endl;
    }
    else
    {
        std::cout << "Key " << key << " not found." << std::endl;
    }
}
```

As we can see, most of the job is done by calling the **lookup** function. We just need to validate the result and reset the value to remove it from the table.

7. For insertion, we shall implement the actual logic in a different function because it will be recursive. One more thing we want to do is avoid cycles. However, keeping a record of all the values that are visited can be costly. To avoid that, we will simply stop the function once it is called more than n times. Since the threshold of the recursion depth of n is dependent on our memory (or hash table size), this gives good performance:

```
void insert(int key)
{
    insert_impl(key, 0, 1);
}
```

```cpp
void insert_impl(int key, int cnt, int table)
{
    if(cnt >= size)
    {
        std::cout << "Cycle detected, while inserting " << key << ".
Rehashing required." << std::endl;
        return;
    }

    if(table == 1)
    {
int hash = hash1(key);
        if(data1[hash] == -1)
        {
            std::cout << "Inserted key " << key << " in table " << table
<< std::endl;
            data1[hash] = key;
        }
        else
        {
            int old = data1[hash];
            data1[hash] = key;
            std::cout << "Inserted key " << key << " in table " << table
<< " by replacing " << old << std::endl;
            insert_impl(old, cnt + 1, 2);
        }
    }
    else
    {
int hash = hash2(key);
        if(data2[hash] == -1)
        {
            std::cout << "Inserted key " << key << " in table " << table
<< std::endl;
            data2[hash] = key;
        }
        else
        {
            int old = data2[hash];
```

```
        data2[hash] = key;
        std::cout << "Inserted key " << key << " in table " << table
    << " by replacing " << old << std::endl;
        insert_impl(old, cnt + 1, 2);
    }
  }
}
```

As we can see, the implementation takes three parameters – the key, the table in which we want to insert the key, and the count of the recursion call stack to keep track of the number of elements we have changed the positions of.

8. Now, let's write a utility function to print the data inside the hash tables. Although this is not really necessary and shouldn't be exposed, we will do that so that we can get a better understanding of how our insert function is managing the data internally:

```
void print()
{
    std::cout << "Index: ";
    for(int i = 0; i < size; i++)
        std::cout << i << '\t';
    std::cout << std::endl;

    std::cout << "Data1: ";
    for(auto i: data1)
        std::cout << i << '\t';
    std::cout << std::endl;

    std::cout << "Data2: ";
    for(auto i: data2)
        std::cout << i << '\t';
    std::cout << std::endl;
}
};
```

9. Now, let's write the **main** function so that we can use this hash map:

```
int main()
{
    hash_map map(7);
    map.print();

    map.insert(10);
```

```
    map.insert(20);
    map.insert(30);
    std::cout << std::endl;

    map.insert(104);
    map.insert(2);
    map.insert(70);
    map.insert(9);
    map.insert(90);
    map.insert(2);
    map.insert(7);

    std::cout << std::endl;

    map.print();

    std::cout << std::endl;

    map.insert(14);  // This will cause cycle.
}
```

10. You should see the following output:

```
Index: 0    1    2    3    4    5    6
Data1: -1    -1    -1    -1    -1    -1    -1
Data2: -1    -1    -1    -1    -1    -1    -1
Inserted key 10 in table 1
Inserted key 20 in table 1
Inserted key 30 in table 1

Inserted key 104 in table 1 by replacing 20
Inserted key 20 in table 2
Inserted key 2 in table 1 by replacing 30
Inserted key 30 in table 2
Inserted key 70 in table 1
Inserted key 9 in table 1 by replacing 2
Inserted key 2 in table 2
```

```
Inserted key 90 in table 1 by replacing 104
Inserted key 104 in table 2 by replacing 2
Inserted key 2 in table 1 by replacing 9
Inserted key 9 in table 2
Inserted key 2 in table 1 by replacing 2
Inserted key 2 in table 2 by replacing 104
Inserted key 104 in table 1 by replacing 90
Inserted key 90 in table 2
Inserted key 7 in table 1 by replacing 70
Inserted key 70 in table 2

Index: 0    1    2    3    4    5    6
Data1: 7   -1    2   10   -1   -1    104
Data2: 2    9   20   70   30   90   -1

Inserted key 14 in table 1 by replacing 7
Inserted key 7 in table 2 by replacing 9
Inserted key 9 in table 1 by replacing 2
Inserted key 2 in table 2 by replacing 2
Inserted key 2 in table 1 by replacing 9
Inserted key 9 in table 2 by replacing 7
Inserted key 7 in table 1 by replacing 14
Cycle detected, while inserting 14. Rehashing required.
```

As we can see, the output is showing the complete trace of how both the tables are maintained internally. We have printed the internal steps because some values are being moved around. The last insertion of **14** leads to a cycle, as we can see from the trace. The depth of insertion has gone beyond **7**. Simultaneously, we can also see that both the tables are almost full. We've filled **11** elements out of **14**, and hence the chance of replacing values is increasing at each step. We printed the table just before the cycle as well.

Also, the deletion of an element takes O(1) time here because it just uses the **lookup** function and deletes the element, if found. So, the only function that is costly is insertion. Hence, this is an ideal implementation if the number of insertions is quite a bit lower than the number of lookups in any application.

Let's use the following visual aids so that we can understand this better:

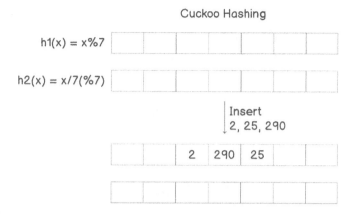

Figure 3.11: Inserting elements in a hash table that uses cuckoo hashing

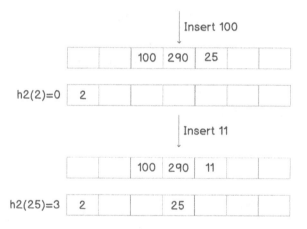

Figure 3.12: Handling collisions in a hash table using cuckoo hashing

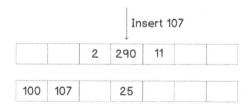

Figure 3.13: Handling collisions in a hash table using cuckoo hashing (continued)

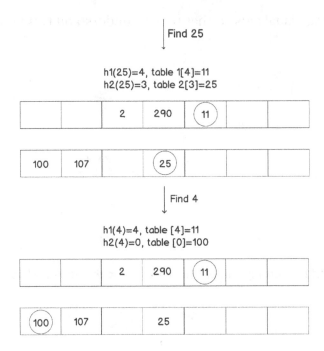

Figure 3.14: Finding values in a hash table that uses cuckoo hashing

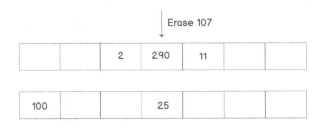

Figure 3.15: Erasing values in a hash table that uses cuckoo hashing

As we can see from the preceding series of figures, first, we try to insert elements in the first table. If there's already another element, we overwrite it and insert the preexisting element in the other table. We repeat this until it is safe to insert the last element.

C++ Hash Tables

As we mentioned previously, the lookup operation is quite frequent in most applications. However, we may not always encounter positive integers, which are quite easy to hash. You are likely to encounter strings most of the time. Consider the example of an English language dictionary that we considered earlier. We can store the dictionary data by using the words as keys and the word definitions as the values. Another example is the hospital records database we considered in *Chapter 1, Lists, Stacks, and Queues*, where the patients' names may be used as keys, and other related information could be stored as values.

The simple modulo function we used earlier to calculate the hash values of integers does not work for strings. An easy option is to calculate the modulo of the sum of the ASCII values of all the characters. However, all the permutations of characters in a string would be quite vast, and this would create a lot of collisions.

C++ provides a function called `std::hash<std::string>(std::string)` that we can use to generate hash values of string. It has a built-in algorithm to take care of the hashing function. Similarly, C++ provides such functions for all the basic types of data.

Now, looking at the hash table we implemented in *Exercise 14, Hash Table with Chaining*, it seems obvious that we can simply templatize it based on the data type and make a generic solution to provide a hash function for any given type of data. STL provides a couple of solutions for this: `std::unordered_set<Key>` and `std::unordered_map<Key, Value>`. An unordered set can only store a set of keys, whereas an unordered map can store the keys and their values. So, each unique key will have a corresponding value in the container.

Both of these containers are implemented in the same way – using hash tables with chaining. Each row in the hash table is a vector that stores the keys (and the values for the map). The rows are known as **buckets**. So, after calculating the hash value for a key, it will be placed into one of the buckets. Each bucket is also a list to support chaining.

By default, these containers have a maximum load factor of 1. As soon as the number of elements exceeds the size of the hash table, the hash function will be changed, the hash values will be recalculated (rehashing), and a larger hash table will be rebuilt to bring down the load factor. We can also use the `rehash` function to do this manually. This default maximum limit of 1 for the load factor can be changed using the `max_load_factor(float)` function. The values will be rehashed once the load factor exceeds the defined maximum limit.

These containers provide commonly useful functions such as **find**, **insert**, and **erase**. They also provide iterators to iterate over all the elements, as well as constructors to create an unordered set and map using other containers, such as vectors and arrays. An unordered map also provides **operator[]** so that it can return the value for a known key.

We'll look at the implementation of unordered sets and maps in the following exercise.

Exercise 16: Hash Tables Provided by STL

In this exercise, we shall implement unordered sets and maps and apply operations such as insertion, deletion, and find on these containers. Let's get started:

1. Include the required headers:

```
#include <iostream>
#include <unordered_map>
#include <unordered_set>
```

2. Now, let's write some simple **print** functions to make our **main** function more readable:

```
void print(const std::unordered_set<int>& container)
{
    for(const auto& element: container)
        std::cout << element << " ";
    std::cout << std::endl;
}

void print(const std::unordered_map<int, int>& container)
{
    for(const auto& element: container)
        std::cout << element.first << ": " << element.second << ", ";
    std::cout << std::endl;
}
```

3. Similarly, add wrappers over the **find** functions to keep the code neat:

```
void find(const std::unordered_set<int>& container, const auto& element)
{
    if(container.find(element) == container.end())
        std::cout << element << " not found" << std::endl;
    else
        std::cout << element << " found" << std::endl;
}

void find(const std::unordered_map<int, int>& container, const auto& element)
```

```
{
    auto it = container.find(element);
    if(it == container.end())
        std::cout << element << " not found" << std::endl;
    else
        std::cout << element << " found with value=" << it->second <<
    std::endl;
}
```

4. Now, write the **main** function so that we can use **unordered_set** and **unordered_map**,

and then perform various operations on it. We shall find, insert, and erase the elements:

```
int main()
{
    std::cout << "Set example: " << std::endl;
    std::unordered_set<int> set1 = {1, 2, 3, 4, 5};
    std::cout << "Initial set1: ";
    print(set1);

    set1.insert(2);
    std::cout << "After inserting 2: ";
    print(set1);

    set1.insert(10);
    set1.insert(351);
    std::cout << "After inserting 10 and 351: ";
    print(set1);

    find(set1, 4);
    find(set1, 100);
    set1.erase(2);
    std::cout << "Erased 2 from set1" << std::endl;
    find(set1, 2);

    std::cout << "Map example: " << std::endl;
    std::unordered_map<int, int> squareMap;

    squareMap.insert({2, 4});
    squareMap[3] = 9;
    std::cout << "After inserting squares of 2 and 3: ";
```

```
    print(squareMap);

    squareMap[30] = 900;
    squareMap[20] = 400;
    std::cout << "After inserting squares of 20 and 30: ";
    print(squareMap);

    find(squareMap, 10);
    find(squareMap, 20);
    std::cout << "Value of map[3]=" << squareMap[3] << std::endl;
    std::cout << "Value of map[100]=" << squareMap[100] << std::endl;
}
```

5. One of the possible outputs of this program is as follows. The order of elements in a set and a map can be different, and hence is called an *unordered* set/map:

```
Set example:
Initial set1: 5 4 3 2 1
After inserting 2: 5 4 3 2 1
After inserting 10 and 351: 351 10 1 2 3 4 5
4 found
100 not found
Erased 2 from set1
2 not found
Map example:
After inserting squares of 2 and 3: 3: 9, 2: 4,
After inserting squares of 20 and 30: 20: 400, 30: 900, 2: 4, 3: 9,
10 not found
20 found with value=400
Value of map[3]=9
Value of map[100]=0
```

As we can see, we can insert, find, and erase elements from both containers. These operations are working as expected. If we benchmark these operations against other containers, such as vector, list, array, deque, and so on, performance will be much faster here.

We can store key-value pairs and access the value for any given key using `operator[]`, as shown in this exercise. It returns a reference and hence also allows us to set the value, and not just retrieve it.

> **Note**
>
> Since `operator[]` returns a reference, if the key is not found, it will add the default value to the entry.

In the last line, we are getting `map[100]` = `0`, even if `100` was never inserted in the map. This is because `operator[]` is returning the default value.

If we want to keep track of the number of buckets as they change based on rehashing, we can do that using the `bucket_count()` function. There are other functions for getting details about other internal parameters as well, such as `load_factor`, `max_bucket_count`, and so on. We can also rehash manually using the `rehash` function.

Since these containers are implemented using chaining, they are actually storing the key/value pairs in different buckets. So, while searching the keys in any bucket, we need to compare them for equality. Hence, we need to define the equality operator for the key type. Alternatively, we can pass it as another template parameter.

As we can have seen in this exercise, unordered sets and maps do not allow duplicate keys. If we need to store duplicate values, we can use `unordered_multiset` or `unordered_multimap`. To support multiple values, the insert function does not check whether the key already exists in the container. Also, it supports some extra functions to retrieve all the items with a particular key. We won't look at any more details regarding these containers as it is out of the scope of this book.

STL provides hash functions for all the basic data types supported by C++. So, if we want a custom class or struct as the key type for any of the aforementioned containers, we need to implement a hash function inside the `std` namespace. Alternatively, we can pass it as a template parameter. However, writing a hash function on our own every time is not a good idea because the performance heavily depends on it. Designing a hash function requires quite a bit of research and understanding of the problem at hand, as well as mathematical skills. Hence, we are leaving it out of the scope of this book. For our purposes, we can simply use the `hash_combine` function provided in the `boost` library, as shown in the following example:

```
#include <boost/functional/hash.hpp>

struct Car
```

```cpp
{
    std::string model;
    std::string brand;
    int buildYear;
};

struct CarHasher
{
    std::size_t operator()(const Car& car) const
    {
        std::size_t seed = 0;
        boost::hash_combine(seed, car.model);
        boost::hash_combine(seed, car.brand);
        return seed;
    }
};

struct CarComparator
{
    bool operator()(const Car& car1, const Car& car2) const
    {
    return (car1.model == car2.model) && (car1.brand == car2.brand);
    }
};

// We can use the hasher as follows:
std::unordered_set<Car, CarHasher, CarComparator> carSet;
std::unordered_map<Car, std::string, CarHasher, CarComparator>
carDescriptionMap;
```

As we can see, we've defined a hashing struct with **operator()**, which will be used by unordered containers. We have also defined the comparator struct with **operator()** to support relevant functions. We have passed these structs as template parameters. This also allows us to have different types of comparators and hashers for different objects.

Apart from simple hash functions such as modulo, there are some complex hash functions, known as cryptographic hash functions, such as MD5, SHA-1, and SHA-256. These algorithms are very complex, and they can take any kind of data – even a file – as the input value. An important characteristic of cryptographic functions is that it is very difficult to determine the actual data from a given hash value (also known as reverse hashing), and hence they are used in some of the most secure systems. For example, the Bitcoin blockchain uses the SHA-256 algorithm to store an important proof of authenticity of the transaction records. Each *block* in the blockchain contains an SHA-256 hash value of its previous linked block, and the current block's hash is included in the subsequent block. Illegally modifying any block invalidates the entire blockchain from that block onwards, since now the modified block's hash value will not match with the value that was stored in the next block. Even with some of the fastest supercomputers in the world, it would take hundreds of years to break this and create forged transaction records.

Activity 6: Mapping Long URLs to Short URLs

In this activity, we'll create a program to implement a service similar to https://tinyurl.com/. It can take a very long URL and map it to a small URL that is easy and convenient to share. Whenever we enter the short URL, it should retrieve the original URL.

We want the following functionalities:

- Store the original and corresponding smaller URL provided by the user efficiently

- Retrieve the original URL based on the given smaller URL if found; otherwise, return an error

These high-level steps should help you solve this activity:

1. Create a class that contains **unordered_map** as the main data member.

2. Add a function to insert values. This function should take two parameters: the original URL and the smaller version of it.

3. Add a function to find the actual URL based on a given small URL if present.

> **Note**
>
> The solution to this activity can be found on page 498.

Bloom Filters

Bloom filters are extremely space-efficient compared to hash tables, but at the cost of deterministic answers; that is, we get an answer that is unsure. It only guarantees that there won't be any false negatives, but there may be false positives. In other words, if we get a positive hit, the element may or may not be present; but if we get a negative, then the element is definitely not present.

Just like cuckoo hashing, we will use multiple hash functions here. However, we'll keep three functions, as two functions cannot achieve decent accuracy. The fundamental idea is that instead of storing the actual values, we store an array of Booleans indicating whether or not a value is (maybe) present.

To insert an element, we compute the value of all the hash functions and set the bits corresponding to all three hash values in the array to 1. For lookup, we compute the value of all the hash functions and check whether all the corresponding bits are set to 1. If so, we return *true*; otherwise, we return *false* (the element is not present).

The obvious question is – why is lookup indeterministic? The reason is that any bit can be set by multiple elements. So, there is a relatively significant probability that all the relevant bits for a particular value (call it x) are set to 1 because of some other elements that were inserted earlier, although x was not inserted at all. In that case, the lookup function will still return *true*. Hence, we can expect some false positives. The more elements we insert, the higher the chances of false positives. However, if one of the bits for x is not set, then we can say that the element is not present with confidence. So, false negatives cannot be a possibility.

The array will be saturated when all the bits in the Boolean array are set to 1. So, the lookup function will always return *true*, and the insertion function will not have any effect at all since all the bits are already set to 1.

The following diagrams make this clearer:

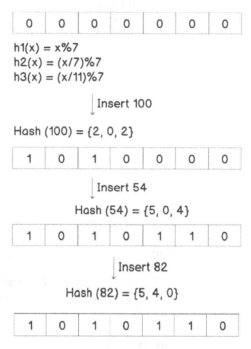

Figure 3.16: Inserting elements in a bloom filter

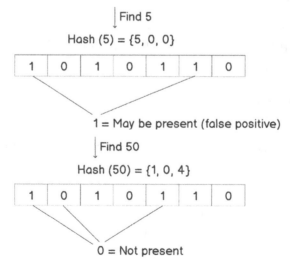

Figure 3.17: Finding elements in a bloom filter

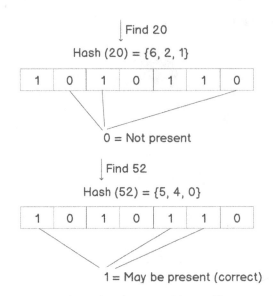

Figure 3.18: Finding elements in a bloom filter (continued)

As shown in the preceding diagrams, we are setting the relevant bits based on the hash functions, and for insertion, we're doing a bitwise **AND** for lookup of the element, as we explained earlier.

We'll implement a Bloom filter in C++ in the following exercise.

Exercise 17: Creating Bloom Filters

In this exercise, we shall create a Bloom filter and try out some basic operations. We shall also test for false positives in lookup. Let's get started:

1. Let's include the required headers:

```
#include <iostream>
#include <vector>
```

2. Now, let's create a class for our Bloom filter and add the required data members:

```
class bloom_filter
{
    std::vector<bool> data;
    int nBits;
```

3. Now, let's add the required hash functions. Again, we'll use very basic hash functions:

```
int hash(int num, int key)
{
    switch(num)
    {
    case 0:
        return key % nBits;
    case 1:
        return (key / 7) % nBits;
    case 2:
        return (key / 11) % nBits;
    }
    return 0;
}
```

As you can see, we're using single functions, with a parameter called **num** determining the hash function, to avoid unnecessary **if-else** blocks in other functions. This is also easy to expand; we just need to add a case for every hash function.

4. Let's add a constructor for the Bloom filter:

```
public:
bloom_filter(int n) : nBits(n)
{
    data = std::vector<bool>(nBits, false);
}
```

5. Now, let's add a **lookup** function:

```
void lookup(int key)
{
    bool result = data[hash(0, key)] & data[hash(1, key)] & data[hash(2,
key)];
    if(result)
    {
        std::cout << key << " may be present." << std::endl;
    }
    else
    {
        std::cout << key << " is not present." << std::endl;
    }
}
```

The **lookup** function is really simple, as expected. It checks whether all the required bits are set to **1**. If there are a variable number of hash functions, we can always loop over all of them to check whether all the corresponding bits are set to **1**. To make our words more accurate, we are also saying that a key *may be present* due to the possibility of false positives. On the other hand, we are completely sure that a key is not present if **lookup** returns negative.

6. Even the insertion function is equally simple:

```
void insert(int key)
{
    data[hash(0, key)] = true;
    data[hash(1, key)] = true;
    data[hash(2, key)] = true;
    std::cout << key << " inserted." << std::endl;
}
};
```

7. Let's add the **main** function so that we can use this class:

```
int main()
{
bloom_filter bf(11);
bf.insert(100);
bf.insert(54);
bf.insert(82);
bf.lookup(5);
bf.lookup(50);
bf.lookup(2);
bf.lookup(100);
bf.lookup(8);
bf.lookup(65);
}
```

8. You should see the following output:

```
100 inserted.
54 inserted.
82 inserted.
5 may be present.
50 is not present.
2 is not present.
100 may be present.
8 is not present.
65 may be present.
```

As we can see, there are a couple of false positives, but no false negatives.

Unlike the previous techniques, this structure only required 11 bits to store this information, as we can see from the constructor of the Bloom filter. Thus, we can easily increase the size of the filter and also update the hash functions accordingly to achieve much better results. For example, we can increase the size of the array to 1,000 (1,023 is used frequently as it is a prime number), and we'll still be using less than 130 bytes, which is much less than most other techniques. With the increase in the size of the hash table, our hash functions will also become %1023 or similar and will provide better results and a better distribution of numbers.

One important point to note here is that since we are not storing the actual data in the container, we can use this as a heterogeneous structure; that is, as long as our hash functions are good enough, we can insert different types of data, such as integers, strings, and doubles, simultaneously in the same Bloom filter.

There are some really good use cases of this in real life, especially when the amount of data is too huge to search even with hash tables, and some false positives would be acceptable. For example, when creating a new email address with an email provider such as Gmail or Outlook, there is a check to see whether the email address already exists. There are billions of email addresses present in the database, and an accurate check for such a basic and frequent query would be very expensive. Fortunately, even if the email address is not already taken, it is okay to sometimes say that it is taken as it doesn't do any harm. The user will simply choose something else. In such cases, using a Bloom filter is a feasible option. We'll see this in action in *Activity 7, Email Address Validator*.

Another example is the recommendation algorithm for showing new ads that are used by services, such as Facebook ads. It will show you a new ad every time you check your feed. It can simply store the IDs of ads you have watched in a Bloom filter. Then, the ID of a particular ad can be checked against it before showing it on your feed. If the check returns that you have watched a particular ad even though you haven't (false positive), it will not show that ad. However, this is fine since you wouldn't know about it as you haven't seen that ad anyway. This way, you can get new ads every time with a very fast lookup.

Activity 7: Email Address Validator

In this activity, we'll create a validator for emails, similar to what we find in a lot of email service provides (such as Gmail and Outlook) while signing up. We'll use a Bloom filter to check whether an email address has already been taken by someone else.

These high-level steps should help you complete this activity:

1. Create a `BloomFilter` class that can take a number of hash functions and the size of the Bloom.

2. For hashing, use the MD5 algorithm from the OpenSSL library to generate a hash value of a given email. MD5 is a 128-bit hashing algorithm. For multiple hash functions, we can use each byte as a separate hash value.

3. To add an email in the Bloom filter, we need to set all the bits to *true* that are coming from each byte of the hash value we calculated in *step 2*.

4. To find any email, we need to check whether all the relevant bits are *true* based on the hash value we calculated in *step 2*.

> **Note**
>
> The solution to this activity can be found on page 503.

Summary

As we mentioned in the introduction, the lookup problem is encountered in most applications in one way or the other. We can use deterministic as well as probabilistic solutions as per our needs. In this chapter, we implemented and saw how we can use both of them. In the end, we also looked at an example of built-in containers for hashing in C++. These containers are extremely useful while we're writing applications as we don't need to implement them ourselves every time and for every type. A simple rule of thumb is this: if we can see a lot of function calls to the `find` function for the container, we should go for a lookup-based solution.

So far, we've seen how we can store data in various types of data structures and perform some basic operations. In the upcoming chapters, we'll look at various types of algorithm design techniques so that we can optimize those operations, starting with divide and conquer.

4

Divide and Conquer

Learning Objectives

By the end of this chapter, you will be able to:

- Describe the divide-and-conquer design paradigm
- Implement standard divide-and-conquer algorithms such as merge sort, quicksort, and linear time selection
- Solve problems using the MapReduce programming model
- Learn how to use a multithreaded C++ MapReduce implementation

In this chapter, we shall study the divide-and-conquer algorithm design paradigm and learn how to use it to solve computational problems.

Introduction

In the previous chapter, we studied some commonly used data structures. Data structures are organizations of data in different forms, and a data structure enables and controls the cost of access to the data stored inside it. However, what makes software useful is not just the ability to store and retrieve data in various formats, but the ability to make transformations on data in order to solve computational problems. For a given problem, the precise definition and order of transformations on data is determined by a sequence of instructions called an **algorithm**.

An algorithm takes in a set of inputs that define an instance of a problem, applies a series of transformations, and outputs a set of results. If these results are the correct solutions to the computational problem at hand, our algorithm is said to be *correct*. The *goodness* of an algorithm is determined by its efficiency, or how few instructions the algorithm needs to perform to produce correct results:

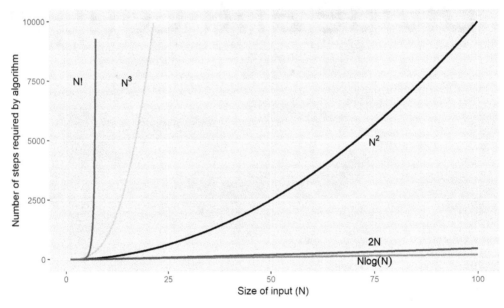

Figure 4.1: Scaling of steps taken by an algorithm with respect to the size of the input

The preceding diagram shows the growth in the number of steps required by an algorithm as a function of the size of the input. Algorithms that are more complex grow more quickly with the size of the input, and with sufficiently large inputs they can become infeasible to run, even on modern computer systems. For instance, let's assume that we have a computer that can perform a million operations per second. For an input of size 50, an algorithm that takes $N \log(N)$ steps will take 283 microseconds to complete; an algorithm that takes N^2 steps will take 2.5 milliseconds; and an algorithm that takes $N!$ (factorial of N) steps would take approximately 9,637,644,561,599,544,267,0 27,654,516,581,964,749,586,575,812,734.82 **centuries** to run!

An algorithm is said to be efficient if, for the size of input N, it solves the problem in a number of steps that is a polynomial of N.

The problems that express **polynomial-time algorithms** as solutions are also said to belong to the class P (polynomial) of computational complexity. There are several other computational complexities that problems can be divided into, a few examples of which are given here:

- **NP** (**Non-Deterministic Polynomial Time**) problems have solutions that can be verified in polynomial time, but do not have any known polynomial-time solutions.

- **EXPTIME** (**Exponential Time**) problems have solutions that run in time exponential to the size of the input.

- **PSPACE** (**Polynomial Space**) problems require a polynomial amount of space.

Finding out whether the set of problems in P is exactly the same as the set of problems in NP is the famous P = NP problem, which remains unsolved after decades of efforts and even carries a $1 million prize for anyone who can solve it. We shall take another look at P and NP-type problems in *Chapter 9, Dynamic Programming II.*

Algorithms have been studied as mathematical objects by computer scientists for several decades and a set of general approaches (or **paradigms**) to design efficient algorithms have been identified that can be used to solve a wide variety of problems. One of the most widely applicable algorithm design paradigms is called *divide and conquer* and shall be our subject of study in this chapter.

A **divide-and-conquer** type algorithm breaks the given problem into smaller parts, tries to solve the problem for each part, and, finally, combines the solution for each part into the solution for the whole problem. Several widely used algorithms fall into this category, for example, binary search, quicksort, merge sort, matrix multiplication, Fast Fourier Transform, and the skyline algorithms. These algorithms appear in almost all the major applications that are used today, including databases, web browsers, and even language runtimes such as the Java Virtual Machine and the V8 JavaScript engine.

In this chapter, we will show you what it means to solve problems using divide and conquer, and how you can identify whether your problem is amenable to such a solution. Next, we will practice thinking recursively and show you the tools that the modern C++ Standard Library gives you so that you can solve your problems using divide and conquer. We'll end this chapter by looking at MapReduce, including a discussion on why and how it scales, and how you can use the same paradigm to scale up your programs using both CPU-level and machine-level parallelization.

Let's dive into a basic algorithm that uses the divide-and-conquer approach – binary search.

Binary Search

Let's start with the standard search problem: say we are given a sorted sequence of positive integers and are required to find out if a number, N, exists in the sequence. There are several places where the search problem shows up naturally; for example, a receptionist looking for a customer's file in a set of files that are kept ordered by customer IDs or a teacher looking for the marks obtained by a student in their register of students. They are both, in effect, solving the search problem.

Now, we can approach the problem in two different ways. In the first approach, we iterate over the entire sequence, checking whether each element is equal to N. This is called a **linear search** and is shown in the following code:

```cpp
bool linear_search(int N, std::vector<int>& sequence)

{

    for (auto i : sequence)

    {

        if (i == N)

            return true;      // Element found!

    }


    return false;

}
```

One benefit of this approach is that it works for all arrays, sorted or unsorted. However, it is inefficient and does not take into account that the given array is sorted. In terms of its algorithmic complexity, it is an O(N) algorithm.

An alternative solution that exploits the fact that the sequence is sorted is as follows:

1. Start with the whole sequence in **range**.

2. Compare the middle element of the current **range** with N. Let this middle element be M.

3. If M = N, we have found N in the sequence and, therefore, the search stops.

4. Otherwise, we modify the **range** according to two rules:

   - If N < M, it means that if N were to be present in the **range**, it would be to the left of M and, therefore, we can safely remove all the elements to the right of M from the **range**.

   - If N > M, the algorithm removes all the elements to the left of M from the **range**.

5. If more than 1 element remains in the **range**, go to *step* 2.

6. Otherwise, N does not exist in the sequence and the search stops.

To illustrate this algorithm, we'll show how binary search works where S is a sorted sequence of integers from 1 to 9 and N = 2:

1. The algorithm starts with putting all the elements of S in range. The middle element in this step is found to be 5. We compare N and 5:

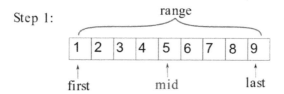

Figure 4.2: Binary search algorithm – step 1

2. Since N < 5, if N was present in the sequence, it would have to be to the left of 5. Therefore, we can safely discard all the elements of the sequence lying toward the right of 5 from our search. Our range now has elements only between 1 and 5, and the middle element is now 3. We can now compare N and 3:

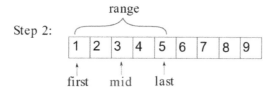

Figure 4.3: Binary search algorithm – step 2

3. We find that the current middle element, 3, is still greater than N, and the range can further be pruned to contain elements only between 1 and 3. The new middle element is now 2, which is equal to N, and the search terminates:

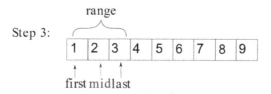

Figure 4.4: Binary search algorithm – step 3

In the following exercise, we shall look at the implementation of the binary search algorithm.

Exercise 18: Binary Search Benchmarks

In this exercise, we will write and benchmark a binary search implementation. Follow these steps to complete this exercise:

1. Begin by adding the following headers:

```
#include <iostream>
#include <vector>
#include <chrono>
#include <random>
#include <algorithm>
#include <numeric>
```

2. Add the linear search code like so:

```
bool linear_search(int N, std::vector<int>& S)
{
    for (auto i : S)
    {
        if (i == N)
            return true;        // Element found!
    }

    return false;
}
```

3. Add the binary search code shown here:

```
bool binary_search(int N, std::vector<int>& S)
{
    auto first = S.begin();
    auto last = S.end();

    while (true)
    {
        // Get the middle element of current range
        auto range_length = std::distance(first, last);
        auto mid_element_index = first + std::floor(range_length / 2);
        auto mid_element = *(first + mid_element_index);

        // Compare the middle element of current range with N
```

```
            if (mid_element == N)
                return true;
            else if (mid_element > N)
                std::advance(last, -mid_element_index);
            if (mid_element < N)
                std::advance(first, mid_element_index);

            // If only one element left in the current range
            if (range_length == 1)
                return false;
        }
    }
```

4. To evaluate the performance of binary search, we will implement two functions. First, write the small test:

```
void run_small_search_test()
{
    auto N = 2;
    std::vector<int> S{ 1, 3, 2, 4, 5, 7, 9, 8, 6 };

    std::sort(S.begin(), S.end());

    if (linear_search(N, S))
        std::cout << "Element found in set by linear search!" <<
std::endl;
    else
        std::cout << "Element not found." << std::endl;

    if (binary_search(N, S))
        std::cout << "Element found in set by binary search!" <<
std::endl;
    else
        std::cout << "Element not found." << std::endl;
}
```

5. Now, add the large test function, as follows:

```
void run_large_search_test(int size, int N)
{
    std::vector<int> S;
    std::random_device rd;
    std::mt19937 rand(rd());
```

```
        // distribution in range [1, size]
        std::uniform_int_distribution<std::mt19937::result_type> uniform_
    dist(1, size);

        // Insert random elements
        for (auto i=0;i<size;i++)
            S.push_back(uniform_dist(rand));

        std::sort(S.begin(), S.end());

        // To measure the time taken, start the clock
        std::chrono::steady_clock::time_point begin = std::chrono::steady_
    clock::now();


        bool search_result = binary_search(111, S);

        // Stop the clock
        std::chrono::steady_clock::time_point end = std::chrono::steady_
    clock::now();

        std::cout << "Time taken by binary search = " <<
    std::chrono::duration_cast<std::chrono::microseconds>
    (end - begin).count() << std::endl;

        if (search_result)
            std::cout << "Element found in set!" << std::endl;
        else
            std::cout << "Element not found." << std::endl;
    }
```

6. Lastly, add the following driver code, which searches for the number **36543** in randomly generated vectors of different sizes:

```
int main()
{
    run_small_search_test();

    run_large_search_test(100000, 36543);
    run_large_search_test(1000000, 36543);
```

```
    run_large_search_test(10000000, 36543);

    return 0;
}
```

7. Compile the program in x64-Debug mode and run it. The output should look like the following:

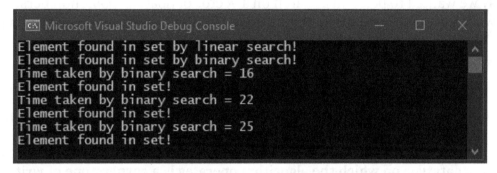

Figure 4.5: Binary search with debugging enabled

Notice that each of the three input arrays are all 10 times bigger than the previous arrays, so the third array is a hundred times larger than the first array, which itself contains a hundred thousand elements. Still, the time taken to search in the arrays using binary search increases only by 10 microseconds.

In the previous test, we did not allow any compiler optimizations and ran with the debugger attached to the program. Now, let's see what happens when our compiler is allowed to optimize the C++ code with no debugger attached. Try compiling the code in *Exercise 18*, *Binary Search Benchmarks*, in x64-Release mode and run it. The output should look as follows:

Figure 4.6: Binary search with compiler optimizations turned on

The binary search takes approximately equal time in all three cases, even with vastly different vector sizes!

Note that our implementation of binary search uses iterators and the C++ Standard Library functions such as **std::distance()** and **std::advance()**. This is considered good practice in modern C++ since it helps keep our code agnostic of the underlying data type and safe from index out-of-bounds errors.

Now, say we wanted to perform a search on a vector of floating-point numbers. How would we modify our functions in the previous exercise? The answer is exceedingly simple. We can modify the function signatures as follows:

```
bool linear_search(float N, std::vector<float>& S)

bool binary_search(float N, std::vector<float>& S)
```

The rest of the code inside of the search functions can still remain exactly the same since it is completely independent of the underlying datatype and depends only on the behavior of a container datatype. **This separation of core algorithm logic from the underlying datatype on which the algorithm operates is a cornerstone of writing reusable code in modern C++.** We shall see several examples of such separation in the duration of this book and dive into more functions that the Standard Library provides that can help us write reusable and robust code.

Activity 8: Vaccinations

Imagine that it is flu season and health department officials are planning to visit a school to ensure that all the enrolled children are administered their flu shot. However, there is a problem: a few children have already taken their flu shots but do not remember if they have been vaccinated against the specific category of flu that the health officials plan to vaccinate all the students against. Official records are sought out and the department is able to find a list of students that have already been administered the vaccine. A small excerpt of the list is shown here:

First name	Last name	Flu shot administered?
1	3	Yes
2	2	No
2	3	Yes

Figure 4.7: Excerpt of vaccination records

Assume that all the names are positive integers and that the given list is sorted. Your task is to write a program that can look up the vaccination status of a given student in the list and outputs to the officials whether the student needs to be vaccinated. Students need to be vaccinated in case of two conditions:

- If they are not present in the list

- If they are present in the list but have not been administered a flu shot

Since the list can have a large number of students, your program should be as fast and efficient as possible. The final output of your program should look as follows:

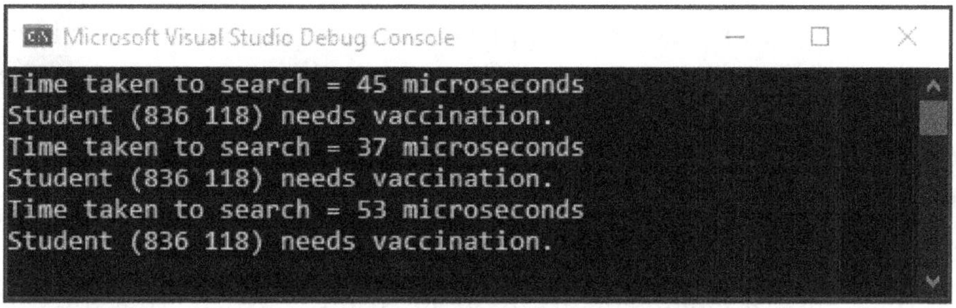

Figure 4.8: Sample output of Activity 8

High-level Steps

The solution to this activity uses a slightly modified version of the binary search algorithm. Let's get started:

1. Represent each student as an object of the **Student** class, which can be defined as follows:

   ```
   class Student
   {
       std::pair<int, int> name;

       bool vaccinated;
   }
   ```

2. Overload the required operators for the **Student** class so that a vector of students can be sorted using the Standard Library's **std::sort()** function.

3. Use a binary search to see if the student is present on the list.

4. If the student isn't present in the list, your function should return *true* since the student needs to be administered the vaccine.

5. Otherwise, if the student is present in the list but has not been administered the vaccine, return *true*.

6. Else, return *false*.

> **Note**
>
> The solution to this activity can be found on page 506.

Understanding the Divide-and-Conquer Approach

At the core of the divide-and-conquer approach is a simple and intuitive idea: if you don't know how to solve a large instance of a problem, find a small part of the problem that you can solve, and then solve it. Then, iterate for more such parts, and once you have solved all the parts, combine the results into a large coherent solution to the original problem. There are three steps to solving a problem using the divide-and-conquer approach:

1. **Divide**: Take the original problem and divide it into parts so that the same problem needs to be solved for each part.

2. **Conquer**: Solve the problem for each part.

3. **Combine**: Take the solutions for the different parts and combine them into a solution for the original problem.

In the previous section, we looked at an example of using divide and conquer to search within a sequence. At each step, binary search tries to search in only a part of the sequence, which is marked as the **range**. The search terminates when either the element is found or there is no longer a way to further divide the **range** into smaller parts. However, the search problem differs from most divide-and-conquer algorithms in the following manner: in the search problem, if an element can be found in a smaller **range** of the sequence, then it also definitely exists in the complete sequence. In other words, the solution to the problem in a smaller part of the sequence gives us the solution to the whole problem. Therefore, the solution does not need to implement the combination step of the general divide-and-conquer approach. This property, unfortunately, is not exhibited by the vast majority of computational problems that can be solved using a divide-and-conquer approach. In the following section, we shall dive deeper and look at more examples of using the divide-and-conquer approach to solve problems.

Sorting Using Divide and Conquer

We shall now explore how to implement the divide-and-conquer approach when it comes to solving another standard problem – sorting. The importance of having an efficient sorting algorithm cannot be overstated. In the early days of computing in the 1960s, computer manufacturers estimated that 25% of all CPU cycles in their machines were spent sorting elements of arrays. Although the computing landscape has changed significantly over the years, sorting is still widely studied today and remains a fundamental operation in several applications. For instance, it is the key idea behind indexes in databases, which then allow quick access to the stored data using a logarithmic time search, which is similar to binary search.

The general requirements for an implementation of a sorting algorithm are as follows:

- The implementation should be able to work with any datatype. It should be able to sort integers, floating-point decimals, and even C++ structures or classes where an order among different elements can be defined.

- The sorting algorithm should be able to handle large amounts of data, that is, the same algorithm should work with sizes of data even greater than the main memory of a computer.

- The sorting algorithm should be fast, both asymptotically and in practice.

While all three listed goals are desirable, in practice, it is hard to achieve the second and third objectives simultaneously. The second objective requires external sorting, that is, sorting data that does not reside on the main memory of a computer. External sorting algorithms can work while holding only a small subset of the whole data in memory at any point during execution.

In this section, we will introduce two sorting algorithms: merge sort and quicksort. Merge sort is an external sorting algorithm and, therefore, achieves our second objective, while quicksort, as its name suggests, is one of the fastest known sorting

algorithms in practice and appears as a part of the C++ Standard Library's `std::sort()` function.

Merge Sort

Merge sort is one of the oldest known sorting algorithms and appeared in reports in the late 1940s. The computers of that time had a few hundred bytes of main memory and were often used for complex mathematical analyses. Therefore, it was crucial for sorting algorithms to be able to work, even when all the data to be operated upon could not be held in the main memory. Merge sort solved this problem by exploiting a simple idea – sorting a large set of elements is the same as sorting a small subset of elements, and then merging the sorted subsets so that the increasing or decreasing order of elements is maintained:

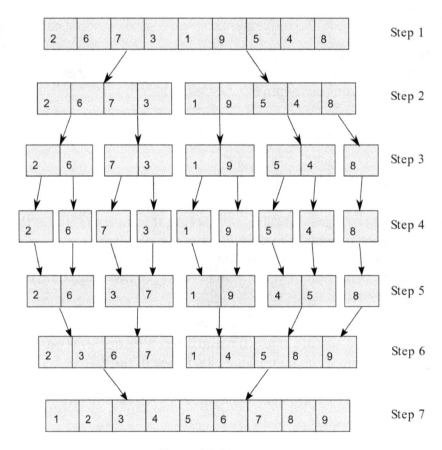

Figure 4.9: Merge sort

The preceding diagram shows an example of sorting an array of integers using merge sort. First, the algorithm divides the original array into subarrays until each subarray only consists of one element (*steps 1 to 4*). In all the subsequent steps, the algorithm merges elements into larger arrays, keeping elements in each subarray in increasing order.

Exercise 19: Merge Sort

In this exercise, we shall implement the merge sort algorithm. The steps are as follows:

1. Import the following headers:

```
#include <iostream>
#include <vector>
#include <chrono>
#include <random>
#include <algorithm>
#include <numeric>
```

2. The C++ code for the merge operation on two vectors is as follows. Write the **merge()** function like so:

```
template <typename T>
std::vector<T> merge(std::vector<T>& arr1, std::vector<T>& arr2)
{
    std::vector<T> merged;

    auto iter1 = arr1.begin();
    auto iter2 = arr2.begin();

    while (iter1 != arr1.end() && iter2 != arr2.end())
    {
        if (*iter1 < *iter2)
        {
            merged.emplace_back(*iter1);
            iter1++;
        }
        else
        {
            merged.emplace_back(*iter2);
            iter2++;
        }
    }

    if (iter1 != arr1.end())
    {
        for (; iter1 != arr1.end(); iter1++)
```

```
            merged.emplace_back(*iter1);
    }
    else
    {
        for (; iter2 != arr2.end(); iter2++)
            merged.emplace_back(*iter2);
    }

    return merged;
}
```

The templatized **merge()** function takes in references to two vectors of type **T** and returns a new vector containing the elements in input arrays, but sorted in increasing order.

3. We can now use the merge operation to write a recursive merge sort implementation, as shown here:

```
template <typename T>
std::vector<T> merge_sort(std::vector<T> arr)
{
    if (arr.size() > 1)
    {
        auto mid = size_t(arr.size() / 2);
        auto left_half = merge_sort<T>(std::vector<T>(arr.begin(), arr.
begin() + mid));
        auto right_half = merge_sort<T>(std::vector<T>(arr.begin() + mid,
arr.end()));

        return merge<T>(left_half, right_half);
    }

    return arr;
}
```

4. Add the following function to print the vector:

```
template <typename T>
void print_vector(std::vector<T> arr)


{
    for (auto i : arr)
        std::cout << i << " ";

    std::cout << std::endl;
}
```

5. The following function allows us to test our implementation of the merge sort algorithm:

```
void run_merge_sort_test()
{
    std::vector<int>    S1{ 45, 1, 3, 1, 2, 3, 45, 5, 1, 2, 44, 5, 7 };
    std::vector<float>  S2{ 45.6f, 1.0f, 3.8f, 1.01f, 2.2f, 3.9f, 45.3f,
    5.5f, 1.0f, 2.0f, 44.0f, 5.0f, 7.0f };
    std::vector<double> S3{ 45.6, 1.0, 3.8, 1.01, 2.2, 3.9, 45.3, 5.5,
    1.0, 2.0,  44.0, 5.0, 7.0 };
    std::vector<char>   C{ 'b','z','a','e','f','t','q','u','y' };

    std::cout << "Unsorted arrays:" << std::endl;
    print_vector<int>(S1);
    print_vector<float>(S2);
    print_vector<double>(S3);
    print_vector<char>(C);
    std::cout << std::endl;

    auto sorted_S1 = merge_sort<int>(S1);


    auto sorted_S2 = merge_sort<float>(S2);
    auto sorted_S3 = merge_sort<double>(S3);
    auto sorted_C = merge_sort<char>(C);

    std::cout << "Arrays sorted using merge sort:"
                << std::endl;
    print_vector<int>(sorted_S1);
    print_vector<float>(sorted_S2);
    print_vector<double>(sorted_S3);
    print_vector<char>(sorted_C);
```

```
        std::cout << std::endl;
    }

    int main()
    {
        run_merge_sort_test();
        return 0;
    }
```

6. Compile and run the program. The output should look like the following:

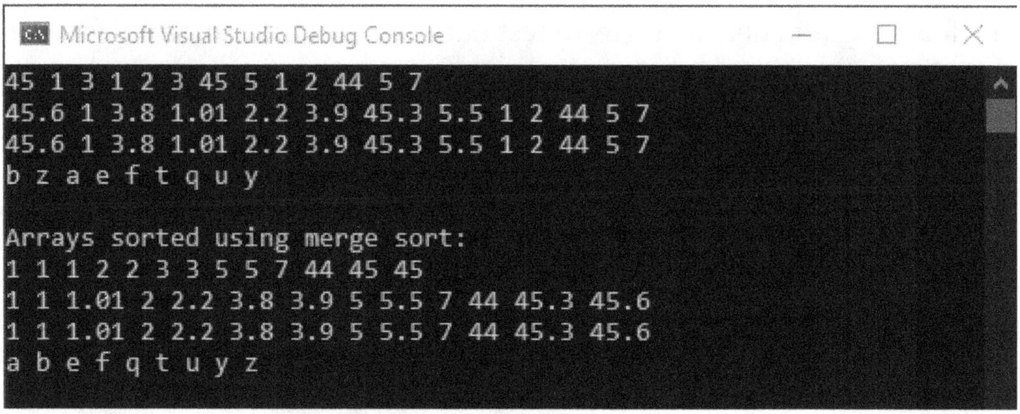

Figure 4.10: Sorting by merge sort

Our implementation of merge sort in this exercise continues our theme of not tying implementations of algorithms to underlying datatypes and relying only on the functions exposed by the containers.

Quicksort

While the goal in the case of merge sort was to sort large amounts of data, quicksort tries to reduce the average-case running time. The underlying idea in quicksort is also the same as merge sort – divide the original input array into smaller subarrays, sort the subarrays, and merge the results to get the sorted array. However, the fundamental operation that quicksort uses is **partition** and not merge.

Working of the Partition Operation

Given an array and a **pivot element**, P, in the array, the **partition operation** does two things:

1. It divides the original array into two subarrays, L and R, where L contains all the elements of the given array that are less than or equal to P, and R contains all elements of the given array that are greater than P.

2. It reorganizes the elements in the array in the order L, P, R.

The following diagram shows the result of a partition that was applied to an unsorted array, with the first element chosen as the pivot:

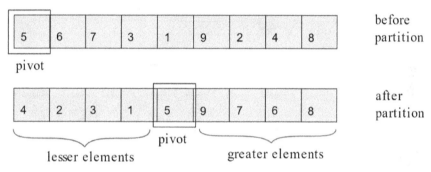

Figure 4.11: Selecting a pivot and partitioning the vector around it

A useful property of the partition operation is that after it is applied, the new position of the pivot, P, in the vector becomes the position that P would have if the vector were sorted. For example, the element 5 appears at the 5th position in the array after we apply the partition operation, which is the same position that element 5 would have been in if the array was sorted in increasing order.

The preceding property is also the core idea behind the quicksort algorithm, which works as follows:

1. If the input array, A, has more than 1 element in it, apply the partition operation on A. It results in subarrays L and R.

2. Use L as an input to *step 1*.

3. Use R as an input to *step 1*.

Steps 2 and 3 are recursive calls to the partition operation on the arrays that are generated by the partition operation and applied to the original input array. This simple recursive application of the partition operation results in sorting elements in increasing order. Since the quicksort recursion trees can quickly become deep, the following diagram shows an example of applying quicksort on a small array of six elements, {5, 6, 7, 3, 1, 9}:

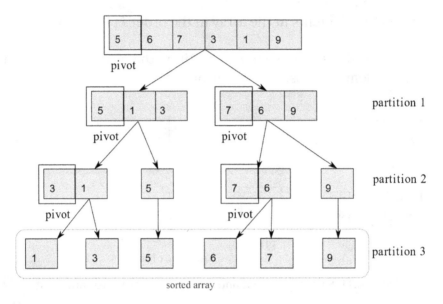

Figure 4.12: Visualization of the quicksort algorithm

Each iteration of the algorithm shows the result of the partition operation being applied to the subarrays generated in the previous step using the highlighted pivots. It should be noted that our choice of the first element of the array as the pivot is arbitrary. Any element of the array can be chosen as the pivot without affecting the correctness of the quicksort algorithm.

Exercise 20: Quicksort

In this exercise, we shall implement and test our implementation of quicksort. Let's get started:

1. Import the following headers:

```
#include <iostream>
#include <vector>
#include <chrono>
#include <random>
#include <algorithm>
#include <numeric>
```

2. The C++ code for the partition operation is as follows. Write the **partition()** function as shown here:

```cpp
template <typename T>
auto partition(typename std::vector<T>::iterator begin,
          typename std::vector<T>::iterator last)
{
    // Create 3 iterators,

    // one pointing to the pivot, one to the first element and
    // one to the last element of the vector.
    auto pivot_val = *begin;
    auto left_iter = begin+1;
    auto right_iter = last;

    while (true)
    {
        // Starting from the first element of vector, find an element that
is greater than pivot.
        while (*left_iter <= pivot_val &&
                std::distance(left_iter, right_iter) > 0)
            left_iter++;
        // Starting from the end of vector moving to the beginning, find an
element that is lesser than the pivot.
        while (*right_iter > pivot_val &&
                std::distance(left_iter, right_iter) > 0)
            right_iter--;

        // If left and right iterators meet, there are no elements left to
swap. Else, swap the elements pointed to by the left and right iterators
        if (left_iter == right_iter)
            break;
        else

            std::iter_swap(left_iter, right_iter);
    }
    if (pivot_val > *right_iter)
        std::iter_swap(begin, right_iter);

    return right_iter;
}
```

The implementation shown here takes in only the iterators over an underlying container object and returns another iterator that points to the index of the partition in the array. This means that all the elements of the vector are greater than the pivot in the right partition, and all the elements less than or equal to the pivot are in the left partition.

3. The quicksort algorithm uses the partition operation recursively, as shown in the following code:

```cpp
template <typename T>
void quick_sort(typename std::vector<T>::iterator begin,
        typename std::vector<T>::iterator last)
{
    // If there are more than 1 elements in the vector
    if (std::distance(begin, last) >= 1)
    {
        // Apply the partition operation
        auto partition_iter = partition<T>(begin, last);

        // Recursively sort the vectors created by the partition operation
        quick_sort<T>(begin, partition_iter-1);
        quick_sort<T>(partition_iter, last);
    }
}
```

4. **print_vector()** is used to print a vector to the console and is implemented as follows:

```cpp
template <typename T>
void print_vector(std::vector<T> arr)
{
    for (auto i : arr)
        std::cout << i << " ";

    std::cout << std::endl;
}
```

5. Adapt the driver code from *Exercise 19, Merge Sort*, as follows:

```cpp
void run_quick_sort_test()
{
    std::vector<int> S1{ 45, 1, 3, 1, 2, 3, 45, 5, 1, 2, 44, 5, 7 };
    std::vector<float>  S2{ 45.6f, 1.0f, 3.8f, 1.01f, 2.2f, 3.9f, 45.3f,
5.5f, 1.0f, 2.0f, 44.0f, 5.0f, 7.0f };
    std::vector<double> S3{ 45.6, 1.0, 3.8, 1.01, 2.2, 3.9, 45.3, 5.5,
1.0, 2.0,  44.0, 5.0, 7.0 };
    std::vector<char> C{ 'b','z','a','e','f','t','q','u','y'};

    std::cout << "Unsorted arrays:" << std::endl;
    print_vector<int>(S1);
    print_vector<float>(S2);
    print_vector<double>(S3);
    print_vector<char>(C);
    std::cout << std::endl;
    quick_sort<int>(S1.begin(), S1.end() - 1);
    quick_sort<float>(S2.begin(), S2.end() - 1);
    quick_sort<double>(S3.begin(), S3.end() - 1);
    quick_sort<char>(C.begin(), C.end() - 1);


    std::cout << "Arrays sorted using quick sort:" << std::endl;
    print_vector<int>(S1);
    print_vector<float>(S2);
    print_vector<double>(S3);
    print_vector<char>(C);
    std::cout << std::endl;
}
```

6. Write a **main()** function that calls **run_quick_sort_test()**:

```cpp
int main()
{
    run_quick_sort_test();
    return 0;
}
```

7. Your final output should look as follows:

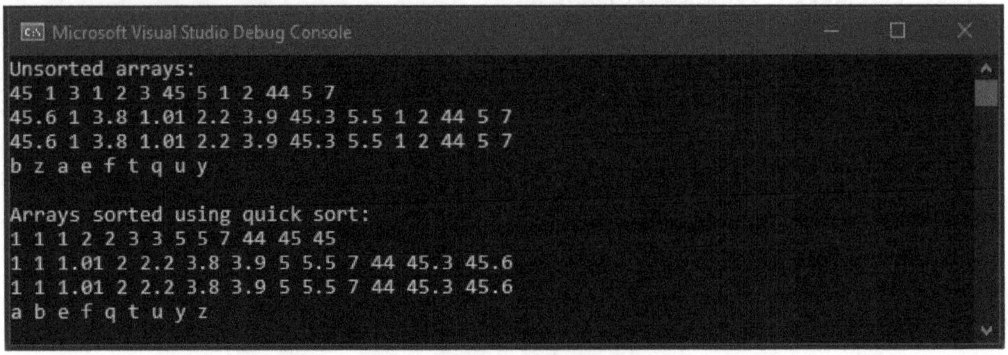

Figure 4.13: Sorting by quicksort

However, the runtime of quicksort does depend on how "good" our choice of pivot is. The best case for quicksort is when the pivot at any step is the median element of the current array; in such a case, quicksort is able to partition the elements into vectors of equal sizes at each step, and, therefore, the depth of the recursion tree is exactly $log(n)$. If the medians are not chosen as pivots, it results in an imbalance in the partition sizes and, therefore, a deeper recursion tree and greater running time.

The asymptotic complexity of quicksort and merge sort is shown here:

Algorithm	Best case	Average case	Worst case
Merge sort	$O(n \log n)$	$O(n \log n)$	$O(n \log n)$
Quicksort	$O(n \log n)$	$O(n \log n)$	$O(n^2)$

Figure 4.14: Asymptotic complexity of quicksort and merge sort

Activity 9: Partial Sorting

In the last two exercises, we have implemented **total sorting** algorithms that order all the elements of a vector in an increasing (or decreasing) order. However, this can be overkill in several problem instances. For example, imagine that you are given a vector containing the ages of all humans on earth and are asked to find the median age of the oldest 10% of the population.

A naïve solution to this problem is to sort the vector of ages, extract the ages of the oldest 10% people from the vector, and then find the median of the extracted vector. However, this solution is wasteful as it does far more than is strictly needed in order to compute the solution, that is, it sorts the entire array to ultimately use only 10% of the sorted array for the required solution.

A better solution to such problems can be derived by specializing the total sorting algorithms such as merge sort and quicksort into **partial sorting algorithms**. A partial sorting algorithm sorts only a specified number of elements in a given vector and leaves the rest of the vector unsorted.

The partial quicksort is described as follows:

1. Assume that we are given a vector, V, and we are required to create a sorted

    subvector of k elements.

2. Apply the partition operation on V, assuming the first element of V as the pivot (again, this choice is completely arbitrary). The result of the partition operation are two vectors, L and R, where L contains all the elements of V that are less than the pivot and R contains all the elements greater than the pivot. Also, the new position of the pivot is the "correct" position of the pivot in the sorted array.

3. Use L as input to *step 1*.

4. If the new position of pivot in *step 2* is less than k, use R as input to *step 1*.

Your task in this activity is to implement the partial quicksort algorithm that uses randomly generated arrays to test the output of the algorithm. The final output with a vector of size 100 and k = 100 should look as follows:

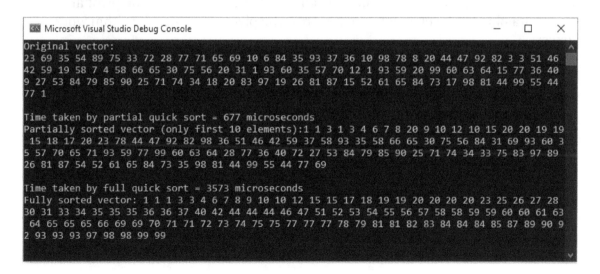

Figure 4.15: Sample output of Activity 9

Note

The solution to this activity can be found on page 510.

Linear Time Selection

In the previous section, we looked at simple examples of algorithms that use the divide-and-conquer paradigm and were introduced to the partition and merge operations. So far, our view of divide-and-conquer algorithms has been restricted to ones that recursively divide each intermediate step into exactly two subparts. However, there are certain problems where dividing each step into more subparts can yield substantial benefits. In the following section, we shall study one such problem – linear time selection.

Imagine that you are in charge of organizing a marching band parade for your school. To ensure that all the band members look uniform, it is important that the heights of students be the same. Moreover, students from all grades are required to participate. To solve these problems, you come up with the following solution – you will select only the 15th shortest student in every grade to participate in the parade. The problem can be formalized as follows: given a randomly ordered set of elements, S, you are asked to find the ith smallest element in S. A simple solution could be sorting the input and then selecting the ith element. However, the algorithmic complexity of this solution is $O(n \log n)$. In this section, we will work through a divide-and-conquer solution that solves the problem in $O(n)$.

Our solution hinges on using the partition operation correctly. The partition operation we introduced in the previous subsection takes in a vector and a pivot, and then divides the vector into two parts, one containing all the elements less than the pivot and the other containing all the elements greater than the pivot. The final algorithm works as follows:

1. Assume that we are given an input vector, V, and we need to find the *ith* smallest element.

2. Divide the input vector, V, into vectors V^1, V^2, V^3, ... , $V^{n/5}$, each containing five elements (the last vector can have less than five elements, if necessary).

3. Next, we sort each V^i.

4. For each V^i, find the median, m^i, and collect all medians into a set, M, as shown here:

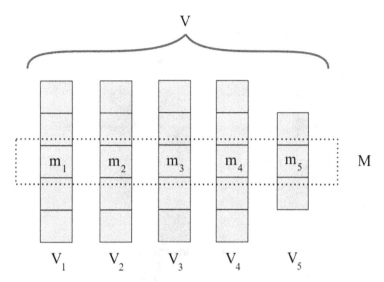

Figure 4.16: Finding the medians of each subvector

5. Find the median element, q, of M:

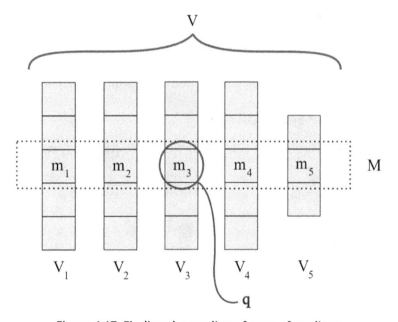

Figure 4.17: Finding the median of a set of medians

6. Use the partition operation on V using q as the pivot to get two vectors, L and R:

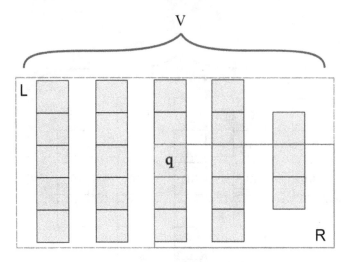

Figure 4.18: Partitioning the whole vector

7. By the definition of the partition operation, L contains all the elements less than q and R contains all the elements greater than q. Let's say L has $(k - 1)$ elements:

   - If $i = k$, then q is the ith element in V.
   - If $i < k$, set V = L and go to *step 1*.
   - If $i > k$, set V = R and $i = i - k$, and go to *step 1*.

The following exercise demonstrates the implementation of this algorithm in C++.

Exercise 21: Linear Time Selection

In this exercise, we shall implement the linear time selection algorithm. Let's get started:

1. Import the following headers:

```cpp
#include <iostream>
#include <vector>
#include <chrono>
#include <random>
#include <algorithm>
#include <numeric>
```

2. Write the helper function shown here:

```
template<typename T>
auto find_median(typename std::vector<T>::iterator begin, typename
std::vector<T>::iterator last)
{
    // Sort the array
    quick_sort<T>(begin, last);

    // Return the middle element, i.e. median
    return begin + (std::distance(begin, last)/2);
}
```

3. In *Exercise 20*, *Quicksort*, our partition function assumed that the first element in a given vector was always the pivot to be used. We now need a more general form of the partition operation that can work with any pivot element:

```
template <typename T>
auto partition_using_given_pivot(
typename std::vector<T>::iterator begin,
typename std::vector<T>::iterator end,
typename std::vector<T>::iterator pivot)
{
        // Since the pivot is already given,
        // Create two iterators pointing to the first and last element of
the vector respectively

        auto left_iter = begin;
        auto right_iter = end;

        while (true)
        {
        // Starting from the first element of vector, find an element that
is greater than pivot.
                while (*left_iter < *pivot && left_iter != right_iter)
                    left_iter++;

        // Starting from the end of vector moving to the beginning, find an
element that is lesser than the pivot.
                while (*right_iter >= *pivot &&
                        left_iter != right_iter)
                    right_iter--;
```

```
            // If left and right iterators meet, there are no elements left to
    swap. Else, swap the elements pointed to by the left and right iterators.
            if (left_iter == right_iter)
                break;
            else
                std::iter_swap(left_iter, right_iter);
        }
        if (*pivot > *right_iter)
            std::iter_swap(pivot, right_iter);

        return right_iter;
    }
```

4. Use the following code to implement our linear time search algorithm:

```
// Finds ith smallest element in vector V
template<typename T>
typename std::vector<T>::iterator linear_time_select(
typename std::vector<T>::iterator begin,
typename std::vector<T>::iterator last, size_t i)
{
    auto size = std::distance(begin, last);

    if (size > 0 && i < size) {

        // Get the number of V_i groups of 5 elements each
        auto num_Vi = (size+4) / 5;
        size_t j = 0;

        // For each V_i, find the median and store in vector M
        std::vector<T> M;
        for (; j < size/5; j++)
        {
            auto b = begin + (j * 5);
            auto l = begin + (j * 5) + 5;

            M.push_back(*find_median<T>(b, l));
        }
        if (j * 5 < size)
        {
            auto b = begin + (j * 5);
            auto l = begin + (j * 5) + (size % 5);
```

```
        M.push_back(*find_median<T>(b, 1));
    }

    // Find the middle element ('q' as discussed)
        auto median_of_medians = (M.size() == 1)? M.begin():
    linear_time_select<T>(M.begin(),
                            M.end()-1, M.size() / 2);

        // Apply the partition operation and find correct position 'k' of
    pivot 'q'.

        auto partition_iter = partition_using_given_pivot<T>(begin, last,
    median_of_medians);
        auto k = std::distance(begin, partition_iter)+1;

        if (i == k)
            return partition_iter;
        else if (i < k)
            return linear_time_select<T>(begin, partition_iter - 1, i);
        else if (i > k)
            return linear_time_select<T>(partition_iter + 1, last, i-k);
    }
    else {
        return begin;
    }
}
```

5. Add the merge sort implementation shown in the following code. We shall use the sorting algorithm to demonstrate the correctness of our implementation:

```
template <typename T>
std::vector<T> merge(std::vector<T>& arr1, std::vector<T>& arr2)
{
    std::vector<T> merged;

    auto iter1 = arr1.begin();
    auto iter2 = arr2.begin();

    while (iter1 != arr1.end() && iter2 != arr2.end())
    {
        if (*iter1 < *iter2)
        {
```

```cpp
                merged.emplace_back(*iter1);
                iter1++;
            }
            else
            {
                merged.emplace_back(*iter2);
                iter2++;
            }
        }

        if (iter1 != arr1.end())
        {
            for (; iter1 != arr1.end(); iter1++)
                merged.emplace_back(*iter1);
        }
        else
        {
            for (; iter2 != arr2.end(); iter2++)
                merged.emplace_back(*iter2);
        }

        return merged;
    }

template <typename T>
std::vector<T> merge_sort(std::vector<T> arr)
{
    if (arr.size() > 1)
    {
        auto mid = size_t(arr.size() / 2);
        auto left_half = merge_sort(std::vector<T>(arr.begin(),
            arr.begin() + mid));
        auto right_half = merge_sort(std::vector<T>(arr.begin() + mid,
            arr.end()));

        return merge<T>(left_half, right_half);
    }

    return arr;
}
```

6. Lastly, add the following driver and test functions:

```
void run_linear_select_test()

{
    std::vector<int> S1{ 45, 1, 3, 1, 2, 3, 45, 5, 1, 2, 44, 5, 7 };
    std::cout << "Original vector:" << std::endl;
    print_vector<int> (S1);

    std::cout << "Sorted vector:" << std::endl;
    print_vector<int>(merge_sort<int>(S1));


    std::cout << "3rd element: "
              << *linear_time_select<int>(S1.begin(), S1.end() - 1, 3)
    << std::endl;
    std::cout << "5th element: "
              << *linear_time_select<int>(S1.begin(), S1.end() - 1, 5)
    << std::endl;
    std::cout << "11th element: "
              << *linear_time_select<int>(S1.begin(), S1.end() - 1, 11)
    << std::endl;
}


int main()
{
    run_linear_select_test();
    return 0;
}
```

7. Compile and run the code. Your final output should look like this:

Figure 4.19: Finding the 3rd, 5th, and 11th elements using linear time selection

While a detailed theoretical analysis of the given algorithm is beyond the scope of this chapter, the runtime of the algorithm merits some discussion. The basic idea why the preceding algorithm works is that every time `linear_time_select()` is called with an input, V, a partition operation is applied, and the function then recursively calls itself on only one of the partitions. At each recursion step, the size of the problem reduces by at least 30%. Since finding a median of five elements is a constant time operation, the recurrence equation that's obtained by the preceding algorithm can be then solved using induction to see that the runtime is indeed O(n).

> **Note**
>
> An interesting property of the linear time selection algorithm is that its well-known asymptotic complexity (linear) is achieved when *V* is divided into subvectors of five elements each. Finding a constant size of subvectors that results in better asymptotic complexity remains an open problem.

C++ Standard Library Tools for Divide and Conquer

In the previous section, we manually implemented the necessary functions for divide-and-conquer algorithms. However, the C++ standard library comes bundled with a large set of predefined functions that can save us a lot of work when programming. The following table provides a handy list of the most commonly used functions that are used while implementing algorithms that use the divide-and-conquer paradigm. We are briefly describing these functions for reference, but the detailed implementation is left out of the scope of this chapter for brevity. Feel free to explore more about these functions; you should be able to understand them based on the concepts we've covered in this chapter:

STL function	Description of the function
`std::binary_search()`	Searches for a single element in a container using binary search.
`std::search()`	Searches for a range of elements in a container.
`std::upper_bound()`	Returns an iterator to the first element in a container that is greater than a given value.
`std::lower_bound()`	Returns an iterator to the first element in a container that is not less than a given value.
`std::partition()`	Applies the partition operation, reordering the elements in a container so that all the elements less than the pivot are positioned left of the pivot and all the elements greater than the pivot appear to the right.
`std::partition_copy()`	Applies the partition operation but returns two separate arrays as results.
`std::is_partitioned()`	Checks if the partition operation has been applied to the given container with respect to a given pivot.
`std::stable_partition()`	Applies the partition operation while ensuring that the order of elements after partitioning is controlled by the input predicate, that is, the elements for which the input predicate is true appear before the elements for which it is false.
`std::sort()`	Sorts the container. Internally, it uses a combination of different sorting techniques.
`std::stable_sort()`	Sorts the container while keeping the order of equal elements the same as that in the input container.
`std::partial_sort()`	Sorts only a portion instead of the entire container.
`std::merge()`	Merges two input containers so that the order of elements is maintained as they appear in the original containers.
`std::nth_element()`	Returns the nth smallest element in the container.

STL function	Description of the function
std::accumulate()	Computes the sum of a given value and all the elements in the given container. It also accepts an external reduction operator.
std::transform()	Given a container and a function, it applies the function on each element in the container, thus modifying its values.
std::reduce() (only for C++ 17 onwards)	Takes in a reduction operator, applies it to the given range, and returns the result.

Figure 4.20: Some useful STL functions for algorithms

Dividing and Conquering at a Higher Abstraction Level – MapReduce

So far in this chapter, we have looked at divide and conquer as an algorithm design technique and used it to solve our problems using a predefined set of divide-conquer-merge steps. In this section, we'll take a slight detour and see how the same principle of dividing a problem into smaller parts and solving each part separately can be particularly helpful when we need to scale software beyond the computational power of a single machine and use clusters of computers to solve problems.

The original **MapReduce** paper starts as follows:

"MapReduce is a programming model and an associated implementation for processing and generating large datasets. Users specify a map function that processes a key-value pair to generate a set of intermediate key/value pairs, and a reduce function that merges all the intermediate values associated with the same intermediate key."

> **Note**
>
> You can refer to the original research paper about the MapReduce model, which was published by Jeffrey Dean and Sanjay Ghemawat in 2004, here: https://static.googleusercontent.com/media/research.google.com/en/us/archive/mapreduce-osdi04.pdf.

Since the original paper first appeared, several open source implementations of the MapReduce programming model have appeared, the most notable of which is Hadoop. Hadoop provides a programming toolkit for the user to write map and reduce functions that can be applied to data stored in a distributed filesystem called the Hadoop Distributed File System (HDFS). Since HDFS can easily scale up to a cluster of several thousand machines connected over a network, MapReduce programs are therefore capable of scaling with the size of the cluster.

In this section, however, we are interested not in Hadoop, but in MapReduce as a programming paradigm, and its association with the topic at hand, that is, the divide-and-conquer technique. Instead of Hadoop, we will stick to an open source single-machine implementation of MapReduce that uses multithreading to emulate the original worker model for task parallelization.

The Map and Reduce Abstractions

The terms *map* and *reduce* have their origins in functional programming languages such as Lisp.

Map is an operation that takes in a container, C, and applies a given function, $f(x)$, to each element of C. An example of using $f(x) = x^2$ is shown in the following diagram:

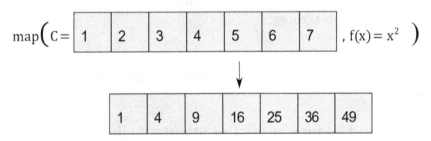

Figure 4.21: Mapping the values of a container

Reduce is an operation that aggregates values in a container, C, by applying a given function, *f(acc, x)*, to each element, *x*, of C, and returning a single value. This is shown in the following diagram:

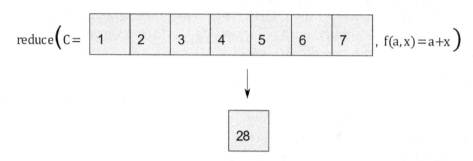

Figure 4.22: Reducing the values of a container

The C++ Standard Library contains map and reduce operations, that is, `std::transform()` and `std::accumulate()`, respectively (`std::reduce()` is also available in C++ 17).

> **Note**
>
> `std::accumulate()` is a restricted form of the reduce operation that uses only the addition function. The newer compilers also provide `std::reduce()`, which is more general and can be parallelized.

The following exercise demonstrates the implementation of MapReduce using the C++ Standard Library.

Exercise 22: Map and Reduce in the C++ Standard Library

In this exercise, we shall see how we can use these functions to further understand the map and reduce operations. Let's get started:

1. Import the following headers:

```
#include <iostream>
#include <vector>
#include <chrono>
#include <random>
#include <algorithm>
#include <numeric>
```

2. Begin by creating an array with random elements:

```
void transform_test(size_t size)
{
    std::vector<int> S, Tr;
    std::random_device rd;
    std::mt19937 rand(rd());
    std::uniform_int_distribution<std::mt19937::result_type> uniform_
dist(1, size);

    // Insert random elements
    for (auto i = 0; i < size; i++)
        S.push_back(uniform_dist(rand));

    std::cout << "Original array, S: ";
    for (auto i : S)
        std::cout << i << " ";
    std::cout << std::endl;
    std::transform(S.begin(), S.end(), std::back_inserter(Tr),
                   [](int x) {return std::pow(x, 2.0); });

    std::cout << "Transformed array, Tr: ";
    for (auto i : Tr)
        std::cout << i << " ";
    std::cout << std::endl;

    // For_each
    std::for_each(S.begin(), S.end(), [](int &x) {x = std::pow(x, 2.0);
});

    std::cout << "After applying for_each to S: ";
    for (auto i : S)
            std::cout << i << " ";
    std::cout << std::endl;
}
```

3. The **transform_test()** function randomly generates a vector of a given size and applies a transformation, $f(x) = x^2$, to the vector.

> **Note**
>
> **std::transform()** does not change the original vector and instead returns the result in a separate vector, while **std::for_each()** modifies the input vector. Another difference between the two is that **std::transform()** does not guarantee that the input function, f, will be applied from the first to the last element of the container; that is, the order of function application does not necessarily match the order of elements. Starting with C++ 17, **std::transform()** also supports native parallelization by accepting **ExecutionPolicy** as the first argument.

The reduce operation is implemented in the C++ Standard Library as **std::accumulate()** and **std::reduce()** (available only in C++ 17 and later):

```cpp
void reduce_test(size_t size)
{
    std::vector<int> S;
    std::random_device rd;
    std::mt19937 rand(rd());
    std::uniform_int_distribution<std::mt19937::result_type> uniform_
dist(1, size);

    // Insert random elements
    for (auto i = 0; i < size; i++)
        S.push_back(uniform_dist(rand));

    std::cout << std::endl << "Reduce test== " << std::endl << "Original
array, S: ";
    for (auto i : S)
        std::cout << i << " ";
    std::cout << std::endl;
    // Accumulate
    std::cout<<"std::accumulate() = " << std::accumulate(S.begin(),
S.end(), 0, [](int acc, int x) {return acc+x; });

    std::cout << std::endl;
}
```

4. Add the following driver code:

```
int main()
{
    transform_test(10);
    reduce_test(10);
    return 0;
}
```

5. Compile and run the code. Your output should look as follows:

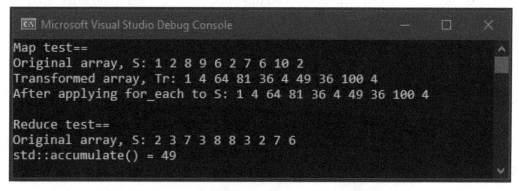

Figure 4.23: Mapping and reducing an array

Integrating the Parts – Using a MapReduce Framework

To write a program using the MapReduce model, we must be able to express our desired computation in a series of two stages: **Map** (also referred to as **Partition**), where the program reads the input and creates a set of intermediate *<key,value>* pairs, and **Reduce**, where the intermediate *<key,value>* pairs are then combined in the required manner to generate the final result. The following diagram illustrates this idea:

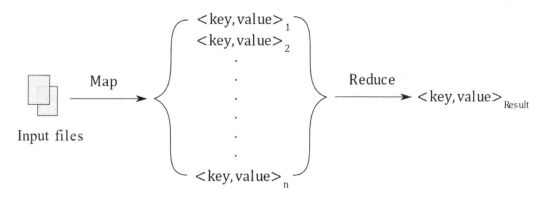

Figure 4.24: Generalized MapReduce framework

The main value that frameworks such as Hadoop add to the MapReduce programming model is that they make the map and reduce operations distributed and highly scalable so that the computation runs on a cluster of machines and the total time taken is reduced.

We shall use the MapReduce framework to execute a sample task in the following exercise.

> **Note**
>
> The following exercise and activity need the Boost C++ libraries to be installed on your system. Follow these links to get the Boost libraries:
>
> Windows: https://www.boost.org/doc/libs/1_71_0/more/getting_started/windows.html
>
> Linux/macOS: https://www.boost.org/doc/libs/1_71_0/more/getting_started/unix-variants.html

Exercise 23: Checking Primes Using MapReduce

Given a positive integer, N, we wish to find out the prime numbers between 1 and N. In this exercise, we shall see how we can implement this using the MapReduce programming model and solve the problem using multiple threads. Let's get started:

1. Let's begin by including the required libraries and defining a function to check whether a given number is prime using prime factorization:

```cpp
#include <iostream>
#include "mapreduce.hpp"

namespace prime_calculator {

    bool const is_prime(long const number)
    {
        if (number > 2)
        {
            if (number % 2 == 0)
                return false;

            long const n = std::abs(number);
```

```cpp
            long const sqrt_number = static_cast<long>(std::sqrt(
    static_cast<double>(n)));

            for (long i = 3; i <= sqrt_number; i += 2)
            {
                if (n % i == 0)
                    return false;
            }
        }
        else if (number == 0 || number == 1)
            return false;

        return true;
    }
```

2. The following class is used to generate a range of numbers with a given difference between consecutive numbers (also called the **step size**):

```cpp
    template<typename MapTask>
    class number_source : mapreduce::detail::noncopyable
    {
    public:
        number_source(long first, long last, long step)
            : sequence_(0), first_(first), last_(last), step_(step)
        {
        }

        bool const setup_key(typename MapTask::key_type& key)
        {
            key = sequence_++;
            return (key * step_ <= last_);
        }

        bool const get_data(typename MapTask::key_type const& key,
    typename MapTask::value_type& value)
        {
            typename MapTask::value_type val;

            val.first = first_ + (key * step_);
            val.second = std::min(val.first + step_ - 1, last_);
```

```
                std::swap(val, value);
                return true;
        }

    private:
        long sequence_;
        long const step_;
        long const last_;
        long const first_;
    };
```

3. The following function defines the steps to be performed in the map stage:

```
    struct map_task : public mapreduce::map_task<long, std::pair<long,
long> >
    {
        template<typename Runtime>
        void operator()(Runtime& runtime, key_type const& key,
value_type const& value) const
        {
            for (key_type loop = value.first;
                loop <= value.second; loop++)
            runtime.emit_intermediate(is_prime(loop), loop);
        }
    };
```

4. Now, let's implement the reduce stage:

```
    struct reduce_task : public mapreduce::reduce_task<bool, long>
    {
        template<typename Runtime, typename It>
        void operator()(Runtime& runtime, key_type const& key, It it, It
ite) const
        {
            if (key)
                std::for_each(it, ite, std::bind(&Runtime::emit,
&runtime, true, std::placeholders::_1));
        }
    };

    typedef
```

```
          mapreduce::job<
               prime_calculator::map_task,
               prime_calculator::reduce_task,
               mapreduce::null_combiner,
               prime_calculator::number_source<prime_calculator::map_task>>
     job;


} // namespace prime_calculator
```

The preceding namespace has three functions: first, it defines a function that checks whether a given number is prime; second, it defines a function that generates a range of numbers within given bounds; third, it defines the map and reduce tasks. The map function, as defined earlier, emits < k, v > pairs, where both k and v are of the **long** type, where k is 1 if v is a prime, and 0 if v is not a prime number. The reduce function then acts as a filter and outputs < k, v > pairs only where $k = 1$.

5. The following driver code then sets the relevant parameters and starts the MapReduce computation:

```
int main()
{
     mapreduce::specification spec;

     int prime_limit = 1000;

     // Set number of threads to be used
     spec.map_tasks = std::max(1U, std::thread::hardware_concurrency());
     spec.reduce_tasks = std::max(1U, std::thread::hardware_concurrency());

     // Set the source of numbers in given range
     prime_calculator::job::datasource_type datasource(0, prime_limit,
prime_limit / spec.reduce_tasks);

     std::cout << "\nCalculating Prime Numbers in the range 0 .. " <<
prime_limit << " ..." << std::endl;

std::cout << std::endl << "Using "
          << std::max(1U, std::thread::hardware_concurrency()) << " CPU
cores";

     // Run mapreduce
     prime_calculator::job job(datasource, spec);
```

```
    mapreduce::results result;

    job.run<mapreduce::schedule_policy::cpu_parallel<prime_
calculator::job> >(result);

    std::cout << "\nMapReduce finished in "
<< result.job_runtime.count() << " with "
<< std::distance(job.begin_results(), job.end_results())
<< " results" << std::endl;


// Print results
    for (auto it = job.begin_results(); it != job.end_results(); ++it)
        std::cout << it->second << " ";

    return 0;
}
```

The driver code sets the parameters that are required for the MapReduce framework, runs the computation, collects results from the reduce function, and, finally, outputs the results.

6. Compile and run the preceding code. Your output should look as follows:

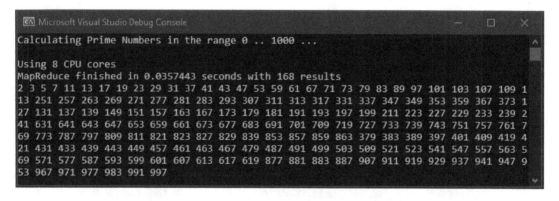

Figure 4.25: Calculating prime numbers using the MapReduce framework

The main benefit of programming using the MapReduce model is that it results in software that is massively scalable. The MapReduce framework we used in this exercise was one that only used multithreading on a single machine to achieve parallelization. But had it been able to support distributed systems, the same code we wrote here could have run on a large cluster of servers, enabling the computation to scale to massive sizes. Porting the preceding code to systems such as Hadoop is a trivial exercise in Java, but beyond the scope of this book.

Activity 10: Implementing WordCount in MapReduce

In this chapter, we have seen how powerful the idea behind the divide-and-conquer technique can be as an exceedingly useful algorithm design technique, as well as in providing useful tools to handle large and complex computations. In this activity, we shall practice dividing a large problem into smaller parts, solving the smaller parts, and merging the subsequent results by using the MapReduce model that was presented in the preceding section.

Our problem definition has been taken from the original MapReduce paper, and is given as follows: given a set of files containing text, find the frequency of each word that appears in the files. For example, let's say you are given two files with the following contents:

File 1:

```
The quick brown fox jumps over a rabbit
```

File 2:

```
The quick marathon runner won the race
```

Considering the input files, our program should output the following result:

The	2
quick	2
a	1
brown	1
fox	1
jumps	1
marathon	1
over	1
rabbit	1
race	1
runner	1
the	1
won	1

Such problems often arise in indexing workloads, that is, when you are given a large corpus of text and are required to index the contents so that subsequent searches on the text can be made faster. Search engines such as Google and Bing heavily use such indexes.

In this activity, you are required to implement the map and reduce stages of the word count problem. Since this involves a significant portion of code that is specific to our library, boilerplate code has been provided for you in `mapreduce_wordcount_skeleton.cpp`.

Activity Guidelines:

1. Read through and understand the given code in `mapreduce_wordcount_skeleton.cpp`. You will notice that we need to import the Boost libraries in the header. Another thing to note is that the map stage in the given code creates $< k, v >$ pairs, where k is a string and v is set to 1. For example, say your set of input files contained a random combination of words, $w^1, w^2, w^3, ..., w^n$. If so, the map stage should output $< k, 1>$ pairs with $k = \{w^1, w^2, w^3, ..., w^n\}$, as illustrated in the following diagram:

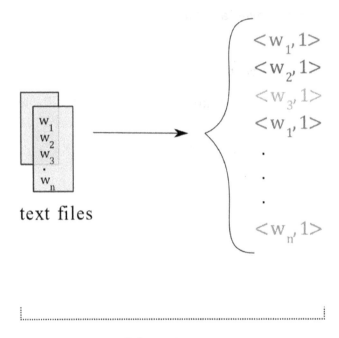

Map stage

Figure 4.26: Mapping stage

2. The skeleton code for the map stage looks as follows:

```
struct map_task : public mapreduce::map_task<
    std::string,                          // MapKey (filename)
    std::pair<char const*, std::uintmax_t>> // MapValue (memory mapped file
                                            // contents)
{
template<typename Runtime>
```

```
void operator()(Runtime& runtime, key_type const& key,
                              value_type& value) const
{
    // Write your code here.
    // Use runtime.emit_intermediate() to emit <k,v> pairs
}
};
```

3. Since the map stage of the problem generated $< k, 1 >$ pairs, the reduce task of our program should now combine the pairs with matching values of k, as shown here:

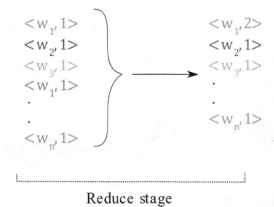

Reduce stage

Figure 4.27: Reducing stage

4. In the given code, the reduce task accepts two iterators, which can be used to iterate over the elements with the same key, that is, all the elements between **it** and **ite** are guaranteed to have the same key. Your reduce phase should then create a new $< k, v >$ pair, with k set to the key of the input pairs and v equal to the number of input pairs:

```
template<typename KeyType>
struct reduce_task : public mapreduce::reduce_task<KeyType, unsigned>
{
    using typename mapreduce::reduce_task<KeyType, unsigned>::key_type;

    template<typename Runtime, typename It>
    void operator()(Runtime& runtime, key_type const& key, It it, It const
ite) const
    {
        // Write your code here.
        // Use runtime.emit() to emit the resulting <k,v> pairs
    }
};
```

5. You are given a set of test data in **testdata/**. Compile and run your code. The output should look as follows:

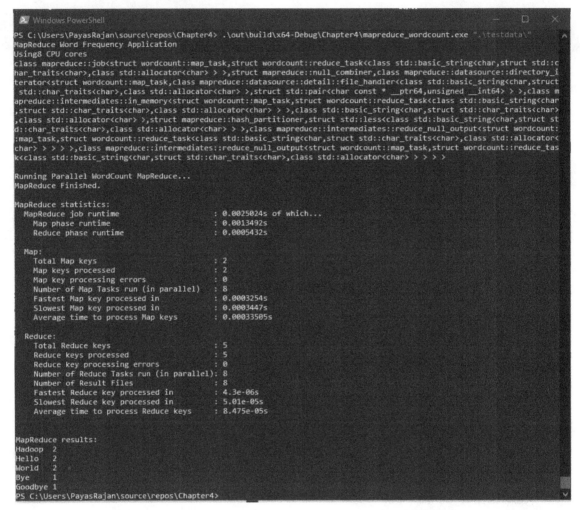

Figure 4.28: Getting the frequency of words in the given input files

---

Note

The solution to this activity can be found on page 514.

Summary

In this chapter, we discussed divide and conquer in two different ways: first as an algorithm design paradigm, and then its use in designing other tools that help us in scaling our software. We covered some standard divide-and-conquer algorithms (merge sort and quicksort). We also saw how simple operations such as **partition** underlie the solutions to different problems such as partial sorting and linear time selection.

An important idea to keep in mind while implementing these algorithms in practice is the separation of data structures that hold data from the implementation of the algorithm itself. Using C++ templates is often a good way to achieve this separation. We saw that the C++ Standard Library comes with a large set of primitives that can be used for implementing divide-and-conquer algorithms.

The simplicity of the underlying idea behind divide and conquer makes it an incredibly useful tool in solving problems and allows for the creation of parallelization frameworks such as MapReduce. We also saw an example of using the MapReduce programming model to find prime numbers in a given range.

In the next chapter, we shall cover the greedy algorithm design paradigm, which results in solutions such as Dijkstra's algorithm to find the shortest paths in graphs.

5

Greedy Algorithms

Learning Objectives

By the end of this chapter, you will be able to:

- Describe the greedy approach to algorithm design
- Identify the optimal substructure and greedy choice properties of a problem
- Implement greedy algorithms such as fractional knapsack and greedy graph coloring
- Implement Kruskal's Minimum Spanning Tree algorithm using a disjoint-set data structure

In this chapter, we will look at various 'greedy' approaches to algorithm design and see how they can be applied in order to solve real-world problems.

Introduction

In the previous chapter, we discussed the divide-and-conquer algorithm design technique, which solves a given problem by dividing the input into smaller subproblems, solving each subproblem, and subsequently merging the results. Continuing our theme of algorithm design paradigms, we will now look at our next topic: the **greedy approach**.

On each iteration, a greedy algorithm is one that picks the 'seemingly best' alternative. In other words, a greedy solution to a problem composes a globally optimal solution to the given problem from a series of locally optimal solutions. For example, the following screenshot shows the shortest path that a car can take from Dulles International Airport in Washington DC to an office building in East Riverdale. Naturally, the path shown is also the shortest for any two points on the path that are not the starting and ending points:

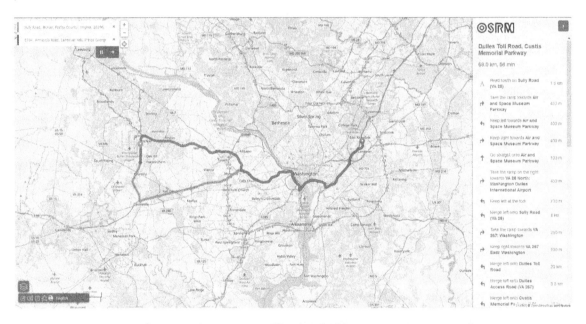

Figure 5.1: A route from an airport to an office in Washington DC (Source: project-osrm.org)

Therefore, we can infer that the whole shortest path, P, is, in effect, a concatenation of several shortest paths between the vertices of the road network that lie along P. So, if we were asked to design a shortest path algorithm, one possible strategy would be as follows: start from the origin vertex and draw a path to the closest vertex that hasn't been explored yet, and then repeat until we reach the destination vertex. Congratulations – you have just solved the shortest path problem using Dijkstra's algorithm, which is the same one that powers commercial software such as Google Maps and Bing Maps!

Expectedly, the simple approach taken by greedy algorithms makes them applicable only to a small subset of algorithmic problems. However, the simplicity of the greedy approach often makes it an excellent tool for 'first attack', by which we can understand the properties and behavior of the underlying problem, which can then be solved using other, more complex approaches.

In this chapter, we will study the conditions under which a given problem is suitable for a greedy solution – the optimal substructure and greedy choice properties. We will see that when a problem can be shown to have these two properties, a greedy solution is guaranteed to yield the correct results. We will also see a few examples of real-world problems for which greedy solutions are used in practice, and we will end this chapter with a discussion of the minimum spanning tree problem, which commonly arises in cases of telecommunication and water supply networks, electrical grids, and circuit design. But first, let's start by taking a look at some simpler problems that can be solved using greedy algorithms.

Basic Greedy Algorithms

In this section, we will study two standard problems that can be solved using the greedy approach: **shortest-job-first scheduling** and the **fractional knapsack** problem.

Shortest-Job-First Scheduling

Say you are standing in a queue at your bank. It's a busy day and there are N people in the queue, but the bank has only one counter open (it's also a really bad day!). Let's assume that it takes a person, p^i, the amount of time of a^i to get served at the counter. Since the people in the queue are quite rational, everyone agrees to reorder their places in the queue so that the *average waiting time* for everyone in the queue is minimized. You are tasked with finding a way of reordering the people in the queue. How would you solve this problem?

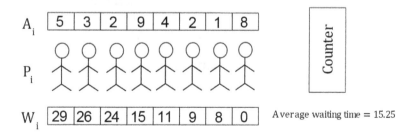

Figure 5.2: The original queue

To take this problem apart further, let's look at an example. The preceding figure shows an example of the original queue, where A^i shows the service time and W^i shows the waiting time for the ith person. The person closest to the counter can start getting served immediately, so the waiting time for them is 0. The person who's second in the queue must wait until the first person is done, so they have to wait for $a^1 = 8$ units of time before getting served. Continuing in a similar fashion, the ith person has a waiting time equal to the sum of the service times for all of the $i - 1$ people before them in the queue.

A clue to solving this problem is as follows: since we are looking to minimize the *average waiting time*, we must find a way to reduce the waiting time for the largest possible set of people, as much as possible. One way to reduce the waiting time for all people is the job that can be completed the quickest. By repeating this idea for all the people in the queue, our solution results in the following reordered queue:

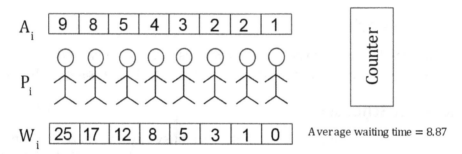

Figure 5.3: The reordered queue with the minimum average waiting time

Notice that our reordered queue has an average waiting time of 8.87 units versus 15.25 units for the original ordering, which is an improvement by a factor of approximately 2.

Exercise 24: Shortest-Job-First Scheduling

In this exercise, we will implement a shortest-job-first scheduling solution by taking a similar example to the one shown in the preceding figure. We will consider 10 people in a queue and try to minimize the average waiting time for all of them. Let's get started:

1. Begin by adding the required headers and creating functions for computing the waiting times and input/output:

```
#include <iostream>
#include <algorithm>
#include <vector>
#include <random>
#include <numeric>

// Given a set of service times, computes the service times for all users
```

```cpp
template<typename T>
auto compute_waiting_times(std::vector<T>& service_times)
{
    std::vector<T> W(service_times.size());
    W[0] = 0;

    for (auto i = 1; i < service_times.size(); i++)
        W[i] = W[i - 1] + service_times[i - 1];

    return W;
}

// Generic function to print a vector
template<typename T>
void print_vector(std::vector<T>& V)
{
    for (auto& i : V)
        std::cout << i << " ";
    std::cout << std::endl;
}

template<typename T>
void compute_and_print_waiting_times(std::vector<T>& service_times)
{
    auto waiting_times = compute_waiting_times<int>(service_times);

    std::cout << "Service times: " << std::endl;
    print_vector<T>(service_times);

    std::cout << "Waiting times: " << std::endl;
    print_vector<T>(waiting_times);

    std::cout << "Average waiting time = "
        << std::accumulate(waiting_times.begin(),
            waiting_times.end(), 0.0) /
        waiting_times.size();

    std::cout<< std::endl;
}
```

2. Add the main solver and driver code, as shown here:

```
void shortest_job_first(size_t size)
{
    std::vector<int> service_times;
    std::random_device rd;
    std::mt19937 rand(rd());
    std::uniform_int_distribution<std::mt19937::result_type> uniform_
dist(1, size);

    // Insert random elements as service times
    service_times.reserve(size);
    for (auto i = 0; i < size; i++)
        service_times.push_back(uniform_dist(rand));

    compute_and_print_waiting_times<int>(service_times);

    // Reorder the elements in the queue
    std::sort(service_times.begin(), service_times.end());

    compute_and_print_waiting_times<int>(service_times);
}

int main(int argc, char* argv[])
{
    shortest_job_first(10);
}
```

3. Compile and run the code! Your output should look as follows:

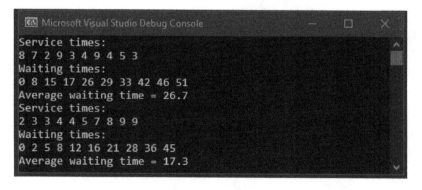

Figure 5.4: Output of the program to schedule the shortest job first

The Knapsack Problem(s)

In this section, we will discuss the standard **knapsack problem**, also known as the 0-1 knapsack problem, which is known to be NP-complete, and thereby does not allow us to have any polynomial-time solution. Then, we will turn our discussion toward a version of the knapsack problem called the **fractional knapsack problem**, which can be solved using a greedy approach. Our focus in this section is to demonstrate how even subtle differences between how a problem is defined can lead to large changes in the solution strategies.

The Knapsack Problem

Suppose you are given a set of objects, $O = \{O^1, O^2, ..., O^n\}$, with each having a certain weight, W^i, and a value of V^i. You are also given a bag (or a knapsack) that can carry only a total weight of T units. Now, say you are tasked with finding out about a set of objects to keep in your bag so that the total weight is less than or equal to T, and the total value of the objects is the maximum it can possibly be.

A real-world example of this problem can be understood if you imagine a traveling trader who earns a fixed percentage profit on all their trades. They would want to carry the maximum value of goods to maximize their profit, but their vehicle (or knapsack) can hold only up to T units of weight. The trader knows the exact weight and value of each object. Which set of objects should they carry so that the total value of the objects carried for trade is the maximum possible?

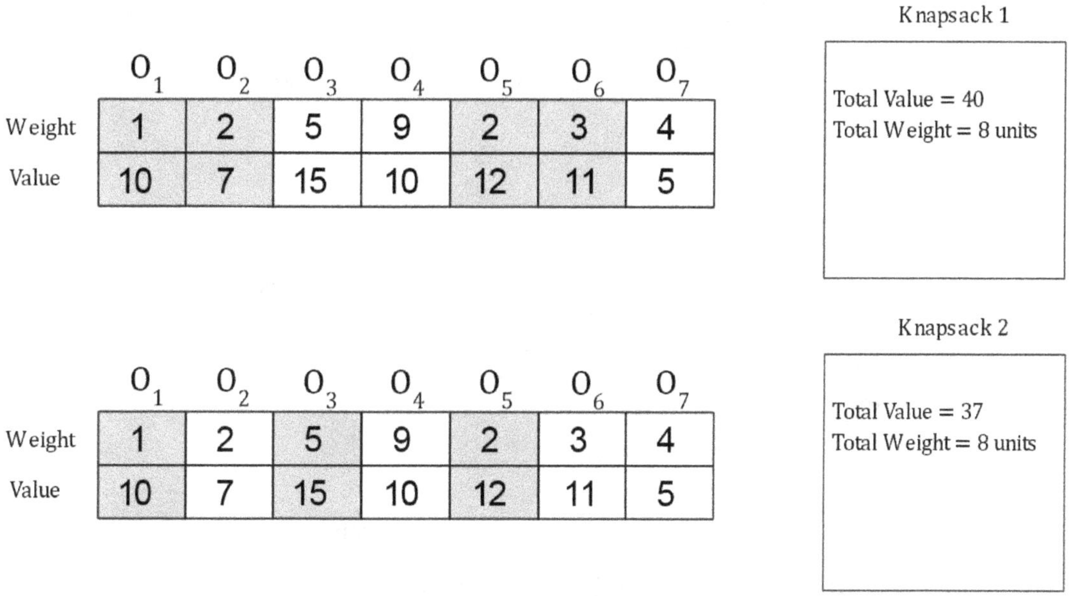

Knapsack 1

	O_1	O_2	O_3	O_4	O_5	O_6	O_7
Weight	1	2	5	9	2	3	4
Value	10	7	15	10	12	11	5

Total Value = 40
Total Weight = 8 units

Knapsack 2

	O_1	O_2	O_3	O_4	O_5	O_6	O_7
Weight	1	2	5	9	2	3	4
Value	10	7	15	10	12	11	5

Total Value = 37
Total Weight = 8 units

Figure 5.5: The knapsack problem

The problem that's presented in the preceding figure is the well-known knapsack problem and has been proven to be NP-complete. In other words, there is no known polynomial-time solution to this problem. As a result, we must look at all the possible combinations of the objects to find the combination that has the greatest value while having a total weight of only T units. The preceding diagram shows two ways a knapsack with a capacity of 8 units can be filled. The objects shown in grey are the ones that have been chosen to be put in the knapsack. We can see that the first set of objects has a total value of 40, the second set of objects has a total value of 37, and that the total weight in both cases is 8 units. Therefore, the second set of objects is a better choice than the first. To find the best possible set of objects, we must list all possible combinations and choose the one with the maximum value.

The Fractional Knapsack Problem

Now, we will make a small change to the knapsack problem that was given in the previous subsection: let's say we are now allowed to break each object into as many parts as we need, and then we can choose what fraction of each object we want to keep in the knapsack.

In terms of the real-world analogy, let's say that the trader in our previous analogy is trading items such as oil, grains, and flour. The trader may take any smaller measure of weight.

Contrary to the NP-completeness of the standard knapsack, the fractional knapsack problem has a simple solution: order the elements according to their value per weight ratio and 'greedily' choose as many objects as possible with the maximum ratio. The following figure shows the optimal selection of a given set of objects when the knapsack's capacity is set to 8 units. Notice that the chosen objects are the ones with the highest value per weight ratio:

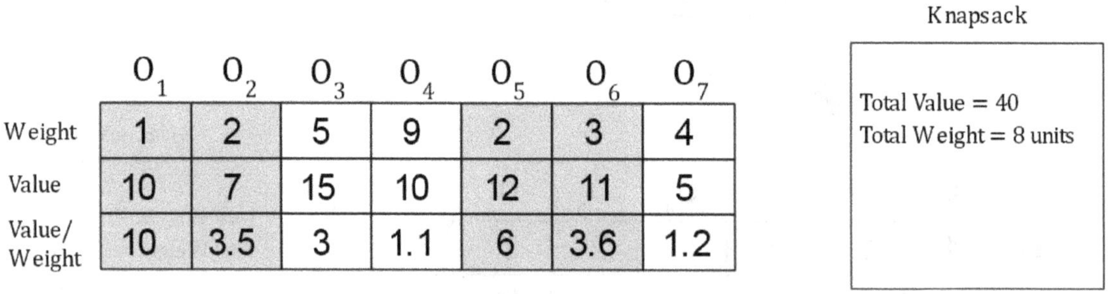

	O_1	O_2	O_3	O_4	O_5	O_6	O_7
Weight	1	2	5	9	2	3	4
Value	10	7	15	10	12	11	5
Value/Weight	10	3.5	3	1.1	6	3.6	1.2

Knapsack

Total Value = 40
Total Weight = 8 units

Figure 5.6: The fractional knapsack problem

We will implement this solution in the following exercise.

Exercise 25: Fractional Knapsack Problem

In this exercise, we will consider 10 items and try to maximize the value in our knapsack, which can hold a maximum weight of 25 units. Let's get started:

1. First, we will begin by adding the required headers and defining an **Object** struct that will represent one object in our solution:

```cpp
#include <iostream>
#include <algorithm>
#include <vector>
#include <random>
#include <numeric>

template <typename weight_type,
    typename value_type,
    typename fractional_type>
struct Object
{
    using Wtype = weight_type;
    using Vtype = value_type;
    using Ftype = fractional_type;

    Wtype weight;
    Vtype value;
    Ftype value_per_unit_weight;

    // NOTE: The following overloads are to be used for std::sort() and
I/O
    inline bool operator< (const Object<Wtype,Vtype,Ftype>& obj) const
    {
        // An object is better or worse than another object only on the
        // basis of its value per unit weight
        return this->value_per_unit_weight < obj.value_per_unit_weight;
    }

    inline bool operator== (const Object<Wtype, Vtype, Ftype>& obj) const
    {
        // An object is equivalent to another object only if
        // its value per unit weight is equal
        return this->value_per_unit_weight == obj.value_per_unit_weight;
    }
```

```
    // Overloads the << operator so an object can be written directly to a
stream
    // e.g. Can be used as std::cout << obj << std::endl;

    template <typename Wtype,
        typename Vtype,
        typename Ftype>
    friend std::ostream& operator<<(std::ostream& os,
                        const Object<Wtype,Vtype,Ftype>& obj);
};

template <typename Wtype,
    typename Vtype,
    typename Ftype>
std::ostream& operator<<(std::ostream& os, const
Object<Wtype,Vtype,Ftype>& obj)

{
    os << "Value: "<<obj.value
    << "\t Weight: " << obj.weight
        <<"\t Value/Unit Weight: " << obj.value_per_unit_weight;
    return os;
}
```

Note that we have overloaded the < and == operators since we will use **std::sort()** over a vector of **objects**.

2. The code for the fractional knapsack solver is as follows:

```
template<typename weight_type,
    typename value_type,
    typename fractional_type>
auto fill_knapsack(std::vector<Object<weight_type, value_type,fractional_
type>>& objects,
                        weight_type knapsack_capacity)
{

    std::vector<Object<weight_type, value_type, fractional_type>>
knapsack_contents;
    knapsack_contents.reserve(objects.size());

    // Sort objects in the decreasing order
    std::sort(objects.begin(), objects.end());
```

```
    std::reverse(objects.begin(), objects.end());

    // Add the 'best' objects to the knapsack
    auto current_object = objects.begin();
    weight_type current_total_weight = 0;
    while (current_total_weight <= knapsack_capacity &&
current_object != objects.end())
    {
        knapsack_contents.push_back(*current_object);

        current_total_weight += current_object->weight;
        current_object++;
    }

    // Since the last object overflows the knapsack, adjust weight
    auto weight_of_last_obj_to_remove = current_total_weight - knapsack_
capacity;

    knapsack_contents.back().weight -= weight_of_last_obj_to_remove;
    knapsack_contents.back().value -= knapsack_contents.back().value_per_
unit_weight *
                        weight_of_last_obj_to_remove;

    return knapsack_contents;
}
```

The preceding function sorts the objects in decreasing order of their value/weight ratio and then picks all the fractions of objects that can fit in the knapsack until the knapsack is full.

3. Finally, to test our implementation, add the following test and driver code:

```
void test_fractional_knapsack(unsigned num_objects, unsigned knapsack_
capacity)
{
    using weight_type = unsigned;
    using value_type = double;
    using fractional_type = double;

    // Initialize the Random Number Generator
    std::random_device rd;
    std::mt19937 rand(rd());
    std::uniform_int_distribution<std::mt19937::result_type>
```

```
        uniform_dist(1, num_objects);

            // Create a vector of objects
            std::vector<Object<weight_type, value_type, fractional_type>> objects;
            objects.reserve(num_objects);
            for (auto i = 0; i < num_objects; i++)
            {
                // Every object is initialized with a random weight and value
                auto weight = uniform_dist(rand);
                auto value = uniform_dist(rand);
                auto obj = Object<weight_type, value_type, fractional_type> {
                    static_cast<weight_type>(weight),
                    static_cast<value_type>(value),
                    static_cast<fractional_type>(value) / weight
                };

                objects.push_back(obj);
            }

            // Display the set of objects
            std::cout << "Objects available: " << std::endl;
            for (auto& o : objects)
                std::cout << o << std::endl;
            std::cout << std::endl;

            // Arbitrarily assuming that the total knapsack capacity is 25 units
            auto solution = fill_knapsack(objects, knapsack_capacity);

            // Display items selected to be in the knapsack
            std::cout << "Objects selected to be in the knapsack (max capacity = "
                << knapsack_capacity<< "):" << std::endl;
            for (auto& o : solution)
                std::cout << o << std::endl;
            std::cout << std::endl;
        }

        int main(int argc, char* argv[])
        {
            test_fractional_knapsack(10, 25);
        }
```

The preceding function creates objects and initializes them with random data from the STL random number generator. Next, it calls our implementation of the fractional knapsack solver and then displays the results.

4. Compile and run this code! Your output should look as follows:

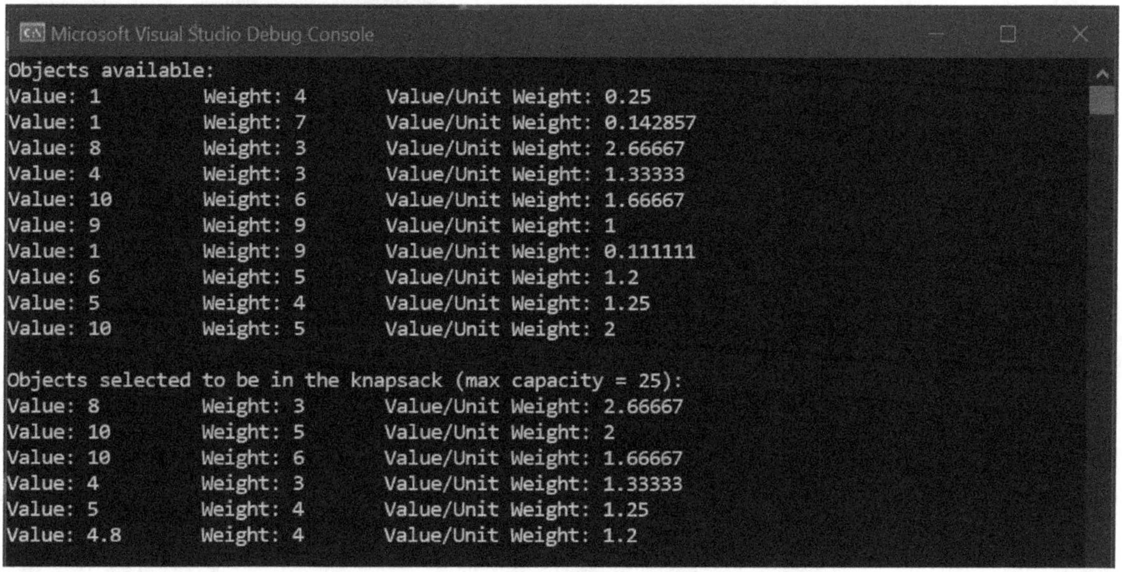

Figure 5.7: Output of Exercise 25

Note how the solver took a fraction, that is, only 4 of the 5 units of the last object by weight. This is an example of how objects can be partitioned before being chosen to be kept in the knapsack, which differentiates the fractional knapsack from the 0-1 (standard) knapsack problem.

Activity 11: The Interval Scheduling Problem

Imagine that you have a set of tasks on your to-do list (doing the dishes, going to the supermarket to buy groceries, working on a secret project for world domination, and other similar chores). Each task is identified by an ID and can be completed only between a particular start and end time. Let's say you wish to complete the maximum number of tasks. On what subset, and in what order, should you work on your tasks to achieve your objective? Assume that you can work on only one task at any point in time.

As an example, consider the problem instance shown in the following figure. We have been given four different tasks that we could possibly spend our time working on (the rectangular boxes represent the time interval in which the task can be completed):

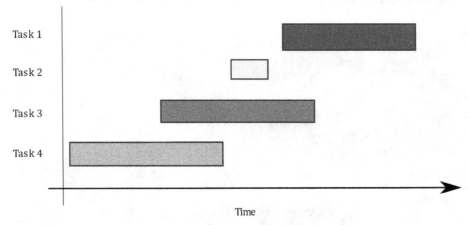

Figure 5.8: Given task schedules

The following figure shows the optimal scheduling of tasks, which maximizes the total number of tasks completed:

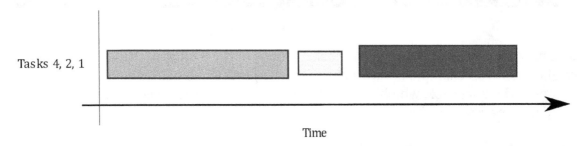

Figure 5.9: Optimal selection of tasks

Notice how not completing task 3 allows us to complete tasks 1 and 2 instead, increasing the total number of completed tasks. In this activity, you will need to implement this greedy interval scheduling solution.

The high-level steps for solving this activity are as follows:

1. Assume that each task has a start time, an end time, and an ID. Create a struct that describes a task. We will represent different tasks with different instances of this struct.

2. Implement a function that creates an **std::list** of N tasks, set their IDs sequentially from 1 to N, and use the values from a random number generator for the start and end times.

3. Implement the scheduling function as follows:

a. Sort the list of tasks in increasing order of their ending times.

b. Greedily choose to complete the task with the earliest ending time.

c. Remove all the tasks that overlap with the currently chosen task (all the tasks that start before the current task ends).

d. If tasks remain on the list, go to *step b*. Otherwise, return the chosen vector of tasks.

Your final output should look similar to the following:

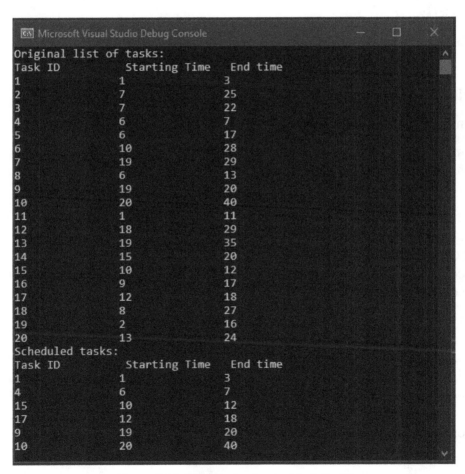

Figure 5.10: Expected output of Activity 11

> **Note**
> The solution for this activity can be found on page 516.

Requirements for Greedy Algorithms

In the previous section, we looked at examples of problems where the greedy approach gives optimal solutions. However, a problem can be optimally solved using the greedy approach if and only if it has two properties: the **optimal substructure** property and the **greedy choice** property. In this section, we will attempt to understand these properties and show you how to identify whether a problem exhibits them.

Optimal substructure: When an optimal solution to a given problem, P, is composed of the optimal solutions to its subproblems, then P is said to have an optimal substructure.

Greedy choice: When an optimal solution to a given problem, P, can be reached by selecting the locally optimal solution on each iteration, P is said to have the greedy choice property.

To understand the optimal substructure and greedy choice properties, we will implement Kruskal's minimum spanning tree algorithm.

The Minimum Spanning Tree (MST) Problem

The minimum spanning tree problem can be stated as follows:

"Given a graph, G = < V, E >, where V is the set of vertices and E is the set of edges, each associated with an edge weight, find a tree, T, that spans all the vertices in V and has the minimum total weight."

A real-life application of the MST problem is the design of water supply and transportation networks since the designers typically wish to minimize the total length of the pipeline that's used or the roads that are created and still make sure that the services reach all designated users. Let's try to take the problem apart with the following example.

Let's say that you are given the locations of 12 villages on a map and are asked to find the minimum total length of road that would need to be built so that all the villages are reachable from one another, and that the roads do not form a cycle. Assume that each road can be traversed in either direction. A natural representation of villages in this problem is using a graph data structure. Let's assume that the vertices of the following graph, G represent the locations of the 12 given villages and that the edges of G represent the distances between the vertices:

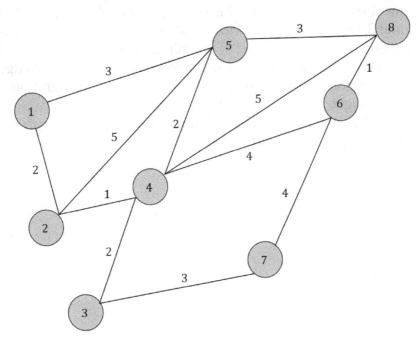

Figure 5.11: Graph G representing the villages and distances between them

A simple greedy algorithm to construct the minimum spanning tree, T, could be as follows:

1. Add all the edges of G in a min-heap, H.

2. From H, pop an edge, e. Naturally, e has the minimum cost among all edges in H.

3. If both vertices of e are already in T, this means that adding e would create a cycle in T. Therefore, discard e and go to step 2. Otherwise, proceed to the next step.

4. Insert e in the minimum spanning tree, T.

Let's take a moment to think about why this strategy works. At each iteration of the loop in steps 2 and 3, we take the edge with the lowest cost and check whether it adds any vertex to our solution. This is stored in the minimum spanning tree, T. If it does, we add the edge to T; otherwise, we discard that edge and choose another edge with the minimum value. Our algorithm is greedy in the sense that at each iteration, it chooses the minimum edge weight to add to the solution. The preceding algorithm was invented in 1956 and is called **Kruskal's minimum spanning tree algorithm**. Applying this algorithm to the graph shown in *figure* 5.11 gives the following result:

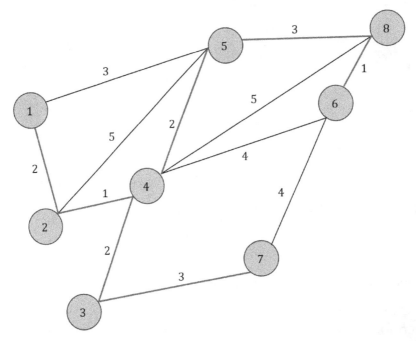

Figure 5.12: Graph G showing the minimum spanning tree, T (with red edges)

The total weight of edges in the minimum spanning tree, T, is $(2 \times 1) + (3 \times 2) + (2 \times 3) = 14$ units. Therefore, the answer to our problem is that at least 12 units of road would need to be built.

How do we know that our algorithm is indeed correct? We need to return to the definitions of optimal substructure and greedy choice and show that the MST problem exhibits these two properties. While a rigorous mathematical proof of the properties is beyond the ambit of this book, here are the intuitive ideas behind the proofs:

Optimal substructure: We will prove this by using contradiction. Let's assume that the MST problem does not exhibit an optimal substructure; that is, a minimum spanning tree was not composed of a set of smaller minimum spanning trees:

1. Let's say we are given a minimum spanning tree, T, over the vertices of graph G Let's remove any edge, e, from T. Removing e decomposes T into smaller trees, T^1 and T^2.

2. Since we assumed that the MST problem does not exhibit optimal substructure, there must exist a spanning tree with a lesser total weight over the vertices of T^1. Take this spanning tree and add the edges e and T^2 to it. This new tree will be T'.

3. Now, since the total weight of T' is less than that of T, this contradicts our original assumption that T is an MST. Therefore, the MST problem must exhibit the optimal substructure property.

Greedy choice: If the MST problem exhibits greedy choice property, then for a vertex, v, the minimum weight edge connecting v to the rest of the graph, G, should always be a part of the minimum spanning tree, T. We can prove this hypothesis by contradiction, as follows:

1. Say an edge (u, v) is the minimum weight edge connecting v to any other vertex in G. Assume that (u, v) is not a part of T.

2. If (u, v) is not a part of T, then T must consist of some other edge connecting v to the rest of G. Let this edge be (x, v). Since (u, v) is the minimum weight edge, by definition, the weight of (x, v) is greater than the weight of (u, v).

3. A tree with a lesser total weight than T can be obtained if (x, v) is replaced with (u, v) in T. This contradicts our assumption that T is the minimum spanning tree. Therefore, the MST problem must exhibit the greedy choice property.

> **Note**
>
> As we mentioned earlier, we can also take a rigorous mathematical approach to show that the MST problem exhibits the optimal substructure property and is suitable for the greedy choice property. You can find it here: https://ocw.mit.edu/courses/electrical-engineering-and-computer-science/6-046j-design-and-analysis-of-algorithms-spring-2015/lecture-notes/MIT6_046JS15_lec12.pdf.

Let's think about how to implement Kruskal's algorithm. We covered graph and heap data structures in *Chapter 2, Trees, Heaps, and Graphs*, so we know how to implement steps 1 and 2. Step 3 is somewhat more complicated. We need a data structure that stores the edges of the graph and tells us whether adding a new edge would create a cycle with any possible combination of the edges already stored in it. This problem can be solved using a disjoint-set data structure.

Disjoint-Set (or Union-Find) Data Structures

A **disjoint-set data structure** consists of a forest (a set of trees) of elements, where each element is represented by a numerical ID, has a 'rank,' and contains a pointer to its parent. When the data structure is initialized, it starts with N independent elements of rank 0, each of which is a part of a tree that contains only the element itself. The data structure supports two other operations:

- A **find** operation on a tree returns the root element of that tree

- A **union** operation applied on two trees merges the smaller trees into a larger tree, where the size of the tree is stored as the rank of its root.

More precisely, the disjoint-set data structure supports the following operations:

- **Make-Set**: This initializes the data structure with N elements, setting the rank of each element to 0, and the parent pointer to itself. The following figure shows an example of a disjoint-set DS initialized with five elements. The digits inside the circles show the element IDs, the digit in parentheses shows the rank, and the arrows represent the pointer to the root element:

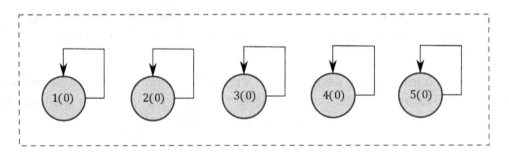

Figure 5.13: Initializing disjoint set with five elements

At this stage, the data structure consists of five trees, each consisting of one element.

- **Find**: Starting from a given element, x, the **find** operation follows the parent pointers of elements until the root of the tree is reached. The parent of a root element is the root itself. In the example in the previous set, each element is the root of the tree, and hence this operation will return the lone element in the tree.

- **Union**: Given two elements, x and y, the **union** operation finds the roots of x and y. If the two roots are the same, this means that x and y belong to the same tree. Therefore, it does nothing. Otherwise, it sets the root with a higher rank as the parent of the root with a lower rank. The following figure shows the result of implementing the **Union(1, 2)** and **Union(4, 5)** operations on DS:

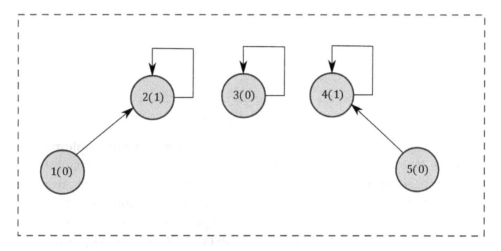

Figure 5.14: Merging 1,2 and 4,5

As subsequent union operations are applied, more trees merge into fewer (but larger) trees. The following figure shows the trees in DS after applying **Union(2, 3)**:

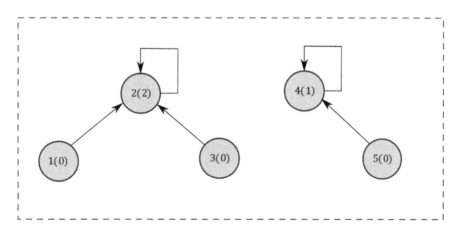

Figure 5.15: Merging 2,3

The following diagram shows the trees in DS after applying **Union(2, 4)**:

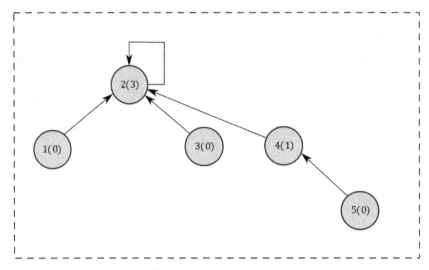

Figure 5.16: Merging 2,4

Now, let's understand how the disjoint-set data structure helps us implement Kruskal's algorithm. At the start of the algorithm, before step 1, we initialize a disjoint-set data structure with N equal to the number of vertices in our graph, G. Then, step 2 takes an edge from the min heap and step 3 checks whether the edge under consideration forms a cycle. Notice that this check for cycles can be implemented using the **union** operation on DS, which is applied to the two vertices of the edge. If the **union** operation succeeds in merging the two trees, then the edge is added to the MST; otherwise, the edge can safely be discarded as it would introduce a cycle in the MST. The following illustrated steps explain this logic:

1. First, we begin by initializing a disjoint-set data structure, DS, containing all of the given vertices in the graph:

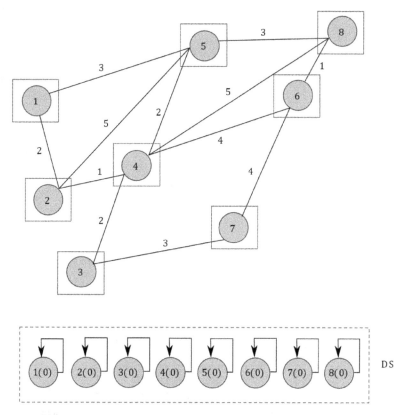

Figure 5.17: Step 1 of Kruskal's algorithm – initialization

2. Let's proceed to add the edge with the lowest weight to our MST. As you can see from the following figure, as we add *edge* (2,4), we also apply **Union(2,4)** to the elements in DS:

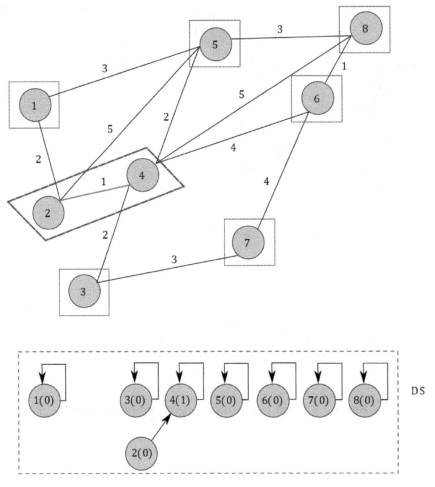

Figure 5.18: Adding edge (2, 4) to the MST after applying Union (2, 4) to the disjoint-set

3. As we proceed with adding edges as per the algorithm, we reach *edge (1,5)*. As you can see, in DS, the corresponding elements are in the same tree. Hence, we cannot add that edge. As you can see from the following graph, adding that would have created a cycle:

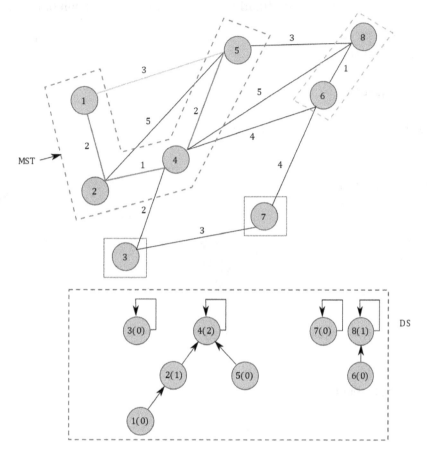

Figure 5.19: Trying to add edge (1, 5) to MST fails because vertices 1 and 5 are in the same tree in DS

In the following exercise, we will implement Kruskal's minimum spanning tree algorithm using the disjoint-set data structure.

Exercise 26: Kruskal's MST Algorithm

In this exercise, we will implement the disjoint-set data structure and Kruskal's algorithm to find an MST in the graph. Let's get started:

1. Begin by adding the following headers and declaring the **Graph** data structure:

```
#include<iostream>
#include<vector>
#include<algorithm>
#include<queue>
#include<map>
template <typename T> class Graph;
```

2. First, we will implement the disjoint set:

```
template<typename T>
class SimpleDisjointSet
{
private:
    struct Node
    {
        T data;

        Node(T _data) : data(_data)
        {}

        bool operator!=(const Node& n) const
        {
            return this->data != n.data;
        }
    };

    // Store the forest
    std::vector<Node> nodes;
    std::vector<size_t> parent;
    std::vector<size_t> rank;
```

3. Add the constructor for the class and implement the **Make-set** and **Find** operations, as shown here:

```cpp
public:
    SimpleDisjointSet(size_t N)
    {
        nodes.reserve(N);
        parent.reserve(N);
        rank.reserve(N);
    }

    void add_set(const T& x)
    {
        nodes.emplace_back(x);
        parent.emplace_back(nodes.size() - 1);    // the parent is the
node itself
        rank.emplace_back(0);               // the initial rank for all nodes is
0
    }

    auto find(T x)
    {
        // Find the node that contains element 'x'
        auto node_it = std::find_if(nodes.begin(), nodes.end(),
            [x](auto n)
            {return n.data == x; });
        auto node_idx = std::distance(nodes.begin(), node_it);
        auto parent_idx = parent[node_idx];

        // Traverse the tree till we reach the root
        while (parent_idx != node_idx)
        {
            node_idx = parent_idx;
            parent_idx = parent[node_idx];
        }

        return parent_idx;
    }
```

4. Next, we will implement the **Union** operation between two trees in the disjoint-set, as shown here:

```
// Union the sets X and Y belong to
void union_sets(T x, T y)
{
    auto root_x = find(x);
    auto root_y = find(y);

    // If both X and Y are in the same set, do nothing and return
    if (root_x == root_y)
    {
        return;
    }
    // If X and Y are in different sets, merge the set with lower rank
    // into the set with higher rank
    else if (rank[root_x] > rank[root_y])
    {
        parent[root_y] = parent[root_x];
        rank[root_x]++;
    }
    else
    {
        parent[root_x] = parent[root_y];
        rank[root_y]++;
    }
}
};
```

5. Now that our implementation of the disjoint set is complete, let's start implementing the graph. We will use an edge-list representation. The **edge** struct is defined as follows:

```
template<typename T>
struct Edge
{
    size_t src;
    size_t dest;
    T weight;

    // To compare edges, only compare their weights,
    // and not the source/destination vertices
    inline bool operator< (const Edge<T>& e) const
```

```
    {
        return this->weight < e.weight;
    }

    inline bool operator> (const Edge<T>& e) const
    {
        return this->weight > e.weight;
    }
};
```

Since our implementation of an edge is templatized, the edge weights are allowed to be of any datatype that implements the < and > operations.

6. The following function allows a graph to be serialized and output to streams:

```
template <typename T>
std::ostream& operator<<(std::ostream& os, const Graph<T>& G)
{
    for (auto i = 1; i < G.vertices(); i++)
    {
        os << i <<":\t";

        auto edges = G.edges(i);
        for (auto& e : edges)
            os << "{" << e.dest << ": " << e.weight << "}, ";

        os << std::endl;
    }

    return os;
}
```

7. The graph data structure can now be implemented with the following code:

```
template<typename T>
class Graph
{
public:
    // Initialize the graph with N vertices
    Graph(size_t N): V(N)
    {}

    // Return number of vertices in the graph
    auto vertices() const
```

```cpp
{
    return V;
}

// Return all edges in the graph
auto& edges() const
{
    return edge_list;
}

void add_edge(Edge<T>&& e)
{
    // Check if the source and destination vertices are within range
    if (e.src >= 1 && e.src <= V && e.dest >= 1 && e.dest <= V)
        edge_list.emplace_back(e);
    else
        std::cerr << "Vertex out of bounds" << std::endl;
}

// Returns all outgoing edges from vertex v
auto edges(size_t v) const
{
    std::vector<Edge<T>> edges_from_v;
    for(auto& e:edge_list)
    {
        if (e.src == v)
            edges_from_v.emplace_back(e);
    }
    return edges_from_v;
}

// Overloads the << operator so a graph be written directly to a
stream
```

```
    // Can be used as std::cout << obj << std::endl;

    template <typename T>
    friend std::ostream& operator<< <>(std::ostream& os, const Graph<T>&
G);
private:
    size_t V;          // Stores number of vertices in graph
    std::vector<Edge<T>> edge_list;
};
```

> **Note**
>
> Our implementation of the graph does not allow changing the number of vertices
> in the graph after it has been created. Also, although we can add as many edges
> as needed, the deletion of edges is not implemented since it is not needed in this
> exercise.

8. Now, we can implement Kruskal's algorithm like so:

```
    // Since a tree is also a graph, we can reuse the Graph class
    // However, the result graph should have no cycles

    template<typename T>
    Graph<T> minimum_spanning_tree(const Graph<T>& G)
    {
        // Create a min-heap for the edges
        std::priority_queue<Edge<T>,
            std::vector<Edge<T>>,
            std::greater<Edge<T>>> edge_min_heap;

        // Add all edges in the min-heap
        for (auto& e : G.edges())
            edge_min_heap.push(e);

        // First step: add all elements to their own sets
        auto N = G.vertices();
        SimpleDisjointSet<size_t> dset(N);
        for (auto i = 0; i < N; i++)
            dset.add_set(i);

        // Second step: start merging sets
        Graph<T> MST(N);
```

```
    while (!edge_min_heap.empty())
    {
        auto e = edge_min_heap.top();
        edge_min_heap.pop();
```

```
// Merge the two trees and add edge to the MST only if the two vertices of
the edge belong to different trees in the MST
```

```
        if (dset.find(e.src) != dset.find(e.dest))
        {
            MST.add_edge(Edge <T>{e.src, e.dest, e.weight});
            dset.union_sets(e.src, e.dest);
        }
    }
```

```
    return MST;
}
```

9. Lastly, add the driver code shown here:

```
int main()
{
    using T = unsigned;

    Graph<T> G(9);

    std::map<unsigned, std::vector<std::pair<size_t, T>>> edges;
    edges[1] = { {2, 2}, {5, 3} };
    edges[2] = { {1, 2}, {5, 5}, {4, 1} };
    edges[3] = { {4, 2}, {7, 3} };
    edges[4] = { {2, 1}, {3, 2}, {5, 2}, {6, 4}, {8, 5} };
    edges[5] = { {1, 3}, {2, 5}, {4, 2}, {8, 3} };
    edges[6] = { {4, 4}, {7, 4}, {8, 1} };
    edges[7] = { {3, 3}, {6, 4} };
    edges[8] = { {4, 5}, {5, 3}, {6, 1} };

    for (auto& i : edges)
        for(auto& j: i.second)
```

```
        G.add_edge(Edge<T>{ i.first, j.first, j.second });

    std::cout << "Original Graph" << std::endl;
    std::cout << G;

    auto MST = minimum_spanning_tree(G);
    std::cout << std::endl << "Minimum Spanning Tree" << std::endl;
    std::cout << MST;

    return 0;
}
```

10. Finally, run the program! Your output should look as follows:

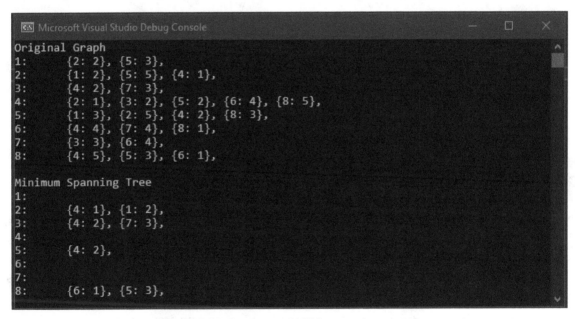

Figure 5.20: Getting an MST from a given graph

Verify that the output of our algorithm is indeed the MST that was shown in *figure* 5.12.

The complexity of Kruskal's algorithm without using the disjoint set is O(E *log* E), where E is the number of edges in the graph. With the disjoint set, however, the total complexity comes down to O(Eα(V)), where α(v) is the inverse of the Ackermann function. Since the inverse Ackermann function grows much slower than the logarithm function, the difference in the performance of the two implementations is small for graphs with a few vertices but can be notably large for larger graph instances.

The Vertex Coloring Problem

The vertex coloring problem can be stated as follows:

"Given a graph, G, assign a color to each vertex of the graph so that no two adjacent vertices have the same color."

As an example, the following figure shows a valid coloring of the graph that was shown in *figure 5.11*:

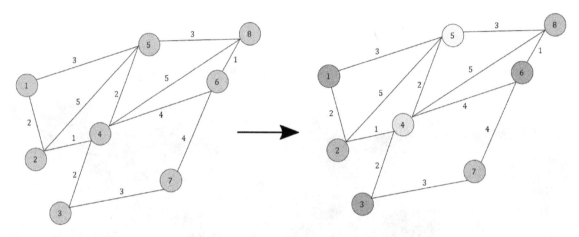

Figure 5.21: Coloring an uncolored graph

Graph coloring has applications in solving a large variety of problems in the real world – making schedules for taxis, solving sudoku puzzles, and creating timetables for exams can all be mapped to finding a valid coloring of the problem, modeled as a graph. However, finding the minimum number of colors required to produce a valid vertex coloring (also called the chromatic number) is known to be an NP-complete problem. Thus, a minor change in the nature of the problem can make a massive difference to its complexity.

As an example of the applications of the graph coloring problem, let's consider the case of sudoku solvers. Sudoku is a number-placement puzzle where the objective is to fill a 9 × 9 box with numbers from 1 to 9 with no number being repeated in each row. Each column is a 3 × 3 block. An example of a sudoku puzzle is shown here:

5	3			7				
6			1	9	5			
	9	8					6	
8				6				3
4			8		3			1
7				2				6
	6					2	8	
			4	1	9			5
				8			7	9

5	3	4	6	7	8	9	1	2
6	7	2	1	9	5	3	4	8
1	9	8	3	4	2	5	6	7
8	5	9	7	6	1	4	2	3
4	2	6	8	5	3	7	9	1
7	1	3	9	2	4	8	5	6
9	6	1	5	3	7	2	8	4
2	8	7	4	1	9	6	3	5
3	4	5	2	8	6	1	7	9

Figure 5.22: (Left) a sudoku puzzle, (Right) its solution

We can model an instance of the puzzle to the graph coloring problem as follows:

- Represent each cell in the puzzle by a vertex in graph G.

- Add edges between the vertices that are in the same column, row, or are in the same 3 × 3 block.

- A valid coloring of G then gives us a solution to the original sudoku puzzle.

We will take a look at the implementation of graph coloring in the following exercise.

Exercise 27: Greedy Graph Coloring

In this exercise, we will implement a greedy algorithm that produces a graph coloring for the graph shown in *figure 5.21* when the maximum number of colors that can be used is six. Let's get started:

1. Begin by including the required header files and declaring the **Graph** data structure, which we will implement later in this exercise:

```
#include <unordered_map>
#include <set>
#include <map>
#include <string>
#include <vector>
#include <iostream>

template <typename T> class Graph;
```

2. The following struct implements an edge in our graph:

```cpp
template<typename T>
struct Edge
{
    size_t src;
    size_t dest;
    T weight;

    // To compare edges, only compare their weights,
    // and not the source/destination vertices
    inline bool operator< (const Edge<T>& e) const
    {
        return this->weight < e.weight;
    }

    inline bool operator> (const Edge<T>& e) const
    {
        return this->weight > e.weight;
    }
};
```

3. The following function allows us to write the graph directly to the output stream:

```cpp
template <typename T>
std::ostream& operator<<(std::ostream& os, const Graph<T>& G)
{
    for (auto i = 1; i < G.vertices(); i++)
    {
        os << i << ":\t";

        auto edges = G.outgoing_edges(i);
        for (auto& e : edges)
            os << "{" << e.dest << ": " << e.weight << "}, ";

        os << std::endl;
    }

    return os;
}
```

4. Implement the graph as an edge list, as shown here:

```cpp
template<typename T>
class Graph
{
public:
    // Initialize the graph with N vertices
    Graph(size_t N) : V(N)
    {}

    // Return number of vertices in the graph
    auto vertices() const
    {
        return V;
    }

    // Return all edges in the graph
    auto& edges() const
    {
        return edge_list;
    }

    void add_edge(Edge<T>&& e)
    {
        // Check if the source and destination vertices are within range
        if (e.src >= 1 && e.src <= V &&
            e.dest >= 1 && e.dest <= V)
            edge_list.emplace_back(e);
        else
            std::cerr << "Vertex out of bounds" << std::endl;
    }

    // Returns all outgoing edges from vertex v
    auto outgoing_edges(size_t v) const
    {
        std::vector<Edge<T>> edges_from_v;
        for (auto& e : edge_list)
        {
            if (e.src == v)
                edges_from_v.emplace_back(e);
        }
        return edges_from_v;
```

```
        }

        // Overloads the << operator so a graph be written directly to a
    stream
        // Can be used as std::cout << obj << std::endl;
        template <typename T>
        friend std::ostream& operator<< <>(std::ostream& os, const Graph<T>&
    G);

    private:
        size_t V;           // Stores number of vertices in graph
        std::vector<Edge<T>> edge_list;
    };
```

5. The following hash map stores the list of colors that will be used by our coloring algorithm:

```
    // Initialize the colors that will be used to color the vertices
    std::unordered_map<size_t, std::string> color_map = {
        {1, "Red"},
        {2, "Blue"},
        {3, "Green"},
        {4, "Yellow"},
        {5, "Black"},
        {6, "White"}
    };
```

6. Next, let's implement a helper function that prints the colors that have been assigned to each vertex:

```
    void print_colors(std::vector<size_t>& colors)
    {
        for (auto i=1; i<colors.size(); i++)
        {
            std::cout << i << ": " << color_map[colors[i]] << std::endl;
        }
    }
```

7. The following function implements our coloring algorithm:

```cpp
template<typename T>
auto greedy_coloring(const Graph<T>& G)
{
    auto size = G.vertices();
    std::vector<size_t> assigned_colors(size);

    // Let us start coloring with vertex number 1.
    // Note that this choice is arbirary.
    for (auto i = 1; i < size; i++)
    {
        auto outgoing_edges = G.outgoing_edges(i);
        std::set<size_t> neighbour_colors;

        for (auto e : outgoing_edges)
        {
            auto dest_color = assigned_colors[e.dest];
            neighbour_colors.insert(dest_color);
        }

        // Find the smallest unassigned color
        // that is not currently used by any neighbor
        auto smallest_unassigned_color = 1;
        for (;
            smallest_unassigned_color <= color_map.size();
            smallest_unassigned_color++)
        {
          if (neighbour_colors.find(smallest_unassigned_color) ==
              neighbour_colors.end())
                break;
        }

        assigned_colors[i] = smallest_unassigned_color;
    }

    return assigned_colors;
}
```

8. Finally, add the driver code, as shown here:

```cpp
int main()
{
    using T = size_t;


    Graph<T> G(9);

    std::map<unsigned, std::vector<std::pair<size_t, T>>> edges;
    edges[1] = { {2, 2}, {5, 3} };
    edges[2] = { {1, 2}, {5, 5}, {4, 1} };
    edges[3] = { {4, 2}, {7, 3} };
    edges[4] = { {2, 1}, {3, 2}, {5, 2}, {6, 4}, {8, 5} };
    edges[5] = { {1, 3}, {2, 5}, {4, 2}, {8, 3} };
    edges[6] = { {4, 4}, {7, 4}, {8, 1} };
    edges[7] = { {3, 3}, {6, 4} };
    edges[8] = { {4, 5}, {5, 3}, {6, 1} };

    for (auto& i : edges)
        for (auto& j : i.second)
            G.add_edge(Edge<T>{ i.first, j.first, j.second });

    std::cout << "Original Graph: " << std::endl;
    std::cout << G << std::endl;

    auto colors = greedy_coloring<T>(G);
    std::cout << "Vertex Colors: " << std::endl;
    print_colors(colors);

    return 0;
}
```

9. Run the implementation! Your output should look as follows:

```
Microsoft Visual Studio Debug Console                    —    □    ✕
Original Graph:
1:      {2: 2}, {5: 3},
2:      {1: 2}, {5: 5}, {4: 1},
3:      {4: 2}, {7: 3},
4:      {2: 1}, {3: 2}, {5: 2}, {6: 4}, {8: 5},
5:      {1: 3}, {2: 5}, {4: 2}, {8: 3},
6:      {4: 4}, {7: 4}, {8: 1},
7:      {3: 3}, {6: 4},
8:      {4: 5}, {5: 3}, {6: 1},

Vertex Colors:
1: Red
2: Blue
3: Red
4: Green
5: Yellow
6: Red
7: Blue
8: Blue
```

Figure 5.23: Output of the graph coloring implementation

Our implementation always starts coloring the vertices starting with vertex ID 1. However, this choice is arbitrary, and starting the greedy coloring algorithm with different vertices even on the same graph is very likely to result in different graph colorings that require a different number of colors.

The quality of a graph coloring is usually measured by how few colors it uses to color the graph. While finding the optimal graph coloring that uses the least possible number of colors is NP-complete, greedy graph coloring often serves as a useful approximation. For example, when designing a compiler, graph coloring is used to allocate CPU registers to the variables of the program that's being compiled. The greedy coloring algorithm is used with a set of heuristics to arrive at a "good enough" solution to the problem, which is desirable in practice since we need compilers to be fast in order to be useful.

Activity 12: The Welsh-Powell Algorithm

An improvement to the simple approach of starting greedy coloring with a fixed vertex ID is to color the vertices in decreasing order of the number of edges incident on the vertices (or in decreasing order of the degree of vertices).

The algorithm works as follows:

1. Sort all the vertices in decreasing order of degree and store them in an array.

2. Take the first uncolored vertex in the sorted array and assign to it the first color that hasn't been assigned to any of its neighbors. Let this color be C.

3. Traverse the sorted array and assign the color C to each uncolored vertex that doesn't have any neighbors who have been assigned C.

4. If any uncolored vertices remain in the array, go to step 2. Else, end the program. The colors that have been assigned to the vertices so far is the final output.

The following is an illustrated example of the four iterations of the algorithm that are required to find a valid coloring of the graph shown in *figure 5.21*:

1. Here is the graph that we start with:

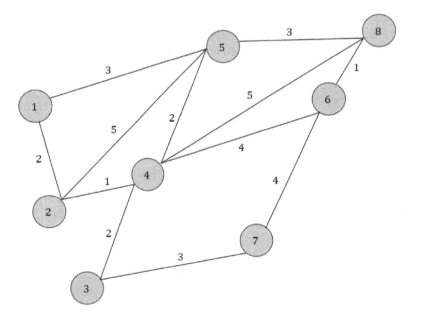

Vertex colors:
1: No color
2: No color
3: No color
4: No color
5: No color
6: No color
7: No color
8: No color

Figure 5.24: Starting with an uncolored graph

2. Next, we sort by decreasing order of vertices, and start by coloring red:

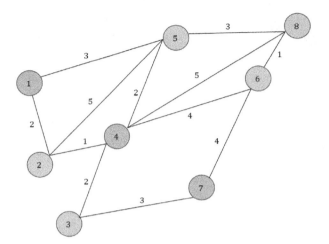

Decreasing order of vertices by degree:
4, 5, 2, 6, 8, 1, 3, 7

Vertex colors:
1: Red
2: Cannot be red, connected to 4
3: Cannot be red, connected to 4
4: Red
5: Cannot be red, connected to 4
6: Cannot be red, connected to 4
7: Red
8: Cannot be red, connected to 4

Figure 5.25: Coloring red

3. In the next round, we start coloring blue:

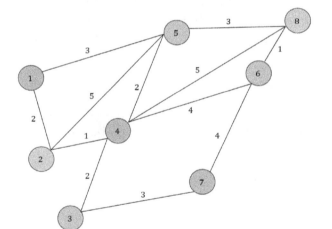

Decreasing order of vertices by degree:
4, 5, 2, 6, 8, 1, 3, 7

Vertex colors:
1: Red
2: Cannot be blue, connected to 5
3: Blue
4: Red
5: Blue
6: Blue
7: Red
8: Cannot be red, connected to 5, 6

Figure 5.26: Coloring blue

4. In the last round, we color green:

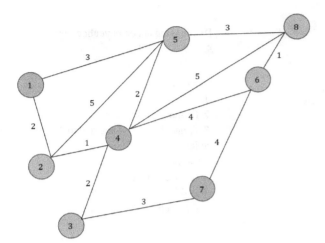

Decreasing order of vertices by degree:
4, 5, 2, 6, 8, 1, 3, 7

Vertex colors:
1: Red
2: Green
3: Blue
4: Red
5: Blue
6: Blue
7: Red
8: Green

Figure 5.27: Coloring green

The high-level steps to complete this activity are as follows:

1. Assume that each edge of the graph holds the source vertex ID, destination vertex ID, and the edge weight. Implement a struct that represents an edge of the graph. We will use instances of this struct to create different edges in our graph representation.

2. Implement a graph using the edge list representation.

3. Implement a function that implements the Welsh–Powell graph coloring and returns a vector of colors. The color at index *i* in the vector should be the one that's assigned to vertex ID *i*.

4. Add the driver and input/output code as required to create the graph shown in *figure 5.24*. It is okay to assume that the coloring always starts with vertex ID 1.

Your output should look as follows:

```
Microsoft Visual Studio Debug Console                    —    □    ×
Original Graph
1:      {2: 2}, {5: 3},
2:      {1: 2}, {5: 5}, {4: 1},
3:      {4: 2}, {7: 3},
4:      {2: 1}, {3: 2}, {5: 2}, {6: 4}, {8: 5},
5:      {1: 3}, {2: 5}, {4: 2}, {8: 3},
6:      {4: 4}, {7: 4}, {8: 1},
7:      {3: 3}, {6: 4},
8:      {4: 5}, {5: 3}, {6: 1},
The vertices will be colored in the following order:
Vertex ID       Degree
4               5
5               4
2               3
6               3
8               3
1               2
3               2
7               2
Vertex Colors:
1: Red
2: Green
3: Blue
4: Red
5: Blue
6: Blue
7: Red
8: Green
```

Figure 5.28: Expected output of Activity 12

Note

The solution for this activity can be found on page 518.

Summary

The greedy approach is simple: at each iteration of the algorithm, pick the seemingly best alternative out of all the possible alternatives. In other words, greedy solutions to problems are applicable when choosing the locally 'best' alternative at each iteration leads to the globally optimal solution to the problem.

In this chapter, we looked at examples of problems where the greedy approach is optimal and leads to correct solutions to the given problem; that is, shortest-job-first scheduling. We also discussed how slightly modified versions of NP-complete problems such as the 0-1 knapsack and the graph coloring problem can have simple greedy solutions. This makes the greedy approach an important algorithm design tool for difficult problems. For problems that have a greedy solution, it is likely to be the simplest way to solve them; and even for problems that do not have a greedy solution, it can often be used to solve relaxed versions of the problem that might be 'good enough' in practice (for example, greedy graph coloring is used while allocating registers to variables in programming language compilers).

Next, we discussed the greedy choice and optimal substructure properties and looked at an example of proof that a given problem exhibits these properties. We concluded this chapter with two solutions to the minimum spanning tree problem: Kruskal's algorithm and the Welsh-Powell algorithm. Our discussion of Kruskal's algorithm also introduced the disjoint-set data structure.

In the next chapter, we will focus on graph algorithms, starting with breadth-first and depth-first search, and then move on to Dijkstra's shortest path algorithm. We will also look at another solution to the minimum spanning tree problem: Prim's algorithm.

Graph Algorithms I

Learning Objectives

By the end of this chapter, you will be able to:

- Describe the utility of graphs for solving various real-world problems
- Choose and implement the right traversal method to find an element in a graph
- Solve the minimum spanning tree (MST) problem using Prim's algorithm
- Identify when to use the Prim's and Kruskal's algorithms to solve the MST problem
- Find the shortest path between two vertices/nodes in a graph using Dijkstra's algorithm

In this chapter, we will study the basic and most commonly used algorithms for solving problems that can be represented in the form of graphs, which shall then be discussed further in the next chapter.

Introduction

In the previous two chapters, we discussed two algorithm design paradigms: divide and conquer and the greedy approach, which led us to well-known solutions to widely used and important computational problems such as sorting, searching, and finding the minimum weight spanning tree on a graph. In this chapter, we shall discuss some algorithms that are specifically applicable to the graph data structure.

A **graph** is defined as a set of **vertices** and **edges** that connect a pair of vertices. Mathematically, this is often written as G = < V, E >, where V denotes the set of vertices and E denotes the set of edges that constitute a graph. Edges that point from one node to another are called *directed*, while edges that have no direction are called *undirected*. Edges may also be associated with a *weight* or be *unweighted*, as we saw in *Chapter 2, Trees, Heaps, and Graphs*.

> **Note**
>
> The terms "node" and "vertex" can be used interchangeably when we talk about graphs. In this chapter, we shall stick with "vertex."

Graphs are some of the most versatile data structures – so much so that other linked data structures such as trees and linked lists are known to be just special cases of graphs. What makes graphs useful is that they are the general representation of *relationships* (represented as **edges**) between *objects* (represented as **nodes**). Graphs can have multiple edges between the same pair of nodes, or even have multiple edge weights on a single edge, and nodes can also have edges from themselves to themselves (also known as self edges). The graph shown in the following diagram shows how these features can be present in a graph. Variants of graphs, called "hypergraphs," are also allowed to have edges that connect multiple nodes, and another set of variants called "mixed graphs" are also allowed to have both directed and undirected edges within the same graph:

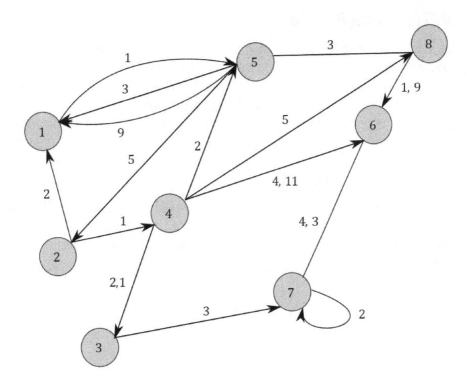

Figure 6.1: A graph with multiple edge weights, self edges (also called loops), and both directed and undirected edges

As a result of the high degree of generality that graphs offer, they find use in several applications. Theoretical computer scientists use graphs to model finite state machines and automata, artificial intelligence and machine learning experts use graphs to extract information from changes in the structure of different kinds of networks over time, and traffic engineers use graphs to study the flow of traffic through road networks.

In this chapter, we shall restrict ourselves to studying algorithms that use weighted, directed graphs, and if needed, positive edge weights. We shall first study the **graph traversal problem** and cover two solutions to it: **breadth-first search** (**BFS**) and **depth-first search** (**DFS**). Next, we shall revert to the minimum spanning tree problem we introduced in the previous chapter and provide a different solution to it called Prim's algorithm. Finally, we shall cover the single-source shortest path problem that powers navigation applications such as Google Maps and the OSRM route planner.

Let's begin by taking a look at the basic problem of traversing a graph.

The Graph Traversal Problem

Imagine that you have recently moved into an apartment in a new neighborhood. As you meet your new neighbors and make new friends, people often recommend restaurants to dine at in the vicinity. You wish to visit all the recommended restaurants, so you pull out a map of the neighborhood and mark all the restaurants and your home on the map, which already has all the roads marked on it. If we represent each restaurant and your home as a vertex, and the roads connecting the restaurants as edges in a graph, the problem of visiting all the vertices in the graph, when starting from a given vertex, is called the graph traversal problem.

In the following figure, the numbers in blue are assumed vertex IDs. Vertex 1 is *Home*, and the restaurants are labeled from R1 to R7. None of the edges have arrows since the edges are assumed to be bidirectional, that is, you can travel on the roads in either direction:

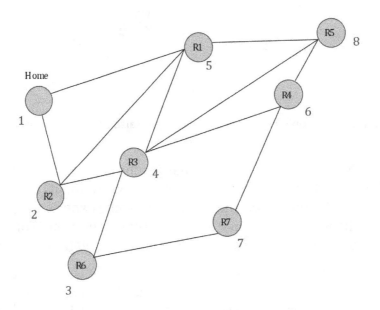

Figure 6.2: Representing a neighborhood map as a graph

In mathematical notation, given a graph, $G = <V, E>$, the graph traversal problem is to visit all $v \in V$ starting from a given vertex, s. The graph traversal problem is also called **the graph search problem** since it can be used to "find" a vertex in the graph. Different graph traversal algorithms give different orders for visiting the vertices in the graph.

Breadth-First Search

A "breadth-first" search or breadth-first traversal of the graph starts by adding the starting vertex to a **frontier** that consists of the set of previously visited vertices and

then iteratively exploring the vertices adjacent to the current frontier. The following illustrated steps should help you understand this idea:

1. First, the *Home* vertex, which is the starting point, is visited. R1 and R2 are the neighbors of the vertices in the current frontier, which is represented by a blue dotted line in the following figure:

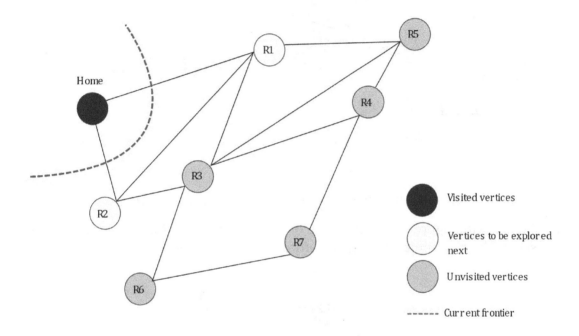

Figure 6.3: Initialization of the BFS frontier

2. The following figure shows BFS after visiting R1 and R1, either of which can be visited before the other. The order of visiting vertices that are at the same distance from the source vertex is irrelevant; however, the vertices with lower distance from the source are always visited first:

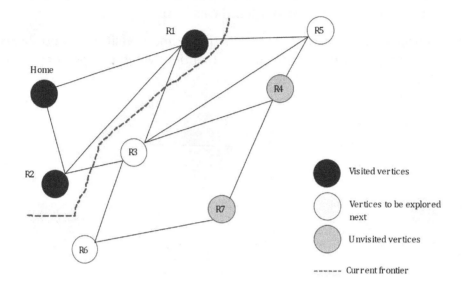

Figure 6.4: The BFS frontier after visiting the R1 and R2 vertices

3. The following figure shows the state of BFS after visiting R3, R5, and R6. This is essentially the penultimate stage before the entire graph is traversed:

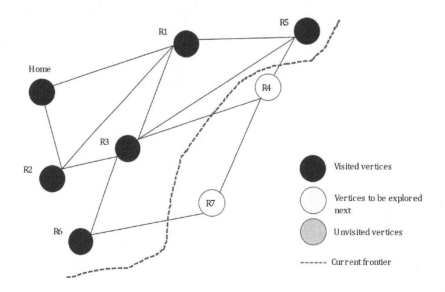

Figure 6.5: The BFS frontier after visiting R3, R5, and R6

A useful property of BFS is that for every vertex that is visited, all of its children vertices are visited before any grandchildren vertices. However, while implementing BFS, the frontier is typically not explicitly maintained in a separate data structure. Instead, a queue of vertex IDs is used to ensure that the vertices that are closer to the source vertex are always visited before the vertices that are farther away. In the following exercise, we shall implement BFS in C++.

Exercise 28: Implementing BFS

In this exercise, we shall implement the breadth-first search algorithm using an edge list representation of the graph. To do so, perform the following steps:

1. Add the required header files and declare the graph, as follows:

```
#include <string>
#include <vector>
#include <iostream>
#include <set>
#include <map>
#include <queue>

template<typename T> class Graph;
```

2. Write the following struct, which represents an edge in our graph:

```
template<typename T>
struct Edge
{
    size_t src;
    size_t dest;
    T weight;

    // To compare edges, only compare their weights,
    // and not the source/destination vertices
    inline bool operator< (const Edge<T>& e) const
    {
        return this->weight < e.weight;
    }

    inline bool operator> (const Edge<T>& e) const
    {
        return this->weight > e.weight;
    }
};
```

Since our definition of an edge uses templates, the edges can be easily made to have an edge weight of any data type that's needed.

3. Next, overload the **<<** operator for the **Graph** data type in order to display the contents of the graph:

```cpp
template <typename T>
std::ostream& operator<<(std::ostream& os, const Graph<T>& G)
{
    for (auto i = 1; i < G.vertices(); i++)
    {
        os << i << ":\t";

        auto edges = G.outgoing_edges(i);
        for (auto& e : edges)
            os << "{" << e.dest << ": " << e.weight << "}, ";

        os << std::endl;
    }

    return os;
}
```

4. Write a class to define our graph data structure, as shown here:

```cpp
template<typename T>
class Graph
{
public:
    // Initialize the graph with N vertices
    Graph(size_t N) : V(N)
    {}

    // Return number of vertices in the graph
    auto vertices() const
    {
        return V;
    }

    // Return all edges in the graph
    auto& edges() const
```

```cpp
    {
        return edge_list;
    }

    void add_edge(Edge<T>&& e)
    {
        // Check if the source and destination vertices are within range
        if (e.src >= 1 && e.src <= V &&
            e.dest >= 1 && e.dest <= V)
            edge_list.emplace_back(e);
        else
            std::cerr << "Vertex out of bounds" << std::endl;
    }

    // Returns all outgoing edges from vertex v
    auto outgoing_edges(size_t v) const
    {
        std::vector<Edge<T>> edges_from_v;
        for (auto& e : edge_list)
        {
            if (e.src == v)
                edges_from_v.emplace_back(e);
        }
        return edges_from_v;
    }

    // Overloads the << operator so a graph be written directly to a
stream
    // Can be used as std::cout << obj << std::endl;
    template <typename T>
    friend std::ostream& operator<<(std::ostream& os, const Graph<T>& G);

private:
    size_t V;          // Stores number of vertices in graph
    std::vector<Edge<T>> edge_list;
};
```

5. For this exercise, we shall test our implementation of BFS on the following graph:

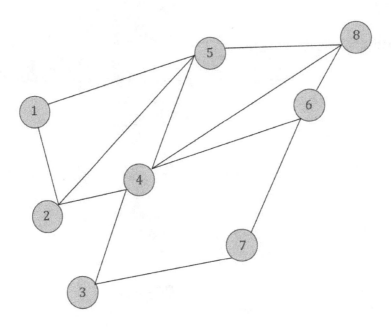

Figure 6.6: Graph for implementing BFS traversal in Exercise 28

We need a function to create and return the required graph. Note that while edge weights are assigned to each edge in the graph, this is not necessary since the BFS algorithm does not need to use edge weights. Implement the function as follows:

```
template <typename T>
auto create_reference_graph()
{
    Graph<T> G(9);

    std::map<unsigned, std::vector<std::pair<size_t, T>>> edges;
    edges[1] = { {2, 2}, {5, 3} };
    edges[2] = { {1, 2}, {5, 5}, {4, 1} };
    edges[3] = { {4, 2}, {7, 3} };
    edges[4] = { {2, 1}, {3, 2}, {5, 2}, {6, 4}, {8, 5} };
    edges[5] = { {1, 3}, {2, 5}, {4, 2}, {8, 3} };
    edges[6] = { {4, 4}, {7, 4}, {8, 1} };
    edges[7] = { {3, 3}, {6, 4} };
```

```
        edges[8] = { {4, 5}, {5, 3}, {6, 1} };

        for (auto& i : edges)
            for (auto& j : i.second)
                G.add_edge(Edge<T>{ i.first, j.first, j.second });

        return G;
    }
```

6. Implement the breadth-first search like so:

```cpp
template <typename T>
auto breadth_first_search(const Graph<T>& G, size_t dest)
{
    std::queue<size_t> queue;
    std::vector<size_t> visit_order;
    std::set<size_t> visited;
    queue.push(1); // Assume that BFS always starts from vertex ID 1

    while (!queue.empty())
    {
        auto current_vertex = queue.front();
        queue.pop();

        // If the current vertex hasn't been visited in the past
        if (visited.find(current_vertex) == visited.end())
        {
            visited.insert(current_vertex);
            visit_order.push_back(current_vertex);

            for (auto e : G.outgoing_edges(current_vertex))
                queue.push(e.dest);
        }
    }

    return visit_order;
}
```

7. Add the following test and driver code that creates the reference graph, runs BFS starting from vertex 1, and outputs the results:

```cpp
template <typename T>
void test_BFS()
{
    // Create an instance of and print the graph
    auto G = create_reference_graph<unsigned>();
    std::cout << G << std::endl;

    // Run BFS starting from vertex ID 1 and print the order
    // in which vertices are visited.
    std::cout << "BFS Order of vertices: " << std::endl;
    auto bfs_visit_order = breadth_first_search(G, 1);
    for (auto v : bfs_visit_order)
        std::cout << v << std::endl;
}

int main()
{
    using T = unsigned;
    test_BFS<T>();

    return 0;
}
```

8. Run the preceding code. Your output should look as follows:

```
Microsoft Visual Studio Debug Console
1:      {2: 2}, {5: 3},
2:      {1: 2}, {5: 5}, {4: 1},
3:      {4: 2}, {7: 3},
4:      {2: 1}, {3: 2}, {5: 2}, {6: 4}, {8: 5},
5:      {1: 3}, {2: 5}, {4: 2}, {8: 3},
6:      {4: 4}, {7: 4}, {8: 1},
7:      {3: 3}, {6: 4},
8:      {4: 5}, {5: 3}, {6: 1},

BFS Order of vertices:
1
2
5
4
8
3
6
7
```

Figure 6.7: Expected output of Exercise 28

The following figure shows the order of vertices that our BFS implementation visits. Notice that the search starts from vertex 1 and then gradually visits vertices farther away from the source. In the following figure, the integers in red show the order, and the arrows show the direction in which our BFS implementation visits the vertices of the graph:

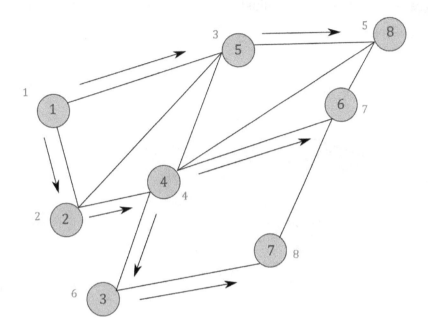

Figure 6.8: BFS implementation in Exercise 28

The time complexity of the BFS is $O(V + E)$, where V is the number of vertices and E is the number of edges in the graph.

Depth-First Search

While BFS starts from the source vertex and gradually expands the search outward to vertices farther away, DFS starts from the source vertex and iteratively visits vertices as far away as possible along a certain path, returning to earlier vertices to explore vertices along a different path in the graph. This method of searching the graph is also called **backtracking**. The following illustrated steps show the working of DFS:

1. Naturally, we begin our traversal by visiting the *Home* vertex, as shown in the following figure:

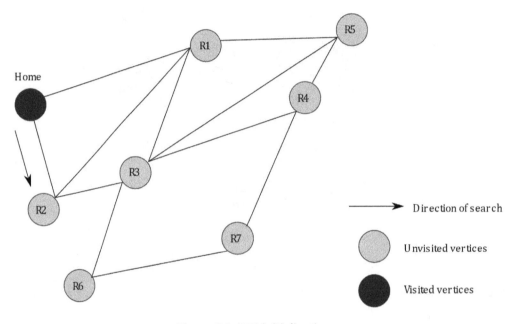

Figure 6.9: DFS initialization

2. Next, we visit vertex R2. Note that R2 is chosen arbitrarily over R1 since both are adjacent to *Home*, and either could have been chosen without affecting the correctness of the algorithm:

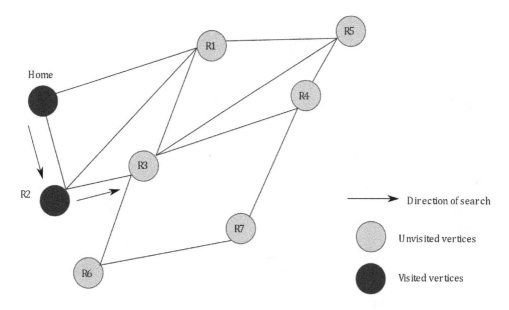

Figure 6.10: DFS after visiting R2

3. Next, we visit vertex R3, as shown in the following figure. Again, either of R3 or R1 could have been chosen arbitrarily, as both are adjacent to R2:

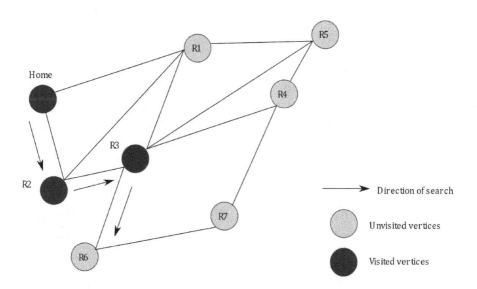

Figure 6.11: DFS after visiting R3

4. The search continues by visiting an arbitrary unvisited neighbor vertex at each iteration. After R1 is visited, the search tries to look for the next unvisited vertex. Since there are none left, the search terminates:

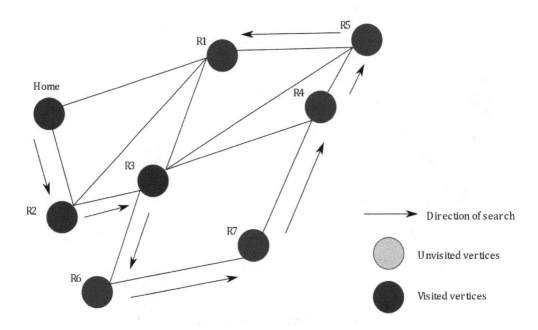

Figure 6.12: DFS after visiting all the vertices in the graph

While implementing the BFS, we used a queue to keep track of unvisited vertices. Since a queue is a **First-In, First-Out** (**FIFO**) data structure where vertices are removed from the queue in the same order as they are added to the queue, it was used by the BFS algorithm to ensure that vertices closer to the starting vertex are visited before the vertices farther away. Implementing DFS is remarkably similar to implementing BFS, except for one difference: instead of using a queue as a container for the list of vertices to be visited, we can now use a stack, while the rest of the algorithm remains the same. This approach works because on each iteration, DFS visits an unvisited neighbor of the current vertex, which can easily be tracked using a stack, which is a **Last-In, First-Out** (**LIFO**) data structure.

Exercise 29: Implementing DFS

In this exercise, we shall implement the DFS algorithm in C++ and test it on the graph shown in *figure 6.2*. The steps are as follows:

1. Include the required header files, as follows:

```
#include <string>
#include <vector>
#include <iostream>
#include <set>
#include <map>
#include <stack>

template<typename T> class Graph;
```

2. Write the following struct in order to implement an edge in our graph:

```
template<typename T>
struct Edge
{
    size_t src;
    size_t dest;
    T weight;

    // To compare edges, only compare their weights,
    // and not the source/destination vertices
    inline bool operator< (const Edge<T>& e) const
    {
        return this->weight < e.weight;
    }

    inline bool operator> (const Edge<T>& e) const
    {
        return this->weight > e.weight;
    }
};
```

Again, since our implementation uses a templatized version of the struct, it allows us to assign edge weights of any data type required. However, for the purposes of DFS, we shall use null values as placeholders for the edge weights.

3. Next, overload the **<<** operator for the graph so that it can be printed out using the following function:

```
template <typename T>
std::ostream& operator<<(std::ostream& os, const Graph<T>& G)
{
    for (auto i = 1; i < G.vertices(); i++)
    {
        os << i << ":\t";

        auto edges = G.outgoing_edges(i);
        for (auto& e : edges)
            os << "{" << e.dest << ": " << e.weight << "}, ";

        os << std::endl;
    }

    return os;
}
```

4. Implement the graph data structure that uses an edge list representation as follows:

```
template<typename T>
class Graph
{
public:
    // Initialize the graph with N vertices
    Graph(size_t N) : V(N)
    {}

    // Return number of vertices in the graph
    auto vertices() const
    {
        return V;
    }

    // Return all edges in the graph
    auto& edges() const
    {
        return edge_list;
    }
```

```cpp
    void add_edge(Edge<T>&& e)
    {
        // Check if the source and destination vertices are within range
        if (e.src >= 1 && e.src <= V &&
            e.dest >= 1 && e.dest <= V)
            edge_list.emplace_back(e);
        else
            std::cerr << "Vertex out of bounds" << std::endl;
    }

    // Returns all outgoing edges from vertex v
    auto outgoing_edges(size_t v) const
    {
        std::vector<Edge<T>> edges_from_v;
        for (auto& e : edge_list)
        {
            if (e.src == v)
                edges_from_v.emplace_back(e);
        }
        return edges_from_v;
    }

    // Overloads the << operator so a graph be written directly to a
stream
    // Can be used as std::cout << obj << std::endl;
    template <typename T>
    friend std::ostream& operator<< <>(std::ostream& os, const Graph<T>&
G);

private:
    size_t V;         // Stores number of vertices in graph
    std::vector<Edge<T>> edge_list;
};
```

5. Now, we need a function to perform DFS for our graph. Implement it as follows:

```cpp
template <typename T>
auto depth_first_search(const Graph<T>& G, size_t dest)
{
    std::stack<size_t> stack;
    std::vector<size_t> visit_order;
    std::set<size_t> visited;
    stack.push(1); // Assume that DFS always starts from vertex ID 1

    while (!stack.empty())
    {
        auto current_vertex = stack.top();
        stack.pop();

        // If the current vertex hasn't been visited in the past
        if (visited.find(current_vertex) == visited.end())
        {
            visited.insert(current_vertex);
            visit_order.push_back(current_vertex);

            for (auto e : G.outgoing_edges(current_vertex))
            {
                // If the vertex hasn't been visited, insert it in the
stack.
                if (visited.find(e.dest) == visited.end())
                {
                    stack.push(e.dest);
                }
            }
        }
    }

    return visit_order;
}
```

6. We shall test our implementation of the DFS on the graph shown here:

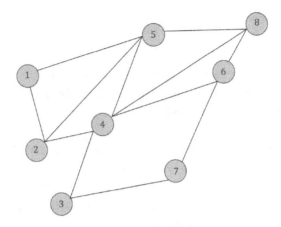

Figure 6.13: Graph for implementing DFS traversal in Exercise 29

Use the following function to create and return the graph:

```cpp
template <typename T>
auto create_reference_graph()
{
    Graph<T> G(9);

    std::map<unsigned, std::vector<std::pair<size_t, T>>> edges;
    edges[1] = { {2, 0}, {5, 0} };
    edges[2] = { {1, 0}, {5, 0}, {4, 0} };
    edges[3] = { {4, 0}, {7, 0} };
    edges[4] = { {2, 0}, {3, 0}, {5, 0}, {6, 0}, {8, 0} };
    edges[5] = { {1, 0}, {2, 0}, {4, 0}, {8, 0} };
    edges[6] = { {4, 0}, {7, 0}, {8, 0} };
    edges[7] = { {3, 0}, {6, 0} };
    edges[8] = { {4, 0}, {5, 0}, {6, 0} };

    for (auto& i : edges)
        for (auto& j : i.second)
            G.add_edge(Edge<T>{ i.first, j.first, j.second });

    return G;
}
```

Note the use of null values for edge weights since DFS does not require edge weights. A simpler implementation of the graph could have omitted the edge weights entirely without affecting the behavior of our DFS algorithm.

7. Finally, add the following test and driver code, which runs our DFS implementation and prints the output:

```cpp
template <typename T>
void test_DFS()
{
    // Create an instance of and print the graph
    auto G = create_reference_graph<unsigned>();
    std::cout << G << std::endl;

    // Run DFS starting from vertex ID 1 and print the order
    // in which vertices are visited.
    std::cout << "DFS Order of vertices: " << std::endl;
    auto dfs_visit_order = depth_first_search(G, 1);
    for (auto v : dfs_visit_order)
        std::cout << v << std::endl;
}

int main()
{
    using T = unsigned;
    test_DFS<T>();

    return 0;
}
```

8. Compile and run the preceding code. Your output should look as follows:

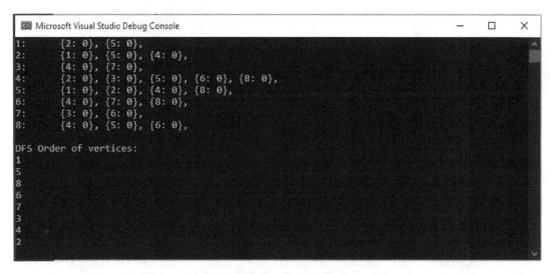

Figure 6.14: Expected output of Exercise 29

The following figure shows the order in which the vertices were visited by our DFS implementation:

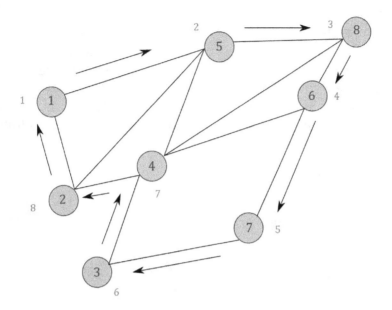

Figure 6.15: The order of vertices visited and the direction of DFS

The time complexity of both BFS and DFS is O(V + E). However, there are several important differences between the two algorithms. The following list summarizes the differences between the two and points out some cases where one should be preferred over the other:

- BFS is more suited to finding vertices that are closer to the source vertex, whereas DFS is often more suited to finding vertices that are farther away from the source.

- Once a vertex is visited in BFS, the path that's found from the source to the vertex is guaranteed to be the shortest path, while no such guarantees exist for DFS. This is the reason why all single-source and multiple-source shortest path algorithms use some variant of BFS. This shall be explored in the upcoming sections of this chapter.

- As BFS visits all the vertices adjacent to the current frontier, the search trees that are created by BFS are short and wide, and require comparatively more memory, whereas the search trees that are created by DFS are long and narrow, and require comparatively less memory.

Activity 13: Finding out Whether a Graph is Bipartite Using DFS

A bipartite graph is one where the vertices can be divided into two sets so that any edges in the graph must connect a vertex from one set to a vertex from the other set.

Bipartite graphs can be used to model several different practical use cases. For instance, if we are given a list of students and a list of classes, the relationship between students and classes can be modeled as a bipartite graph containing an edge between a student and a class if the student is enrolled in that class. As you would imagine, edges leading from one student to another, or from one subject to another, would not make sense. Therefore, such edges are not allowed in a bipartite graph. The following figure illustrates such a model:

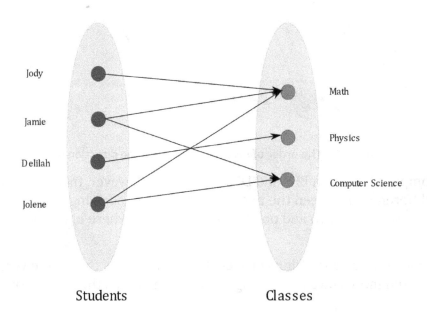

Figure 6.16: A sample bipartite graph representing student enrollment in different classes

Once a model such as the one shown here has been prepared, it can be used to create a schedule of classes so that no two classes that have been enrolled by the same student overlap. For example, if Jolene is enrolled in *Math* and *Computer Science*, these two classes should not be scheduled at the same time to avoid a conflict. Minimizing such conflicts in timetables can be achieved through solving a maximum flow problem in graphs. Several standard algorithms are known for the maximum flow problem: Ford-Fulkerson's, Dinic's, and the push-relabel algorithms are some examples. However, such algorithms are often complex and, therefore, beyond the scope of this book.

Another use case of modeling relationships between entities using a bipartite graph is between the viewers and the list of movies maintained by large video streaming platforms such as Netflix and YouTube.

An interesting property of bipartite graphs is that some operations such as finding a maximum matching and vertex cover, which are NP-*complete* for general graphs, can be solved in polynomial time for bipartite graphs. Therefore, it is useful to determine whether a given graph is bipartite or not. In this activity, you are required to implement a C++ program that checks whether a given graph, G, is bipartite.

The bipartite checking algorithm uses a slightly modified version of DFS and works as follows:

1. Assume that the DFS starts with vertex 1. Add the vertex ID, 1, to the stack.

2. If unvisited vertices remain on the stack, pop a vertex from the stack and set it as the current vertex.

3. If the color that was assigned to the parent vertex was blue, assign the current vertex red; otherwise, assign the current vertex blue.

4. Add all the unvisited adjacent vertices of the current vertex to the stack and mark the current vertex as visited.

5. Repeat *steps* 2, 3, and 4 until all the vertices have been assigned a color. If all the vertices are colored when the algorithm terminates, the given graph is bipartite.

6. If, while running *step* 2, the search encounters a vertex that has already been visited and assigned a color that is different from the color that it would have been assigned in *step* 3 (the inverse of the color assigned to its parent vertex in the search tree), the algorithm terminates immediately and the given graph is not bipartite.

The following figures illustrate the working of the preceding algorithm:

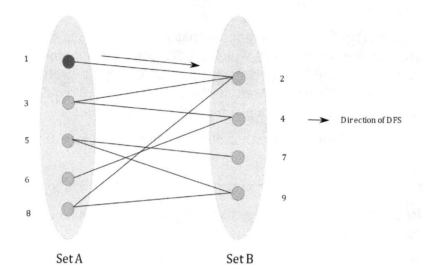

Figure 6.17: Initialization

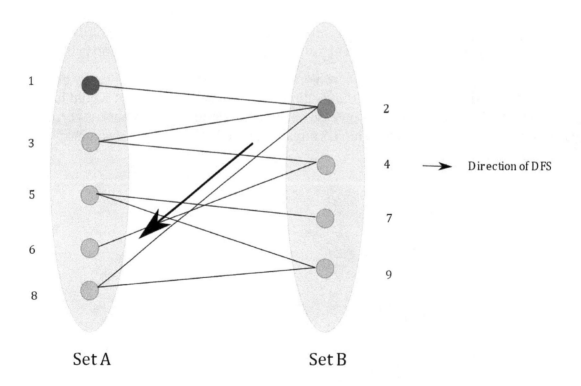

Figure 6.18: Since vertex 1 was assigned blue, we color vertex 2 red

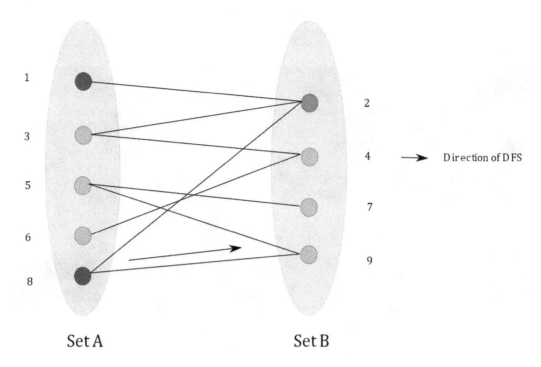

Figure 6.19: Since vertex 2 was colored red, we color vertex 8 blue.

As can be observed from the preceding set of figures, the algorithm zigzags through the graph, assigning alternate colors to each vertex that's visited. If all the vertices can be colored this way, the graph is bipartite. If DFS reaches two vertices that have already been assigned the same color, the graph can be safely declared to be not bipartite.

Using the graph in *figure 6.17* as input, your final output should look as follows:

```
Microsoft Visual Studio Debug Console                          —    □    ×
1:        {2: 0},
2:        {1: 0}, {3: 0}, {8: 0},
3:        {2: 0}, {4: 0},
4:        {3: 0}, {6: 0},
5:        {7: 0}, {9: 0},
6:        {1: 0}, {4: 0},
7:        {5: 0},
8:        {2: 0}, {9: 0},
9:        {5: 0},

Coloring vertex 1 BLUE
Coloring vertex 2 RED
Coloring vertex 8 BLUE
Coloring vertex 9 RED
Coloring vertex 5 BLUE
Coloring vertex 7 RED
Coloring vertex 3 BLUE
Coloring vertex 4 RED
Coloring vertex 6 BLUE
The graph is bipartite
```

Figure 6.20: Expected output of Activity 13

> **Note**
>
> The solution to this activity can be found on page 524.

Prim's MST Algorithm

The MST problem was introduced in *Chapter 5, Greedy Algorithms*, and is defined as follows:

"Given a graph, G = < V, E >, where V is the set of vertices and E is the set of edges, each associated with an edge weight, find a tree, T, that spans all vertices in V and has the minimum total weight."

In *Chapter 5, Greedy Algorithm*, we discussed the practical applications of the MST problem and Kruskal's algorithm, which finds an MST in a given graph. Kruskal's algorithm adds all the edges of the graph to a min-heap and greedily adds minimum-cost edges to MST, checking that no cycles are formed in the tree on each addition.

The idea behind Prim's algorithm (also known as Jarvik's algorithm) is similar to that of BFS. The algorithm starts by adding the starting vertex to a *frontier*, which consists of the set of previously visited vertices and then iteratively explores the vertices adjacent to the current frontier. However, while choosing the vertex to be visited on each iteration, the vertex with the lowest cost edge from the frontier is picked.

While implementing Prim's algorithm, we attach a *label* to each vertex of the graph, which stores its distance from the starting vertex. The algorithm works as follows:

1. First, it initializes the labels on all the vertices and sets all the distances to infinity. Since the distance from the starting vertex to itself is 0, it sets the label of the starting vertex to 0. Then, it adds all the labels to a min-heap, H.

    In the following figure, the numbers shown in red represent the estimated distance from the starting vertex, which is assumed to be vertex 1; the numbers shown in black represent edge weights:

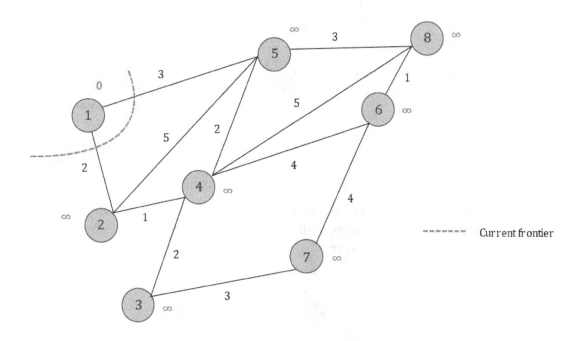

Figure 6.21: Initializing Prim's MST algorithm

2. Next, it pops a vertex, U, from H. Naturally, U is the vertex with a minimum distance from the starting vertex.

3. For all vertices, V, adjacent to U, if the label of V > edge weight of (U, V), set the label of V = edge weight of (U, V). This step is called *settling* or *visiting* vertex U:

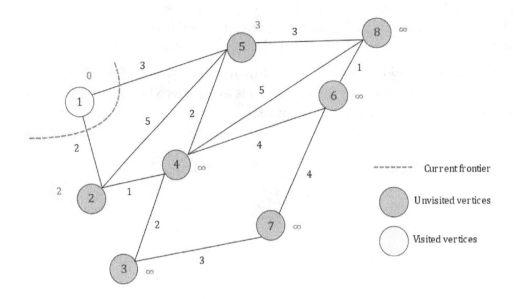

Figure 6.22: The status of the graph after visiting vertex 1

4. While unvisited vertices remain in the graph, go to *step* 2. The following figure shows the state of the graph after visiting vertex 2, where the edge shown in green is the sole edge in our MST so far:

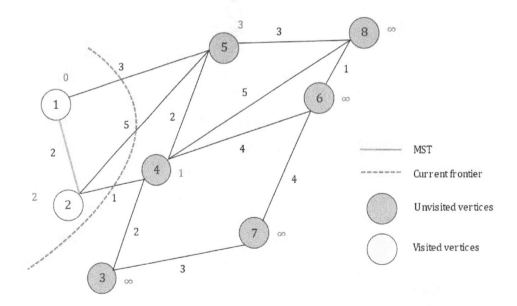

Figure 6.23: The status of the graph after visiting vertex 2

5. The final MST after all vertices have been settled is shown here:

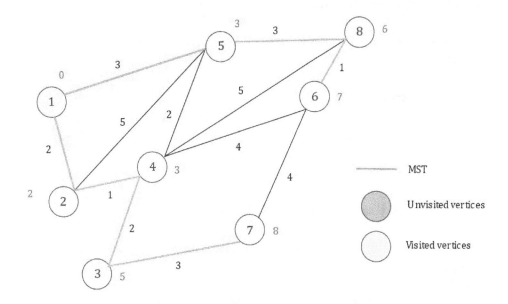

Figure 6.24: MST for our graph

Exercise 30: Prim's Algorithm

In this exercise, we shall implement Prim's algorithm to find the MST in the graph shown in *figure 6.22*. Follow these steps to complete this exercise:

1. Add the required header files, as shown here:

```
#include <set>
#include <map>
#include <queue>
#include <limits>
#include <string>
#include <vector>
#include <iostream>
```

2. Implement an edge in the graph by using the following struct:

```cpp
template<typename T> class Graph;

template<typename T>
struct Edge
{
    size_t src;
    size_t dest;
    T weight;

    // To compare edges, only compare their weights,
    // and not the source/destination vertices
    inline bool operator< (const Edge<T>& e) const
    {
        return this->weight < e.weight;
    }

    inline bool operator> (const Edge<T>& e) const
    {
        return this->weight > e.weight;
    }
};
```

3. Use the following function to overload the **<<** operator for the **Graph** class so that we can output the graph to C++ streams:

```cpp
template <typename T>
std::ostream& operator<<(std::ostream& os, const Graph<T>& G)
{
    for (auto i = 1; i < G.vertices(); i++)
    {
        os << i << ":\t";

        auto edges = G.outgoing_edges(i);
        for (auto& e : edges)
            os << "{" << e.dest << ": " << e.weight << "}, ";

        os << std::endl;
    }

    return os;
}
```

4. Add an edge list-based graph implementation, as shown here:

```cpp
template<typename T>
class Graph
{
public:
    // Initialize the graph with N vertices
    Graph(size_t N) : V(N)
    {}

    // Return number of vertices in the graph
    auto vertices() const
    {
        return V;
    }

    // Return all edges in the graph
    auto& edges() const
    {
        return edge_list;
    }

    void add_edge(Edge<T>&& e)
    {
        // Check if the source and destination vertices are within range
        if (e.src >= 1 && e.src <= V &&
            e.dest >= 1 && e.dest <= V)
            edge_list.emplace_back(e);
        else
            std::cerr << "Vertex out of bounds" << std::endl;
    }

    // Returns all outgoing edges from vertex v
    auto outgoing_edges(size_t v) const
    {
        std::vector<Edge<T>> edges_from_v;
        for (auto& e : edge_list)
        {
            if (e.src == v)
                edges_from_v.emplace_back(e);
        }
        return edges_from_v;
```

```
    }

    // Overloads the << operator so a graph be written directly to a
stream
    // Can be used as std::cout << obj << std::endl;
    template <typename T>
    friend std::ostream& operator<< <>(std::ostream& os, const Graph<T>&
G);

private:
    size_t V;          // Stores number of vertices in graph
    std::vector<Edge<T>> edge_list;
};
```

5. Make a function to create and return the graph shown in *figure 6.22* by using the
    following code:

```
template <typename T>
auto create_reference_graph()
{
    Graph<T> G(9);

    std::map<unsigned, std::vector<std::pair<size_t, T>>> edges;
    edges[1] = { {2, 2}, {5, 3} };
    edges[2] = { {1, 2}, {5, 5}, {4, 1} };
    edges[3] = { {4, 2}, {7, 3} };
    edges[4] = { {2, 1}, {3, 2}, {5, 2}, {6, 4}, {8, 5} };
    edges[5] = { {1, 3}, {2, 5}, {4, 2}, {8, 3} };
    edges[6] = { {4, 4}, {7, 4}, {8, 1} };
    edges[7] = { {3, 3}, {6, 4} };
    edges[8] = { {4, 5}, {5, 3}, {6, 1} };

    for (auto& i : edges)
        for (auto& j : i.second)
            G.add_edge(Edge<T>{ i.first, j.first, j.second });

    return G;
}
```

6. Next, we shall implement the **Label** structure, an instance of which is assigned to each vertex in the graph in order to store its distance from the frontier. Use the following code to do so:

```cpp
template<typename T>
struct Label
{
    size_t vertex_ID;
    T distance_from_frontier;

    Label(size_t _id, T _distance) :
        vertex_ID(_id),
        distance_from_frontier(_distance)
    {}

    // To compare labels, only compare their distances from source
    inline bool operator< (const Label<T>& l) const
    {
        return this->distance_from_frontier < l.distance_from_frontier;
    }

    inline bool operator> (const Label<T>& l) const


    {
        return this->distance_from_frontier > l.distance_from_frontier;
    }

    inline bool operator() (const Label<T>& l) const
    {
        return this > l;
    }
};
```

7. Write a function to implement Prim's MST algorithm, as shown here:

```cpp
template <typename T>
auto prim_MST(const Graph<T>& G, size_t src)
{
    std::priority_queue<Label<T>, std::vector<Label<T>>,
std::greater<Label<T>>> heap;
    std::set<int> visited;

    std::vector<T> distance(G.vertices(), std::numeric_limits<T>::max());
```

```cpp
    std::vector<size_t> MST;

    heap.emplace(src, 0);

    // Search for the destination vertex in the graph
    while (!heap.empty())
    {
        auto current_vertex = heap.top();
        heap.pop();

        // If the current vertex hasn't been visited in the past
        if (visited.find(current_vertex.vertex_ID) == visited.end())
        {
            std::cout << "Settling vertex ID "
<< current_vertex.vertex_ID << std::endl;
            MST.push_back(current_vertex.vertex_ID);

            // For each outgoing edge from the current vertex,
            // create a label for the destination vertex and add it to the
heap
            for (auto e : G.outgoing_edges(current_vertex.vertex_ID))
            {
                auto neighbor_vertex_ID = e.dest;
                auto new_distance_to_frontier = e.weight;

        // Check if the new path to the vertex is shorter
        // than the previously known best path.
        // If yes, update the distance
                if (new_distance_to_frontier < distance[neighbor_vertex_
ID])
                {
heap.emplace(neighbor_vertex_ID,  new_distance_to_frontier);
                    distance[e.dest] = new_distance_to_frontier;
                }
            }

            visited.insert(current_vertex.vertex_ID);
        }
    }

    return MST;
}
```

8. Finally, add the following code, which runs our implementation of Prim's algorithm and outputs the results:

```cpp
template<typename T>
void test_prim_MST()
{
    auto G = create_reference_graph<T>();
    std::cout << G << std::endl;

    auto MST = prim_MST<T>(G, 1);

    std::cout << "Minimum Spanning Tree:" << std::endl;
    for (auto v : MST)
        std::cout << v << std::endl;
    std::cout << std::endl;
}

int main()
{
    using T = unsigned;
    test_prim_MST<T>();

    return 0;
}
```

9. Run the program. Your output should look as follows:

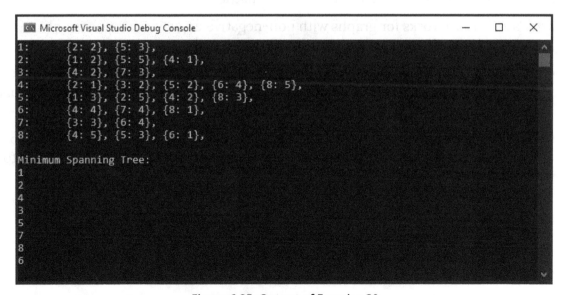

Figure 6.25: Output of Exercise 30

The time complexity of Prim's algorithm is O(E *log* V) when using a binary min-heap and an adjacency list for storing the MST, which can be improved to O(E + V *log* V) when using a type of heap called the "Fibonacci min-heap."

While both Prim's and Kruskal's are examples of greedy algorithms, they differ in important ways, some of which are summarized here:

Kruskal's algorithm	Prim's algorithm
Starts building MST by adding the minimum-cost edge in the graph to the MST	Starts building MST from any starting vertex in the graph
Best known time complexity is $O(E \log V)$	Best known time complexity is $O(E + V \log V)$
Typically preferred for sparse graphs with a small number of edges	Typically preferred for dense graphs with a large number of edges

Figure 6.26: Table comparing Kruskal's and Prim's algorithms

Dijkstra's Shortest Path Algorithm

The single-source shortest path problem on a graph is solved every time a user requests a route on a route planning application such as Google Maps or in the navigation software built into cars. The problem is defined as follows:

"Given a directed graph, G – < V, E > where V is the set of vertices and E is the set of edges, each of which is associated with an edge weight, a source vertex, and a destination vertex, find a minimum-cost path from a source to a destination."

Dijkstra's algorithm works for graphs with non-negative edge weights and is only a slight modification of Prim's MST algorithm, with two major changes:

- Instead of setting labels on every vertex equal to the minimum distance from the frontier, Dijkstra's algorithm sets the labels on each vertex with the distance equal to the total distance of the vertex from the source.

- Dijkstra's algorithm terminates if the destination vertex is popped from the heap, whereas Prim's algorithm terminates only when there are no more vertices left to be settled on the heap.

The working of the algorithm is illustrated in the following steps:

1. First, it initializes the labels on all the vertices and sets all the distances to infinity. Since the distance from the starting vertex to itself is 0, it sets the label of the starting vertex to 0. Then, it adds all the labels to a min-heap, H.

   In the following diagram, the numbers shown in red represent the current best-known distances from the source (vertex 2) and the destination (vertex 6):

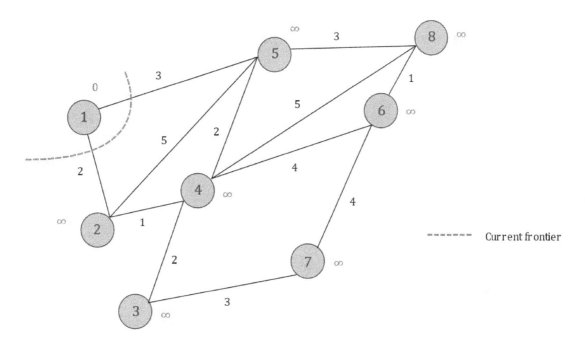

Figure 6.27: Initializing Dijkstra's algorithm

2. Then, it pops a vertex, U, from H. Naturally, U is the vertex with the minimum distance from the starting vertex. If U is the required destination, we have found our shortest path and the algorithm terminates.

3. For all vertices, V, adjacent to U, if the label of V > (label of U + edge weight of (U, V)), we have found a path to V that is shorter than the previously known minimum-cost path. Therefore, set the label of V to (label of U + edge weight of (U, V)). This step is called **settling** or **visiting** the vertex U:

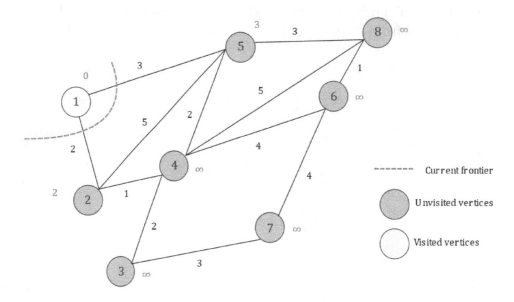

Figure 6.28: The state of the algorithm after settling vertex 1

4. While unvisited vertices remain in the graph, go to *step* 2. The following figure shows the state of the graph after settling vertex 2:

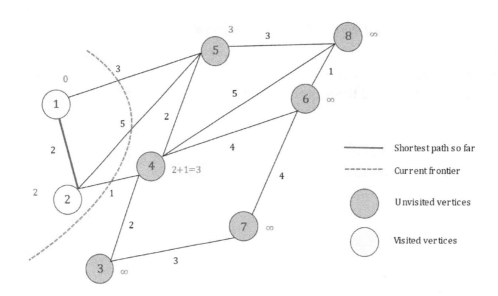

Figure 6.29: The state of the algorithm after settling vertex 2

5. The algorithm terminates when the destination vertex (vertex ID 6) is popped from H. The shortest path that's found by the algorithm from 1 to 6 is shown in the following figure. Also, the labels on other settled vertices show the shortest distance from 1 to that vertex:

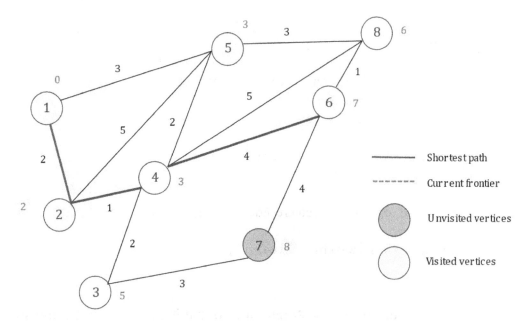

Figure 6.30: The shortest path from 1 to 6

Exercise 31: Implementing Dijkstra's Algorithm

In this exercise, we shall implement Dijkstra's algorithm to find the shortest path in the graph shown in *figure 6.28*. Follow these steps to complete this exercise:

1. Include the required header files and declare the graph data structure, as shown here:

```
#include <string>
#include <vector>
#include <iostream>
#include <set>
#include <map>
#include <limits>
#include <queue>

template<typename T> class Graph;
```

2. Write the following struct to implement an edge in our graph implementation:

```cpp
template<typename T>
struct Edge
{
    size_t src;
    size_t dest;
    T weight;

    // To compare edges, only compare their weights,
    // and not the source/destination vertices
    inline bool operator< (const Edge<T>& e) const
    {
        return this->weight < e.weight;
    }

    inline bool operator> (const Edge<T>& e) const
    {
        return this->weight > e.weight;
    }
};
```

3. Overload the **<<** operator for the **Graph** class so that it can be output using streams, as shown here:

```cpp
template <typename T>
std::ostream& operator<<(std::ostream& os, const Graph<T>& G)
{
    for (auto i = 1; i < G.vertices(); i++)
    {
        os << i << ":\t";

        auto edges = G.outgoing_edges(i);
        for (auto& e : edges)
            os << "{" << e.dest << ": " << e.weight << "}, ";

        os << std::endl;
    }

    return os;
}
```

4. Implement the graph, as shown here:

```cpp
template<typename T>
class Graph
{
public:
    // Initialize the graph with N vertices
    Graph(size_t N) : V(N)
    {}

    // Return number of vertices in the graph
    auto vertices() const
    {
        return V;
    }


    // Return all edges in the graph
    auto& edges() const
    {
        return edge_list;
    }

    void add_edge(Edge<T>&& e)
    {
        // Check if the source and destination vertices are within range
        if (e.src >= 1 && e.src <= V &&
            e.dest >= 1 && e.dest <= V)
            edge_list.emplace_back(e);
        else
            std::cerr << "Vertex out of bounds" << std::endl;
    }

    // Returns all outgoing edges from vertex v
    auto outgoing_edges(size_t v) const
    {
        std::vector<Edge<T>> edges_from_v;
        for (auto& e : edge_list)
        {
            if (e.src == v)
                edges_from_v.emplace_back(e);
        }
```

```
            return edges_from_v;
        }

        // Overloads the << operator so a graph be written directly to a
    stream
        // Can be used as std::cout << obj << std::endl;
        template <typename T>
        friend std::ostream& operator<< <>(std::ostream& os, const Graph<T>&
    G);

    private:
        size_t V;        // Stores number of vertices in graph
        std::vector<Edge<T>> edge_list;
    };
```

5. Write a function to create the reference graph shown in *figure 6.28* using the **Graph** class, as shown here:

```
template <typename T>
auto create_reference_graph()
{
    Graph<T> G(9);

    std::map<unsigned, std::vector<std::pair<size_t, T>>> edges;
    edges[1] = { {2, 2}, {5, 3} };
    edges[2] = { {1, 2}, {5, 5}, {4, 1} };
    edges[3] = { {4, 2}, {7, 3} };
    edges[4] = { {2, 1}, {3, 2}, {5, 2}, {6, 4}, {8, 5} };
    edges[5] = { {1, 3}, {2, 5}, {4, 2}, {8, 3} };
    edges[6] = { {4, 4}, {7, 4}, {8, 1} };
    edges[7] = { {3, 3}, {6, 4} };
    edges[8] = { {4, 5}, {5, 3}, {6, 1} };

    for (auto& i : edges)
        for (auto& j : i.second)
            G.add_edge(Edge<T>{ i.first, j.first, j.second });

    return G;
}
```

6. Implement Dijkstra's algorithm, as shown here:

```cpp
template <typename T>
auto dijkstra_shortest_path(const Graph<T>& G, size_t src, size_t dest)
{
    std::priority_queue<Label<T>, std::vector<Label<T>>,
std::greater<Label<T>>> heap;
    std::set<int> visited;
    std::vector<size_t> parent(G.vertices());
    std::vector<T> distance(G.vertices(), std::numeric_limits<T>::max());
    std::vector<size_t> shortest_path;

    heap.emplace(src, 0);
    parent[src] = src;

    // Search for the destination vertex in the graph
    while (!heap.empty()) {
        auto current_vertex = heap.top();
        heap.pop();

        // If the search has reached the destination vertex
        if (current_vertex.vertex_ID == dest) {
            std::cout << "Destination " <<
current_vertex.vertex_ID << " reached." << std::endl;
            break;
        }
        if (visited.find(current_vertex.vertex_ID) == visited.end()) {
            std::cout << "Settling vertex " <<
current_vertex.vertex_ID << std::endl;
            // For each outgoing edge from the current vertex,
            // create a label for the destination vertex and add it to the
heap
            for (auto e : G.outgoing_edges(current_vertex.vertex_ID)) {
                auto neighbor_vertex_ID = e.dest;
                auto new_distance_to_dest=current_vertex.distance_from_
source
+ e.weight;

                // Check if the new path to the destination vertex
// has a lower cost than any previous paths found to it, if // yes, then
this path should be preferred
                if (new_distance_to_dest < distance[neighbor_vertex_ID]) {
```

```
                            heap.emplace(neighbor_vertex_ID, new_distance_to_
    dest);
                        parent[e.dest] = current_vertex.vertex_ID;
                        distance[e.dest] = new_distance_to_dest;
                    }
                }
                visited.insert(current_vertex.vertex_ID);
            }
        }
        // Construct the path from source to the destination by backtracking
        // using the parent indexes
        auto current_vertex = dest;
        while (current_vertex != src) {
            shortest_path.push_back(current_vertex);
            current_vertex = parent[current_vertex];
        }
        shortest_path.push_back(src);
        std::reverse(shortest_path.begin(), shortest_path.end());
        return shortest_path;
    }
```

Our implementation works in two phases – it searches for the destination vertex starting from the source and uses the backtracking phase, where the shortest path is found by following the parent pointers from the destination back to the source.

7. Finally, add the following code to test our implementation of Dijkstra's algorithm by finding the shortest path between vertices 1 and 6 in the graph:

```
template<typename T>
void test_dijkstra()
{
    auto G = create_reference_graph<T>();
    std::cout << "Reference graph:" << std::endl;
    std::cout << G << std::endl;

    auto shortest_path = dijkstra_shortest_path<T>(G, 1, 6);

    std::cout << "The shortest path between 1 and 6 is:" << std::endl;
    for (auto v : shortest_path)
        std::cout << v << " ";
```

```
        std::cout << std::endl;
    }

    int main()
    {
        using T = unsigned;
        test_dijkstra<T>();

        return 0;
    }
```

8. Run the program. Your output should look as follows:

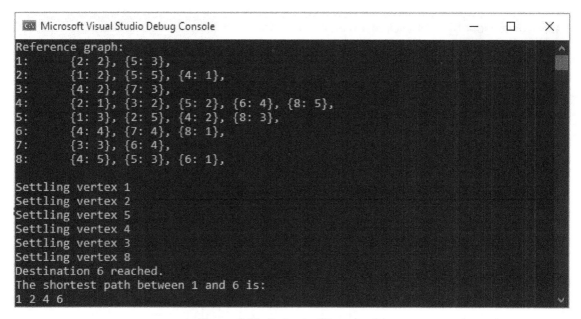

Figure 6.31: Output of Exercise 31

As you can see in the preceding output, our program traces the vertices along the shortest path between vertices 1 and 6. The best known running time of Dijkstra's algorithm is $O(E + V \log V)$ when Fibonacci min-heaps are used.

Activity 14: Shortest Path in New York

In this activity, you are required to implement Dijkstra's algorithm in C++ so that it can be used to find the shortest path in the given road network of New York. Our road graph consists of 264,326 vertices and 733,846 directed edges, and the edge weight is the Euclidean distance between the vertices. The steps for this activity are as follows:

1. Download the road graph file from the following link: https://raw.githubusercontent.com/TrainingByPackt/CPP-Data-Structures-and-Algorithm-Design-Principles/master/Lesson6/Activity14/USA-road-d.NY.gr.

> **Note**
>
> If the file is not automatically downloaded, and instead is opened in your browser, download it by right-clicking on any blank space and selecting "**Save as...**"

2. If you're running Windows, move the downloaded file to **\<project directory\>/out/x86-Debug/Chapter6**.

   If you're running Linux, move the downloaded file to **\<project directory\>/build/Chapter6**.

> **Note**
>
> The directory structure may vary based on your IDE. The file needs to be placed in the same directory as your compiled binary. Alternatively, you may tweak the implementation to accept a path to the file.

3. The road graph is a text file with three different kinds of rows:

Example of row	Description
c	Comment line. Should be ignored.
p sp N M.	Problem line. Sp refers to the shortest path problem. N is the number of vertices and M is the number of edges in the graph.
a U V W	An edge in the graph from vertex U to V with the weight, W.

Figure 6.32: Table describing the road graph file for New York

4. Implement a weighted edge graph. It is okay to assume that once the graph is created, no vertices can be added or deleted from the graph.

5. Implement a function to parse the road graph file and populate the graph.

6. Implement Dijkstra's algorithm and test your implementation by finding the shortest path between vertices **913** and **542**. Your output should look as follows:

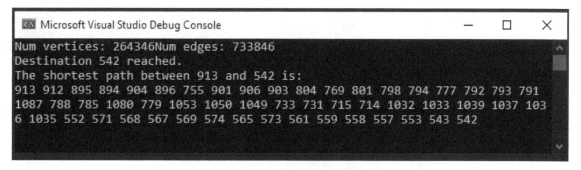

Figure 6.33: Expected output of Activity 14

> **Note**
>
> The solution to this activity can be found on page 530.

Summary

We covered three major graph problems in this chapter: first, the graph traversal problem for which two solutions were introduced, breadth-first search (BFS) and depth-first search (DFS). Second, we revisited the minimum spanning tree (MST) problem and solved it using Prim's algorithm. We also compared it with Kruskal's algorithm and discussed the conditions under which one should be preferred over the other. Finally, we introduced the single-source shortest path problem, which finds a minimum-cost shortest path in graphs, and covered Dijkstra's shortest path algorithm.

However, Dijkstra's algorithm only works for graphs with positive edge weights. In the next chapter, we shall seek to relax this constraint and introduce a shortest path algorithm that can handle negative edge weights. We shall also generalize the shortest path problem to find the shortest paths between all the pairs of vertices in graphs.

Graph Algorithms II

Learning Objectives

By the end of this chapter, you will be able to:

- Describe the inherent problems of Dijkstra's algorithm and demonstrate how it can be modified and/or combined with other algorithms to circumvent those issues

- Find the shortest path in a graph using the Bellman-Ford and Johnson's algorithms

- Describe the significance of strongly connected components in a garaph

- Use Kosaraju's algorithm to find strongly connected components in a graph

- Describe the difference between connectivity in directed and undirected graphs

- Implement depth-first search for complicated problems

- Evaluate negative weight cycles in a graph

This chapter builds upon the previous chapter by introducing some more advanced algorithms for graphs. You will also learn how to deal with negative weights and handle the exceptions of negative weight cycles.

Introduction

So far, we have explored a variety of common programming structures and paradigms. Now, we are going to delve into several techniques that expand on the topics we discussed previously, beginning with an assortment of advanced graph problems, and then shifting focus toward the expansive subject of dynamic programming.

In this chapter, we will discuss three well-known algorithms, namely the Bellman-Ford algorithm, Johnson's algorithm, and Kosaraju's algorithm. All of these algorithms share clear similarities with ones we have already covered in this book but extend and combine them in various ways to solve potentially complex problems with much greater efficiency than suboptimal implementations would allow. In addition to learning these specific techniques, this chapter should also increase your general familiarity with the use of fundamental graph-related techniques and provide greater insight into how those fundamentals can be applied to a diverse range of different problems.

Revisiting the Shortest Path Problem

We previously discussed several ways to find the shortest path between two nodes in a graph. We began by exploring the most standard forms of graph traversal, namely depth-first search and breadth-first search, and eventually discussed how to approach the more problematic case of graphs containing weighted edges. We demonstrated how Dijkstra's algorithm could be used to efficiently find the shortest distances in weighted graphs by greedily prioritizing each step in the traversal according to the best option immediately available. However, despite the improvement in performance that Dijkstra's algorithm provides, it is not applicable to every situation.

Consider a Wi-Fi signal that is being broadcast through a network; as it travels beyond the point at which it is originally transmitted, its strength is likely to be affected by numerous factors, such as the distance it travels and the number of walls and other obstacles it must pass through. If you wanted to determine the path that the signal will take to each destination that will minimize its deterioration, you could create a weighted graph with each point in the network represented by a node and the degree of signal loss between any two points represented by weighted edges. You could then calculate the shortest distances in the graph using Dijkstra's algorithm to determine the least costly paths in the network.

Now, suppose that a repeater/booster is installed in the network to increase the strength of the signal at a particular point – how might this addition be represented in your graph? The most obvious approach would be to set the outgoing edge weights from the booster's node to negative values (equivalent to the degree by which it increases the signal strength), which would decrease the total distance/deterioration of any path passing through it. How might this affect our results if we used Dijkstra's algorithm on the network's graph?

As we discussed in the previous chapter, Dijkstra's algorithm takes a greedy approach in terms of how it selects each vertex in the traversal. At every step, it finds the closest unvisited vertex and adds it to the visited set, excluding it from further consideration. The assumption that's being made by Dijkstra's algorithm is that the shortest path to every vertex that's been considered so far has already been found, so searching for better alternatives would be pointless. However, in graphs containing negative edge weights, this approach would not explore the possibilities that lead to the optimal solution if they produced a higher sum in the early stages of the traversal.

Consider a graph with a negative edge weight, as shown in the following figure:

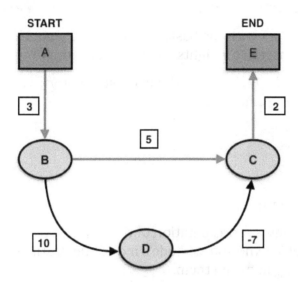

Figure 7.1: Applying Dijkstra's algorithm to a graph with a negative weight

In the preceding figure, the path that's traversed by Dijkstra's algorithm is indicated in red. Assuming we start at vertex A, there will be two potential options after the first move from node A to node B: B –> C, which has an edge weight of 5, and B –> D, which has an edge weight of 10. Because of Dijkstra's greedy approach, C will be chosen as the next node in the shortest path, but we can clearly see that the other option (B –> D –> C = 10 + –7 = 3) is actually the optimal choice.

When faced with negative edge weights, the inherent optimizations in Dijkstra's algorithm that enable its high level of efficiency ultimately lead to its downfall. Thankfully, for such graphs, we can employ an alternative approach that is quite similar to Dijkstra's algorithm and arguably simpler to implement.

The Bellman-Ford Algorithm

We can use the **Bellman-Ford algorithm** to handle graphs with negative weights. It replaces Dijkstra's method of greedy selection with an alternative approach of iterating across every edge in the graph V – 1 times (where V is equal to the total number of vertices) and finding progressively optimal distance values from the source node across each iteration. Naturally, this gives it a higher asymptotic complexity than Dijkstra's algorithm, but it also allows it to produce correct results for graphs that Dijkstra's algorithm would misinterpret. The following exercise shows how to implement the Bellman-Ford algorithm.

Exercise 32: Implementing the Bellman-Ford Algorithm (Part I)

In this exercise, we will work with the basic Bellman-Ford algorithm to find the shortest distance in a graph with negative weights. Let's get started:

1. First, set up your code by including the necessary libraries (as well as the **namespace std** for convenience):

```
#include <iostream>
#include <vector>
#include <climits>

using namespace std;
```

2. Let's begin by defining a representation of the edges in our graph, which will require three variables: the source node's index, the destination node's index, and the cost of traversing between them:

```
struct Edge
{
    int start;     // The starting vertex
    int end;       // The destination vertex
    int weight;    // The edge weight

    // Constructor
    Edge(int s, int e, int w) : start(s), end(e), weight(w) {}
};
```

3. To implement the Bellman-Ford algorithm, we will need to have some representation of our graph. For the sake of simplicity, let's assume that our graph can be represented by an integer, **V**, the total number of vertices in the graph, and a vector, **edges** (a collection of pointers to 'edge' objects that define the graph's adjacencies). Let's also define an integer constant, **UNKNOWN**, which we can set to some arbitrary high value that will always be greater than the sum of any subset of edge weights in the graph (the **INT_MAX** constant defined in `climits` works well for this purpose):

```
const int UNKNOWN = INT_MAX;

vector<Edge*> edges;    // Collection of edge pointers
int V;                  // Total number of vertices in the graph
int E;                  // Total number of edges in the graph
```

4. Let's also write some code for collecting the graph's data as user input:

```
int main()
{
    cin >> V >> E;

    for(int i = 0; i < E; i++)
    {
        int node_a, node_b, weight;
        cin >> node_a >> node_b >> weight;

        // Add a new edge using the defined constructor
        edges.push_back(new Edge(node_a, node_b, weight));
    }

    // Choose a starting node

    int start;
    cin >> start;

    // Run the Bellman-Ford algorithm on the graph for
    // the chosen starting vertex

    BellmanFord(start);

    return 0;
}
```

5. Now, we can start implementing the Bellman-Ford algorithm itself. For our purposes, let's create a function called **BellmanFord()** that takes one argument – **start** (the starting node from which we want to find the shortest paths in the graph) – and returns **void**. Then, we will define a distance array of size **V**, with every element initialized to **UNKNOWN** except for the starting node, whose index is initialized to **0**:

```cpp
void BellmanFord(int start)
{
    vector<int> distance(V, UNKNOWN);

    distance[start] = 0;
```

6. The bulk of the work is done in the next step, where we define a loop that lasts for **V - 1** iterations and iterates through the entire set of edges on every repetition. For each edge, we check to see whether its source node's current distance value is not equal to **UNKNOWN** (which, in the first iteration, only applies to the starting node). Assuming this is true, we then compare the current distance value of its destination node to the sum of the source node's distance with the weight of the edge. If the result of adding the edge weight to the current node's distance is less than the stored distance of the destination node, we replace its value in the distance array with the new sum:

```cpp
// Perform V - 1 iterations
for(int i = 0; i < V; i++)
{
    // Iterate over entire set of edges
    for(auto edge : edges)
    {
        int u = edge->start;
        int v = edge->end;
        int w = edge->weight;

        // Skip nodes which have not yet been considered
        if(distance[u] == UNKNOWN)
        {
            continue;
        }


        // If the current distance value for the destination
        // node is greater than the sum of the source node's
        // distance and the edge's weight, change its distance
```

```
        // to the lesser value.

        if(distance[u] + w < distance[v])
        {
            distance[v] = distance[u] + w;
        }
    }
}
```

7. At the end of our function, we can now iterate through the **distance** array and output the shortest distances from the source to every other node in the graph:

```
cout << "DISTANCE FROM VERTEX " << start << ":\n"

for(int i = 0; i < V; i++)
{
    cout << "\t" << i << ": ";

    if(distance[i] == UNKNOWN)
    {
        cout << "Unvisited" << endl;

        continue;
    }

    cout << distance[i] << endl;
}
```

8. Now, we can return to our **main()** method and make a call to our newly implemented **BellmanFord()** function. Let's test our implementation on the example graph from *figure 7.1*. To do so, we should run our code and enter the following input:

```
5 5
0 1 3
1 2 5
1 3 10
3 2 -7
2 4 2
0
```

9. Our program should output the following:

```
DISTANCE FROM VERTEX 0:
     0:  0
     1:  3
     2:  6
     3:  13
     4:  8
```

As we can see, Bellman-Ford avoids the trap that would lead Dijkstra's algorithm to evaluate the shortest paths incorrectly. However, there is still another significant problem to contend with, which we will discuss in the next section.

The Bellman-Ford Algorithm (Part II) – Negative Weight Cycles

Consider the graph shown in the following figure:

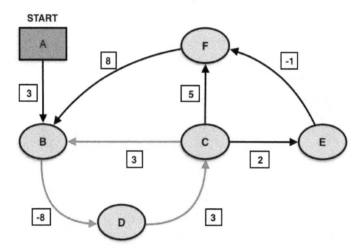

Figure 7.2: Graph with a negative weight cycle

The edges highlighted in red indicate a negative weight cycle or a cycle in the graph where the combined edge weights produce a negative sum. In such a situation, this cycle would be considered repeatedly, and the final results would be skewed.

For the sake of comparison, consider a graph with only positive edge weights. A cycle in such a graph would never be considered in the solution because the shortest distance to the first node in the cycle would have been found already. To demonstrate this, imagine that the edge weight between nodes B and D in the preceding figure is positive. Starting from node A, the first iteration through the edges would determine that the shortest distance to node B is equal to 3. After two more iterations, we would also know the shortest distance from A to C (A –> B –> D –> C), which is equal to 14 (3 + 8 + 3).

Obviously, no positive number can be added to 14 that will produce a sum of less than 3. As there can be at most | V – 1 | steps in any graph traversal where each node is visited only once, we can be certain that | V – 1 | iterations through the graph's edges are sufficient to determine every possible shortest distance. By extension, we can conclude that the only way an even shorter path can exist after | V – 1 | iterations is if a node is revisited and the edge weight leading to it is negative. Thus, the final step of the Bellman-Ford algorithm consists of performing one more iteration through the edges to check for the existence of such cycles.

We can accomplish this with the same logic we used to find the shortest paths: by checking whether the sum of each edge's weight with the distance value of its source node is less than the currently stored distance to its destination node. If a shorter path is found during this step, we terminate the algorithm and report the existence of a negative cycle.

We will explore this implementation of the algorithm in the following exercise.

Exercise 33: Implementing the Bellman-Ford Algorithm (Part II)

In this exercise, we will modify the implementation in *Exercise 32, Implementing the Bellman-Ford Algorithm (Part I)*, to deal with a graph with negative weight cycles. Let's get started:

1. We can essentially copy our code from the previous step verbatim. However, this time, we will replace the code under the condition that determines whether a shorter path has been found with some sort of output indicating that the graph contains a negative cycle, thus rendering it invalid:

```
// Iterate through edges one last time
for(auto edge : edges)
{
    int u = edge->start;
    int v = edge->end;
    int w = edge->weight;

    if(distance[u] == UNKNOWN)
    {
        continue;
    }
```

2. If we can still find a path shorter than the one we have already found, the graph must contain a negative cycle. Let's check for a negative weight cycle with the following **if** statement:

```
if(distance[u] + w < distance[v])
{
    cout << "NEGATIVE CYCLE FOUND" << endl;
    return;
}
}
```

3. Now, let's insert this block of code in-between the end of the first **for** loop and the first output line:

```
void BellmanFord(int start)
{
    vector<int> distance(V, UNKNOWN);

    distance[start] = 0;

    for(int i = 1; i < V; i++)
    {
        for(auto edge : edges)
        {
            int u = edge->start;
            int v = edge->end;
            int w = edge->weight;

            if(distance[u] == UNKNOWN)
            {
                continue;
            }

            if(distance[u] + w < distance[v])
            {
```

```cpp
                distance[v] = distance[u] + w;
            }
        }
    }
    for(auto edge : edges)
    {
        int u = edge->start;
        int v = edge->end;
        int w = edge->weight;

        if(distance[u] == UNKNOWN)
        {
            continue;
        }

        if(distance[u] + w < distance[v])
        {
            cout << "NEGATIVE CYCLE FOUND" << endl;
            return;
        }
    }

    cout << "DISTANCE FROM VERTEX " << start << ":\n";

    for(int i = 0; i < V; i++)
    {
        cout << "\t" << i << ": ";

        if(distance[i] == UNKNOWN)
        {
            cout << "Unvisited" << endl;
            continue;
        }
        cout << distance[i] << endl;
    }
}
```

4. To test the logic we've added, let's run the algorithm on the following input:

```
6 8
0 1 3
1 3 -8
2 1 3
2 5 5
3 2 3
2 4 2
4 5 -1
5 1 8
0
```

5. Our program should output the following:

```
NEGATIVE CYCLE FOUND
```

Activity 15: Greedy Robot

You are developing a pathfinding robot that must find the most efficient path through an obstacle course. For testing purposes, you have designed several courses, each in the shape of a square grid. Your robot is able to traverse any obstacle it encounters, but this also requires a greater expenditure of power. Assuming your robot starts in the top-left corner of the grid and can move in any of the four cardinal directions (north, south, east, and west), you must implement an algorithm that determines the maximum amount of energy your robot can finish the course with.

Since the amount of energy that's required to perform this traversal can be high, you have interspersed power stations throughout the grid, which your robot has the capability of using to recharge itself. Unfortunately, it appears that your robot is quite greedy in terms of energy consumption – if it can reach an energy station multiple times without having to backtrack, it will continually return to the same location until it inevitably overcharges and explodes! Because of this, you will need to predict whether your robot will end up revisiting a power station and abort the traversal attempt before disaster ensues.

Input

- The first line contains a single integer, N, which is the height and width of the course.

- The next N² - 1 lines each contain the **directions** string and an integer called **power**. Each set of N lines corresponds to a single row, beginning from the top of the grid, where each cell's data is defined from left to right (for example, in a 3 x 3 grid, 0 –> [0, 0], 1 –> [0, 1], 2 –> [0, 2], 3 –> [1, 0], 4 –> [1, 1], and so on).

- **directions** contains 0-3 characters from the set { 'N', 'S', 'E', 'W' }, which represent the cells that your robot can visit from each point. Thus, if the **directions** string is SW, then the robot can move south or west from that point. **power** represents the energy expenditure required to cross the cell. Positive values for **power** indicate that a charging station is located within the cell.

Output

- If traversing the course causes the robot to explode, print a single line – **TRAVERSAL ABORTED.**

- Otherwise, print the maximum amount of energy your robot can have upon reaching the bottom-right cell of the course, relative to the amount of energy it started with. For example, if the robot can finish the maze with 10 more units of energy than it started with, print **10**; if it finishes the maze with 10 fewer units of energy than it started with, print **-10**.

Example

Let's say we had the following input:

```
3
SE -10
SE -8
S -6
S 7
E -10
S 20
E -1
NE 5
```

The grid's layout would look like this:

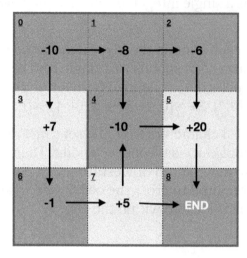

Figure 7.3: Grid for the robot's traversal

The path that reaches the bottom-right cell with the most energy is as follows:

```
0 -> 3 (-10)
3 -> 6 (+7)
6 -> 7 (-1)
7 -> 4 (+5)
4 -> 5 (-10)
5 -> 8 (+20)

(-10) + 7 + (-1) + 5 + (-10) + 20
= 11 more units of energy
```

Therefore, your program should output **11**.

Test Cases

The following test cases should help you understand this problem better:

Input	Output
3	11
SE -10	
SE -8	
S -6	
S 7	
E -10	
S 20	
E -1	
NE 5	

Figure 7.4: Test case 1 for Activity 15

Input	Output
3	TRAVERSAL ABORTED
E -1	
E -5	
S 6	
S -2	
W 15	
W -10	
E -5	
NE 5	

Figure 7.5: Test case 2 for Activity 15

Input	Output
4	-352
S -83	
E -77	
SE -93	
S 86	
SE -49	
N -62	
SE -90	
S -63	
S 40	
NW -72	
SW -11	
W 67	
E -82	
N -62	
E -67	

Figure 7.6: Test case 3 for Activity 15

Input	Output
5	TRAVERSAL ABORTED
SE -83	
SE -77	
E -93	
S 86	
W -49	
E -62	
SE -90	
N -63	
SEW 40	
NS -72	
S -11	
W 67	
NW -82	
W -62	
SW -67	
S 29	
W 22	
SW 69	
W -93	
SW -11	
E 29	
E -21	
E -84	
E -98	

Figure 7.7: Test case 4 for Activity 15

Input	Output
5	25
S 8	
E -2	
SEW -15	
SE 4	
S 25	
S -26	
NEW 19	
NS 7	
SEW -56	
S 11	
E 25	
N -86	
SEW 11	
NE 26	
S -78	
NS -11	
NSW -76	
SW 33	
NSW 4	
SW -40	
E 8	
E 11	
E 36	
E -2	

Figure 7.8: Test case 5 for Activity 15

Activity Guidelines

- No algorithms beyond what was covered in *Exercise 33, Implementing the Bellman-Ford Algorithm (Part II)*, are required.

- You may need to reinterpret some of the input so that it corresponds to the actual problem you are trying to solve.

- There is no need to represent the grid as two-dimensional.

> **Note**
>
> The solution to this activity can be found on page 537.

We have now established that Bellman-Ford is more versatile than Dijkstra's algorithm since it possesses the capability to produce correct solutions in cases where Dijkstra's algorithm would yield incorrect results. However, if the graph we are considering does not contain any negative edge weights, Dijkstra's algorithm is the obvious choice between the two due to the potentially significant efficiency advantages afforded by its greedy approach. Now, we will explore how Bellman-Ford can be used in conjunction with Dijkstra's algorithm so that it can be used for graphs with negative weights.

Johnson's Algorithm

Having compared the relative merits and disadvantages of the Bellman-Ford algorithm and Dijkstra's algorithm, we will now discuss an algorithm that combines both of them to retrieve the shortest paths between every pair of vertices in a graph. **Johnson's algorithm** provides us with the advantage of being able to utilize the efficiency of Dijkstra's algorithm while still producing correct results for graphs with negative edge weights.

The concept behind Johnson's algorithm is quite novel – to contend with Dijkstra's limitations when dealing with negative weights, Johnson's algorithm simply reweights the edges in the graph so they are uniformly non-negative. This is accomplished with the rather creative use of Bellman-Ford combined with some particularly elegant mathematical logic.

The first step in Johnson's algorithm is to add a new 'dummy' vertex to the graph, which is subsequently connected to every other vertex by zero-weighted edges. Bellman-Ford is then used to find the shortest paths between the new vertex and the rest, and the distances are stored for later use.

Consider the implications of the addition of this new vertex: because it has a 0-weighted edge connecting it to every other node in the graph, none of its shortest path distances will ever be positive. Furthermore, its connectivity to every node in the graph ensures that its distance values maintain a constant relation across all the potential traversal paths, which causes the sum that's formed by these values and their corresponding edge weights to 'telescope', in other words, subsequent terms in the sequence cancel each other out, making the summation equivalent to the difference of the first and last terms. Take a look at the following figure:

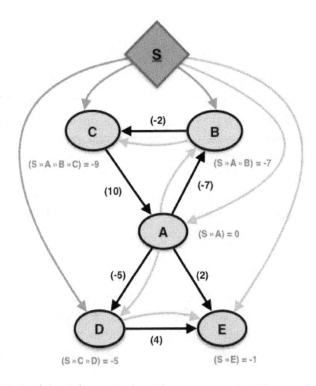

Figure 7.9: Applying Johnson's algorithm on a graph with negative weights

In the preceding graph, the diamond-shaped node labeled **S** represents the dummy vertex, the black parenthesized numbers represent edge weights, the red text represents the shortest paths from **S** to each node, the orange arrows represent the optimal paths traversed from **S**, and the blue arrows represent 0-weighted edges branching from **S** that are not included in any of **S**'s shortest paths.

Let's take the new distance values and arrange them in a sequence according to their appearance in this traversal of the graph – **A** --> **B** --> **C** --> **A** --> **D** --> **E**:

	A	B	C	A	D	E	
{	0	-7	-9	0	-5	-1	}

Figure 7.10: Distance for traversing at each node

If we insert the original edge weights in-between the distance values of the nodes they connect to, the sequence will be as follows:

	A		B		C		A		D		E	
{	0	(-7)	-7	(-2)	-9	(10)	0	(-5)	-5	(4)	-1	}
		AB		BC		CA		AD		DE		

Figure 7.11: Calculating the distance that's been traversed

Now, let's apply the following formula to the edge values:

```
W(uv) = w(uv) + d[s, u] - d[s, v]
```

Here, **w(uv)** represents the original edge weight between nodes **u** and **v**, **d[s, u]** and **d[s, v]** represent the shortest path distances between **S** and **u/v**, and **W(uv)** represents the transformed edge weight values. Applying this formula yields the following result:

```
AB -> (-7) +   0 - (-7) = 0
BC -> (-2) + (-7) - (-9) = 0
CA ->  10  + (-9) -   0  = 1
AD -> (-5) +   0 - (-5) = 0
DE ->   4  + (-5) - (-1) = 0
```

Notice how the third term in the expression is always canceled out by the middle term in subsequent iterations; this demonstrates the "telescoping" property of the formula. Because of this property, the following two expressions representing the distance between node A and E are equivalent:

```
(w(AB) + d[s, A] - d[s, B]) + (w(BC) + d[s, B] - d[s, C]) + … + (w(DE) +
d[s, D] - d[s, E])
```

```
(w(AB) + w(BC) + w(CA) + w(AD) + w(DE)) + d[s, A] - d[s, E]
```

This implies that the amount of weight being added to any path in the graph is equal to the amount of weight being added to its subpaths. We know that the results of adding these values will always be non-negative because the distance array that's returned by Bellman-Ford ensures that we have `d[s, u] + weight(u, v) >= d[s, v]` for any pair, `u,v`. Thus, the value of `w(u, v) + d[s, u] - d[s, v]` can never be less than 0.

As a result of the applied transformation, each edge that will be traversed in any shortest path in the graph will be reweighted to zero, which leaves us with non-negative weight values that, quite remarkably, have still retained their original shortest path orderings! We can now perform Dijkstra's algorithm on the graph using these new weight values to efficiently retrieve the shortest paths for every pair of nodes.

We will explore the implementation of Johnson's algorithm in the following exercise.

Exercise 34: Implementing Johnson's Algorithm

In this exercise, we will implement Johnson's algorithm to find the shortest distance from each node to every other node in a graph with negative weights. Let's get started:

1. We can reuse most of our code from the previous exercise, including our **Edge** structure, **UNKNOWN** constant, and graph data:

```
#include <iostream>
#include <vector>
#include <climits>

using namespace std;

struct Edge
{
    int start;
    int end;
    int weight;

    Edge(int s, int e, int w) : start(s), end(e), weight(w) {}
};

const int UNKNOWN = INT_MAX;

vector<Edge*> edges;
int V;
int E;
```

2. We should modify our function declaration for Bellman-Ford so that it accepts two arguments (an integer, **V**, and a vector or **Edge** pointers, **edges**) and returns an integer vector. We can also remove the **start** parameter:

```
vector<int> BellmanFord(int V, vector<Edge*> edges)
```

3. We will begin by adding the dummy vertex, **S**, to the graph. Because **S** essentially has no influence on the rest of the graph, this is as simple as increasing the distance array's size to | V + 1 | and adding an edge between **S** and every other node:

```
vector<int> distance(V + 1, UNKNOWN);

int s = V;

for(int i = 0; i < V; i++)
{
    edges.push_back(new Edge(s, i, 0));
}

distance[s] = 0;
```

4. We proceed to apply the standard implementation of Bellman-Ford to the modified graph, using **S** as the source node:

```
for(int i = 1; i < V; i++)
{
    for(auto edge : edges)
    {
        int u = edge->start;
        int v = edge->end;
        int w = edge->weight;

        if(distance[u] == UNKNOWN)
        {
            continue;
        }
        if(distance[u] + w < distance[v])
        {
            distance[v] = distance[u] + w;
        }
    }
}
```

5. This time, let's move the final check for negative cycles into its own function:

```cpp
bool HasNegativeCycle(vector<int> distance, vector<Edge*> edges)
{
    for(auto edge : edges)
    {
        int u = edge->start;
        int v = edge->end;
        int w = edge->weight;

        if(distance[u] == UNKNOWN) continue;

        if(distance[u] + w < distance[v])
        {
            return true;
        }
    }
    return false;
}
```

6. Now, we can call it at the end of the original function and return an empty array if a negative cycle is found:

```cpp
if(HasNegativeCycle(distance, edges))
{
    cout << "NEGATIVE CYCLE FOUND" << endl;

    return {};
}
```

7. After ensuring that the graph has no negative cycles, we can return the resultant set of distance values to the calling function and apply the reweighting formula to every edge in the graph. But first, let's implement Dijkstra's algorithm:

```cpp
vector<int> Dijkstra(int V, int start, vector<Edge*> edges)
```

8. Now, let's declare an integer vector, **distance**, and a Boolean vector, **visited**. As usual, every index of **distance** will be initialized to UNKNOWN (except for the starting vertex), and every index of **visited** will be initialized to false:

```
vector<int> distance(V, UNKNOWN);
vector<bool> visited(V, false);

distance[start] = 0;
```

9. Our implementation of Dijkstra's algorithm will utilize a simple iterative approach using a **for** loop. As you may recall from earlier chapters, Dijkstra's algorithm needs to find the node with the minimum distance value at each step in the traversal. While this is often done via a priority queue, we will accomplish this by coding another short function, **GetMinDistance()**, which will take the distance and visited arrays as arguments and return the index of the node with the shortest path value:

```
// Find vertex with shortest distance from current position and
// return its index

int GetMinDistance(vector<int> &distance, vector<bool> &visited)
{
    int minDistance = UNKNOWN;
    int result;

    for(int v = 0; v < distance.size(); v++)
    {
        if(!visited[v] && distance[v] <= minDistance)
        {
            minDistance = distance[v];
            result = v;
        }
    }
    return result;
}
```

10. We can now finish implementing Dijkstra's algorithm:

```
for(int i = 0; i < V - 1; i++)
{
    // Find index of unvisited node with shortest distance
    int curr = GetMinDistance(distance, visited);
```

```
            visited[curr] = true;

            // Iterate through edges
            for(auto edge : edges)
            {
                // Only consider neighboring nodes
                if(edge->start != curr) continue;

                // Disregard if already visited
                if(visited[edge->end]) continue;

                if(distance[curr] != UNKNOWN && distance[curr] + edge->weight <
        distance[edge->end])
                {
                distance[edge->end] = distance[curr] + edge->weight;
                }
            }
        }

        return distance;
```

11. We now have everything we need to perform Johnson's algorithm. Let's declare a new function, **Johnson()**, which also takes **V** and **edges** as arguments:

    ```
    void Johnson(int V, vector<Edge*> edges)
    ```

12. We start by creating an integer vector, **h**, and setting it to the output of **BellmanFord()**:

    ```
    // Get distance array from modified graph
    vector<int> h = BellmanFord(V, edges);
    ```

13. We check whether **h** is empty. If it is, we terminate the function:

    ```
    if(h.empty()) return;
    ```

14. Otherwise, we apply the reweighting formula:

    ```
    for(int i = 0; i < edges.size(); i++)
    {
        edges[i]->weight += (h[edges[i]->start] - h[edges[i]->end]);
    }
    ```

15. To store the shortest path distances for every pair of nodes, we initialize a matrix with **V** rows (so that each pair of two-dimensional indices, **[i, j]**, represents the shortest path between vertex **i** and vertex **j**). We then perform **V** calls to Dijkstra's algorithm, which returns the **distance** array for each starting node:

```
// Create a matrix for storing distance values
vector<vector<int>> shortest(V);

// Retrieve shortest distances for each vertex
for(int i = 0; i < V; i++)
{
    shortest[i] = Dijkstra(V, i, edges);
}
```

16. Unsurprisingly, the results we have accumulated in this step are quite inaccurate. Every distance value is now positive as a result of our reweighting operation. However, this can be rectified quite simply by applying the same formula to each result in reverse:

```
// Reweight again in reverse to get original values
for(int i = 0; i < V; i++)
{
    cout << i << ":\n";

    for(int j = 0; j < V; j++)
    {
        if(shortest[i][j] != UNKNOWN)
        {
            shortest[i][j] += h[j] - h[i];

            cout << "\t" << j << ": " << shortest[i][j] << endl;
        }
    }
}
```

17. Now, let's return to our **main()** function and implement the code for handling input. After we have collected the edges of the input graph, we simply need to perform a single call to **Johnson()** and our work is done:

```
int main()
{
    int V, E;
    cin >> V >> E;
```

```
            vector<Edge*> edges;

            for(int i = 0; i < E; i++)
            {
                int node_a, node_b, weight;
                cin >> node_a >> node_b >> weight;

                edges.push_back(new Edge(node_a, node_b, weight));
            }

            Johnson(V, edges);

            return 0;
        }
```

18. Let's test our algorithm using the following input:

```
7 9
0 1 3
1 2 5
1 3 10
1 5 -4
2 4 2
3 2 -7
4 1 -3
5 6 -8
6 0 12
```

19. The output should be as follows:

```
0:
        0: 0
        1: 3
        2: 6
        3: 13
        4: 8
        5: -1
        6: -9
1:
        0: 0
        1: 0
        2: 3
        3: 10
        4: 5
```

```
        5: -4
        6: -12
    2:
        0: -1
        1: -1
        2: 0
        3: 9
        4: 2
        5: -5
        6: -13
    4:
        0: -3
        1: -3
        2: 0
        3: 7
        4: 0
        5: -7
        6: -15
    5:
        0: 4
        1: 7
        2: 10
        3: 17
        4: 12
        5: 0
        6: -8
    6:
        0: 12
        1: 15
        2: 18
        3: 25
        4: 20
        5: 11
        6: 0
```

As you can see from the preceding output, we have successfully printed the shortest distance from each node to every other node.

Activity 16: Randomized Graph Statistics

You are a developer at a well-known software company that receives a high volume of new job applicants every year. As such, it is a requirement for every employee to participate in the process of conducting technical interviews. Before every interview, you are given a set of three programming problems, each containing a short description, and two to three test cases of increasing difficulty.

It was recently brought to your attention that a number of interviewees managed to acquire the test cases for certain interview questions in advance. As a result, the powers that be have called on you to create new sets of test cases every couple of weeks. Producing decent test cases for most problems is not particularly challenging, except for questions concerning graph theory. You have noticed that the process of designing a graph that is both valid and relevant to the problem can be a bit time-consuming, so you have become determined to automate the process.

The most common graph-related interview question your company uses is the all-pairs shortest path problem, which requires the interviewee to find the shortest distances between every pair of vertices in a directed graph with weighted edges. Because of the nature of this problem, you want the graphs that are produced by your generator utility to be useful in assessing the interviewees' understanding of the problem. You've decided that a graph will be useful for technical interviews if it meets the following criteria:

- It is a directed graph that can contain both positive and negative edge weights.

- There should only be one edge between any pair of nodes, and no node should have an edge to itself.

- Every node should have at least one incoming or outgoing edge.

- The absolute value of any edge weight should be less than 100.

The utility should take the following inputs:

- **seed**: A seed value for random number generation

- **iterations**: The number of graphs to generate

- **V**: The number of vertices

- **E**: The number of edges

The utility should handle the generation of every edge using calls to **std::rand()**. In the event that it attempts to create a second edge between the same pair of nodes, it should stop generating new edges until a valid pair is found.

Graph generation should be done as follows:

1. Receive input (**seed**, **iterations**, **V**, and **E**)

2. Set the random number generator's seed value

3 For each iteration, do the following:

- Set **i = 0**

  - Attempt to create an edge by performing three calls to **rand()** in order to generate the values for the source node, destination node, and edge weight (in that order).

  - Check whether the next value that's generated by **rand()** is evenly divisible by **3**; if so, make the edge weight negative.

- If an edge between the source and destination nodes already exists, try again:

  - Add **edge(source, destination, weight)** to the set of edges and increment **i**.

  - If after **E** edges have been created there is a node that is not part of an edge, the graph is considered invalid.

If the generated graph is valid, you should find the shortest paths between every pair of nodes in the graph, as we would be expected to do during an interview. For each node in the graph, you want to find the average shortest distance across all of its paths (that is, the sum of distance values divided by the number of reachable nodes). The average distance of the graph will be defined as the average of these values.

You are also interested in which sets of values tend to produce the greatest number of "interesting" graphs. You consider graphs to be interesting when the average distance of the graph is less than half of that of the highest-valued edge weight. Your algorithm should, therefore, output the ratio of interesting graphs to the total number of valid graphs as a percentage (rounded to two decimal places). Note that for this particular purpose, you consider a connected graph with negative weight cycles to be valid but not interesting.

Input Format

One line containing four integers; that is, **seed**, **iterations**, **V**, and **E**, respectively.

Output Format

Two lines, the first containing the **INVALID:** string, followed by the number of invalid graphs, and the second containing the **PERCENT INTERESTING:** string, followed by the ratio of interesting to valid graphs, displayed as a percentage rounded to two decimal places.

Activity Guidelines

Calls to **std::rand()** will not necessarily produce the same value in every environment. To ensure consistency, you can copy/paste the following code into your program (taken from the C standard):

```
static unsigned long int randNext = 1;


int rand(void) // RAND_MAX assumed to be 32767
{
    randNext = randNext * 1103515245 + 12345;
    return (unsigned int)(randNext/65536) % 32768
}


void srand(unsigned int seed)
{
    randNext = seed;
}
```

When implementing the graph generation utility, make sure that the steps are followed in the exact order described in the problem description.

Test Cases

Here are some sample inputs and outputs that should help you understand the problem better:

Input	Output
42 1000 15 10	INVALID: 996
	PERCENT INTERESTING: 0.00%
11111 400 5 5	INVALID: 55
	PERCENT INTERESTING: 0.58%
1125 100 10 20	INVALID: 1
	PERCENT INTERESTING: 3.03%
0 300 15 30	INVALID: 29
	PERCENT INTERESTING: 1.11%
51 1000 5 10	INVALID: 0
	PERCENT INTERESTING: 14.10%
1000000007 200 10 20	INVALID: 7
	PERCENT INTERESTING: 5.07%
1000000000 500 8 20	INVALID: 0
	PERCENT INTERESTING: 4.80%

Figure 7.12: Test cases for Activity 16

> **Note**
>
> The solution to this activity can be found on page 541.

Strongly Connected Components

In the previous chapters, we discussed several classifications of graphs. Among the most common ways of describing the characteristics of a graph is stating whether it is directed or undirected. The latter defines graphs in which the edges are bidirectional by default (if node A has an edge connecting to node B, then node B has an edge connecting to node A), while the former describes graphs with edges oriented toward specific 'directions'.

Imagine you are an employee for a video hosting website and are tasked with producing statistics about commonalities between subscribers to various channels. Your company is particularly interested in discovering patterns between the individuals who subscribe to certain channels and the subscriptions of the channels' respective owners, hoping to gain greater insight into how their targeted advertising service should be directed. The service your company provides has become rather expansive recently, so you need a method of organizing the relevant data in a way that is clear enough to produce useful statistical information.

Let's visualize the channels of every user of the site as nodes in a directed graph, with the adjacencies between them representing the other channel's respective owner that they're subscribed to. We would likely notice that even among large groups of users that share subscriptions to the same channels, the amount of diversity in all of their individual sets of subscriptions would greatly complicate our ability to find any distinguishing similarities between them. Ideally, we would want to untangle the massive jumble of connections in our graph and place the data into distinct groups in which every user's subscriptions are somehow related to the other users'.

We can unravel the complexity of this particular problem by observing certain characteristics that are common to directed graphs. Because the edges of a directed graph are not guaranteed to be bidirectional, we can logically conclude that access to certain parts of the graph could potentially be restricted depending on which node you start traversing from. If you were to divide a graph into distinct sets so that any pair of vertices in the same set has a connective path between them, the resulting groups would represent the graph's strongly connected components.

Connectivity in Directed and Undirected Graphs

An undirected graph's connected components can be described as the set of maximum-sized subgraphs comprising the primary graph in which every node within the same group is 'connected' to the others (that is, access between any two nodes in a single component is unrestricted). In a connected graph, every node can be reached, regardless of where a traversal begins, so we can deduce that such graphs consist of a single connected component (the entire graph). Conversely, any graph that has restricted access from one point to another is described as disconnected.

So-called 'strong' connectivity, on the other hand, is a characteristic that's exclusive to directed graphs. To comparatively understand the difference in terms of how 'strong connectivity' is defined, observe the following example of an undirected graph:

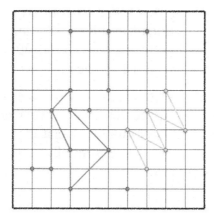

Figure 7.13: Graph with different connected components

The three colored subgraphs each represent a separate connected component. As we stated previously, their connectivity is defined by the fact that every vertex has a path connecting it to the others within the same group. Furthermore, no vertex from one component has a path that connects it to a different component. From the preceding figure, we can see that the connected components of an undirected graph are divided into distinctly separate groups, where the sets of nodes and edges of any component are cut off completely from the others.

Strongly connected components, by contrast, don't need to be completely isolated from the other components in the graph – that is to say, paths can exist that overlap between components:

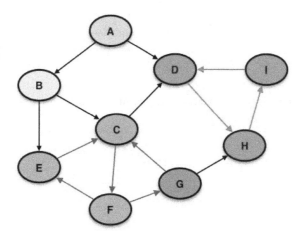

Figure 7.14: Graph with different strongly connected components

In the preceding figure, we can see that there are four strongly connected components: A, B, CEFG, and DHI. Notice that nodes A and B are the only members in their respective sets. By investigating node A further, we can see that though A has a path to every node in the DHI set, none of the nodes in set DHI have any path leading to node A.

Returning to our video hosting website example, we could define the network graph's strongly connected components as groups in which every channel can be found by navigating through the 'path' of subscriptions associated with other users' channels within the same group. Breaking apart the potentially vast amount of data in this way could potentially help in isolating relevant sets of graph relations from those that have no distinguishing similarities:

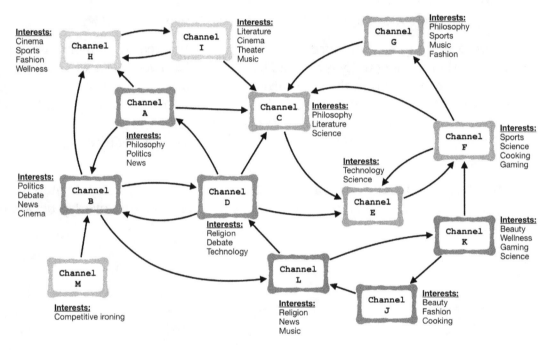

Figure 7.15: Example dataset represented as a graph with different strongly connected components

Kosaraju's Algorithm

One of the most common and conceptually easy to grasp methods of finding the strongly connected components of a graph is Kosaraju's algorithm. Kosaraju's algorithm works by performing two independent sets of DFS traversals, first exploring the graph in its original form, and then doing the same with its transpose.

> **Note**
>
> Though DFS is the type of traversal typically used in Kosaraju's algorithm, BFS is also a viable option. For the explanations and exercises included in this chapter, however, we will stick with the traditional DFS-based approach.

The transpose of a graph is essentially identical to the original graph, except that the source/destination vertices in each of its edges are swapped (that is, if there is an edge from node A to node B in the original graph, the transposed graph will have an edge from node B to node A):

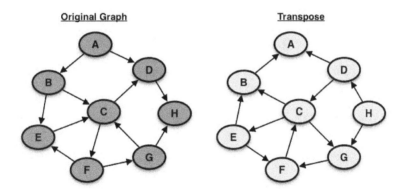

Figure 7.16: Transpose of a graph

The first step of the algorithm (after initialization) is to iterate through the vertices of the graph and perform a DFS traversal, starting from each node that has not yet been visited in a previous traversal. At the beginning of each point in the DFS, the current node is marked as visited, and then all of its unvisited neighbors are explored. After each current node's adjacencies have been investigated, it is added to the top of a stack before the current recursive subtree is terminated.

After exploring every vertex in the original graph, the same is done with its transpose, starting from each unvisited node, which is popped from the top of the stack. At this point, the set of nodes that are encountered during each subsequent DFS traversal with a unique starting point represents a strongly connected component of the graph.

Kosaraju's algorithm is quite effective in terms of how it intuitively simplifies a potentially complex problem, reducing it into something rather straightforward to implement. Additionally, assuming that the input graph has an adjacency list representation, it is also quite efficient since it has a linear asymptotic complexity of $O(V + E)$.

> **Note**
>
> The use of adjacency matrices with this algorithm is not recommended due to the significant amount of additional iterations required to find the neighbors of each vertex in the traversal.

We will take a look at the implementation of Kosarju's algorithm in the following exercise.

Exercise 35: Implementing Kosaraju's Algorithm

In this exercise, we will find the strongly connected components in a graph using Kosaraju's algorithm. Let's get started:

1. For our implementation of Kosaraju's algorithm, we will need to include the following headers:

   ```cpp
   #include <iostream>
   #include <vector>
   #include <stack>
   ```

2. Let's define a function called **Kosaraju()** that takes two arguments – an integer, **V**, (the number of vertices) and a vector of integer vectors, **adj** (an adjacency list representation of the graph) – and returns a vector of integer vectors representing the set of node indices in each strongly connected component of the input graph:

   ```cpp
   vector<vector<int>> Kosaraju(int V, vector<vector<int>> adj)
   ```

3. Our first step is to declare our stack container and visited array (with every index initialized to **false**). We then iterate through each node of the graph, beginning our DFS traversals at every index that has not yet been marked as **visited**:

```
vector<bool> visited(V, false);
stack<int> stack;

for(int i = 0; i < V; i++)
{
    if(!visited[i])
    {
        FillStack(i, visited, adj, stack);
    }
}
```

4. Our first DFS function, **FillStack()**, takes four arguments: an integer node (the index of the vertex at the current point in the traversal), a Boolean vector called **visited** (the set of nodes that were previously traversed), and two integer vectors, **adj** (the graph's adjacency list) and **stack** (a list of visited node indices, ordered according to when they were explored). The last three arguments will be passed by reference from the calling function. The DFS is implemented in the standard way, except with an additional step in which the current node's index is pushed to the stack at the end of each function call:

```
void FillStack(int node, vector<bool> &visited,
vector<vector<int>> &adj, stack<int> &stack)
{
    visited[node] = true;

    for(auto next : adj[node])
    {
        if(!visited[next])
        {
            FillStack(next, visited, adj, stack);
        }
    }
    stack.push(node);
}
```

5. Now, let's define another function, **Transpose()**, which takes the parameters of the original graph as arguments and returns an adjacency list of its transpose:

```
vector<vector<int>> Transpose(int V, vector<vector<int>> adj)
{
    vector<vector<int>> transpose(V);

    for(int i = 0; i < V; i++)
    {
        for(auto next : adj[i])
        {
            transpose[next].push_back(i);
        }
    }
    return transpose;
}
```

6. In preparation for the next set of traversals, we declare the adjacency list transpose (initialized to the output of our **Transpose()** function) and reinitialize our visited array to **false**:

```
vector<vector<int>> transpose = Transpose(V, adj);

fill(visited.begin(), visited.end(), false);
```

7. For the second half of our algorithm, we will need to define our second DFS function, **CollectConnectedComponents()**, which takes the same arguments as **FillStack()**, except the fourth parameter is now replaced with a reference to an integer vector component. This vector component is where we will store the node indices of each strongly connected component in the graph. The implementation of the traversal is also almost identical to the **FillStack()** function, except we remove the line that pushes nodes to the stack. Instead, we include a line at the beginning of the function that collects the traversed nodes in the component vector:

```
void CollectConnectedComponents(int node, vector<bool> &visited,
vector<vector<int>> &adj, vector<int> &component)
{
    visited[node] = true;
    component.push_back(node);

    for(auto next : adj[node])
    {
        if(!visited[next])
```

```
            {
                CollectConnectedComponents(next, visited, adj, component);
            }
        }
    }
```

8. Returning to our **Kosaraju()** function, we define a vector of integer vectors called **connectedComponents**, which is where we will store the result of each traversal we perform on the transpose. We then iteratively pop elements from the stack in a **while** loop, once again beginning each DFS traversal exclusively from unvisited nodes. Before each call to the DFS function, we declare the component vector that is referenced by **CollectConnectedComponents()** and then push it to **connectedComponents** upon completion of the traversal. The algorithm is complete when the stack is empty, after which we return **connectedComponents**:

```
vector<vector<int>> connectedComponents;

while(!stack.empty())
{
    int node = stack.top();

    stack.pop();

    if(!visited[node])
    {
        vector<int> component;

        CollectConnectedComponents(node, visited, transpose, component);
        connectedComponents.push_back(component);
    }
}

return connectedComponents;
```

9. From our `main()` function, we can now output the results of each strongly connected component by printing the values of each vector on a separate line:

```cpp
int main()
{
    int V;
    vector<vector<int>> adj;

    auto connectedComponents = Kosaraju(V, adj);

    cout << "Graph contains " << connectedComponents.size() << " strongly
connected components." << endl;

    for(auto component : connectedComponents)
    {
        cout << "\t";

        for(auto node : component)
        {
            cout << node << " ";
        }
        cout << endl;
    }
}
```

10. To test the functionality of our newly implemented algorithm, let's create an adjacency list representation based on the following graph:

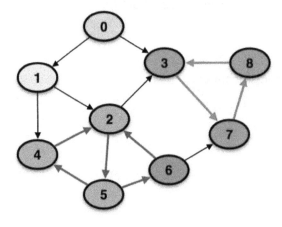

Figure 7.17: Graphical representation of sample input data

11. In **main()**, **V** and **adj** would be defined as follows:

```
int V = 9;

vector<vector<int>> adj =
{
    { 1, 3 },
    { 2, 4 },
    { 3, 5 },
    { 7 },
    { 2 },
    { 4, 6 },
    { 7, 2 },
    { 8 },
    { 3 }
};
```

12. Upon executing our program, the following output should be displayed:

```
Graph contains 4 strongly connected components.
0
1
2 4 5 6
3 8 7
```

Activity 17: Maze-Teleportation Game

You are designing a game where multiple players are placed randomly in a maze of rooms. Each room contains one or more teleportation devices that the players can use to travel between different parts of the maze. Every teleporter has a value associated with it, which is added to any player's score who uses it. Players alternately take turns traversing the maze until every room has been visited at least once, at which point the round ends and the player with the lowest score is the winner.

You have implemented a system that procedurally generates a new maze at the beginning of every game. Unfortunately, you recently discovered that some of the generated mazes contained loops that a player could use to endlessly reduce their score. You also noticed that players frequently had an unfair advantage, depending on the room they started in. Worst of all, the teleporters are often dispersed in such a way that a player can end up being cut off from the rest of the maze for the duration of the round.

You want to implement a testing procedure to make sure that the generated maze is fair and properly balanced. Your test should first determine whether the maze contains a path that can be used to endlessly lower a player's score. If so, it should output **INVALID MAZE**. If the maze is valid, you should find the lowest scores that can be achieved from each starting point and report them (or **DEAD END**, in the case of a room that has no teleporter).

Additionally, you would like to prevent the possibility of getting stuck in a particular section of the maze, and so your test should also output any groups of rooms from which players are unable to access other portions of the maze.

Expected Input

Each test should receive the following input:

- The number of rooms in the maze

- The number of teleporters in the maze

- The source room, destination room, and the number of points associated with each teleporter

Expected Output

For each test, the program should first determine whether there are any paths in the maze that can be used to infinitely reduce a player's score. If so, it should print a single line: **INVALID MAZE**.

If the maze is valid, your program should output the lowest score that can be achieved, starting from each room (or **DEAD END**, if the room does not have a teleporter), assuming that at least one move is made and that the entire maze can only be traversed once. Finally, your program should list any groups of rooms in which players can get 'stuck' (that is, they are completely restricted from accessing other parts of the maze); for every such group, your program should print the indices of all the rooms within each one on a separate line.

Sample Input and Output

Here are a few sample inputs that should help you understand this problem better:

Input	Output
7 9	INVALID MAZE
0 1 50	
1 0 -10	
1 2 -50	
2 0 0	
3 0 3	
3 4 0	
4 5 1	
5 3 -2	
6 0 -25	

Figure 7.18: Test case 1 for Activity 17

Input	Output
8 16	0: 54
0 3 54	1: -5
1 0 -5	2: -44
1 3 6	3: 91
2 0 -44	4: -44
2 3 -38	5: -33
2 1 -17	6: 18
3 1 96	7: 68
4 0 -44	0 1 3
4 3 15	
5 2 11	
5 0 44	
5 3 91	
6 1 53	
6 2 62	
6 0 77	
7 3 68	

Figure 7.19: Test case 2 for Activity 17

Input	Output
10 17	INVALID MAZE
0 1 90	
1 2 -16	
1 0 79	
1 3 95	
2 3 -89	
3 1 -23	
3 0 -38	
4 1 -34	
5 3 -38	
6 0 59	
6 2 85	
7 4 47	
7 1 85	
7 0 -44	
8 0 -25	
8 2 11	
9 4 -95	

Figure 7.20: Test case 3 for Activity 17

Input	Output
15 26	0: -40
0 4 -40	1: 15
1 6 92	2: 7
2 3 77	3: -70
3 1 61	4: 93
3 6 7	5: 48
3 2 81	6: -77
4 2 93	7: -1
5 2 48	8: -119
6 0 -27	9: -69
6 4 -77	10: -17
7 5 -1	11: -97
8 3 -49	12: -62
8 6 52	13: -89
8 1 70	14: 63
9 6 20	0 6 1 3 2 4
9 0 95	
9 3 1	
10 5 -17	
11 1 75	
11 0 -57	
12 1 -62	
12 4 -5	
13 3 -19	
13 6 17	
13 4 94	
14 1 63	

Figure 7.21: Test case 4 for Activity 17

Input	Output
9 14	0: -3
0 1 5	1: -7
0 3 -3	2: -7
1 2 3	3: 10
1 4 5	4: -12
2 3 -7	5: 0
2 5 8	6: -13
3 7 10	7: 5
4 2 -5	8: 4
5 4 12	3 8 7
5 6 13	
6 2 -6	
6 7 8	
7 8 5	
8 3 4	

Figure 7.22: Test case 5 for Activity 17

Input	Output
18 39	0: 1
0 4 1	1: 1
1 7 1	2: 1
2 0 1	3: 1
2 4 1	4: 1
2 5 1	5: 1
3 5 1	6: 1
3 8 1	7: 1
3 13 1	8: 1
3 14 1	9: 1
3 16 1	10: 1
4 2 1	11: 1
5 4 1	12: 1
5 6 1	13: 1
6 0 1	14: 1
6 4 1	15: 1
7 1 1	16: DEAD END
8 11 1	17: 1
9 5 1	16

Input	Output
9 6 1	8 10 11 12 17
9 15 1	1 7
10 8 1	0 2 4 5 6
10 11 1	
10 12 1	
10 17 1	
11 8 1	
11 10 1	
12 8 1	
12 11 1	
13 1 1	
13 7 1	
14 3 1	
14 6 1	
14 9 1	
14 15 1	
15 13 1	
15 17 1	
17 8 1	
17 10 1	
17 11 1	

Figure 7.23: Test case 6 for Activity 17

Input	Output
13 24	0: -96
0 2 37	1: 33
0 5 -96	2: -133
0 9 72	3: -142
1 5 33	4: -131
2 9 -36	5: 14
3 2 15	6: -164
3 4 -11	7: -111
4 2 46	8: -41
4 7 -20	9: -97
4 10 26	10: -119
5 1 14	11: DEAD END
6 2 -1	12: -64
6 3 83	11
6 10 -45	5 1
7 8 70	
7 12 -47	
8 7 81	
8 11 -41	
9 0 -1	
10 3 23	
10 6 61	
10 7 32	
12 8 40	
12 11 -64	

Figure 7.24: Test case 7 for Activity 17

Activity Guidelines

- Do not get distracted by irrelevant information. Ask yourself what specifically needs to be accomplished.

- The first condition of the problem (determining whether or not the maze contains a path that can infinitely reduce our score) can also be expressed as follows: if the maze is represented as a weighted graph, does a cycle exist on any path that produces a negative sum? Clearly, this is a problem we are well-equipped to handle! You probably also recognize that the second condition (finding the minimum scores that can be acquired by a player starting at a given point) is closely related to the first.

- The last condition is a bit more challenging. Consider how you might redefine being "stuck" in a section of the maze according to the graph terminology we have discussed in this chapter. What might a maze with this property look like?

- Consider drawing one or several of the input graphs on paper. What characterizes the groups of rooms in which a player can get stuck?

> **Note**
>
> The solution to this activity can be found on page 550.

Choosing the Right Approach

By now, it is probably apparent that there is rarely a single 'perfect' approach to implementing graph structures. The characteristics of the data we are representing, combined with the details of the problem we are trying to solve, can make certain approaches unreasonably inefficient, despite the fact that they may be perfectly acceptable under different sets of conditions.

Whenever you are trying to determine whether to use adjacency lists versus matrices, classes/structs versus simple arrays, Bellman-Ford versus Johnson's algorithm, BFS versus DFS, and so on, the final decision should be primarily dependent upon the specifics of the data and how you intend to use it. For example, if you want to find the shortest distances between every pair of nodes in a graph, Johnson's algorithm would be an excellent choice. However, if you only need to sporadically find the shortest distances for a single starting node, Johnson's algorithm would perform quite a bit of unnecessary work, whereas a single call to Bellman-Ford would be sufficient.

It is a beneficial exercise to try writing each of the algorithms we've discussed in this chapter using different forms of graph representations. For example, Bellman-Ford can be just as easily implemented by replacing the vector of **Edge** pointers that we used in the first exercise with an adjacency list and a two-dimensional matrix of edge weights. In some cases, the efficiency potential that's offered by one implementation may only be marginally better than another; at other times, the difference can be quite significant. And then, sometimes, the value of a certain approach has more to do with simplicity and readability than any measurable performance benchmark. Comparing how the performance of various algorithms scales across different data sets and scenarios can be very informative and is often an essential practice in real-world development.

In your endeavors to develop a better understanding of graph theory and implementation, we offer the following recommendations:

- Resist the urge to use the 'copy-paste' approach to implementing a new algorithm. If you do not understand the underlying principles behind why an algorithm works, you will have a very high likelihood of using it incorrectly. Furthermore, even if it functions the way you want it to, it is important to remember that graph implementations are highly specific to the context. Blindly using any algorithm means you will lack the understanding that's necessary to extend the functionality of the solution across different sets of parameters.

- When putting new concepts into practice, avoid relying entirely on abstract, non-contextual implementations. After using a certain algorithm on purely theoretical data, try to modify it to fit some sort of actual data model (even if that data itself is hypothetical). Imagining real scenarios in which you can use your newly acquired algorithmic knowledge will increase the probability that you will know when and how to use it on the job.

Avoid implementing your graph before you have really considered the following:

- Its fundamental purpose(s) and the essential functionality required to accomplish that purpose (that is, the data it describes, the types of queries it needs to perform, how dynamic it needs to be, and so on)

- The most basic components it needs to represent the relevant information about the problem

Failure to evaluate these key ideas could lead to cluttered and overly verbose code, packed with unnecessary data and functions that essentially contribute nothing of value to the actual solution. Planning out the necessary components of your graph prior to writing any code will potentially save you quite a bit of confusion and tedious refactoring.

Ultimately, developing a comprehensive understanding of graph programming is a skill that extends far beyond the scope of simply learning all the right algorithms. A simple web search related to any non-trivial graphing problem will lead to a plethora of deeply analytical research articles, a comparative evaluation of different approaches, and conjectured solutions for which a reasonable implementation has yet to be discovered. As always, consistent practice is the best method for mastering any programming skillset; and graph theory, being a vast and dynamic subject of study, is certainly no exception!

Summary

So far, we have covered graphs in fairly comprehensive detail. You should now have a solid understanding of some of the basic uses of graph theory in software development, as well as an appreciation for how graph-based solutions can be used to encapsulate complex data in a way that allows us to query and manipulate it with relative ease. Having learned the fundamentals of graph structures and traversals in *Chapter 6, Graph Algorithms I*, and then extended them to solve more advanced problems in this chapter, you should now be well-equipped to explore much deeper graph implementations in the future since these basic concepts are at the core of all of them.

Though this chapter does not completely conclude our discussion of graph algorithms for this book, we will now take a break from graphs to explore one of the most powerful and challenging programming techniques in the modern developer's repertoire. Like graph algorithms, the subject we will cover next is so expansive and conceptually abstract that it will span two separate chapters. However, because of its usefulness (and its difficulty), it is a favorite of many software companies during technical interviews.

8

Dynamic Programming I

Learning Objectives

By the end of this chapter, you will be able to:

- Analyze whether the dynamic programming approach can be applied to a given problem
- Compare and choose the right approach between memoization and tabulation
- Choose an appropriate caching solution using memoization
- Analyze a problem using a naive brute-force approach
- Develop a dynamic programming solution by implementing progressively optimized algorithms

In this chapter, you will be introduced to the dynamic programming approach. This chapter will guide you through implementing this approach for solving some well-known problems in computer science.

Introduction

Loved and feared in equal measure by many programmers, **<u>dynamic programming</u>** (**<u>DP</u>**) is a conceptual extension of the divide-and-conquer paradigm that pertains to a specific class of problems. The difficulties involved in dynamic programming problems are multi-faceted and often require creativity, patience, and the ability to visualize abstract concepts. However, the challenges these problems pose frequently have elegant and surprisingly simple solutions, which can provide a programmer with insights that reach far beyond the scope of the immediate task.

In the previous chapter, we discussed several techniques, such as the divide-and-conquer and the greedy approach. These approaches, though quite effective in the right circumstances, will not produce optimal results in certain situations. For example, in the previous chapter, we discussed how Dijkstra's algorithm does not produce optimal results for graphs with negative edge weights, whereas the Bellman-Ford algorithm does. For problems that can be solved recursively, but cannot be solved using the aforementioned techniques, a DP solution may often be the best approach.

DP problems are also encountered in a wide variety of situations. Here are just a few broad examples:

- Combinatorics (counting the number of combinations/permutations of a sequence matching certain criteria)

- Strings/arrays (edit distance, longest common subsequence, longest increasing subsequence, and so on)

- Graphs (shortest path problem)

- Machine learning (speech/face recognition)

Let's begin by understanding the basic idea of dynamic programming.

What Is Dynamic Programming?

The best way to answer this question is by example. To illustrate the purpose of dynamic programming, let's consider the Fibonacci sequence:

```
{ 0, 1, 1, 2, 3, 5, 8, 13, 21, 34, 55, … }
```

By observing the preceding sequence, we can see that, beginning with the third element, each term is equal to the sum of the two preceding terms. This can be simply expressed with the following formula:

```
F(0) = 0
F(1) = 1

...

F(n) = F(n-1) + F(n-2)
```

As we can clearly see, the terms of this sequence have a recursive relationship – the current term, $F(n)$, is based on the results of previous terms, $F(n-1)$ and $F(n-2)$, and thus the preceding equation, that is, $F(n) = F(n-1) + F(n-2)$, is described as the **recurrence relation** of the sequence. The initial terms, $F(0)$ and $F(1)$, are described as the **base cases**, or the points in which a solution is produced without the need to recurse further. These operations are shown in the following figure:

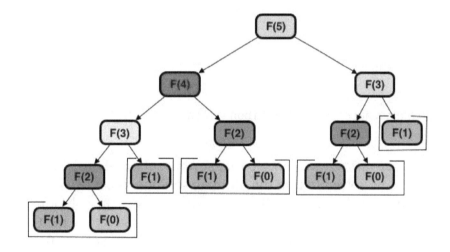

Figure 8.1: Computing the nth term in the Fibonacci sequence

Describing the preceding figure in English might look like this:

```
F5 is equal to:
    F4 + F3, where F4 is equal to:
        F3 + F2, where F3 is equal to:
    .       F2 + F1, where F2 is equal to:
    .   .       F1 + F0, where F1 = 1 and F0 = 0.
    .   .   .
```

- . . ...and F1 = 1.
- . ...and F2 is equal to:
- . F1 + F0, where F1 = 1 and F0 = 0.
...and F3 is equal to:
  F2 + F1, where F2 is equal to:
  - . F1 + F0, where F1 = 1 and F0 = 0
  ...and F1 = 1.

We describe the preceding approach as a **top-down solution** because it begins at the top of the recursion tree (that is, the solution) and traverses down its branches until it reaches the base cases. In C++, this could be written using the following recursive function:

```cpp
int Fibonacci(int n)
{
    if(n < 2)
    {
        return n;
    }
    return Fibonacci(n - 1) + Fibonacci(n - 2);
}
```

By observing the tree further, we can see that several **subproblems**, or intermediate problems that must be solved to find the ultimate solution, must be solved more than once. For example, the solution for $F(2)$ must be found to get the solution for $F(4)$ [$F(3)$ + $F(2)$] and $F(3)$ [$F(2)$ + $F(1)$]. Thus, the Fibonacci sequence is said to exhibit a property known as **overlapping subproblems**. This is one of the defining characteristics that separate a standard divide-and-conquer problem from a dynamic programming problem; in the former, subproblems tend to be unique, whereas in the latter, the same subproblems must be solved repeatedly.

We can also see that several of the solution branches are completely identical to each other. For example, finding the solution for $F(2)$ is going to require the same set of calculations, regardless of whether you need it to solve $F(4)$ or $F(3)$. This demonstrates the second defining characteristic of dynamic programming problems, which is known as the optimal substructure. A problem is said to exhibit an **optimal substructure** when the optimal solution to the overall problem can be formed through some combination of the optimal solutions of its subproblems.

For a problem to be solvable using dynamic programming, it must possess these two properties. Because of the overlapping subproblems property, the complexity of these problems tends to increase exponentially as the input increases; however, exploiting the optimal substructure property makes it possible to reduce the complexity significantly. So, in essence, the purpose of DP is to devise a method of caching previous solutions as a means to avoid the repeated calculation of previously solved subproblems.

Memoization – The Top-Down Approach

No, this is not "memorization," though that would also describe this technique quite accurately. Using memoization, we can reformulate the top-down solution we described previously to make use of the optimal substructure property exhibited by the Fibonacci sequence. Our program logic will essentially be the same as it was before, only now, after having found the solution at every step, we will cache the results in an array, indexed according to the current value of n (in this problem, n represents the **state** or set of parameters defining the current recursive branch). At the very beginning of each function call, we will check to see whether we have a solution available in the cache for state $F(n)$. If so, we will simply return the cached value:

```
const int UNKNOWN = -1;
const int MAX_SIZE = 100000;


vector<int> memo(MAX_SIZE, UNKNOWN);


int Fibonacci(int n)
{
    if(n < 2)
    {
        return n;
    }
    if(memo[n] != UNKNOWN)
    {
        return memo[n];
    }
```

```
    int result = Fibonacci(n - 1) + Fibonacci(n - 2);
    memo[n] = result;


    return result;
}
```

The recursion tree now looks like this:

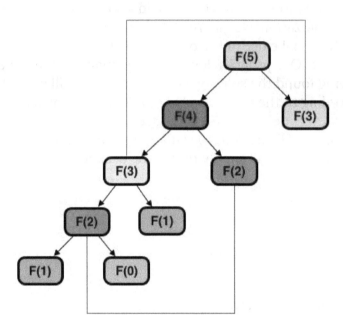

Figure 8.2: Computing the nth term in the Fibonacci sequence using cached solutions

By doing this, we have eliminated quite a bit of redundant work. This technique of recursively caching solutions in a top-down manner is known as **memoization**, and can essentially be employed for any DP problem, assuming the following are true:

1. You can devise a caching scheme that exploits the similarity of different states while preserving their uniqueness.

2. You can accumulate the solutions for the requisite subproblems before exceeding the available stack space.

The first point means that the method of indexing results for later use should be both valid and useful. In order for a caching scheme to be valid, it must only be considered a match for states whose solutions are derived from the same series of subproblems; in order for it to be useful, it must not be so state-specific that it cannot be effectively used (for example, if every subproblem is assigned a unique index in the cache, the conditional `"if(memo[KEY] != UNKNOWN)"` will never be true).

The second point refers to the possibility of causing a stack overflow error, which is a fundamental limitation of any top-down approach if the number of recursive calls is likely to be very high. A stack overflow occurs when a program exceeds the allotted amount of memory that's available on the call stack. Depending on the nature of a given problem, it is possible that the depth of recursion that's required may prevent memoization from being a viable option; as always, it is quite beneficial to assess the potential complexity of the task at hand before choosing an approach.

Memoization is frequently a decent optimization method for DP problems. However, in many cases, a better option is available, which we will study in the following section.

Tabulation – the Bottom-Up Approach

The *heart* of dynamic programming is tabulation, which is the inverse approach to memoization. In fact, though the term *dynamic programming* is sometimes applied to both memoization and tabulation, its use is generally assumed to refer specifically to the latter.

The standard implementation of tabulation consists of storing the solutions for the base cases and then iteratively filling a table with the solutions for every subproblem, which can then be reused to find the solutions for other subproblems. Tabulated solutions are generally considered to be a bit harder to conceptualize than memoized ones because the state of each subproblem must be represented in a way that can be expressed iteratively.

A tabulated solution to computing the Fibonacci sequence would look like this:

```
int Fibonacci(int n)
{
        vector<int> DP(n + 1, 0);

        DP[1] = 1;

        for(int i = 2; i <= n; i++)
        {
```

```
            DP[i] = DP[i-1] + DP[i-2];
        }
        return DP[n];
    }
}
```

In the Fibonacci example, the state is quite simple since it's one-dimensional and unconditional – the formula always holds that, for any n greater than 1, F(n) = F(n-1) + F(n-2). However, DP problems often contain several dimensions that define a given state and may have multiple conditions that affect how states transition between each other. In such cases, determining how to represent the current state may require a fair amount of creativity, in addition to a comprehensive understanding of the problem.

The advantages of tabulation, however, are significant. In addition to the fact that tabulated solutions frequently tend to be much more efficient in terms of memory, they also produce a complete lookup table encompassing every given state. Therefore, if you are likely to receive queries about any state of the problem, tabulation is likely to be your best option.

Interestingly, any problem that can be solved with memoization can theoretically be reformulated into a tabulated solution, and vice versa. Using the former can often provide immense insight into how to approach the latter. Over the next few sections, we will explore several classical examples of dynamic programming problems and demonstrate how employing multiple approaches (beginning with naive brute force) can lead you to the level of understanding that's required for the tabulated solution.

Subset Sum Problem

Imagine that you are implementing the logic for a digital cash register. Whenever a customer needs change, you would like to display a message that tells the cashier whether or not the money currently in the register can be combined in some way so that its sum is equal to the amount of change required. For example, if a product costs $7.50 and the customer pays $10.00, the message would report whether the money in the register can be used to produce exactly $2.50 in change.

Let's say that the register currently contains ten quarters (10 x $0.25), four dimes (4 x $0.10), and six nickels (6 x $0.05). We can easily conclude that the target sum of $2.50 can be formed in the following ways:

```
10 quarters                      -> $2.50


9 quarters, 2 dimes, 1 nickel  -> $2.25 + $0.20 + $0.05
9 quarters, 1 dime,  3 nickels -> $2.25 + $0.10 + $0.15
```

```
9 quarters, 5 nickels               -> $2.25 + $0.25


8 quarters, 4 dimes, 2 nickels -> $2.00 + $0.40 + $0.10

8 quarters, 3 dimes, 4 nickels -> $2.00 + $0.30 + $0.20

8 quarters, 2 dimes, 6 nickels -> $2.00 + $0.20 + $0.30
```

With these parameters, the problem is rather straightforward and can be solved by simply trying all the available combinations of money until a sum matching $2.50 is found. But what if the change that's required is $337.81, and the register contains 100 banknotes/coins divided into denominations of $20.00, $10.00, $5.00, $1.00, $0.25, $0.10, $0.05, and $0.01? We can clearly see that trying every possible sum becomes quite impractical as the complexity increases. This is an example of a classic problem known as the subset sum problem.

In its most basic form, the **subset sum problem** asks the following question: given a set of non-negative integers, **S**, and an integer, **x**, is there a subset of **S**'s elements whose sum is equal to **x**? Take a look at the following example:

```
S = { 13, 79, 45, 29 }

x = 42 -> True (13 + 29)

x = 25 -> False
```

Using the preceding set as an example, we can find the following 16 subsets:

```
{ }


{ 13 }
{ 79 }
{ 45 }
{ 29 }


{ 13, 79 }
{ 13, 45 }
{ 13, 29 }
{ 79, 45 }
{ 79, 29 }
{ 45, 29 }
```

```
{ 13, 79, 45 }
{ 13, 79, 29 }
{ 13, 45, 29 }
{ 79, 45, 29 }
```

```
{ 13, 79, 45, 29 }
```

By listing the total amount of subsets that can be produced for sets of different sizes, we get the following numbers:

```
0: 1
1: 2
2: 4
3: 8
4: 16
5: 32
6: 64
7: 128
...
```

From this list, we can deduce that the total number of subsets that can be formed from a set of size **n** is equal to 2^n, which demonstrates that the number of subsets to consider increases exponentially with the size of n. Assuming the number of elements in S is small, say 10 elements or less, a brute-force approach to this problem could find the solution rather quickly; but if we reconsider the example of a cash register containing 100 different banknotes/coins, the size of S would be equal to 100, which would require exploring 1,267,650,600,228,229,401,496,703,205,376 subsets!

Solving the Subset Sum Problem – Step 1: Evaluating the Need for DP

Our first step when faced with a problem like this is to determine whether it can (and/or should) be solved with DP. To reiterate, a problem is solvable with DP if it has the following properties:

- **Overlapping subproblems**: Like the standard divide-and-conquer approach, the final solution can be derived by combining the solutions of smaller subproblems in some way; in contrast to divide and conquer, however, certain subproblems will be encountered multiple times.

- **Optimal substructure**: The optimal solution for a given problem can be produced by the optimal solutions of its subproblems.

Let's analyze the preceding example in terms of whether or not it possesses these characteristics:

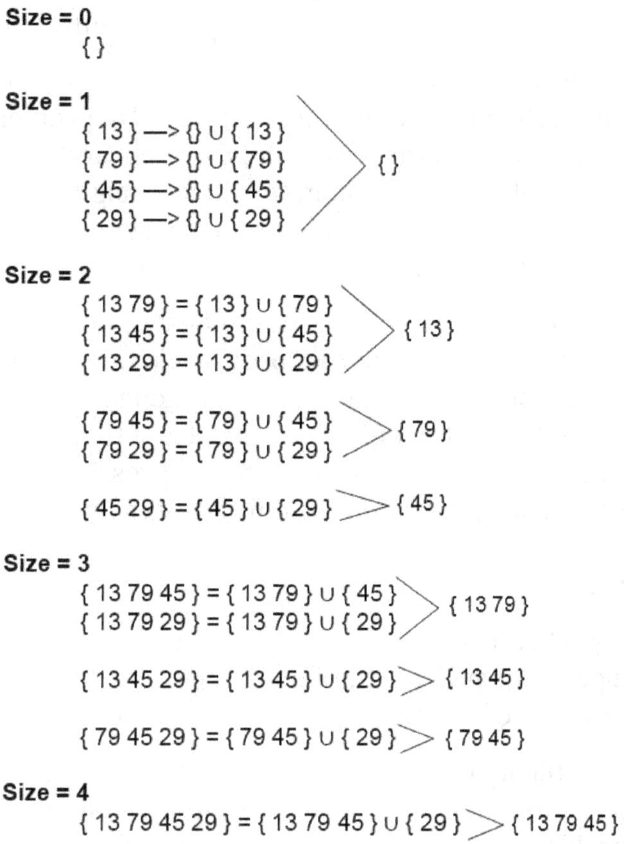

Size = 0

{ }

Size = 1

{ 13 } —> {} ∪ { 13 }
{ 79 } —> {} ∪ { 79 }
{ 45 } —> {} ∪ { 45 }   } { }
{ 29 } —> {} ∪ { 29 }

Size = 2

{ 13 79 } = { 13 } ∪ { 79 }
{ 13 45 } = { 13 } ∪ { 45 }   } { 13 }
{ 13 29 } = { 13 } ∪ { 29 }

{ 79 45 } = { 79 } ∪ { 45 }   } { 79 }
{ 79 29 } = { 79 } ∪ { 29 }

{ 45 29 } = { 45 } ∪ { 29 }   > { 45 }

Size = 3

{ 13 79 45 } = { 13 79 } ∪ { 45 }   } { 13 79 }
{ 13 79 29 } = { 13 79 } ∪ { 29 }

{ 13 45 29 } = { 13 45 } ∪ { 29 }   > { 13 45 }

{ 79 45 29 } = { 79 45 } ∪ { 29 }   > { 79 45 }

Size = 4

{ 13 79 45 29 } = { 13 79 45 } ∪ { 29 }   > { 13 79 45 }

Figure 8.3: Optimal substructure and overlapping subproblems

Reformatting the collection of subsets as shown clearly illustrates how each new subset of size n is formed by appending a single new element to a subset of size **n - 1**. This is the optimal approach for constructing a new subset and holds true for every subset of size greater than 0. Thus, the subset sum problem has an **optimal substructure**. We can also see that several subsets are derived from the same "subsubset" (for example, both { 13 79 45 } and { 13 79 29 } are based on { 13 79 }). Therefore, the problem also has **overlapping subproblems**.

Having satisfied both of our criteria, we can conclude that this problem can be solved with dynamic programming.

Step 2 – Defining the States and the Base Cases

Having determined that this is a DP problem, we now must determine what constitutes a state within the context of this problem. In other words, in terms of the question that we are trying to answer, what makes one possible solution different from another?

Though it is generally advisable to consider these aspects of the problem early in the process, it is often quite difficult to define the states of a DP problem without having a clear understanding of how the ultimate result is formed, and thus it is often quite helpful to start by implementing a solution in the most straightforward way possible. Therefore, we will develop our understanding of the subset sum problem's base case(s) and states by solving it in two different ways that are much simpler to implement.

Throughout our exploration of dynamic programming, we will consider a total of four different approaches to each problem: **brute force**, **backtracking**, **memoization**, and **tabulation**. As with any DP problem, all of these approaches are capable of producing the correct result, but the first three quickly demonstrate their limitations as the size of the input increases. Nevertheless, implementing progressively optimized solutions in this way can be used to great effect when tackling any dynamic programming problem.

Step 2.a: Brute Force

Despite its inefficiency, a brute-force solution can be quite informative in developing an understanding of the problem at hand. Implementing brute-force approaches can be an essential step in the process of forming a DP solution for several reasons:

- **Simplicity**: The simplicity of writing a solution without any consideration of its efficiency can be an excellent way to develop an understanding of the fundamental aspects of the problem; it can also lead to insights about the problem's nature that may otherwise be missed in the act of trying to comprehend its complexity without sufficient context.

- **The certainty of solution correctness**: Oftentimes, a particularly complex DP solution will require quite a bit of redesign as the problem is better understood. Because of this, it is essential to have a way to compare your solution's output to the correct answer.

- **Ability to visualize the subproblems**: A brute-force solution will generate every potential solution and then choose the ones that meet the criteria of the problem. This provides an effective means for visualizing how a correct solution is formed, which can then be inspected for essential patterns that can be used in later approaches.

The following exercise demonstrates the implementation of the brute-force approach.

Exercise 36: Solving the Subset Sum Problem by Using the Brute-Force Approach

In this exercise, we shall find a solution to the subset sum problem using the brute-force approach. Let's get started:

1. Let's begin by including the following headers (and the **std** namespace for convenience):

```
#include <iostream>
#include <vector>
#include <algorithm>

using namespace std;
```

2. Additionally, let's define a preprocessor constant called **DEBUG** and a macro called **PRINT**, which will print to **stderr** only if **DEBUG** is not zero:

```
#define DEBUG 0

#if DEBUG
#define PRINT(x) cerr << x
#else
#define PRINT(x)
#endif
```

3. We will now declare a new function, **SubsetSum_BruteForce()**, that takes two arguments – an array of integers, **set**, and an integer, **sum** – and returns a Boolean:

```
bool SubsetSum_BruteForce(vector<int> set, int sum)
{
    ......
}
```

4. Now, let's declare another function, **GetAllSubsets()**, which takes four arguments – two integer vectors, **set** and **subset**; an integer; **index**; and a three-dimensional vector of integers called **allSubsets** (passed by reference). We will use this function to generate all subsets of S recursively:

```
void GetAllSubsets(vector<int> set, vector<int> subset, int index,
vector<vector<vector<int>>> &allSubsets)
{
    // Terminate if the end of the set is reached
    if(index == set.size())
```

```
    {
        // Add the accumulated subset to the results, indexed by size
        allSubsets[subset.size()].push_back(subset);

        return;
    }

    // Continue without adding element to subset
    GetAllSubsets(set, subset, index + 1, allSubsets);

    // Add element to subset
    subset.push_back(set[index]);
    GetAllSubsets(set, subset, index + 1, allSubsets);
}
```

5. Returning to our **SubsetSum_BruteForce()** function, we can now declare **allSubsets** and call the function:

```
bool SubsetSum_BruteForce(vector<int> set, int target)
{
    vector<vector<vector<int>>> allSubsets(set.size() + 1);

    GetAllSubsets(set, {}, 0, allSubsets);

    ......
```

6. Now, we can iterate through each subset and compare its sum to **target**, returning **true** if a match is found:

```
for(int size = 0; size <= set.size(); size++)
{
    PRINT("SIZE = " << size << endl);

    for(auto subset : allSubsets[size])
    {
        int sum = 0;

        PRINT("\t{ ");

        for(auto number : subset)
        {
            PRINT(number << " ");

            sum += number;
```

```
            }
            PRINT("} = " << sum << endl);

            if(sum == target) return true;
        }
    }
```

7. If a matching sum is not found after checking every subset, we return **false**:

```
    ......

        return false;
    }
```

8. Now, in the **main()** function, let's define our set and target as follows:

```
    int main()
    {
        vector<int> set = { 13, 79, 45, 29 };
        int target = 58;

    ......
    }
```

9. We can now call **SubsetSum_BruteForce()** with these inputs like so:

```
    bool found = SubsetSum_BruteForce(set, target);

    if(found)
    {
        cout << "Subset with sum " << target << " was found in the set." <<
    endl;
    }
    else
    {
        cout << "Subset with sum " << target << " was not found in the set."
    << endl;
    }
```

10. Upon running the preceding code, you should see the following output:

```
    Subset with sum 58 was found in the set.
```

11. Now, let's set **target** to a sum that is not found in the set:

```
    int target = 1000000;
```

12. Running the program again should produce the following output:

```
Subset with sum 1000000 was not found in the set.
```

13. Finally, let's redefine our **DEBUG** constant to 1:

```
#define DEBUG 1
```

14. Running the program now will produce the following output:

```
SIZE = 0
    { } = 0
SIZE = 1
    { 29 } = 29
    { 45 } = 45
    { 79 } = 79
    { 13 } = 13
SIZE = 2
    { 45 29 } = 74
    { 79 29 } = 108
    { 79 45 } = 124
    { 13 29 } = 42
    { 13 45 } = 58
    { 13 79 } = 92
SIZE = 3
    { 79 45 29 } = 153
    { 13 45 29 } = 87
    { 13 79 29 } = 121
    { 13 79 45 } = 137
SIZE = 4
    { 13 79 45 29 } = 166
Subset with sum 1000000 was not found in the set.
```

Thus, we are able to find the required subset using the brute-force approach. Note that we are basically trying out every possibility in order to find the solution. In the following section, we shall apply one layer of optimization over it.

Step 2.b: Optimizing Our Approach – Backtracking

Clearly, the brute-force approach leaves a lot to be desired. In terms of performance, it is about as inefficient as it possibly could be. By indiscriminately checking every possible subset, we consider options long after the point where we could determine that they will never lead to a solution (for example, subsets with sums exceeding the target). To improve our algorithm, we can utilize **backtracking** to exclude all the branches of subproblems that are guaranteed to be invalid.

The main advantage of implementing a backtracking solution before attempting to use DP is that it requires us to determine the base case(s) and intermediate recursive states of the problem. As we defined earlier in this chapter, a base case is a condition in a recursive function that does not rely on further recursion to produce an answer. For further clarification, consider the problem of calculating the factorial of a number (the factorial of a number, n, is equivalent to $n * (n-1) * (n-2) * (n-3) ... * 1$). We could code a C++ function that accomplishes this as follows:

```cpp
int Factorial(int n)
{
    // Base case - stop recursing
    if(n == 1)
    {
        return 1;
    }

    // Recurse until base case is reached
    return n * Factorial(n - 1);
}
```

The structure of this recursive function can be illustrated like so:

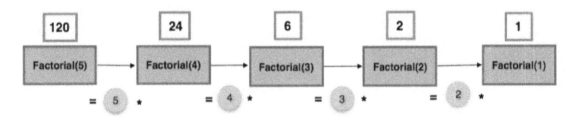

Figure 8.4: Recursively calculating the Nth factorial

The **n = 1** condition is the base case because that is the point at which the solution can be returned without recursing further.

In the subset sum problem, one way to define our base cases would be as follows:

```
If sum of a given subset is equal to target : TRUE
```

Otherwise:

```
    - If sum is greater than target : FALSE
    - If end of set is reached : FALSE
```

Now that we have established base cases, we need to define our intermediate states. Using our brute-force algorithm's output as a reference, we can analyze how subsets of each size group are formed to plot out our state transitions:

```
Base case -> { } [SUM = 0]


{ } -> { 13 } [0 + 13 = 13]
       { 79 } [0 + 79 = 79]
       { 45 } [0 + 45 = 45]
       { 29 } [0 + 29 = 29]
```

Of course, the size **0** and size **1** states are the simplest to understand. We begin with an empty set and we can add any of the elements to it in order to create all subsets of size 1.

```
{ 13 } -> { 13 79 } [13 + 79 = 92]
          { 13 45 } [13 + 45 = 58]
          { 13 29 } [13 + 29 = 42]


{ 79 } -> { 79 45 } [79 + 45 = 124]
          { 79 29 } [79 + 29 = 108]


{ 45 } -> { 45 29 } [45 + 29 = 74]
```

We can follow the same line of logic for size 2 subsets. Simply take each subset of size 1 and append every element whose index is greater than the highest-indexed element already in the subset. This is essentially the approach we took in our brute-force implementation; however, this time, we will consider the sum of each subset as we process them, and terminating them when the current sum exceeds the target:

```
TARGET = 58

SIZE = 2

      { 13 } -> { 13 79 } (92)
                { 13 45 } (58) [*]
                { 13 29 } (42)

      { 79 } -> { 79 45 } (124)
                { 79 29 } (108)

      { 45 } -> { 45 29 } (74)


SIZE = 3
      { 13 79 } -> { 13 79 45 } (137)
                   { 13 79 29 } (121)

      { 13 45 } -> { 13 45 29 } (87)

      { 79 45 } -> { 79 45 29 } (153)

SIZE = 4

      { 13 79 45 } -> { 13 79 45 29 } (166)
```

Figure 8.5: Eliminating values that exceed the target

When **target** is equal to **58**, we can see that none of the subsets of size 3 or 4 need to be considered. Thus, we can describe our intermediate state transition as follows:

```
for element of set at index i and subset ss:


    If sum of ss with set[i] is less than or equal to target:


        1) Append set[i] to ss

        2) Increment i


        Next state -> (i = i + 1, ss = ss U set[i])


    In any case:


        1) Do not append set[i] to ss

        2) Increment i


        Next state -> (i = i + 1, ss = ss)
```

Now, we should ask the following questions:

- What is the minimal amount of data needed to represent this state?
- How can we reformulate the preceding logic to remove unnecessary information?

Consider the specific problem we are trying to solve: finding whether a subset of elements exists within the set whose sum is equal to the target. According to the problem description, our task does not require that we produce the actual subsets, but only their sums. So, our pseudocode could be more succinctly expressed as follows:

```
for element of set at index i and its sum as sum:


    If sum plus set[i] is less than or equal to target:


        1) Add value of set[i] to sum

        2) Increment i
```

```
    Next state -> (i = i + 1, sum = sum + set[i])
```

In any case:

```
    1) Do not add value of set[i] to sum

    2) Increment i
```

```
    Next state -> (i = i + 1, sum = sum)
```

Using this new approach, we can essentially represent each state transition with only two integers, **sum** and **i**, eliminating the need to store 2^n subset arrays in the worst case. Furthermore, we can remove the need to keep track of the target value by inverting the problem (that is, starting at **target** and subtracting **set[i]** at each step). As a final optimization, we can sort the set before calling the function, which allows us to determine that there are no other valid possibilities as soon as the sum exceeds the target. We'll implement this in C++ in the following exercise.

Exercise 37: Solving the Subset Sum Problem by Using Backtracking

In this exercise, we shall solve a problem similar to the one demonstrated in *Exercise 36, Solving the Subset Sum Problem by Using the Brute-Force Approach*, but using a backtracking approach and a more complex input to highlight the differences. Let's get started:

1. To implement the backtracking solution for the subset sum problem, we define a function called **SubsetSum_Backtracking()**, as follows:

    ```
    bool SubsetSum_Backtracking(vector<int> &set, int sum, int i)
    {
        ......
    }
    ```

2. As is often the case in recursive functions, we define our base cases at the very beginning:

    ```
    // The sum has been found
    if(sum == 0)
    {
        return true;
    }

    // End of set is reached, or sum would be exceeded beyond this point
    if(i == set.size() || set[i] > sum)
    ```

```
{
    return false;
}
```

3. At each step, our options are to add the current element's value to the sum, or to keep the sum as-is. We can condense this logic into one line like so:

```
// Case 1: Add to sum
// Case 2: Leave as-is

return SubsetSum_Backtracking(set, sum - set[i], i + 1)
    || SubsetSum_Backtracking(set, sum, i + 1);
```

4. Returning to **main**, let's sort the set and add our call to **SubsetSum_Backtracking()** underneath the call to **SubsetSum_BruteForce()**:

```
sort(set.begin(), set.end());

bool found;

found = SubsetSum_BruteForce(set, target);
found = SubsetSum_Backtracking(set, target, 0);
```

5. For the sake of testing, we will implement a function that will display the time each approach takes to find the solution. First, we will need to include the **<time.h>** and **<iomanip>** headers:

```
#include <iostream>
#include <vector>
#include <algorithm>
#include <time.h>
#include <iomanip>
```

6. We will also define an array of strings called **types**, which we will use to label the results of each approach:

```
vector<string> types =
{
    "BRUTE FORCE",
    "BACKTRACKING",
    "MEMOIZATION",
    "TABULATION"
};

const int UNKNOWN = INT_MAX;
```

7. Now, we will write another function, **GetTime()**, that takes a reference to a **clock_t** object called **timer** and a **string type**, and then returns **void**:

```
void GetTime(clock_t &timer, string type)
{
    // Subtract timer value from current time to get time elapsed
    timer = clock() - timer;

    // Display seconds elapsed
    cout << "TIME TAKEN USING " << type << ": " << fixed << setprecision(5)
<< (float)timer / CLOCKS_PER_SEC << endl;

    timer = clock(); // Reset timer
}
```

8. Now, let's rewrite the **main()** function so that we can perform each function call sequentially and compare the time taken by each approach:

```
int main()
{
    vector<int> set = { 13, 79, 45, 29 };
    int target = 58;
    int tests = 2;

    clock timer = clock();

    sort(set.begin(), set.end());

    for(int i = 0; i < tests; i++)
    {
        bool found;

        switch(i)
        {
            case 0: found = SubsetSum_BruteForce(set, target); break;
            case 1: found = SubsetSum_Backtracking(set, target, 0); break;
        }

        if(found)
        {
            cout << "Subset with sum " << target << " was found in the
set." << endl;
        }
```

```
            else
            {
                cout << "Subset with sum " << target << " was not found in the
    set." << endl;
            }
            GetTime(timer, types[i]);
            cout << endl;
        }
        return 0;
    }
```

9. Finally, let's redefine our input to highlight the difference in efficiency between the two approaches:

```
vector<int> set = { 16, 1058, 22, 13, 46, 55, 3, 92, 47, 7, 98, 367, 807,
106, 333, 85, 577, 9, 3059 };

int target = 6076;
```

10. Your output will produce something along the lines of the following:

```
Subset with sum 6076 was found in the set.
TIME TAKEN USING BRUTE FORCE: 0.89987

Subset with sum 6076 was found in the set.
TIME TAKEN USING BACKTRACKING: 0.00078
```

> **Note**
>
> The actual values for the time taken would vary depending on your system. Please note the difference in the values.

As you can see, in this particular case, the answer was found over 1,000 times faster using the backtracking approach. In the following section, we shall optimize this solution further by making use of caching.

Step 3: Memoization

Though significantly better than brute force, the backtracking solution is still far from ideal. Consider a case where the target sum is high and not in the set – if the target is greater than or equal to the sum of every element in the set, we could easily determine the result by calculating the total in advance and checking that the target is within the valid range. However, if the target sum is just slightly under this amount, our algorithm will still be forced to explore practically every possibility before finishing.

To demonstrate this difference, try running your code from the previous exercise using **6799** as the target (exactly 1 less than the total sum of all the elements of the set). On the author's machine, the backtracking solution took about 0.268 seconds on average to produce the result – nearly 350 times longer than the average time taken with the target value used in the exercise.

Thankfully, we already have all the information we need to devise a top-down solution while utilizing memoization. Even better, we hardly have to modify our previous approach at all to implement it!

Devising a Caching Scheme

The most important aspect of using memoization is to define a caching scheme. Caching results for memoized solutions can be done in a number of ways, but the most common are as follows:

- Simple arrays, with states represented by numerical indices

- Hash tables/maps, with states represented by descriptive strings that are hashed using built-in language features

- Hash tables/maps, with states represented by hash values that are created using an original hashing formula

The choice to make here is largely context-dependent, but here are some general guidelines:

- Arrays/vectors that are accessed by a numerical index tend to be much faster than maps, which must locate a given key in the map in order to determine whether or not it has already been cached.

- Even when states can be represented as integers, if the cache keys are quite large, the memory requirements of an array large enough to encompass them may be unreasonable. In this case, maps are a better option.

- Hash tables (for example, `std::unordered_map`) tend to be much faster than standard map/dictionary structures for locating and retrieving keys (but are still slower than arrays).

- `std::map` is much more versatile than `std::unordered_map` in terms of what types of data can be used as keys. Although `std::unordered_map` can technically offer the same functionality, it requires the programmer to create their own hashing function for data types it is not equipped to store as keys by default.

As you may recall from the introduction to this chapter, a caching scheme should be as follows:

- **Valid**: Cache keys must be represented in a way that avoids collisions between different states that are not used to solve the same set of subproblems.

- **Worthwhile/useful**: If your caching scheme is so specific that it never actually produces any "hits", then it essentially accomplishes nothing.

In the subset sum problem, we may mistakenly come to believe that failing to find the target from a state with a given **sum** value means that it would be impossible to get a true result from any other state with the same sum. Therefore, we may decide to cache every solution based solely on the value of **sum** (that is, `if(memo[sum] != UNKNOWN) return memo[sum];`). This is an example of an invalid caching scheme because it fails to take into account the fact that there may be multiple ways to reach the same sum within the same set, as shown here:

```
{ 1 5 6 2 3 9 }


Sum of { 1 5 } = 6
Sum of { 6 } = 6
Sum of { 1 2 3 } = 6
```

Suppose the target value is **8** in the preceding example. If the third case is encountered first, `memo[6]` would be set to **false**, which is obviously incorrect since the target can be reached from both of the other cases by including the 4th element (**2**).

An example of a useless memoization scheme would be one where the keys are equal to the indices of the subset because every possible state will contain a completely unique key; as a result, states that are formed from the same set of subproblems will not trigger a cache hit.

If you are unsure about the efficacy of your caching scheme, it can be useful to store a counter that increments on every cache hit. If the final value of this counter is equal to 0, or is very low relative to the number of states you have to consider, you can conclude that your caching scheme needs revision.

We shall explore the implementation of memoization with the use of a vector for caching.

Exercise 38: Solving the Subset Sum Problem by Using Memoization

In this exercise, we shall try to implement the same solution that we implemented in *Exercise 37, Solving the Subset Sum Problem by Using Backtracking*, but with the addition of memoization. Let's get started:

1. We will now create another function called **SubsetSum_Memoization()**. The definition for this function will be identical to **SubsetSub_Backtracking()**, except that it will include a reference to a two-dimensional integer vector called **memo**:

```
bool SubsetSum_Memoization(vector<int> &set, int sum, int         i,
vector<vector<int>> &memo)
{
    ......
}
```

2. Much of our code for this function will look quite similar to the backtracking approach. For example, our base cases will be defined exactly like they were previously:

```
if(sum == 0)
{
    return true;
}

if(i == set.size() || set[i] > sum)
{
    return false;
}
```

3. Now, the pivotal difference is that after the base cases, rather than immediately investigating the next two states, we check the **memo** table for cached results:

```
// Is this state's solution cached?
if(memo[i][sum] == UNKNOWN)
{
    // If not, find the solution for this state and cache it

    bool append = SubsetSum_Memoization(set, sum - set[i], i + 1, memo);
    bool ignore = SubsetSum_Memoization(set, sum, i + 1, memo);

    memo[i][sum] = append || ignore;
}
// Return cached value
return memo[i][sum];
```

4. Now, we should insert a call to **SubsetSum_Memoization()** in the **main()** function:

```
int tests = 3;

for(int i = 0; i < tests; i++)
{
    bool found;

    switch(i)
    {
        case 0: found = SubsetSum_BruteForce(set, target); break;

        case 1: found = SubsetSum_Backtracking(set, target, 0); break;

        case 2:
        {
            // Initialize memoization table
            vector<vector<int>> memo(set.size(), vector<int>(7000,
UNKNOWN));

            found = SubsetSum_Memoization(set, target, 0, memo);
            break;
        }
    }

    if(found)
    {
```

```
            cout << "Subset with sum " << target << " was found in the set."
    << endl;
        }
        else
        {
            cout << "Subset with sum " << target << " was not found in the
    set." << endl;
        }
        GetTime(timer, types[i]);
        cout << endl;
    }
```

5. Now, let's define **target** as **6799** and run our code. You should see an output similar to this:

```
Subset with sum 6799 was not found in the set.
TIME TAKEN USING BRUTE FORCE: 1.00100

Subset with sum 6799 was not found in the set.
TIME TAKEN USING BACKTRACKING: 0.26454

Subset with sum 6799 was not found in the set.
TIME TAKEN USING MEMOIZATION: 0.00127
```

Note

The actual values for time taken would vary depending on your system. Please note the difference in the values.

We can see from the output that caching has optimized our problem by an exponential factor.

Step 4: Tabulation

So far, we have implemented three different algorithmic approaches to solving the subset sum problem, each of which has a significant improvement over the one preceding it. However, let's say that we wanted a list of every possible subset sum in a given set. We would have to run our algorithm repeatedly for each sum, from 1 to the total sum of the entire set. For situations such as these, tabulation is often the only efficient option.

Implementing an iterative tabulated solution to a problem like this is often rather hard to conceptualize. Whereas recursive formulations of a problem lend themselves well to multidimensional states and branching conditions, a tabulated solution has to somehow condense the layers of complexity into a simple set of iterations using the standard `for`/`while` loops:

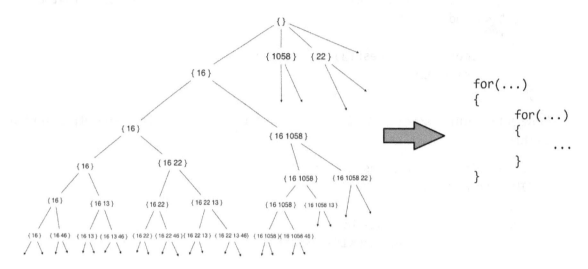

Figure 8.6: Depiction of how the complexity of the subset sum problem's recursive structure is reduced in the tabulated DP solution

There are several methods for tackling this reduction, but ultimately it tends to come down to whether or not you understand the problem well enough to make the correct generalizations.

Like memoization, the first goal after defining the base case(s) and states of the problem is to develop a scheme for storing the solutions for different states. Typically, tabulated approaches use simple arrays/vectors for this purpose. We have already looked at an example of a very simple DP table in the calculation of the Fibonacci sequence:

```
F[n] = F[n - 1] + F[n - 2];
```

Earlier in this chapter, we also discussed how to calculate factorials recursively. A bottom-up approach to filling the table for that problem would look like this:

```
factorial[n] = factorial[n - 1] * n;
```

These are very simple examples because they only contain a single dimension and no conditional logic. Each state has a consistent, predictable formula from beginning to end.

The primary difference between those examples and the subset sum problem is that the minimal way to represent each state uniquely in the latter requires two dimensions – the index in the set and the current sum.

Let's consider some of the insights we have gained about this problem in greater depth:

- Each possible subset of size **k** can be formed by taking new elements and appending them onto every subset of size **k - 1**.

- If a solution has been found at index **i** with a sum value of **x**, then any sequence of state transitions that eventually lead to that same set of conditions will produce an identical result:

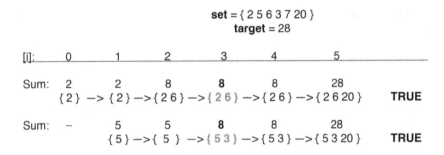

set = { 2 5 6 3 7 20 }
target = 28

[i]:	0	1	2	3	4	5	
Sum:	2	2	8	8	8	28	
	{2} –> {2} –>{26} –>{26} –>{26} –>{26 20}						**TRUE**
Sum:	–	5	5	8	8	28	
	{5} –>{ 5 } –>{5 3} –>{5 3} –>{5 3 20}						**TRUE**

Figure 8.7: Multiple paths with the same sum value on the same index value

Both of these recursive paths have a sum value equal to **8** and an index value equal to **3** at the states indicated in red which, due the optimal substructure of the subset sum problem, means that the solution for that state only needs to be found once – its result will be the same any time those conditions are arrived at, regardless of what occurred before.

With these facts in mind, we can essentially invert our top-down approach to develop the bottom-up approach.

Top-down logic:

1. Start at the target sum and the first index of the set.

2. Iterate through the set:

    - If the sum is reduced to zero, the result is **TRUE**.

    - If the end of the set is reached or the target is exceeded, the result is **FALSE**.

    - Otherwise, you can either subtract the current value from the sum or ignore it.

3. If the target can be found from state **S**, where the sum is equal to **x** and the index is equal to **i**, then the target can also be found from any earlier state that eventually leads to the state **S**.

Bottom-up logic:

1. Start with sum and index values equal to `0`.

2. Iterate through the set:

   - If a sum equal to `x` can be found between indices `0` and `i`, then a sum equal to `x` can also be found between indices `0` and `i+1`.

   - If a sum equal to `x` can be found between indices `0` and `i`, then a sum equal to `x` + `set[i]` can be found between indices `0` and `i+1`.

In terms of how the table is filled, the top-down approach can be described as follows:

If the sum equals `x` and index equals `i` at state S1, the value of `memo(i, x) = true` if either of the following occurs:

   - The target can be found from state S2 (where the sum equals `x` - `set[i]` and index equals `i + 1`), OR...

   - The target can be found from state S3 (where the sum equals `x` and index equals `i + 1`)

      - Otherwise, `memo(i, x) = false`.

The bottom-up version of this logic would be as follows:

If the sum equals `x` and index equals `i`, the value of `DP(i, x) = true` if either of the following occurs:

   - `x` is less than the value of `set[i]` and `DP(i-1, x) = true`

   - `x` is greater than, or equal to, the value of `set[i]` and `DP(i-1, sum) = true` OR `DP(i-1, sum - set[i]) = true`

      - Otherwise, `DP(i, x) = false`.

In other words, if we have already determined that a sum, `x`, can be formed between indices `0` and `i` (inclusive), then clearly, a sum equal to both `x` and `x + set[i]` can be formed between indices `0` and `i + 1`. We'll take a look at the implementation of this in the following exercise.

Exercise 39: Solving the Subset Sum Problem by Using Tabulation

In this exercise, we shall modify the solution for *Exercise 38, Solving the Subset Sum Problem by Using Memoization*, so that we can use tabulation by converting the logic from top-down to bottom-up. Let's get started:

1. We will define a new function called – you guessed it – **SubsetSum_Tabulation()** that takes an integer vector called **set** as an argument and returns a two-dimensional Boolean vector:

```
vector<vector<bool>> SubsetSum_Tabulation(vector<int> set)
{
    ......
}
```

2. We declare a two-dimensional Boolean vector called **DP**. The first dimension's size should be equal to the length of **set**, and the second dimension's size should be equal to the highest possible subset sum in the set (that is, the total sum of all elements) plus one. Every value of DP should be initialized to **false**, except for the base cases (that is, the sum is equal to zero):

```
int maxSum = 0;

for(auto num : set)
{
    maxSum += num;
}

vector<vector<bool>> DP(set.size() + 1, vector<bool>(maxSum + 1, false));

for(int i = 0; i < set.size(); i++)
{
    // Base case - a subset sum of 0 can be found at any index

    DP[i][0] = true;
}
```

3. Now, we iterate across two nested **for** loops, corresponding to the first and second dimensions of the **DP** table:

```
for(int i = 1; i <= set.size(); i++)
{
    for(int sum = 1; sum <= maxSum; sum++)
    {
        ......
    }
}
```

4. Now, to fill the table, use the following code:

```
for(int i = 1; i <= set.size(); i++)
{
    for(int sum = 1; sum <= maxSum; sum++)
    {
        if(sum < set[i-1])
        {
            DP[i][sum] = DP[i-1][sum];
        }
        else
        {
            DP[i][sum] = DP[i-1][sum]
                        || DP[i-1][sum - set[i-1]];
        }
    }
}
return DP;
```

5. Now, we once again modify the **main()** function to include our tabulated solution:

```
int main()
{
    vector<int> set = { 16, 1058, 22, 13, 46, 55, 3, 92, 47, 7, 98, 367,
807, 106, 333, 85, 577, 9, 3059 };

    int target = 6076
    int tests = 4;

    clock_t timer = clock();
```

```
        sort(set.begin(), set.end());

        for(int i = 0; i < tests; i++)
        {
            bool found;

            switch(i)
            {
                ......
                case 3:
                {
                    vector<vector<bool>> DP = SubsetSum_Tabulation(set);
                    found = DP[set.size()][target];
                    break;
                }
            }
        }
        ......
    }
```

6. You should see an output something like the one shown here:

```
Subset with sum 6076 was found in the set.
TIME TAKEN USING BRUTE FORCE: 0.95602

Subset with sum 6076 was found in the set.
TIME TAKEN USING BACKTRACKING: 0.00082

Subset with sum 6076 was found in the set.
TIME TAKEN USING MEMOIZATION: 0.00058

Subset with sum 6076 was found in the set.
TIME TAKEN USING TABULATION: 0.00605
```

Note

The actual values for the time taken will vary depending on your system. Please note the difference in the values.

7. As we can see, the time taken by the tabulated solution is longer than both the memoization and backtracking solutions. However, using the DP table returned by **SubsetSum_Tabulation()**, we can use the following code to find every possible subset sum:

```
int total = 0;

for(auto num : set)
{
    total += num;
}

vector<vector<bool>> DP = SubsetSum_Tabulation(set);

vector<int> subsetSums;

for(int sum = 1; sum <= total; sum++)
{
    if(DP[set.size()][sum])
    {
        subsetSums.push_back(sum);
    }
}
cout << "The set contains the following " << subsetSums.size() << " subset
sums: ";

for(auto sum : subsetSums)
{
    cout << sum << " ";
}
cout << endl;
```

8. The output of this should begin and end like this:

```
The set contains the following 6760 subset sums: 3 7 9 10 12 13 16 19 20
22 ...... 6790 6791 6793 6797 6800
```

Thus, we have optimized the solution and also obtained the sum values of all the states.

Throughout this chapter, we've explored a variety of ways of solving the subset sum problem, which, in turn, demonstrated the clear superiority of the dynamic programming approach; however, despite the comparative advantages that DP solutions have over the alternatives, we also demonstrated how the naive and relatively inefficient approaches can help us better understand the problem, which greatly simplifies the process of devising a solution using DP.

Some of the logic that's required by dynamic programming solutions may initially appear to be quite complex and difficult to grasp. It is highly recommended that you fully understand each solution approach we discussed in this section before proceeding further, since this is a process that can be accelerated by using different input parameters and comparing the results. Additionally, drawing diagrams of how different solutions are formed from given inputs can be particularly helpful.

Activity 18: Travel Itinerary

You are designing a web application for a travel agency that wants to help clients plan their holiday itineraries. A major aspect of this software concerns route planning, which allows users to specify multiple locations they would like to visit and then view a list of cities they would have to pass through en route to their final destination.

Your agency has contracts with specific transportation companies in every major city, and each transportation company has set limits on how far they can travel. Whereas a plane or train can traverse multiple cities and even entire countries, a bus or taxi service may only be willing to travel one or two cities beyond their initial location. When your software produces the list of possible intermediate stops, it also displays the maximum number of cities the transportation company at that location is willing to travel so that clients can plot their course accordingly.

You recently realized that your application needs some method of allowing clients to filter the number of options presented to them since many popular tourist locations are separated by dense clusters of towns. To do this, you want to determine the total number of possible ways to reach the ultimate destination from a given starting location so that you can reduce the amount of information that's displayed when it becomes excessive.

Your application already has the capability to calculate the list of locations on the ideal route between a departure point and destination. From this, you have derived the following data:

- **N**: An integer representing the number of cities between the source and the destination

- **distance**: An array of integers representing the maximum number of cities the transportation company at each location is willing to traverse

Your task is to implement an algorithm that will calculate the total number of possible ways that the destination can be reached by traveling through a sequence of intermediate locations.

Input

The first line contains a single integer, N, the number of cities between the starting point, and the destination.

The second line contains N space-separated integers, where each integer, d^i, represents the maximum distance that can be traveled starting from the city at index i.

Output

Your program should output a single integer and the total number of ways to traverse the cities beginning at index 0 and ending at index N. Because the values get quite large as N increases, output each result as modulo 1000000007.

Example

Suppose you were given the following input:

6

1 2 3 2 2 1

This means there are a total of six cities between the source and target locations. From a given city at index i, you have the option of traveling to any other city within the range of i + 1 to i + distance[i] (inclusive). If we were to think of the sequence of cities as a graph, the adjacencies for the preceding example would be as follows:

[0]: { 1 }

[1]: { 2, 3 }

[2]: { 3, 4, 5 }

[3]: { 4, 5 }

[4]: { 5, 6 }

[5]: { 6 }

Observe the following figure for further clarification:

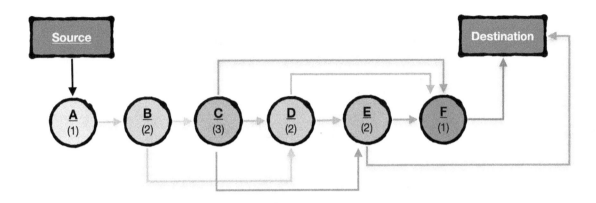

Figure 8.8: Example of city adjacencies

In the preceding example, the destination can be reached in the following ways (with **E** representing the end point):

```
0 > 1 > 2 > 3 > 4 > 5 > E
```

```
0 > 1 > 2 > 3 > 4 > E
0 > 1 > 2 > 3 > 5 > E
0 > 1 > 2 > 4 > 5 > E
0 > 1 > 3 > 4 > 5 > E
```

```
0 > 1 > 2 > 4 > E
0 > 1 > 2 > 5 > E
0 > 1 > 3 > 4 > E
0 > 1 > 3 > 5 > E
```

This gives us an answer of **9**.

In general, the traversal always starts at index **0** and ends at index **N**. It is guaranteed that the sum of a city's index **i** with **distance[i]** will never be greater than **N**, and that every city will have a corresponding distance value of at least **1**.

Test Cases

The following test cases should help you to understand this problem better:

Input:	Output:
3 1 1 1	1

Input:	Output:
6 1 2 3 2 2 1	9

Input:	Output:
15 1 2 5 3 4 2 1 3 6 1 2 1 2 2 1	789

Figure 8.9: Activity 18 simple test cases

Here are some more complex test cases:

Input:	Output:
40 8 5 9 9 11 3 10 9 9 5 1 6 13 3 13 9 8 5 11 8 4 5 10 3 11 4 10 4 12 11 8 9 3 7 6 4 4 3 2 1	47382972

Input:	Output:
100 39 79 34 76 12 28 51 60 53 7 30 48 45 61 66 24 50 64 18 47 7 19 16 72 8 55 72 26 43 57 45 26 68 23 52 28 35 54 2 57 29 59 6 57 8 47 6 44 43 35 50 41 45 4 43 39 44 43 42 26 40 39 32 37 31 20 9 33 30 27 30 29 28 27 26 25 24 23 22 15 20 19 18 17 1 15 14 2 12 11 1 6 8 7 6 5 4 3 2 1	790903754

Figure 8.10: Activity 18 complex test cases

Extra Credit

Assuming you have found an approach that passes the preceding test cases within reasonable time limits, you can truly test the efficiency of your algorithm with one final test case, with **N** equal to **10000000**. Because the number of values would take too much space to print, you can use the following code to generate the array values programmatically:

```
vector<int> Generate(int n)
{
    vector<int> A(n);

    ULL val = 1;

    for(int i = 0; i < n; i++)
    {
        val = (val * 1103515245 + 12345) / 65536;
        val %= 32768;

        A[i] = ((val % 10000) % (n - i)) + 1;
    }
    return A;
}
```

Your program should print **318948158** as the result of this test case. An optimal algorithm should be able to find the result in under one second.

Activity Guidelines

- An optimal approach will run in **O(n)** time and require exactly n iterations.
- If you are completely unsure as to how to formulate the DP solution, use the incremental approach that was described in this chapter, that is, by using brute force first and then progressively optimizing the solution.
- For insights into how the problem's states are formed, consider the recurrence relation exhibited by the Fibonacci sequence.

> **Note**
>
> The solution to this activity can be found on page 556.

Dynamic Programming on Strings and Sequences

So far, our exploration of dynamic programming has primarily focused on combinatorial problems and calculating terms of integer sequences with defined formulae. Now, we will consider another one of DP's most common uses, that is, working with patterns in sequences of data. The most typical scenarios in which a programmer would use DP for this purpose generally concern searching, comparing, and constructing strings.

As software developers, we often work collaboratively with several individuals who all have the ability to make contributions and modifications to the same project. Since the possibility always exists that a programmer may inadvertently introduce a bug into the code, or that the team may try a different approach for a given feature and then decide to return to their original method, it becomes extremely important to have some system of version control. In the event that a feature that was working recently mysteriously develops a glitch, it is essential to have the ability to see the changes that were made to the code, particularly in terms of how they differ from an earlier version. All version control systems therefore have a "diff" feature that analyzes the similarity between two versions of the same code and then displays this in some way to the user.

For example, say you had added the following code to the repository:

```
bool doSomething = true;


void DoStuff()
{
    DoSomething();
    DoSomethingElse();
    DoAnotherThing();
}
```

On the following day, you made some changes:

```
bool doSomething = false;


void DoStuff()
{
    if(doSomething == true)
    {
        DoSomething();
    }
}
```

```
    else

    {

        DoSomethingElse();

    }

}
```

A diff utility would then display something similar to the following:

–	bool doSomething = true;		+	bool doSomething = false;
	void DoStuff()			void DoStuff()
	{			{
			+	if(doSomething == true)
				{
	DoSomething();			DoSomething();
				}
			+	else
			+	{
	DoSomethingElse();			DoSomethingElse();
			+	}
–	DoAnotherThing();			
	}			}

Figure 8.11: Diff utility output

To accomplish this, the utility needs to compute the similarity of the two code files by taking into account the fact that the sequence of text that is common to both versions may not necessarily be contiguous in the string. Additionally, parts of the original text may have been removed or appear in additional locations in the new version. This demonstrates the need for **approximate** (or "**fuzzy**") **string matching**, a technique that frequently makes use of dynamic programming.

The Longest Common Subsequence Problem

The **longest common subsequence problem** (commonly abbreviated as **LCS**) is one of the most famous classical examples of dynamic programming. It answers the following question: given two sequences of data, what is the longest subsequence common to both of them?

As an example, consider two strings, **A** and **B**:

$$A = \text{``ALBOCNDGZEYSXTW''}$$
$$B = \text{``12L45O78N90GE9876S5432T''}$$

Figure 8.12: Two given strings for finding the longest common subsequence

The longest common subsequence would be "**LONGEST**":

$$A = \text{``ALBOCNDGZEYSXTW''}$$
$$B = \text{``12L45078N90GE9876S5432T''}$$

Figure 8.13: Longest common subsequence in the given strings

Equipped with the insights that we've gained from the series of approaches we implemented for the subset sum problem, let's be a bit smarter about how we attack this one. We will start by formulating some ideas about the structure of the problem in advance, starting with the base cases.

Since it tends to be quite difficult to understand the nature of a DP problem for large inputs without first having considered the trivial ones, let's create some examples of different scenarios using small input strings and try to find the length of the longest common subsequence (LCS):

```
Case 1): A or B is empty
```

```
A   = ""
B   = ""
LCS = 0
```

```
A   = "A"
B   = ""
LCS = 0
```

```
A   = ""
B   = "PNEUMONOULTRAMICROSCOPICSILICOVOLCANOCONIOSIS"
LCS = 0
```

In the case where either or both strings are empty, it should be fairly obvious that the length of the longest common subsequence will always be equal to zero:

```
Case 2) Both A and B contain a single character
```

```
A   = "A"
B   = "A"
```

```
LCS = 1


A   = "A"
B   = "B"
LCS = 0
```

```
Case 3) A has one character, B has two characters
```

```
A   = "A"
B   = "AB"
LCS = 1
```

```
A   = "A"
B   = "BB"
LCS = 0
```

These two cases have a simple binary definition – either they have a common character, or they do not:

```
Case 4) Both A and B contain two characters
```

```
A:  = "AA"
B:  = "AA"
LCS = 2
```

```
A   = "BA"
B   = "AB"
LCS = 1
```

```
A   = "AA"
B   = "BB"
LCS = 0
```

Things become a bit more interesting with strings of length 2, but the logic is still quite trivial. Given two strings of length 2, they either are identical, have one character in common, or have no characters in common:

```
Case 5) A and B both contain 3 characters


A    = "ABA"
B    = "AAB"
LCS  = 2


A    = "ABC"
B    = "BZC"
LCS  = 2
```

Now, the complexity of the problem is beginning to emerge. This case demonstrates that the comparisons progressively become much less straightforward:

```
Case 6: A and B both contain 4 characters


A     = AAAB
B     = AAAA


{ "AAA_", "AAA_" }
{ "AAA_", "AA_A" }
{ "AAA_", "A_AA" }
{ "AAA_", "_AAA" }


LCS = 3


A     = AZYB
B     = YZBA
```

```
{ "_Z_B", "_ZB_" }
{ "__YB", "Y_B_" }
```

LCS = 2

By now, it should be fairly obvious that the LCS problem does indeed contain overlapping subproblems. Similar to the previous problem, we can observe that there are 2^n possible subsets of a given string, with **n** being equal to the string's length, except now we have two sequences to contend with. Even worse is the fact that we are not simply considering the subsets of each sequence independently, but must also make comparisons between them:

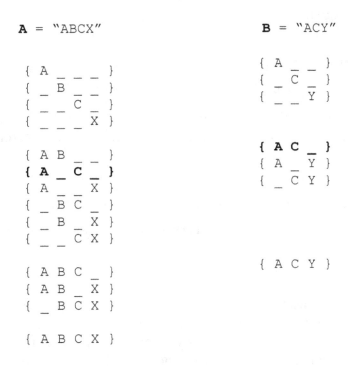

Figure 8.14: All possible character subsequences of two strings, ABCX and ACY

The fact that we are not merely looking for consecutive groups of characters has several implications: firstly, the same sequence of characters can occur multiple times throughout the string and can be spaced across either string in any possible arrangement, assuming the order of the characters is the same. Secondly, there can be many common subsequences beginning from any given index.

Before implementing our brute-force approach, let's also define what constitutes a state for this problem. Let's assume that we are maintaining two pointers, **i** and **j**, which represent character indices in **A** and **B**, respectively, as well as a record of the subsequence of common characters we have found:

```
if i exceeds length of A, or j exceeds length of B:
```

```
- Terminate recursion and return length of subsequence
```

If we have reached the end of either string, there is nothing else to compare because the indices of subsequences are ordered:

```
if A[i] = B[j]:
```

```
- Increase length of subsequence by 1
```

```
- Increment both i and j by 1
```

If the characters are equal, there is no advantage in not including it in our found subsequence. We increment both pointers because any given character can only be considered once per subsequence:

```
Otherwise:

    Option 1) Explore further possibilities with i + 1, and j

    Option 2) Explore further possibilities with i, and j + 1


    LCS from this state is equal to maximum value of Option 1 and Option 2
```

If we have not found a match, we have the choice to either explore the next subset of A's characters, or the next subset of B's characters. We do not include the case of incrementing both indices simultaneously from this state because it would be redundant. That case will be explored by the next function call. Outlining the structure of this recurrence would look like this:

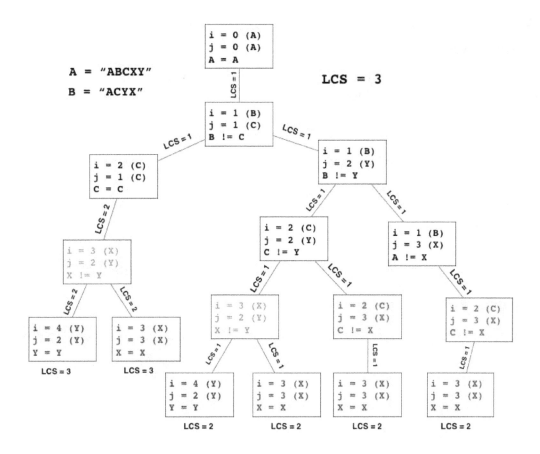

Figure 8.15: Subproblem tree for the longest subsequence problem

In the preceding figure, the overlapping subproblems have been color coded. The optimal substructure of this problem is still not quite clear yet, but we can still make some basic generalizations:

- We only need to compare subsets of equal length.

- From a given state, the possibilities for the next state can be explored by incrementing **i**, **j**, or both.

- Our search always ends when the end of either string is reached.

Hopefully, our preliminary brute-force implementation can provide additional insights. Let's get right to it in the following exercise.

Exercise 40: Finding the Longest Common Subsequence by Using the Brute-Force Approach

In this exercise, we shall use the brute-force approach to solve this problem, just like we did for the subset sum problem in *Exercise 36, Solving the Subset Sum Problem by Using the Brute-Force Approach*. Let's get started:

1. Begin by including the following headers and defining the **DEBUG** and **PRINT** macros that we used in the previous chapter:

```
#include <iostream>
#include <time.h>
#include <iomanip>
#include <algorithm>
#include <utility>
#include <vector>
#include <strings.h>

#define DEBUG 1

#if DEBUG
#define PRINT(x) cerr << x
#else
#define PRINT(x)
#endif

using namespace std;
```

2. Define a function called **LCS_BruteForce()** that takes the following arguments – two strings, **A** and **B**, two integers, **i** and **j**, and a vector of integer pairs, **subsequence** – and returns an integer. Above this function, we will also declare a two-dimensional vector of integer pairs with a global scope, that is, **found**:

```
vector<vector<pair<int, int>>> found;

int LCS_BruteForce(string A, string B, int i, int j, vector<pair<int,
int>> subsequence)
{
    ......
}
```

3. **A** and **B** are, of course, the strings we are comparing, **i** and **j** represent our current positions in **A** and **B**, respectively, and **subsequence** is the collection of index pairs that form each common subsequence, which will be collected in **found** for output.

Since we already have pseudocode to work with, we can implement our function with relative ease by simply inserting each line of pseudocode into our function as comments and translating it into C++ code underneath:

```cpp
// If i exceeds length of A, or j exceeds length of B:
if(i >= A.size() || j >= B.size())
{
    found.push_back(subsequence);

    //Terminate recursion and return length of subsequence
    return subsequence.size();
}

// if A[i] = B[j]:
if(A[i] == B[j])
{
    // Increase length of subsequence by 1
    subsequence.push_back({ i, j });

    // Increment both i and j by 1
    return LCS_BruteForce(A, B, i + 1, j + 1, subsequence);
}
/*
    Option 1) Explore further possibilities with i + 1, and j
    Option 2) Explore further possibilities with i, and j + 1

    LCS from this state is equal to maximum value of Option 1 and Option 2
*/

return max(LCS_BruteForce(A, B, i + 1, j, subsequence),
           LCS_BruteForce(A, B, i, j + 1, subsequence));
```

4. In **main()**, we'll receive input in the form of two strings, and then call our function on it:

```
int main()
{
    string A, B;
    cin >> A >> B;

    int LCS = LCS_BruteForce(A, B, 0, 0, {});

    cout << "Length of the longest common subsequence of " << A << " and "
    << B << " is: " << LCS << endl;

    ...
}
```

5. Like we did in the previous chapter, we will also output the subsequences found to stderr if **DEBUG** is not set to **0**. However, because of the greater complexity of this problem, we will put this output in a separate function, **PrintSubsequences()**:

```
void PrintSubsequences(string A, string B)
{
    // Lambda function for custom sorting logic
    sort(found.begin(), found.end(), [](auto a, auto b)
    {
        // First sort subsequences by length
        if(a.size() != b.size())
        {
            return a.size() < b.size();
        }

        // Sort subsequences of same size by lexicographical order of
    index
        return a < b;
    });

    // Remove duplicates
    found.erase(unique(found.begin(), found.end()), found.end());

    int previousSize = 0;
```

```
        for(auto subsequence : found)
        {
            if(subsequence.size() != previousSize)
            {
                previousSize = subsequence.size();
                PRINT("SIZE = " << previousSize << endl);
            }
            // Fill with underscores as placeholder characters
            string a_seq(A.size(), '_');
            string b_seq(B.size(), '_');

            for(auto pair : subsequence)
            {
                // Fill in the blanks with the characters of each string that
    are part of the subsequence

                a_seq[pair.first] = A[pair.first];
                b_seq[pair.second] = B[pair.second];
            }
            PRINT("\t" << a_seq << " | " << b_seq << endl);
        }
    }
```

6. We can then call this function in **main()**, specifying that it should be ignored unless **DEBUG** is set:

```
int main()
{
    ......

#if DEBUG
    PrintSubsequences();
#endif

    return 0;
}
```

7. Setting **DEBUG** to **1** and using **ABCX** and **ACYXB** as input should produce the following output:

```
Length of the longest common subsequence of ABCX and ACYXB is: 3
SIZE = 1
     A___ A____
SIZE = 2
     AB__ A___B
     A_C_ AC___
     A__X A__X_
SIZE = 3
     A_CX AC_X_
```

This output shows us all the possible combinations of subsequence pairs. Let's analyze this output in the following section and work toward optimizing our solution.

First Steps Toward Optimization – Finding the Optimal Substructure

Let's revisit the logic of our previous approach again to see how it may be optimized. Using the input strings from the previous exercise, **ABCX** and **ACYXB**, if our current state has **i = 0** and **j = 0**, we can clearly see that the only possibility for our next state is as follows:

```
LCS(A, B, 0, 0) = 1 + LCS(A, B, 1, 1)
```

As you may recall, one of our initial insights is that the LCS is equal to **0** if either or both strings are empty. We can also generalize that the LCS of a given prefix of **A** and a given prefix of **B** is equal to the maximum LCS of A's prefix reduced by one character with **B**, and **B**'s prefix reduced by one character with **A**:

```
A = "ABC"
B = "AXB"


LCS of "ABC", "AXB"
= max(LCS of "AB" and "AXB", LCS of "ABC" and "AX")
= LCS of "AB" and "AXB"
= "AB"
```

Using this concept of the LCS for two strings being based on the LCS of their prefixes, we can redefine our logic as follows:

```
If prefix for either string is empty:
    LCS = 0


Otherwise:
    If character in last position of A's prefix is equal to character in last
position of B's prefix:
        LCS is equal to 1 + LCS of prefix of A with last character removed
and prefix of B with last character removed
    Otherwise:
        LCS is equal to maximum of:
            1) LCS of A's current prefix and B's prefix with last character
removed
            2) LCS of B's current prefix and A's prefix with last character
removed
```

Using memoization, we can store our results at every step in a two-dimensional table, with the first dimension equal to the size of **A** and the second dimension equal to the size of **B**. Assuming we have not reached the base case, we can check whether we have a cached result stored in `memo[i - 1][j - 1]`. If we do, we return the result; if not, we recursively explore possibilities in the same way as before and store the results accordingly. We'll implement this in the following activity.

Activity 19: Finding the Longest Common Subsequence by Using Memoization

In solving the subset sum problem, we implemented various approaches, namely brute force, backtracking, memoization, and tabulation. In this activity, your task is to independently implement a solution to the longest common subsequence problem using memoization.

Input

Two strings, A and B, respectively.

Output

The length of the longest common subsequence of A and B.

Test Cases

The following test cases should help you to understand this problem better:

Input:	Output:
123456 QWERTY	0

Input:	Output:
ACBEBC ABCBC	4

Input:	Output:
AZYBYXCXW ZZAYYBXXXCWW	6

Input:	Output:
ABCABDBEFBA ABCBEFBEAB	8

Input:	Output:
ABZCYDABAZADAEA YABAZADBBEAAECYACAZ	10

Figure 8.16: Activity 19 test cases

Activity Guidelines:

- You can represent the state in two dimensions, with the first dimension bound by the length of A, and the second bound by the length of B.

- Very little must be changed to convert the brute-force algorithm into a memoized one.

- Make sure your approach has a way to differentiate between subproblems that have already been cached versus those that have not.

> **Note**
>
> The solution to this activity can be found on page 563.

From Top-Down to Bottom-Up – Converting the Memoized Approach into a Tabulated Approach

If we were to print out the values of the memo table for the pair of strings ABCABDBEFBA and ABCBEFBEAB, it would look like this (note that values of -1 are unknown):

	A	B	C	B	E	F	B	E	A	B
A	1	1	1	1	1	1	1	1	-1	-1
B	1	2	-1	2	2	2	2	2	-1	-1
C	1	2	3	3	3	3	3	3	-1	-1
A	1	2	3	3	3	3	3	3	4	-1
B	1	2	3	4	4	4	4	4	4	-1
D	1	2	3	4	4	4	4	4	4	-1
B	-1	-1	-1	4	4	4	5	5	5	-1
E	-1	-1	-1	-1	5	5	5	6	6	-1
F	-1	-1	-1	-1	-1	6	6	6	6	-1
B	-1	-1	-1	-1	-1	-1	7	7	-1	7
A	-1	-1	-1	-1	-1	-1	-1	-1	8	8

Figure 8.17: Memo table for ABCABDBEFBA and ABCBEFBE

Looking up any of the row/column combinations where the characters are equal (say the 7th row and 7th column), we notice a pattern: the value at memo[i][j] is equal to memo[i - 1][j - 1] + 1.

Now, let's look at the other case (that is, the characters are not equal); the pattern we see is that memo[i][j] is equal to the maximum of memo[i - 1][j] and memo[i][j - 1].

Assuming that we have found the optimal substructure of a problem, it is often quite a simple task to form a solution using tabulation by merely taking the table produced by a memoized solution and devising a scheme to build it from the bottom up. We will need to formulate some of our logic a bit differently, but the general ideas will essentially be the same. The first difference to contend with is the fact that the memo table's values are initialized to UNKNOWN (-1). Remember that a tabulated solution will fill the *entire* table with the appropriate results, and so nothing should be *unknown* by the time the algorithm has finished.

Let's take the unknown value in the second row and third column; what should this be equal to? Assuming the prefixes we are considering at that point are **AB_____** and **ABC_____**, it should be fairly clear that the LCS at this point is equal to **2**. Now, let's consider the unknown value in the 10th row and the 9th column: the prefixes we are considering at this point are **ABCABDBEFB_** and **ABCBEFBEA_**, and the LCS that's found at this point is **ABC_B__EFB_** −> **ABCBEFB___**, which is seven characters long. We can logically deduce that the LCS value at a given state is either equal to the previously found LCS, or one greater than the previously found LCS if the characters are equal. The lowest possible LCS value, of course, should be equal to 0. So, our logic for filling a DP table iteratively would look something like this:

```
If i = 0 or j = 0 (empty prefix):

  LCS(i, j) = 0


Otherwise:

  If the last characters of both prefixes are equal:

    LCS(i, j) = LCS(i - 1, j - 1) + 1

  Otherwise:

    LCS(i, j) = Maximum of:

        LCS(i - 1, j) → LCS for A's current prefix and B's prefix with the
last character removed

        LCS(i, j - 1) → LCS for B's current prefix and A's prefix with the
last character removed
```

Our logic is essentially identical to what it was for the memoized solution, except that rather than recursively finding the values of unexplored states to fill the current state's value in the table, we fill the values for those states first and then simply reuse them as needed. We'll put this logic into code in the following activity.

Activity 20: Finding the Longest Common Subsequence Using Tabulation

In this activity, your task is to implement a bottom-up solution to the longest common subsequence problem using tabulation.

Input

Two strings, A and B, respectively.

Output

The length of the longest common subsequence of A and B.

Extra Credit

In addition to the length of the LCS, also output the actual characters it contains.

Test Cases

The following test cases should help you to understand this problem better:

Input:	Output:
A1B2C3D4E	5
ABCDE	Extra credit: ABCDE

Input:	Output:
ABZCYDABAZADAEA	10
YABAZADBBEAAECYACAZ	Extra credit: YABAZADAEA

Input:	Output:
QWJEHFBEMVJEIIFJEEVFBEHFJXAJXBE	14
BVBQHEJEJCHEEHXBNEBCHHEHHFEHSBE	Extra credit: QHEJEJEEBEHFBE

Input:	Output:
AAA12AAA3AA4AA56AA7AAA8	19
AA1AA2AAA3A4A5A6AA7A89AAA	
	Extra credit: AA12AAA3A4A56AA7AAA

Figure 8.18: Activity 20 test cases

Activity Guidelines

- Like the subset sum problem, the tabulated solution requires iterating over two nested **for** loops.

- For a given state, LCS(I, j), there are three possibilities that need to be handled – either the string's prefix is empty, the last characters of A's and B's prefixes are equal, or the last characters of A's and B's prefixes are not equal.

- Finding the characters of the LCS can be done by backtracking through the DP table.

> **Note**
>
> The solution to this activity can be found on page 568.

Activity 21: Melodic Permutations

> **Note**
>
> This activity is based around the traditional Western 8-note equal temperament scale, although students do not need to know anything about music theory to perform this activity. All the necessary information about the musical aspect is provided here.

Musical set theory is a form of categorization for musical harmonies and melodies according to the intervallic relations of their notes. In musical terminology, an interval can be defined as the distance between two notes in terms of their relative positions when written in musical notation:

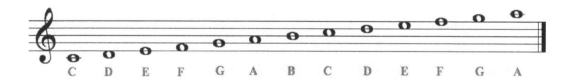

Figure 8.19: Musical notations

The following figure demonstrates the distance between different musical notes when represented as musical notations:

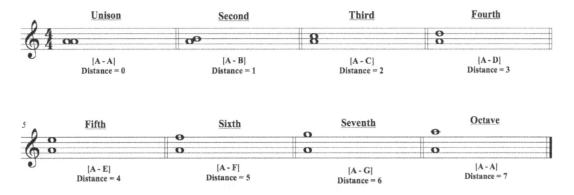

Figure 8.20: Musical intervals

You are a music theorist who is curious about how many times a permutation of a particular note set appears within the melodies of various composers. Given the notes of a complete melody and a set of notes, count the number of times any permutation of the note set appears within the melody. For any valid permutation, notes can be repeated any amount of times and can occur in any order:

```
                0     1     2     3     4    5    6
Melody:      { "A", "B", "C", "C", "E", "C, "A" }
Note set:      { "A", "C", "E" }


Subsets:


    { 0, 2, 4 }      ->     { "A", "C", "E" }
    { 0, 3, 4 }      ->     { "A", "C", "E" }
    { 0, 4, 5 }      ->     { "A", "E", "C" }
    { 2, 4, 6 }      ->     { "C", "E", "A" }
    { 3, 4, 6 }      ->     { "C", "E", "A" }
    { 4, 5, 6 }      ->     { "E", "C", "A" }


    { 0, 2, 3, 4 }      ->     { "A", "C", "C", "E" }
```

```
{ 0, 2, 4, 5 }      ->      { "A", "C", "E", "C" }
{ 0, 2, 4, 6 }      ->      { "A", "C", "E", "A" }
{ 0, 3, 4, 5 }      ->      { "A", "C", "E", "C" }
{ 0, 3, 4, 6 }      ->      { "A", "C", "E", "A" }
{ 0, 4, 5, 6 }      ->      { "A", "E", "C", "A" }
{ 2, 3, 4, 6 }      ->      { "C", "C", "E", "A" }
{ 2, 4, 5, 6 }      ->      { "C", "E", "C", "A" }
{ 3, 4, 5, 6 }      ->      { "C", "E", "C", "A" }


{ 0, 2, 3, 4, 5 }        ->      { "A", "C", "C", "E", "C" }
{ 0, 2, 3, 4, 6 }        ->      { "A", "C", "C", "E", "A" }
{ 0, 2, 4, 5, 6 }        ->      { "A", "C", "E", "C", "A" }
{ 0, 3, 4, 5, 6 }        ->      { "A", "C", "E", "C", "A" }
{ 2, 3, 4, 5, 6 }        ->      { "C", "C", "E", "C", "A" }


{ 0, 2, 3, 4, 5, 6 }     ->      { "A", "C", "C", "E", "C", "A" }
Total Permutations = 21
```

The following notes are described as *enharmonically equivalent* and should be considered identical:

```
C  - B# (B# is pronounced as "B sharp")
C# - Db (Db is pronounced as "D flat")
D# - Eb
E  - Fb
E# - F
F# - Gb
G# - Ab
A# - Bb
B  - Cb
```

The following diagram illustrates this equivalence on a piano:

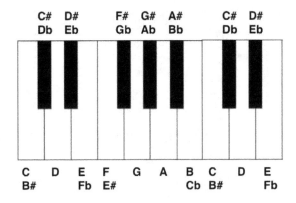

Figure 8.21: Enharmonically equivalent notes represented on a section of a piano

Thus, the following combinations of notes would be considered equivalent:

```
{ A#, B#, C# }    = { Bb, C, Db },
{ Fb, Db, Eb }    = { E, C#, D# },
{ C, B#, E#, F } = { C, C, F, F }
```

And so on...

The following are a few sample inputs and corresponding outputs:

Input:

```
Melody:     { "A", "B", "C", "C", "E", "C, "A" }
Note Set:   { "A", "C", "E" }
```

Output: **21**

Input:

```
Melody:     { "A", "B", "D", "C#", "E", "A", "F#", "B", "C", "C#", "D", "E" }
Note Set:   { "B", "D", "F#", "E" }
```

Output: **27**

Input:

```
Melody:    { "Bb", "Db", "Ab", "G", "Fb", "Eb", "G", "G", "Ab", "A", "Bb",
"Cb", "Gb", "G", "E", "A", "G#" }
Note Set:   { "Ab", "E", "G" }
```

Output: **315**

Input:

```
Melody:    { "C", "C#", "D", "Bb", "E#", "F#", "D", "C#", "A#", "B#", "C#",
"Eb", "Gb", "A", "A#", "Db", "B", "D#" }
Note Set:   { "Bb", "C#", "D#", "B#" }
```

Output: **945**

Input:

```
Melody:    { "A#", "B", "D#", "F#", "Bb", "A", "C", "C#", "Db", "Fb", "G#",
"D", "Gb", "B", "Ab", "G", "C", "Ab", "F", "F#", "E#", "G", "Db" }
Note Set:   { "A", "Db", "Gb", "A#", "B", "F#", "E#" }
```

Output: **1323**

The guidelines for this activity are as follows:

- You do not actually have to know anything about music theory to solve this problem beyond what is explained in the description.

- Is there a better way to represent the notes? Could they be converted into a format that would be more amenable to a tabulated DP solution?

- What is the total count of subsets for *n* elements? Could this bit of information be useful in solving this problem?

> **Note**
>
> The solution to this activity can be found on page 574.

Summary

In this chapter, we have analyzed and implemented two archetypal examples of dynamic programming and learned several methods by which different DP problems may be approached. We have also learned how to identify the characteristics of problems that can be solved with DP, how DP algorithms should be considered conceptually, and how the concepts of states, base cases, and recurrence relations can be used to break a complex problem down into much simpler components.

We have just barely scratched the surface of the dynamic programming technique. Indeed, the two problems we explored in depth are actually quite similar, both conceptually and in terms of how their solutions are implemented. However, many of these similarities serve to demonstrate several commonalities that are encountered in nearly every DP problem, and, as such, they serve as an excellent introduction to a topic that is admittedly quite complex and difficult to master.

Using dynamic programming is a skill that you are unlikely to improve at merely through the act of reading or observing. The only way to truly get better with this technique is through solving as many problems with it as possible, preferably without guidance. At first, certain difficult DP problems may necessitate many attempts before the optimal solution is found, but the experience that you garner through this often arduous process is arguably much greater than what you are likely to gain through simply studying the solutions of any number of DP problems.

The progressive approach to solving DP problems that was demonstrated in this chapter can serve you well in the future, but it is by no means the only way to arrive at the ultimate solution. After having solved a number of DP problems, you will undoubtedly begin to notice certain patterns that will make it possible to devise tabulated solutions from the start. However, these patterns are not likely to be discovered until you have encountered a range of different DP problems. Keep in mind the fact that with DP, just like any challenging skill, continuous practice will make it easier, and, before long, what originally appeared extremely daunting will eventually seem thoroughly manageable, and even quite fun!

In the final chapter, we will learn how to apply dynamic programming to more advanced situations and develop a deeper understanding of how DP problems that appear quite different from one another at first glance are often just variations on the same set of concepts. Finally, we will conclude this book by revisiting the topic of graphs to demonstrate how the DP paradigm can be effectively applied to the shortest path problem.

Dynamic Programming II

Learning Objectives

By the end of this chapter, you will be able to:

- Describe how problems can be solved in polynomial versus non-deterministic polynomial time and the effect this has on our ability to develop efficient algorithms

- Implement solutions for both the 0-1 and unbounded variants of the knapsack problem

- Apply the concept of state space reduction to dynamic programming problems

- Determine every shortest path in a weighted graph using approaches that have been optimized by the dynamic programming paradigm

In this chapter, we will build upon our understanding of the dynamic programming approach and examine how it can be used to optimize the problems we discussed in the previous chapter.

Introduction

From the previous chapter, you should have a basic understanding of dynamic programming, as well as an effective set of strategies for finding a dynamic programming (DP) solution for an unfamiliar problem. In this chapter, we will develop this understanding further by exploring relationships between problems, particularly in terms of how the basic DP logic for one problem can be modified to find the approach to another. We will also discuss the concept of state space reduction, which allows us to exploit certain aspects of a problem to further optimize a working DP solution by decreasing the number of dimensions and/or operations required to find the result. We will conclude this chapter by revisiting the topic of graphs to demonstrate how the DP approach can be applied to the shortest-path problem.

An Overview of P versus NP

In *Chapter 8, Dynamic Programming I*, we demonstrated the significant gains in efficiency that dynamic programming can offer over other approaches, but it may not yet be clear how dramatic the difference can be. It is important to appreciate the extent to which the complexity of certain problems will scale as the input bounds increase because then we can understand the situations in which DP is not just preferable, but necessary.

Consider the following problem:

"Given the terms and operators of a Boolean formula, determine whether or not it evaluates to TRUE."

Take a look at the following example:

```
(0 OR 1)  -> TRUE
(1 AND 0) -> FALSE
(1 NOT 1) -> FALSE
(1 NOT 0) AND (0 NOT 1) -> TRUE
```

This problem is conceptually very simple to solve. All that is required to get the correct result is a linear evaluation of the given formula. However, imagine that, instead, the problem was stated this way:

"Given the variables and operators of a Boolean formula, determine whether there exists an assignment of TRUE/FALSE to each variable so that the formula will evaluate to TRUE."

Take a look at the following example:

```
(a1 OR a2) -> TRUE
```

```
        (0 V 0) = FALSE
        (0 V 1) = TRUE
        (1 V 0) = TRUE
        (1 V 1) = TRUE
```

```
(a1 AND a2) -> TRUE
```

```
        (0 ∧ 0) = FALSE
        (0 ∧ 1) = FALSE
        (1 ∧ 0) = FALSE
        (1 ∧ 1) = TRUE
```

```
(a1 NOT a1) -> FALSE
```

```
        (0 ¬ 0) = FALSE
        (1 ¬ 1) = FALSE
```

```
(a1 NOT a2) AND (a1 AND a2) -> FALSE
```

```
        (0 ¬ 0) ∧ (0 ∧ 0) = FALSE
        (0 ¬ 1) ∧ (0 ∧ 1) = FALSE
        (1 ¬ 0) ∧ (1 ∧ 0) = FALSE
        (1 ¬ 1) ∧ (1 ∧ 1) = FALSE
```

> **Note:**
>
> If you are unfamiliar with logic symbols, ¬ denotes **NOT**, hence **(1 ¬ 1) = FALSE**, and **(1 ¬ 0) = TRUE**. Also, ∧ denotes **AND**, while V denotes **OR**.

The basic underlying concept remains the same, but the difference between these two problems is immense. In the original problem, the complexity of finding the result was dependent only on one factor–the length of the formula–but stated this way, there seems to be no obvious approach to solving it that does not require searching every possible binary subset of variable assignments until a solution is found.

Now, let's consider another problem:

"*Given a graph where every vertex is assigned one of three possible colors, determine whether no two adjacent vertices are the same color.*"

Like our first example, this is quite simple to implement–traverse every vertex of the graph, compare its color to each of its neighbors, and return false only if a matching pair of adjacent colors is found. But now, imagine that the problem is as follows:

"*Given a graph where every vertex is assigned one of three possible colors, determine whether it is possible to color its vertices so that no two neighbors share the same color.*"

Again, this is a very different scenario.

The first versions of these problems are commonly classified as **P**, which simply means that there's a way to solve them in **polynomial time**. When we describe a problem as having a time complexity of $O(n)$, $O(n^2)$, $O(\log n)$, and so on, we are describing a problem within the P class. However, the restated forms–at least as far as anyone has currently been able to prove–have no existing methods for finding a solution that are not essentially exponential in their worst-case complexity. Therefore, we classify their complexity as **NP**, or **non-deterministic polynomial time**.

The relationship between these classes of problems is a subject of considerable debate. The particular matter of interest is that the complexity of computation that's required to *verify* their solutions is "easy," whereas the complexity of *producing* solutions is "hard". This demonstrates one of the most widely discussed unsolved problems in programming: does the fact that the verification of solutions is in class P imply that there is also an approach for producing solutions in polynomial time? In other words, does P = NP? While the generally postulated answer to this question is no (P ≠ NP), this has yet to be proven, and doing so (regardless of what the answer actually is) would be a truly revolutionary advance in the study of algorithms and computation.

Arguably the most interesting group of problems in NP are known as **NP-complete** because they share a remarkable trait: should a solution be discovered that solves any one of these problems efficiently (that is, in polynomial time), that solution can, in fact, be modified to solve all of the other problems in NP efficiently. In other words, if a polynomial solution for the first example (known as the **Boolean satisfiability problem**, or **SAT**) was found, some variant of the same logic could also be used to solve the second example (known as the **graph-coloring problem**), and vice versa.

Keep in mind that not every exponentially complex problem fits into this classification. Consider the problem of determining the next best move in a chess game. You may describe the recursive logic as follows:

```
For each piece, a, belonging to the current player:


    Consider every possible move, m_a, that a can make:


        For each piece, b, belonging to the opponent:


            Consider each possible move m_b that b can make
            in response to m_a.


                for each piece, a, belonging to the
                current player…


            (etc.)


        Count number of ways player_1 can win after this move


Next best move is the one where the probability that player_1 wins is
maximized.
```

The complexity of finding solutions is unquestionably exponential. However, this problem does not meet the criteria of NP-completeness because the basic act of verifying whether a certain move is the best requires the same degree of complexity.

Compare this example to the problem of solving a Sudoku puzzle:

1	5	6	8	2	3	9	7	4
9	7	8	6	4	1	2	5	3
2	4	3	7	5	9	6	1	8
3	2	5	1	7	4	8	9	6
7	6	4	3	9	8	1	2	5
8	1	9	5	6	2	4	3	7
5	3	2	9	8	6	7	4	1
4	8	7	2	1	5	3	6	9
6	9	1	4	3	7	5	8	2

Figure 9.1: A solved Sudoku puzzle

Verification requires scanning each row and column of the matrix and determining that each of the nine outlined 3 x 3 squares contains every digit from 1 – 9, and that no row or column contains the same number more than once. A straightforward implementation of this could use three collections of nine sets, each containing { 1, 2, 3, 4, 5, 6, 7, 8, 9 }, the first of these collections representing the numbers in each row, the second representing the numbers in each column, and the third representing the numbers in each 3 x 3 square. As each cell is scanned, we would check that the number it contains is in each set that corresponds to that cell; if it is, it is removed from the set. Otherwise, the result is FALSE. Once every cell has been considered, the result equals TRUE if every set is empty. Since this approach only requires us to iterate through the matrix once, we can conclude that it can be solved in polynomial time. However, assuming the puzzle that's provided is incomplete and the task is to determine whether a solution exists, we would have to recursively consider each combination of digits for each cell until a valid solution is found, leading to a worst-case complexity of $O(9^n)$, with n equal to the number of empty squares in the original grid; thus, we can conclude that solving a Sudoku puzzle is in NP.

Reconsidering the Subset Sum Problem

In the previous chapter, we discussed the subset sum problem, which we saw possessed exponential complexity in the worst cases. Let's consider the two ways this problem can be expressed – in terms of the relative difficulty of finding a solution and verifying the validity of a solution.

Let's consider the problem of verifying the validity of a solution:

```
Set     -> { 2 6 4 15 3 9 }
Target -> 24


Subset -> { 2 6 4 }
Sum = 2 + 6 + 4 = 12
FALSE


Subset -> { 2 6 15 3 }
Sum = 2 + 6 + 15 + 3 = 24
TRUE


Subset -> { 15 9 }
Sum = 15 + 9 = 24
TRUE


Subset -> { 6 4 3 9 }
Sum = 6 + 4 + 3 + 9 = 22
FALSE
```

There's no question that the complexity of verification is linear regarding the length of each subset–add up all the numbers and compare the sum to the target–which puts it squarely in the P class. We found some seemingly efficient methods for handling the complexity of finding solutions that we may assume to have a polynomial-time complexity of $O(N \times M)$, where N is the size of the set and M is the target sum. This would appear to disqualify this problem as being NP-complete. However, this is actually not the case because M is not the size of the input, but rather its magnitude. Remember that computers represent integers in binary, and integers requiring a greater number of bits to represent them will also require a greater amount of time to process. Thus, every time the maximum value of M is doubled, it will essentially require twice the amount of time to compute.

So, unfortunately, our DP solution does not qualify as having polynomial complexity. We, therefore, define our approach to this problem as running in **pseudo-polynomial time**, and we can conclude that the subset sum problem is in fact NP-complete.

The Knapsack Problem

Now, let's reconsider the knapsack problem we looked at in *Chapter 5, Greedy Algorithms*, which we could describe as the subset sum problem's "big brother." It asks the following:

"Given a knapsack of limited capacity and a collection of weighted items of different values, what set of items can be contained within the knapsack that produces the greatest combined value without exceeding the capacity?"

This problem is also a characteristic example of NP-completeness, and as such, it shares many close ties to the other problems in this class.

Consider the following example:

```
Capacity -> 10
Number of items -> 5
Weights -> { 2, 3, 1, 4, 6 }
Values ->  { 4, 2, 7, 3, 9 }
```

With this data, we can produce the following subsets:

```
{ } | Weight = 0, Value = 0

{ 0 } | Weight = 2, Value = 4
{ 1 } | Weight = 3, Value = 2
{ 2 } | Weight = 1, Value = 7
{ 3 } | Weight = 4, Value = 3
{ 4 } | Weight = 6, Value = 9

{ 0 1 } | Weight = 5, Value = 6
{ 0 2 } | Weight = 3, Value = 11
{ 0 3 } | Weight = 6, Value = 7
{ 0 4 } | Weight = 6, Value = 8
{ 1 2 } | Weight = 4, Value = 9
{ 1 3 } | Weight = 7, Value = 5
{ 1 4 } | Weight = 9, Value = 11
{ 2 3 } | Weight = 5, Value = 7
{ 2 4 } | Weight = 7, Value = 16
{ 3 4 } | Weight = 10, Value = 12

{ 0 1 2 } | Weight = 6, Value = 13
{ 0 1 3 } | Weight = 9, Value = 9
{ 0 1 4 } | Weight = 11, Value = 15
{ 0 2 3 } | Weight = 7, Value = 14
{ 0 2 4 } | Weight = 9, Value = 20
{ 0 3 4 } | Weight = 12, Value = 16
{ 1 2 3 } | Weight = 8, Value = 12
{ 1 2 4 } | Weight = 10, Value = 18
{ 1 3 4 } | Weight = 13, Value = 14
{ 2 3 4 } | Weight = 11, Value = 19

{ 0 1 2 3 } | Weight = 10, Value = 16
{ 0 1 2 4 } | Weight = 12, Value = 22
{ 0 1 3 4 } | Weight = 15, Value = 18
{ 0 2 3 4 } | Weight = 13, Value = 23
{ 1 2 3 4 } | Weight = 14, Value = 21

{ 0 1 2 3 4 } | Weight = 16, Value = 25
```

Figure 9.2: All possible subsets for the given 0-1 knapsack problem

This definitely appears to be familiar territory. Could this require little more than a slight modification to the subset sum algorithm?

0-1 Knapsack – Extending the Subset Sum Algorithm

You may recall from our discussions in *Chapter 6, Graph Algorithms* I, that the previous example is that of the 0-1 knapsack problem. Here, we noticed another clear parallel between the current algorithm and the state logic we used to solve the subset sum problem.

In the subset sum problem, we concluded that for every element, **x**, at index **i** in **set**, we can do the following:

1. Add the value of **x** to a previously found subset sum.

2. Leave the subset sum as is.

This implies that a DP table entry for a new sum, **y**, at index **i + 1** can be marked **TRUE** if it is as follows:

1. An existing sum, **x**, in the previous row of the table, that is, **DP(i, x)**

2. The combined sum of **x** with the current element at **set[i]**, that is, **DP(i, x + set[i])**

In other words, whether or not a sum could be formed with a subset spanning the first **i** elements in the set was dependent on whether it had already been found earlier, or whether it could be found by adding the value of the current element to another previously found sum.

In the current problem, we can observe that for every item, **x**, at index **i** in **set** with weight **w**, we can do either of the following:

1. Add the value of **x** to a previously found subset sum of the item values, as long as the combined total of the corresponding items' weights with **w** is less than or equal to the maximum capacity.

2. Leave the subset sum as is.

This, in turn, implies that the maximum value sum, **y**, that can be found at index **i + 1** of the set of items with a combined weight **W** can be either of the following:

1. An existing maximum value sum, **x**, that had been found within the previous **i** items and had a combined weight of **w**

2. The combined sum of **x** with the value of the item at index **i**, assuming the weight of the item does not exceed capacity when added to **w**

Stated differently, the maximum value sum that can be formed with a subset of items spanning the first **i** items and having a combined weight of **w** is either equal to the maximum sum corresponding to weight **w** for the previous **i - 1** items or the sum produced by adding the current item's value to the total value of a previously found subset.

In pseudocode, we expressed the table-filling scheme for the subset sum problem as follows:

```
for sum (1 <= sum <= max_sum) found at index i of the set:


    if sum < set[i-1]:
     DP(i, sum) = DP(i-1, sum)


    if sum >= set[i-1]:
     DP(i, sum) = DP(i-1, sum) OR DP(i-1, sum - set[i-1])
```

The equivalent logic for the 0-1 knapsack problem would be as follows:

```
for total_weight (1 <= total_weight <= max_capacity) found at index i of the
set:


    if total_weight < weight[i]:
        maximum_value(i, total_weight) = maximum_value(i-1, total_weight)


    if total_weight >= weight[i]:
        maximum_value(i, total_weight) = maximum of:
            1) maximum_value(i-1, total_weight)
            2) maximum_value(i-1, total_weight - weight[i]) + value[i]
```

Here, we can see that the general algorithmic concepts are practically identical: we are traversing a two-dimensional search space bounded by the size of the set and the maximum sum of the set's elements and determining whether new subset sums can be found. The difference is that we are not merely recording whether or not a certain subset sum exists, but rather, we are collecting the maximum corresponding value sums associated with each subset of items and organizing them according to their total combined weights. We'll take a look at its implementation in the following exercise.

Exercise 41: 0-1 Knapsack Problem

We will now implement the preceding logic using the tabulated bottom-up approach. Let's get started:

1. We will begin by including the following headers:

```
#include <iostream>
#include <vector>
#include <algorithm>

using namespace std;
```

2. Our first step will be to handle the input. We will need to declare two integers, **items** and **capacity**, which represent the total number of items to choose from and the weight limit of the knapsack. We will also need two arrays, **value** and **weight**, where we will store the data corresponding to each item:

```
int main()
{
    int items, capacity;

    cin >> items >> capacity;

    vector<int> values(items), weight(items);

    for(auto &v : values) cin >> v;
    for(auto &w : weight) cin >> w;

    ......

}
```

3. Now, we will define the function **Knapsack_01()**, which has parameters corresponding to the input and returns an integer:

```
int Knapsack_01(int items, int capacity, vector<int> value, vector<int>
weight)
{
    ......
}
```

4. Our DP table will be two-dimensional and will correspond quite closely to the table we used in the subset sum problem. In the subset sum table, the first dimension's size was initialized to one greater than the length of the set, while the second dimension's size was initialized to one greater than the maximum sum of all the elements in the set. Here, our first dimension's size will equivalently be initialized to `items + 1`; likewise, the second dimension's size will be initialized to `capacity + 1`:

```
vector<vector<int>> DP(items + 1, vector<int>(capacity + 1, 0));
```

5. We will need to iterate across the length of both dimensions starting from `1`. At the beginning of each iteration of the outer loop, we will define two variables, `currentWeight` and `currentValue`, that correspond to the elements in `weight[i-1]` and `values[i-1]`, respectively:

```
for(int i = 1; i <= items; i++)
{
    int currentWeight = weight[i-1];
    int currentValue = values[i-1];

    for(int totalWeight = 1; totalWeight <= capacity; totalWeight++)
    {
        ......
    }
}
```

6. Now, we will implement our tabulation scheme:

```
if(totalWeight < currentWeight)
{
    DP[i][totalWeight] = DP[i-1][totalWeight];
}
else
{
    DP[i][totalWeight] = max(DP[i-1][totalWeight], DP[i-1][totalWeight -
currentWeight] + currentValue);
}
```

7. At the end of our function, we return the final element of the table:

```
return DP[items][capacity];
```

8. Now, we add a call to **main()** and print the output:

```
int result = Knapsack_01(items, capacity, values, weight);

cout << "The highest-valued subset of items that can fit in the knapsack
is: " << result << endl;

return 0;
```

9. Let's try running our program using the following input:

```
8 66
20 4 89 12 5 50 8 13
5 23 9 72 16 14 32 4
```

The output should be as follows:

```
The highest-valued subset of items that can fit in the knapsack is: 180
```

As we can see, a relatively efficient DP solution to the knapsack problem is little more than a slight modification of the same algorithm we used to solve the subset sum problem.

Unbounded Knapsack

The implementation we explored regarding the knapsack problem is the most traditional version, but as we mentioned earlier in this chapter, there are actually many varieties of this problem that can apply to different scenarios. We will now consider the case where we have unlimited amounts of each item in the set.

Let's consider an example where we find the solution by brute force:

```
Capacity = 25


Values -> { 5, 13, 4, 3, 8  }
Weight -> { 9, 12, 3, 7, 19 }


{ 0 } -> Weight = 9, Value = 5
{ 1 } -> Weight = 12, Value = 13
{ 2 } -> Weight = 3, Value = 4
{ 3 } -> Weight = 7, Value = 3
```

```
{ 4 } -> Weight = 32, Value = 8


{ 0, 0 } -> Weight = 18, Value = 10
{ 0, 1 } -> Weight = 21, Value = 18
{ 0, 2 } -> Weight = 12, Value = 9
{ 0, 3 } -> Weight = 16, Value = 8
{ 0, 4 } -> Weight = 28, Value = 13
{ 1, 1 } -> Weight = 24, Value = 26
{ 1, 2 } -> Weight = 15, Value = 17
{ 1, 3 } -> Weight = 19, Value = 16
{ 1, 4 } -> Weight = 31, Value = 21
{ 2, 2 } -> Weight = 6, Value = 8
{ 2, 3 } -> Weight = 10, Value = 7
{ 2, 4 } -> Weight = 22, Value = 12
{ 3, 3 } -> Weight = 14, Value = 6
{ 3, 4 } -> Weight = 26, Value = 11
{ 4, 4 } -> Weight = 38, Value = 16


{ 0, 0, 0 } -> Weight = 27, Value = 15
{ 0, 0, 1 } -> Weight = 30, Value = 26
{ 0, 0, 2 } -> Weight = 21, Value = 14
{ 0, 0, 3 } -> Weight = 25, Value = 13
{ 0, 0, 4 } -> Weight = 37, Value = 18
{ 0, 1, 1 } -> Weight = 33, Value = 31
```

......

From a brute-force perspective, this problem seems to be significantly more complex. Let's restate our pseudocode logic from the 0-1 knapsack implementation to handle this extra stipulation.

The maximum value sum, **y**, that can be found at index **i** of the set of items with a combined weight `total_weight` can be either of the following:

1. An existing maximum value sum, **x**, that had been found within the previous **i** - 1 items and also had a combined weight equal to `total_weight`

2. Assuming `total_weight` can be formed by adding `current_weight` to some other subset's total weight found within the previous **i** - 1 items:

   a) The sum of the current item's value with the maximum value sum for subsets spanning the previous **i** - 1 items and having a combined weight of `total_weight` - `current_weight`

   b) The sum of the current item's value with some previous **y** found in the recent iteration having a combined weight of `total_weight` - `current_weight`

In terms of the DP table, we can represent the new logic as follows:

```
for total_weight (1 <= total_weight <= max_capacity) found at index i of the
set:


    if total_weight < set[i-1]:

        maximum_value(i, total_weight) = maximum_value(i-1, total_weight)


    if total_weight >= set[i-1]:

        maximum_value(i, total_weight) = maximum of:

            1) maximum_value(i-1, total_weight)

            2) maximum_value(i-1, total_weight - current_weight) + current_value

            3) maximum_value(i, total_weight - current_weight) + current_value
```

We can implement this like so:

```
auto max = [](int a, int b, int c) { return std::max(a, std::max(b, c)); };


for(int i = 1; i <= items; i++)
{
    int current_weight = weight[i-1];
```

```
    int value = values[i-1];


    for(int total_weight = 0; total_weight <= capacity; w++)
    {
        if(total_weight < current_weight)
        {
            DP[i][total_weight] = DP[i-1][total_weight];
        }
        else
        {
            DP[i][total_weight] = max
            (
                DP[i-1][total_weight],
                DP[i-1][total_weight - current_weight] + value,
                DP[i][total_weight - current_weight] + value
            );
        }
    }
}
```

Logically, this approach will work, but it turns out that this is actually not the most efficient implementation. Let's understand its limitations and how to overcome them in the following section.

State Space Reduction

One rather tricky aspect of using DP effectively is the concept of **state space reduction**, which is the act of reformulating a working DP algorithm to use the minimal amount of space required to represent a state. This often comes down to exploiting some pattern or symmetry inherent to the nature of the problem.

To demonstrate this concept, let's consider the problem of finding the value in the nth row and m^{th} column of **Pascal's triangle**, which can be represented as follows:

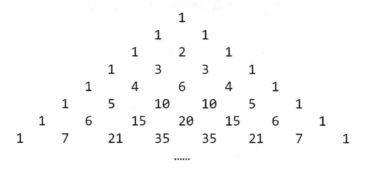

Figure 9.3: Pascal's triangle

Pascal's triangle is built according to the following logic:

```
For m <= n:
```

```
    Base case:
        m = 1, m = n -> triangle(n, m) = 1
```

```
    Recurrence:
        triangle(n, m) = triangle(n-1, m-1) + triangle(n-1, m)
```

In other words, the first value in every row is **1**, and each subsequent column value is equal to the sum of the current and previous columns of the previous row. As you can see from the following figure, in the second column of the second row, we get **2** by adding the elements in the second (**1**) and the first column (**1**) from the previous row:

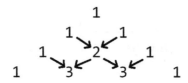

Figure 9.4: Getting the next values in Pascal's triangle

Solving the problem of finding the value in the nth row and m^{th} column using tabulation could be done as follows:

```
vector<vector<int>> DP(N + 1, vector<int>(N + 1, 0));


DP[1][1] = 1;


for(int row = 2; row <= N; row++)
{
    for(int col = 1; col <= row; col++)
    {
        DP[row][col] = DP[row-1][col-1] + DP[row-1][col];
    }
}
```

The DP table that was built in the preceding code would look like this for N = 7:

	0	1	2	3	4	5	6	7
0	0	0	0	0	0	0	0	0
1	0	1	0	0	0	0	0	0
2	0	1	1	0	0	0	0	0
3	0	1	2	1	0	0	0	0
4	0	1	3	3	1	0	0	0
5	0	1	4	6	4	1	0	0
6	0	1	5	10	10	5	1	0
7	0	1	6	15	20	15	6	1

Figure 9.5: Pascal's triangle represented as an N × N DP table

As we can see, this algorithm is quite wasteful both in terms of memory usage and redundant calculations. The immediately apparent problem is the fact that the table has N + 1 columns, despite the fact that only one row ever contains that many values. We could easily reduce space complexity by initializing each row as needed, sized according to the number of elements it requires, which reduces the space required by the table from N^2 to $N \times (N + 1) / 2$. Let's modify our implementation as follows:

```
vector<vector<int>> DP(N + 1);


DP[1] = { 0, 1 };


for(int row = 2; row <= N; row++)
{
    DP[row].resize(row + 1);


    for(int col = 1; col <= row; col++)
    {
        int a = DP[row-1][col-1];
        int b = DP[row-1][min(col, DP[row-1].size()-1)];


        DP[row][col] = a + b;

    }

}
```

We may further observe that there is a symmetrical relationship between the first and second half of each row, which means that we really only need to calculate the values for the first (n/2) columns. Therefore, we have the following:

```
DP(7, 7) ≡ DP(7, 1)
DP(7, 6) ≡ DP(7, 2)
DP(7, 5) ≡ DP(7, 3)
```

We could state this in a generalized way like so:

```
DP(N, M) ≡ DP(N, N - M + 1)
```

Considering this, we could modify our implementation as follows:

```cpp
vector<vector<int>> DP(N + 1);


DP[0] = { 0, 1 };


for(int row = 1; row <= N; row++)
{
    int width = (row / 2) + (row % 2);


    DP[row].resize(width + 2);


    for(int col = 1; col <= width; col++)
    {
        DP[row][col] = DP[row-1][col-1] + DP[row-1][col];
    }


    if(row % 2 == 0)
    {
        DP[row][width+1] = DP[row][width];
    }
}


......


for(int i = 0; i < queries; i++)
{
    int N, M;
    cin >> N >> M;
```

```
    if(M * 2 > N)
    {
        M = N - M + 1;
    }
    cout << DP[N][M] << endl;
}
```

Finally, assuming we were able to receive input queries in advance and precompute the results, we could abandon storing the full table entirely since only the previous row is needed to produce results for the current row. Hence, we could further modify our implementation as follows:

```
map<pair<int, int>, int> results;
vector<pair<int, int>> queries;

int q;
cin >> q;

int maxRow = 0;

for(int i = 0; i < q; i++)
{
    int N, M;
    cin >> N >> M;
    queries.push_back({N, M});

    if(M * 2 > N) M = N - M + 1;

    results[{N, M}] = -1;
    maxRow = max(maxRow, N);
}

vector<int> prev = { 0, 1 };
```

```
for(int row = 1; row <= maxRow; row++)
{
    int width = (row / 2) + (row % 2);

    vector<int> curr(width + 2);

    for(int col = 1; col <= width; col++)
    {
        curr[col] = prev[col-1] + prev[col];

        if(results.find({row, col}) != results.end())
        {
            queries[{row, col}] = curr[col];
        }
    }
    if(row % 2 == 0)
    {
        curr[width + 1] = curr[width];
    }
    prev = move(curr);
}
for(auto query : queries)
{
    int N = query.first, M = query.second;

    if(M * 2 > N) M = N - M + 1;

    cout << results[{N, M}] << endl;
}
```

Now, let's get back to the unbounded knapsack problem:

```
Capacity      ->    12
Values        -> { 5, 1, 6, 3, 4 }
Weight        -> { 3, 2, 4, 5, 2 }
```

The DP table that was constructed by our proposed solution in the previous section would look like this:

	0	1	2	3	4	5	6	7	8	9	10	11	12
0	0	0	0	0	0	0	0	0	0	0	0	0	0
1	0	0	0	5	5	5	10	10	10	15	15	15	20
2	0	0	1	5	5	6	10	10	11	15	15	16	20
3	0	0	1	5	6	6	10	11	12	15	16	17	20
4	0	0	1	5	6	6	10	11	12	15	16	17	20
5	0	0	4	5	8	9	12	13	16	17	20	21	24

Figure 9.6: Two-dimensional DP table constructed by the proposed algorithm

The logic that we used to produce the preceding table was based on the approach we used to solve the 0-1 form of the knapsack problem, and thus, we assumed that the maximum value sum for a given **weight** and **i** types of items, that is, **DP(i, weight)**, could be as follows:

1. The maximum value sum for the same weight and **i** - 1 types of items, without including the current item, that is, **DP(i - 1, weight)**

2. The sum of the current item's `value` with the maximum sum for `i - 1` types of items, that is, `DP(i - 1, weight - w) + value`

3. The sum of the current item's `value` with the maximum sum for `i` types of items if the item is to be included more than once, that is, `DP(i, weight - w) + value`

The first two conditions correspond to the logic of the 0-1 knapsack problem. However, considering them within the context of the unbounded knapsack and checking them against the table that was produced by our algorithm, we can actually conclude that the first two conditions are essentially irrelevant.

In the original problem, we were concerned about the values for `i - 1` items because we needed to decide whether to include or exclude item `i`, but in this problem, we have no reason to exclude any of the items as long as their weight doesn't exceed the knapsack's capacity. In other words, the conditions dictating each state transition are bounded only by the `weight` and are therefore representable in one dimension!

This leads to an important distinction that must be made: the dimensions required to *simulate* a state are not necessarily the same as the dimensions required to *describe* a state. Until now, every DP problem we have examined, when cached, results in a form that was essentially equivalent to the state itself. However, in the unbounded knapsack problem, we can describe each state as follows:

"For each item of weight w and value v, the maximum value of a knapsack of capacity C is equal to v plus the maximum value of a knapsack of capacity C - w."

Consider the following input data:

```
Capacity -> 12
Values   -> { 5, 1, 6, 3, 4 }
Weight   -> { 3, 2, 4, 5, 2 }
```

In the following table, each row represents a weight, w, from 0 to the maximum capacity, and each column represents the index, i, of an item. The number in every cell represents the maximum value sum for each weight after the item at index i has been considered:

	0	1	2	3	4
0	0	0	0	0	0
1	0	0	0	0	0
2	0	1	1	1	4
3	5	5	5	5	5
4	5	5	6	6	8
5	9	9	9	9	9
6	10	10	10	10	12
7	13	13	13	13	13
8	14	14	14	14	16
9	17	17	17	17	17
10	18	18	18	18	20
11	19	19	19	19	21
12	22	22	22	22	24

Figure 9.7: Subproblem results for each weight-index pair

As demonstrated in the preceding table, the allowance of duplicates means that no item needs to be excluded as long as its inclusion fits within the maximum capacity. Therefore, whether or not the weight sum could be found at index 0 or index 1,000 of the collection is irrelevant because we are never going to leave a previously found subset sum as is unless adding to it exceeds the defined bounds of the knapsack. This means that there is no advantage to maintaining a record of the item's index, which allows us to cache our subproblems in a single dimension – the combined weight of any number of items encountered. We'll look at its implementation in the following exercise.

Exercise 42: Unbounded Knapsack

In this exercise, we shall apply the concept of state space reduction to the unbounded knapsack problem by representing our DP table in one dimension. Let's get started:

1. Let's use the same headers and input that we used in the previous exercise:

```
#include <iostream>
#include <vector>
#include <algorithm>
using namespace std;

......

int main()
{
    int items, capacity;

    cin >> items >> capacity;

    vector<int> values(items), weight(items);

    for(auto &v : values) cin >> v;
    for(auto &w : weight) cin >> w;

    ......
}
```

2. Now, we will implement a function called **UnboundedKnapsack()** that returns an integer. Its parameters will be identical to the input:

```
int UnboundedKnapsack(int items, int capacity, vector<int> values,
vector<int> weight)
{
    ......
}
```

3. Our DP table will be represented as an integer vector with size equal to **capacity +** 1, with each index initialized to **0**:

```
vector<int> DP(capacity + 1, 0);
```

4. Like the 0-1 knapsack problem, our state logic will be contained in two nested loops; however, in this variation of the problem, we will invert the nesting of the loops so that the outer loop iterates from **0** to **capacity** (inclusive), and the inner loop iterates through the item indices:

```
for(int w = 0; w <= capacity; w++)
{
    for(int i = 0; i < items; i++)
    {
        ......
    }
}
```

5. Now, we must decide on how to cache our states. Our only concern is that the capacity is not exceeded by the weights of the chosen items. Since our table is only large enough to represent weight values from **0** to **capacity**, we only need to make sure that the difference between **w** and **weight[i]** is non-negative. Thus, all of the assignment logic can be contained within a single **if** statement:

```
for(int w = 0; w <= capacity; w++)
{
    for(int i = 0; i < items; i++)
    {
        if(weight[i] <= w)
        {
            DP[w] = max(DP[w], DP[w - weight[i]] + values[i]);
```

```
        }
      }
    }

    return DP[capacity];
```

6. Now, let's return to **main()**, add a call to **UnboundedKnapsack()**, and output the results:

```
int main()
{
    ......

        int result = UnboundedKnapsack(items, capacity, values, weight);

        cout << "Maximum value of items that can be contained in the knapsack:
    " << result << endl;

        return 0;
}
```

7. Try running your program with the following input:

```
30 335
91 81 86 64 24 61 13 57 60 25 94 54 39 62 5 34 95 12 53 33 53 3 42 75 56 1
84 38 46 62
40 13 4 17 16 35 5 33 35 16 25 29 6 28 12 37 26 27 32 27 7 24 5 28 39 15
38 37 15 40
```

Your output should be as follows:

```
Maximum value of items that can be contained in the knapsack: 7138
```

As demonstrated by the preceding implementation, it is often worth it to consider less costly ways to cache solutions in a DP algorithm. Problems that seem to require complex state representations can often be simplified significantly after closer examination.

Activity 22: Maximizing Profit

You are working for a large chain of department stores. Like any retail business, your company purchases items from wholesale distributors in large quantities and then sells them at a higher price to gain profit. Certain types of products that are being sold in your store can be purchased from multiple different distributors, but the quality and price of the products can vary considerably, which naturally has an effect on its corresponding retail value. Once factors such as exchange rates and public demand are taken into account, products from certain distributors can often be bought at a much lower price per unit than what they can ultimately be sold for. You have been tasked with designing a system that calculates the maximum profit you can gain with an allotted budget.

You have been provided with a catalog of similar products. Each listed product has the following information:

- The wholesale price of the product

- The amount of profit that can be made by selling the same product after markup

- The quantity of the product sold per unit by the distributor

Given that the distributor will only sell the product in the exact quantity specified, your task is to determine the maximum amount of money that can be made by purchasing some subset of the listed products. To ensure that the store offers a variety of choices, each item that's listed can only be purchased once.

Since you only have a limited amount of warehouse space and don't want to overstock a particular type of item, you are also given a restriction on the maximum number of individual units that can be purchased. Therefore, your program should also ensure that the combined number of products that are bought does not exceed this limit.

Example

Say five items are listed in the catalog with the following information:

Product	A	B	C	D	E
Quantity	10	5	12	3	4
Price	20	10	15	50	40
Value	50	20	20	60	80

Figure 9.8: Sample values for profit optimization

You have a budget of $100 and a warehouse capacity of 20 units. The following sets of purchases would be valid:

```
{ A B }     Cost: 30     | Quantity: 15     | Value: 70
{ A D }     Cost: 70     | Quantity: 13     | Value: 110
{ A E }     Cost: 60     | Quantity: 14     | Value: 130
{ B C }     Cost: 25     | Quantity: 17     | Value: 40
{ C D }     Cost: 65     | Quantity: 15     | Value: 80
{ C E }     Cost: 55     | Quantity: 16     | Value: 100
{ D E }     Cost: 90     | Quantity: 7      | Value: 140

{ A B D }   Cost: 80     | Quantity: 18     | Value: 130
{ A B E }   Cost: 70     | Quantity: 19     | Value: 150
{ B C D }   Cost: 75     | Quantity: 20     | Value: 100
{ B D E }   Cost: 100    | Quantity: 12     | Value: 160
```

Thus, the program should output **160**.

Input

The first line contains three integers, **N** as the number of distributors, **budget** as the maximum amount of money that can be spent, and **capacity** as the maximum number of units that can be purchased.

The next **N** lines should contain three space-separated integers:

- **quantity**: The quantity per unit offered by the distributor
- **cost**: The price of the item
- **value**: The amount of profit that can be gained after selling the product

Output

A single integer representing the maximum amount of profit that can be made by choosing some subset of items from the catalog.

Test cases

The following set of test cases should help you understand this problem better:

Input	Output
5 5 5	5
1 1 1	
1 1 1	
1 1 1	
1 1 1	
1 1 1	

Figure 9.9: Activity 22 test case 1

Input	Output
5 30 25	102
6 11 56	
13 34 36	
11 27 31	
9 31 55	
11 17 46	

Figure 9.10: Activity 22 test case 2

Input	Output
10 450 50	3500
2 66 149	
19 59 279	
7 82 474	
5 96 298	
7 72 89	
20 51 573	
2 36 795	
7 30 820	
17 52 155	
3 81 391	

Figure 9.11: Activity 22 test case 3

Input	Output
20 1000 100	3281
33 256 448	
30 249 578	
18 272 773	
36 186 597	
18 262 388	
31 241 372	
13 126 594	
38 220 619	
48 142 454	
14 271 690	
27 157 638	
40 112 715	
26 116 586	
18 287 500	
44 108 523	
26 171 425	
31 133 330	
16 285 399	
47 155 457	
49 206 724	

Figure 9.12: Activity 22 test case 4

Activity Guidelines

- The implementation that's required is very similar to the 0-1 knapsack problem.

- Since there are two constraints (capacity and budget), the DP table will require three dimensions.

> **Note**
>
> The solution to this activity can be found on page 581.

Graphs and Dynamic Programming

In this section, we have discussed advanced graph algorithms and DP as distinctly different topics, but as is often the case, they can be used concurrently depending on the type of problem we are trying to solve and the nature of the graph. Several problems commonly associated with graphs are identified as NP-complete (graph coloring and the vertex cover problem, to name two examples) and can, under the right circumstances, be solved with dynamic programming. However, most of these topics are outside the scope of this book (and are actually worthy of having entire books dedicated specifically to their analysis).

However, one problem in graph theory is particularly well suited to the DP approach, and fortunately, it is one we are already very familiar with: the shortest-path problem. In fact, in *Chapter 7, Graph Algorithms II*, we actually discussed an algorithm that's commonly categorized under the DP umbrella, despite the fact that we never identified it as such.

Reconsidering the Bellman-Ford Algorithm

In our exploration of the Bellman-Ford algorithm, we were viewing it in light of our previous discussions of Dijkstra's algorithm, with which it certainly shares some similarities. But now that we have a solid grasp of the concepts underlying the dynamic programming paradigm, let's reconsider Bellman-Ford according to our new understanding.

In brief, the approach that's used by Bellman-Ford can be described as follows:

Given a source node called **start**, the number of vertices, **V**, and the edges, **E**, of a graph, do the following:

1. Mark distances of each node from **0** to **V - 1** (inclusive) as **UNKNOWN**, except for **start**, which is **0**.

2. Iterate from **1** to **V - 1** (inclusive).

3. On each iteration, consider every edge in **E** and check to see whether the source node's respective distance value is **UNKNOWN**. If not, then compare the neighboring node's currently stored distance to the sum of the source node's distance with the edge weight between them.

4. If the sum of the source node's distance with the edge weight is less than the destination node's distance, update the destination node's distance to the lesser value.

5. After **V - 1** iterations, either the shortest path has been found or the graph has a negative weight cycle, which can be determined with an additional iteration through the edges.

The success of this algorithm is clearly dependent on the fact that the problem exhibits an optimal substructure. We can illustrate the recursive logic behind this concept as follows:

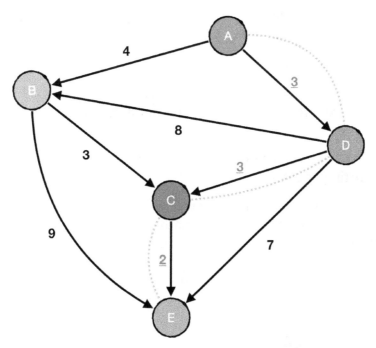

Figure 9.13: Visualizing the Bellman-Ford algorithm

Expressing this as pseudocode would look something like the following:

```
Source -> A
Destination -> E


The shortest path from A to E is equal to:
    ...the edge weight from A to B (4), plus...
        ...the shortest path from B to E, which is:
            ...the edge weight from B to C (3), plus:
                ...the edge weight from C to E (2).
            ...or the edge weight from B to E (9).
    ...or the edge weight from A to D (3), plus:
        ...the shortest path from D to E, which is:
            ...the edge weight from D to B (8), plus:
                ...the shortest path from B to E (9), which is:
```

...the edge weight from B to C (3), plus:

...the edge weight from C to E (2).

...or the edge weight from B to E (9).

...the edge weight from D to C (3), plus:

...the edge weight from C to E (2).

...or the edge weight from D to E (7).

Clearly, the shortest-path problem also possesses the overlapping subproblems property. Bellman-Ford effectively avoids recomputation due to two key observations:

- The maximum number of moves that can be made in a non-cyclic traversal between any two nodes in a graph is | V - 1 | (that is, every node in the graph minus the starting node).

- The shortest path between a source node and every reachable node after N iterations is equivalent to the shortest paths to every node that's reachable after | N - 1 | iterations, plus the edge weights to each of their neighbors.

The following set of figures should help you better visualize the steps in the Bellman-Ford algorithm:

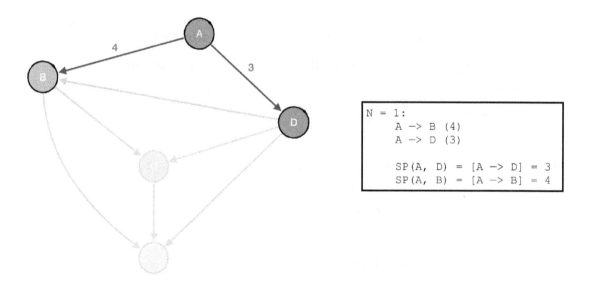

```
N = 1:
    A -> B  (4)
    A -> D  (3)

    SP(A, D)  =  [A -> D]  =  3
    SP(A, B)  =  [A -> B]  =  4
```

Figure 9.14: Bellman-Ford Step 1

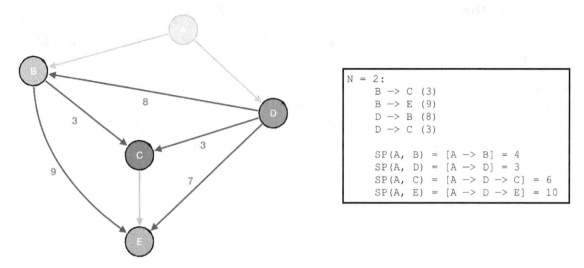

```
N = 2:
     B -> C (3)
     B -> E (9)
     D -> B (8)
     D -> C (3)

     SP(A, B) = [A -> B] = 4
     SP(A, D) = [A -> D] = 3
     SP(A, C) = [A -> D -> C] = 6
     SP(A, E) = [A -> D -> E] = 10
```

Figure 9.15: Bellman-Ford Step 2

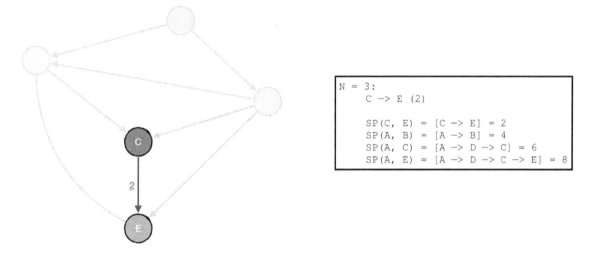

```
N = 3:
     C -> E (2)

     SP(C, E) = [C -> E] = 2
     SP(A, B) = [A -> B] = 4
     SP(A, C) = [A -> D -> C] = 6
     SP(A, E) = [A -> D -> C -> E] = 8
```

Figure 9.16: Bellman-Ford Step 3

The specific problem that Bellman-Ford is said to solve is known as the **single-source shortest path problem** because it is used to find the shortest paths for a single node. In *Chapter 7, Graph Algorithms II*, we discussed Johnson's algorithm, which solves what is known as the **all-pairs shortest path problem** because it finds the shortest paths between every pair of vertices in the graph.

Johnson's algorithm combined the DP approach seen in the Bellman-Ford algorithm with the greedy approach seen in Dijkstra's. In this section, we will explore a complete DP implementation of the all-pairs shortest path problem. However, let's consider the nature of the problem a bit deeper by implementing a top-down solution.

Approaching the Shortest Path Problem as a DP Problem

One way to better understand the logic behind Bellman-Ford is to transform it into a top-down solution. To do this, let's start by considering our base cases.

Bellman-Ford performs V - 1 iterations through the edges of the graph, typically by way of a **for** loop. Since our previous implementations have iterated from 1 to V - 1 inclusive, let's have our top-down solution begin at V - 1 and decrement to 0. In terms of our recurrence structure, let's say that every state can be described as follows:

```
ShortestPath(node, depth)
```

```
node -> the node being considered
depth -> the current iteration in the traversal
```

Therefore, our first base case can be defined as follows:

```
if depth = 0:
```

```
            ShortestPath(node, depth) -> UNKNOWN
```

In other words, if **depth** has been decremented to **0**, we can conclude that no path exists and terminate our search.

The second base case we need to handle is, of course, the point where we find a path from the source to the target. In this case, the depth of the search is irrelevant; the shortest distance from the target to itself will always be **0**:

```
if node = target:
```

```
            ShortestPath(node, depth) -> 0
```

Now, let's define our intermediate states. Let's review what the iterative approach that's used by Bellman-Ford looks like:

```
for i = 1 to V - 1:
```

```
        for each edge in graph:
```

```
                edge -> u, v, weight
```

```
        if distance(u) is not UNKNOWN and distance(u) + weight <
distance(v):

            distance(v) = distance(u) + weight
```

In terms of a recursive traversal, this can be restated as follows:

```
for each edge adjacent to node:


        edge -> neighbor, weight


    if ShortestPath(neighbor, depth - 1) + weight < ShortestPath(node,
depth):

            ShortestPath(node, depth) = ShortestPath(neighbor, depth - 1) +
weight
```

Since every state can be uniquely described according to these two dimensions and the possible existence of cycles means that we are likely to encounter the same states more than once, we can conclude that caching according to node-depth pairs is both valid and useful for memoization purposes:

```
Depth = 7:
    SP(0, 7): 0
    SP(1, 7): 6
    SP(2, 7): UNKNOWN
    SP(3, 7): 12
    SP(4, 7): UNKNOWN
    SP(5, 7): UNKNOWN
    SP(6, 7): 13
    SP(7, 7): UNKNOWN


Depth = 6:
    SP(0, 6): 0
    SP(1, 6): 6
    SP(2, 6): 14
    SP(3, 6): 12
```

```
    SP(4, 6): UNKNOWN
    SP(5, 6): UNKNOWN
    SP(6, 6): 12
    SP(7, 6): 15


Depth = 5:
    SP(0, 5): 0
    SP(1, 5): 6
    SP(2, 5): 14
```

These states are illustrated in the following figure:

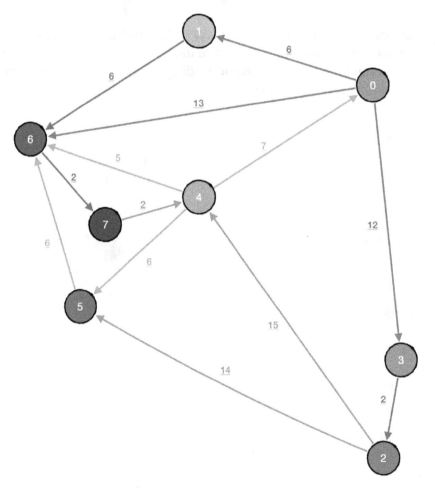

Figure 9.17: All the states for the shortest-path problem

We'll look at the implementation of this approach in the following exercise.

Exercise 43: Single-Source Shortest Paths (Memoization)

In this exercise, we shall take the top-down DP approach to finding a solution to the single-source shortest path problem. Let's get started:

1. Let's begin by including the following headers and the **std** namespace, as well as defining an **UNKNOWN** constant:

```cpp
#include <iostream>
#include <vector>
#include <utility>
#include <map>
using namespace std;

const int UNKNOWN = 1e9;
```

2. Let's also declare **V** and **E** (the number of vertices and the number of edges, respectively), as well as two two-dimensional integer vectors, **adj** (an adjacency list of our graph) and **weight** (a matrix of edge weight values). Finally, we will define a memoization table called **memo**. This time, we will use **std::map** to simplify the differentiation between checking whether a key exists in the cache versus whether its value is unknown:

```cpp
int V, E;

vector<vector<int>> adj;
vector<vector<int>> weight;

map<pair<int, int>, int> memo;
```

3. In the **main()** function, we should handle input so that we receive the graph we wish to apply the algorithm to. The first line of input will contain **V** and **E**, and the following **E** lines will contain three integers: **u**, **v**, and **w** (the source, destination, and weight of each edge, respectively):

```cpp
int main()
{
        int V, E;
        cin >> V >> E;

        weight.resize(V, vector<int>(V, UNKNOWN));
        adj.resize(V);

        for(int i = 0; i < E; i++)
        {
```

```
        int u, v, w;
        cin >> u >> v >> w;

        adj[u].push_back(v);
        weight[u][v] = w;
    }
        …
}
```

4. We will now define a function called **SingleSourceShortestPaths()** that will take one argument—**source**, which is the index of the source vertex—and will return an integer vector:

```
vector<int> SingleSourceShortestPaths(int source)
{
        ……
}
```

5. Now we will need to make some preliminary modifications to our graph. As opposed to traversing from the source node to all the other nodes in the graph, we will instead begin each traversal from the other nodes and calculate the shortest path from the source in reverse. Since our graph is directed, we will have to use its transpose to accomplish this:

```
// Clear table

vector<vector<int>> adj_t(V);
vector<vector<int>> weight_t(V, vector<int>(V, UNKNOWN));

for(int i = 0; i < V; i++)
{
        // Create transpose of graph
        for(auto j : adj[i])
        {
            adj_t[j].push_back(i);
            weight_t[j][i] = weight[i][j];
        }

        // Base case - shortest distance from source to itself is zero at
    any depth
        memo[{source, i}] = 0;
```

```
        if(i != source)
        {
            // If any node other than the source has been reached
            // after V - 1 iterations, no path exists.

            memo[{i, 0}] = UNKNOWN;
        }
    }
}
```

Here, we defined two new two-dimensional integer vectors, **adj_t** and **weight_t**, which will correspond to the adjacency list and weight matrix for the transpose graph. We then used a nested loop to create our modified graph, as well as initialized the values in our **memo** table.

6. We should now define the **ShortestPath_Memoization()** function with four parameters: two integers, **depth** and **node**, and **adj** and **weight** (which, in this case, will be references to the transpose graph):

```
    int ShortestPath_Memoization(int depth, int node, vector<vector<int>>
&adj, vector<vector<int>> &weight)
    {
        ......
    }
```

7. Our algorithm will essentially be a standard depth-first search, except we will cache the results for each **{ node, depth }** pair at the end of each function call. At the top of the function, we will check for a cached result and return it if the key exists in the map:

```
    // Check if key exists in map
    if(memo.find({node, depth}) != memo.end())
    {
        return memo[{node, depth}];
    }

    memo[{node, depth}] = UNKNOWN;

    // Iterate through adjacent edges
    for(auto next : adj[node])
    {
```

```
        int w = weight[node][next];
        int dist = ShortestPath_Memoization(depth - 1, next, adj, weight) + w;

        memo[{node, depth}] = min(memo[{node, depth}], dist);
    }

    return memo[{node, depth}];
```

8. Back in the **SingleSourceShortestPaths()** function, we will define an integer vector called **distance** of size **V** and fill it through successive calls to **ShortestPath_ Memoization()**:

```
vector<int> distance;

for(int i = 0; i < V; i++)
{
    distance[i] = ShortestPath_Memoization(V - 1, i, adj_t, weight_t);
}

return distance;
```

9. Back in **main()**, we will define a two-dimensional integer matrix called **paths**, which will store the distances returned from **SingleSourceShortestPaths()** for each node index from **0** to **V**:

```
vector<vector<int>> paths(V);

for(int i = 0; i < V; i++)
{
    paths[i] = SingleSourceShortestPaths(i);
}
```

10. We can now use the **paths** table to print the distance values for every pair of nodes in the graph:

```
cout << "The shortest distances between each pair of vertices are:" <<
endl;

for(int i = 0; i < V; i++)
{
        for(int j = 0; j < V; j++)
        {
          cout << "\t" << j << ": ";
```

```
            (paths[i][j] == UNKNOWN) ? cout << "- ";
                                     : cout << paths[i][j] << " ";

        }
        cout << endl;
    }
}
```

11. Now, run your code with the following input:

```
8 20
0 1 387
0 3 38
0 5 471
1 0 183
1 4 796
2 5 715
3 0 902
3 1 712
3 2 154
3 6 425
4 3 834
4 6 214
5 0 537
5 3 926
5 4 125
5 6 297
6 1 863
6 7 248
7 0 73
7 3 874
```

The output should be as follows:

```
The shortest distances between each pair of vertices are:
0: 0 387 192 38 596 471 463 711
1: 183 0 375 221 779 654 646 894
2: 1252 1639 0 1290 840 715 1012 1260
3: 746 712 154 0 994 869 425 673
4: 535 922 727 573 0 1006 214 462
5: 537 924 729 575 125 0 297 545
6: 321 708 513 359 917 792 0 248
7: 73 460 265 111 669 544 536 0
```

Unsurprisingly, this is not the preferred way of handling this particular problem, but as with the previous exercises, we can learn quite a bit about how the optimal substructure is formed by implementing recursive solutions like this one. With these insights, we are now equipped to fully understand how the shortest distances between every pair of nodes can be found simultaneously using tabulation.

All-Pairs Shortest Path

Our program from the previous exercise does print the shortest paths for every vertex pair, but its efficiency is roughly equivalent to performing **V** calls to Bellman-Ford, with the added memory-related disadvantages associated with recursive algorithms.

Thankfully, there is a very useful bottom-up algorithm for this problem that is equipped to handle everything that the others can in $O(V^3)$ time and $O(V^2)$ space. It is also quite intuitive, particularly after having implemented the other shortest path algorithms in this book.

The Floyd-Warshall Algorithm

By now, we should have a fairly clear grasp of how the Bellman-Ford algorithm exploits the optimal substructure that's exhibited in the shortest path problem. The key takeaway is that any shortest path between two graph vertices is going to be a combination of some other shortest path beginning from the source and the edge connecting the path's endpoint to the destination vertex.

The **Floyd–Warshall algorithm** uses this same concept to great effect by making an even broader generalization:

"If the shortest distance between Node A and Node B is AB, and the shortest distance between Node B and Node C is BC, then the shortest distance between Node A and Node C is AB + BC."

This logic certainly isn't groundbreaking in and of itself; however, combined with the insight demonstrated by Bellman-Ford—that V iterations across the edges of a graph is sufficient to determine the shortest path from a source node and every other node in a graph—we can use this idea to successively generate the shortest paths between pairs of nodes with **Node A** as the source, and then use those results to generate potential shortest paths for **Node B, C, D**, and so on.

Floyd-Warshall accomplishes this by performing V^3 iterations across the vertices. The first dimension represents a potential midpoint, B, between every possible pair of vertices A and C. The algorithm then checks whether the currently known distance value from A to C is greater than the sum of the shortest known distances from A to B and B to C. If so, it determines that that sum is at least closer to the optimal shortest distance value for A and C, and caches it in a table. Floyd-Warshall makes these sets of comparisons using every node in the graph as a midpoint, continuously improving the accuracy of its results. After every possible start and end point pair has been tested against every possible midpoint, the results in the table contain the correct shortest distance values for every pair of vertices.

Just like any graph-related algorithm, Floyd-Warshall is not guaranteed to be the best choice in every given circumstance, and comparative complexity between Floyd-Warshall and other alternatives should always be considered. A good rule of thumb is to use Floyd-Warshall for dense graphs (that is, graphs containing a large number of edges). Imagine, for example, that you have a graph with 100 vertices and 500 edges. Running the Bellman-Ford algorithm (with a worst-case complexity of $O(V \times E)$) on each starting vertex successively could potentially lead to a total complexity of 500×100×100 (or 5,000,000) operations, whereas Floyd-Warshall would require 100×100×100 (or 1,000,000) operations. Dijkstra's algorithm is usually more efficient than Bellman-Ford and may also be a viable alternative. Nevertheless, one distinct advantage of Floyd-Warshall is the fact that the overall complexity of the algorithm is always exactly $O(V^3)$, regardless of the other properties of the input graph. So, we do not need to know any details about the graph we are using other than the number of vertices to be able to determine exactly how efficient (or inefficient) Floyd-Warshall will be.

A final point to consider is the fact that, like Bellman-Ford (and unlike Dijkstra's algorithm), Floyd-Warshall is equipped to handle graphs with negative edge weights but will also be thwarted by negative edge weight cycles without explicit handling.

We'll implement the Floyd-Warshall algorithm in the following exercise.

Exercise 44: Implementing the Floyd-Warshall Algorithm

In this exercise, we shall find the shortest distance between every pair of vertices using the Floyd-Warshall algorithm. Let's get started:

1. We will begin by including the following headers and defining an **UNKNOWN** constant:

```
#include <iostream>
#include <vector>
using namespace std;

const int UNKNOWN = 1e9;
```

2. Let's begin by handling the input almost exactly like we did in the previous exercise. This time, however, we have no need for an adjacency list representation of the graph:

```
int main()
{
        int V, E;
        cin >> V >> E;

        vector<vector<int>> weight(V, vector<int>(V, UNKNOWN));

        for(int i = 0; i < E; i++)
        {
            int u, v, w;
            cin >> u >> v >> w;

            weight[u][v] = w;
        }
        ......

        return 0;
}
```

3. Our **FloydWarshall()** function will take two arguments—**V** and **weight**—and will return a two-dimensional integer vector of shortest-path distances:

```
vector<vector<int>> FloydWarshall(int V, vector<vector<int>> weight)
{
        ......
}
```

4. Let's define a two-dimensional DP table with the name **distance** and with every value initialized to **UNKNOWN**. Then, we need to assign the initially known shortest distance "estimates" for each pair of nodes (that is, the values in the **weight** matrix), as well as the base case values (that is, the shortest distance from every node to itself, **0**):

```
vector<vector<int>> distance(V, vector<int>(V, UNKNOWN));

for(int i = 0; i < V; i++)
{
    for(int j = 0; j < V; j++)
    {
        distance[i][j] = weight[i][j];
    }
    distance[i][i] = 0;
}
```

5. We will now perform three nested **for** loops from **0** to **V** - **1** (inclusive), with the outer loop representing the current intermediate vertex, **mid**, the middle loop representing the source vertex, **start**, and the innermost loop representing the destination vertex, **end**. We will then compare distance values between every combination of vertices and reassign the distance value from start to end whenever a shorter path is found:

```
for(int mid = 0; mid < V; mid++)
{
    for(int start = 0; start < V; start++)
    {
        for(int end = 0; end < V; end++)
        {
            if(distance[start][mid] + distance[mid][end] < distance[start]
[end])
            {
                distance[start][end] = distance[start][mid] +
distance[mid][end];
            }
        }
    }
}
```

6. Similar to Bellman-Ford, we will need to check for negative cycles if our input is expected to contain negative edge weights. Thankfully, this can be accomplished with great ease using the distance table.

Consider the fact that a graph cycle is a path that has a length greater than zero and is where the start and end vertices are the same. In a table representing distances between each pair of nodes, the shortest path between a node and itself will be contained in **distance[node][node]**. In a graph containing only positive edge weights, the value contained in **distance[node][node]** can clearly only ever be equal to **0**; however, if the graph contains a negative weight cycle, **distance[node][node]** will be negative. Thus, we can test for negative cycles like so:

```cpp
for(int i = 0; i < V; i++)
{
        // If distance from a node to itself is negative, there must be a
negative cycle

        if(distance[i][i] < 0)
        {
            return {};
        }
}

return distance;
```

7. Now that we have finished writing the algorithm, we can perform a call to **FloydWarshall()** in **main()** and output the results:

```cpp
int main()
{
    ......

    vector<vector<int>> distance = FloydWarshall(V, weight);

    // Graphs with negative cycles will return an empty vector
    if(distance.empty())
    {
        cout << "NEGATIVE CYCLE FOUND" << endl;
        return 0;
    }

    for(int i = 0; i < V; i++)
    {
```

```
        cout << i << endl;

        for(int j = 0; j < V; j++)
        {
            cout << "\t" << j << ": ";

            (distance[i][j] == UNKNOWN)
                ? cout << "_" << endl
                : cout << distance[i][j] << endl;
        }
    }
    return 0;
}
```

8. Let's run our program on the following set of input:

   Input:

   ```
   7 9
   0 1 3
   1 2 5
   1 3 10
   1 5 -4
   2 4 2
   3 2 -7
   4 1 -3
   5 6 -8
   6 0 12
   ```

   Output:

   ```
   0:
           0: 0
           1: 3
           2: 6
           3: 13
           4: 8
           5: -1
           6: -9
   ```

```
1:
        0: 0
        1: 0
        2: 3
        3: 10
        4: 5
        5: -4
        6: -12
2:
        0: -1
        1: -1
        2: 0
        3: 9
        4: 2
        5: -5
        6: -13
3:
        0: -8
        1: -8
        2: -7
        3: 0
        4: -5
        5: -12
        6: -20
4:
        0: -3
        1: -3
        2: 0
        3: 7
        4: 0
        5: -7
        6: -15
5:
        0: 4
        1: 7
        2: 10
        3: 17
        4: 12
```

```
                    5: 0
                    6: -8
         6:
                    0: 12
                    1: 15
                    2: 18
                    3: 25
                    4: 20
                    5: 11
                    6: 0
```

9. Now, let's try another set of input:

    Input:

    ```
    6 8
    0 1 3
    1 3 -8
    2 1 3
    2 4 2
    2 5 5
    3 2 3
    4 5 -1
    5 1 8
    ```

    Output:

    ```
    NEGATIVE CYCLE FOUND
    ```

As you can see, Floyd-Warshall is an incredibly useful algorithm that is not only effective but quite easy to implement. In terms of efficiency, whether we should choose Floyd-Warshall or Johnson's algorithm depends entirely on the structure of the graph. But strictly in terms of ease of implementation, Floyd-Warshall is the clear winner.

Activity 23: Residential Roads

You are the head of a real estate development project that is planning on constructing a number of high-end residential communities. You've been given a variety of information about the various properties where developments will be built and are currently tasked with designing a system of roads as cheaply as possible.

Many of the communities are set to be built in areas replete with lakes, forests, and mountains. In these areas, the terrain is often quite rugged, which can make construction much more complicated. You have been warned that the cost of building increases based on the ruggedness of the terrain. For your first drafts, you are told to consider the increase in cost linearly, relative to the ruggedness value of each coordinate where a road may be built.

You've been given the following information:

- Maps of the properties

- The coordinates where properties can be built

- The ruggedness of the terrain at each coordinate

You have also been given the following guidelines for determining how roads should be built:

- Points on the map where a road may be built will be marked with "." characters.

- Roads may only be built between two houses that have a direct vertical, horizontal, or diagonal path between them.

- All the houses in the community should be reachable from every other house.

- Roads may not be built across bodies of water, mountains, forests, and so on.

- The cost of building a road between two houses is equal to the sum of ruggedness values on the path between them.

- A road between two houses should be built only if it is on the path with the lowest possible cost to the designated entry point of the property.

- The entrance point is always the highest indexed house in the input.

Once the positions of the houses and roads have been determined, you should produce a new version of the original map according to the following legend:

- Houses should be labeled with uppercase letters corresponding to the order they were given in input (that is, 0 = A, 1 = B, 2 = C and so on).

- Roads should be indicated with the characters |, -, \, and /, depending on their orientation. If two roads with different orientations intersect, this should be indicated with the + character.

- Everything else on the map should be displayed as it was originally given in the input.

Input Format

The program should take an input in the following format:

- The first line contains two space-separated integers, H and W, representing the height and width of the map.

- The second contains a single integer, N, which is the number of houses to be built.

- The next H lines each contain a string of length W, representing a row on the grid. Valid locations for building roads will be marked with the "." character.

- The next N lines contain two integers, x and y, which are the coordinates of the houses. The final index (that is, N - 1) always represents the entry point to the community.

Output Format

The program should output the same map given in the input, with the following additions:

- The positions of each house should be labeled with uppercase letters corresponding to their zero-based index, with the origin on the top left, relative to N (that is, 0 = A, 1 = B, 2 = C, and so on).

- The roads connecting each pair of houses should be indicated as follows:

  - if the road's orientation is horizontal

  | if the road's orientation is vertical

  / or \ if the road's orientation is diagonal

  + if any number of roads with different orientations intersect at the same point

Hints/Guidelines

- To produce the final result, a number of distinct steps are required. It is recommended that you outline the necessary steps prior to their implementation.

- It may be quite helpful to devise some scheme for debugging and producing test output for each individual part of the program. A mistake early on in the process is likely to cause subsequent steps to fail.

- Study the simpler input and output samples if you are having trouble understanding what needs to be done.

- Start by implementing the algorithms you know you will need, particularly the ones we discussed in the previous chapter. There may be multiple ways to accomplish each part of this task—be creative!

Test Cases

These test cases should help you understand how you need to proceed. Let's begin by taking a simple example:

```
Input:          Output:         Input:              Output:

5 5             A...B           5 5                 A.#.B
5               .\./.           5                   |###|
.....           ..D..           ..#..               |.D.|
.....           ./...           .###.               |/#\|
.....           E---C           .....               E.##C
.....                           ..#..
.....                           ..##.
0 42 68 35 0                    0 42 0 35 0
1 70 25 79 59                   1 0 0 0 59
63 65 0 6 46                    63 65 0 6 46
82 28 62 92 96                  82 28 0 92 96
0 43 28 37 0                    0 43 0 0 0
0 0                             0 0
4 0                             4 0
4 4                             4 4
2 2                             2 2
0 4                             0 4
```

Figure 9.18: Activity 23, test cases 1 (left) and 2 (right)

Let's consider the sample output on the right side of the previous figure. In that example, a path from E(0,4) to C(5,4) cannot be built as impassable obstacles, #, exist. Let's consider a few more samples with more complexity:

Input:	Output:	Input:	Output:
10 10	A-------B.	7 13	.........K--L
11	|\\##......	12	.A--B.../../.
....	|.\\&#&....	....	.|...\\.J../..
..##......	|..\\&C--D.	....	.C....+|.D...
...&#&....	E...\\\|..|.	....	...../.E..\\..
....&.....	|....+..|.	....	....F..|...\\.
....	|@F--++-G.	....	.......G--H.I
....	|.@##|.\\..	....	
.@........	|.#..|.#\\.	....	
..@##.....	I--H.J---K	....	
..#....#..		42 68 35 1 70 25 79 59 63 0	
....		65 6 0	
0 1 1 1 1 1 1 1 0 9		46 0 82 28 0 62 92 96 43 28	
1 1 0 0 9 9 9 9 9 9		37 92 5	
1 9 1 0 0 0 9 9 9 9		3 54 93 83 22 17 19 0 96 48	
1 9 9 1 0 1 1 1 0 9		27 72 39	
0 9 9 9 1 1 9 9 1 9		70 0 13 68 100 36 95 4 12 0	
1 9 9 20 9 1 9 9 1 9		23 34 74	
1 0 0 1 1 1 1 1 0 9		65 42 12 54 69 48 45 0 63	
1 9 0 0 0 1 9 1 9 9		58 38 60 24	
1 9 0 9 0 1 20 0 1 9		42 30 79 17 0 36 91 43 89 7	
0 1 1 0 20 0 1 1 1 0		41 43 65	
0 0		49 47 6 91 30 71 51 0 7 2 0	
8 0		94 0	
5 3		1 1	
8 3		4 1	
0 4		1 3	
2 6		9 3	
8 6		7 4	
3 9		4 5	
0 9		7 6	
5 9		10 6	
9 9		12 6	
		7 2	
		9 0	
		12 0	

Figure 9.19: Activity 23, test cases 3 (left) and 4 (right)

Note that the different symbols are used to represent different types of obstacles. Though the effect of any obstacle is the same, we cannot build a road there. Finally, let's step up the complexity in the following example:

Input:

```
19 25
26
@@@@@@@@@@@@@@@@@@@@@@@@@@
@#.................###@@@
@..@#&.&..........###@@@
@.@##&.&#........######@
&&&#.&.&.#........###@.@
##..&&.&..#........##@.@@
#...#@...........@@@.@@@
#.............@.@@@@.###@
##............@@@@@.####@
.................##@#@@
..........@@@.....##@@@
.....................@
...........###.@.......
..........###@@@@.....
..........#######......
......................
.@....................
@@@...................
@@@@..................
0 0 0 0 0 0 0 0 0 0 0 0 0 0 0 0 0 0 0 0 0 0 0 0 0
0 0 8 0 50 74 0 59 31 73 45 0 79 24 10 41 66 93 43 0 0 0 0 0 0
0 88 4 0 0 0 28 0 30 41 13 4 70 10 58 61 34 100 79 0 0 0 0 0 0
0 0 0 0 0 0 17 0 0 0 36 98 27 0 13 68 11 34 0 0 0 0 0 0 0
0 0 0 0 0 0 80 0 50 0 80 22 68 73 94 37 86 46 29 0 0 0 0 0 0
0 0 92 95 0 0 58 0 2 54 0 0 9 45 69 0 91 25 97 0 0 0 31 0 0
0 4 23 67 0 0 50 25 2 54 78 9 29 34 99 82 36 14 0 0 0 66 0 0 0
0 0 15 64 37 26 0 70 16 95 30 2 18 0 0 96 0 0 0 0 6 0 0 0 0
0 0 5 52 99 89 24 6 83 53 67 17 38 39 0 0 0 0 0 45 0 0 0 0 0
2 98 72 29 38 59 0 78 0 98 95 5 10 0 32 46 76 36 0 0 0 0 0 0 0
99 43 100 69 13 61 58 95 9 96 69 14 0 0 0 31 7 63 43 66 0 0 0 0 0
83 53 68 22 96 13 72 2 91 32 39 58 17 0 91 41 80 36 7 73 99 96 20 0 0
55 24 90 61 6 27 0 24 0 7 14 71 0 0 0 39 0 95 21 45 67 35 27 95 64
```

Output:

```
@@@@@@@@@@@@@@@@@@@@@@@@@@
@#.A--B....C.......###@@@
@./@#&|&../........###@@@
@D@##&|&#E...F....######@
&&&#G&|&.#\./......###@H@
##./&&|&..#I...J...##@/@@
#./.#@|.....\./...@@@/@@@
#K----L------M@.@@@@/###@
##....|\......@@@@@/####@
......N.O----P----Q##@#@@
...../|.|...@@@.....##@@@
..../.|.|....R--------S@
.../..T.U...###.@...../..
../..........###@@@@./...
./..........#######./....
Z----------V.......W.....
.@...........\.....|.....
@@@..........\.....|.....
@@@@..........X----Y.....
```

Figure 9.20: Activity 23, test case 5

Note

The solution to this activity can be found on page 585.

Summary

Now that you have completed this chapter, you should have a fairly high appreciation for the value of dynamic programming. If you initially found this topic to be somewhat anxiety-provoking, you have hopefully come to realize that it is not as complicated as it may have first appeared. Viewing familiar problems through the dynamic programming lens, as we did in this chapter, can certainly help us understand the core ideas that are needed to arrive at a working DP solution. To that end, we encourage you to investigate other variants of the knapsack problem and attempt to implement them using the strategies provided.

And with that, your tour through the vast world of algorithms and data structures in C++ has reached its conclusion. Having arrived at the end of this book, you should have a markedly deepened understanding of how and when to use some of the most useful tools of our trade. Hopefully, you have developed a better sense of the practical applications of the structures and techniques that were covered in this book, as well as an expanded knowledge of the C++ language and its vast collection of features.

It should be noted that the appropriate occasions to use many of these techniques in practice are not necessarily obvious, which is why it is immensely beneficial to apply what you have learned to a range of different contexts. We have endeavored to provide a variety of interesting activities for practicing the concepts in this book, but it is highly recommended that you also try to use these skills in other situations. There are a plethora of online resources offering unique and engaging programming challenges for developers of all levels, which can be invaluable if you wish to train yourself to recognize how certain techniques can be utilized in a variety of circumstances.

Certainly, every topic that we've discussed in this book deserves much deeper study than what can be covered in any single book, and we hope that the information we have provided has made these topics accessible enough to encourage you to explore them deeper. Regardless of whether you are a student, looking for a development job, or already working in the field professionally, you are likely to encounter a use for at least one (and likely many) of the subjects that were covered in this book; and with any luck, you will know exactly what to do when that time comes!

Appendix

About

This section is included to assist the students to perform the activities in the book.
It includes detailed steps that are to be performed by the students to achieve the objectives of the activities.

Chapter 1: Lists, Stacks, and Queues

Activity 1: Implementing a Song Playlist

In this activity, we will implement a tweaked version of a doubly linked list which can be used to store a song playlist and supports the necessary functions. Follow these steps to complete the activity:

1. Let's first include the header and write the node structure with the required data members:

```
#include <iostream>

template <typename T>
struct cir_list_node
{
    T* data;
    cir_list_node *next, *prev;

    ~cir_list_node()
        {
            delete data;
        }
};

template <typename T>
struct cir_list
{
    public:
        using node = cir_list_node<T>;
        using node_ptr = node*;
    private:
        node_ptr head;
        size_t n;
```

2. Now, let's write a basic constructor and size function:

```
public:
cir_list(): n(0)
{
    head = new node{NULL, NULL, NULL};   // Dummy node - having NULL data
    head->next = head;
```

```
        head->prev = head;
    }

    size_t size() const
    {
        return n;
    }
```

We'll discuss why we need a dummy node between the first and the last node later on, in the case of iterating using iterators.

3. Now, let's write the **insert** and **erase** functions. Both will take one value to be inserted or deleted:

```
    void insert(const T& value)
    {
        node_ptr newNode = new node{new T(value), NULL, NULL};
        n++;
    auto dummy = head->prev;
    dummy->next = newNode;
    newNode->prev = dummy;
        if(head == dummy)
        {
            dummy->prev = newNode;
            newNode->next = dummy;
            head = newNode;
            return;
        }
        newNode->next = head;
        head->prev = newNode;
        head = newNode;
    }

    void erase(const T& value)
    {
        auto cur = head, dummy = head->prev;
        while(cur != dummy)
        {
            if(*(cur->data) == value)
            {
                cur->prev->next = cur->next;
                cur->next->prev = cur->prev;
                if(cur == head)
```

```
                head = head->next;
            delete cur;
            n--;
            return;
        }
        cur = cur->next;
    }
}
```

4. Now, let's write a basic structure for the required iterator and add members to access the actual data:

```
struct cir_list_it
{
private:
    node_ptr ptr;
public:
    cir_list_it(node_ptr p) : ptr(p)
    {}

    T& operator*()
    {
        return *(ptr->data);
    }

    node_ptr get()
    {
        return ptr;
    }
```

5. Now, let's implement the core functions of an iterator – pre- and post-increments:

```
cir_list_it& operator++()
{
    ptr = ptr->next;
    return *this;
}

cir_list_it operator++(int)
{
```

```
        cir_list_it it = *this;
        ++(*this);
        return it;
    }
```

6. Let's add the decrement-related operations to make it bidirectional:

```
    cir_list_it& operator--()
    {
        ptr = ptr->prev;
        return *this;
    }

    cir_list_it operator--(int)
    {
        cir_list_it it = *this;
        --(*this);
        return it;
    }
```

7. Let's implement equality-related operators for the iterator, which are essential for range-based loops:

```
    friend bool operator==(const cir_list_it& it1, const cir_list_it& it2)
    {
        return it1.ptr == it2.ptr;
    }

    friend bool operator!=(const cir_list_it& it1, const cir_list_it& it2)
    {
        return it1.ptr != it2.ptr;
    }
};
```

8. Now, let's write the **begin** and **end** functions with their **const** versions as well:

```
cir_list_it begin()
{
    return cir_list_it{head};
}

cir_list_it begin() const
{
```

```
        return cir_list_it{head};
    }

    cir_list_it end()
    {
        return cir_list_it{head->prev};
    }

    cir_list_it end() const
    {
        return cir_list_it{head->prev};
    }
```

9. Let's write a copy constructor, initializer list constructor, and destructor:

```
    cir_list(const cir_list<T>& other): cir_list()
    {

    // Although, the following will insert the elements in a reverse order, it
    won't matter in a logical sense since this is a circular list.
        for(const auto& i: other)
            insert(i);
    }

    cir_list(const std::initializer_list<T>& il): head(NULL), n(0)
    {

    // Although, the following will insert the elements in a reverse order, it
    won't matter in a logical sense since this is a circular list.
        for(const auto& i: il)
            insert(i);
    }

    ~cir_list()
    {
        while(size())
        {
            erase(head->data);
        }
    }
    };
```

10. Now, let's add a class for the music player's playlist for our actual application. Instead of storing the songs, we'll just go ahead and store integers indicating the ID of the song for ease of understanding:

```
struct playlist
{
    cir_list<int> list;
```

11. Let's now implement functions to add and delete songs:

```
void insert(int song)
{
    list.insert(song);
}

void erase(int song)
{
    list.erase(song);
}
```

12. Now, let's implement functions to print all the songs:

```
void loopOnce()
{
    for(auto& song: list)
        std::cout << song << " ";
    std::cout << std::endl;
}
};
```

13. Let's write a **main** function to use the playlist of our music player:

```
int main()
{
    playlist pl;
    pl.insert(1);
    pl.insert(2);
    std::cout << "Playlist: ";
    pl.loopOnce();

    playlist pl2 = pl;
    pl2.erase(2);
```

```
        pl2.insert(3);
        std::cout << "Second playlist: ";
        pl2.loopOnce();
    }
```

14. Upon executing this, you should get output like this:

```
Playlist: 2 1
Second playlist: 3 1
```

Activity 2: Simulating a Card Game

In this activity, we will simulate a card game and implement an efficient data structure to store the information about each player's cards. Follow these steps to complete the activity:

1. First, let's include the necessary headers:

```
#include <iostream>
#include <vector>
#include <array>
#include <sstream>
#include <algorithm>
#include <random>
#include <chrono>
```

2. Now, let's create a class to store the cards and a utility method to print them properly:

```
struct card
{
    int number;
    enum suit
    {
        HEART,
        SPADE,
        CLUB,
        DIAMOND
    } suit;

    std::string to_string() const
    {
        std::ostringstream os;
        if(number > 0 && number <= 10)
            os << number;
```

```
            else
{
switch(number)
{
case 1:
    os << "Ace";
    break;
    case 11:
        os << "Jack";
        break;
    case 12:
        os << "Queen";
        break;
    case 13:
        os << "King";
        break;
    default:
        return "Invalid card";
}
        }
        os << " of ";
        switch(suit)
        {
            case HEART:
                os << "hearts";
                break;
            case SPADE:
                os << "spades";
                break;
            case CLUB:
                os << "clubs";
                break;
            case DIAMOND:
                os << "diamonds";
                break;
        }
        return os.str();
    }
};
```

3. Now, we can create a deck of cards and shuffle the deck to randomly distribute the cards to each of the four players. We'll write this logic inside a **game** class and call the functions later on in the **main** function:

```cpp
struct game
{
    std::array<card, 52> deck;
    std::vector<card> player1, player2, player3, player4;
    void buildDeck()
    {
        for(int i = 0; i < 13; i++)
            deck[i] = card{i + 1, card::HEART};
        for(int i = 0; i < 13; i++)
            deck[i + 13] = card{i + 1, card::SPADE};
        for(int i = 0; i < 13; i++)
            deck[i + 26] = card{i + 1, card::CLUB};
        for(int i = 0; i < 13; i++)
            deck[i + 39] = card{i + 1, card::DIAMOND};
    }

    void dealCards()
    {
        unsigned seed = std::chrono::system_clock::now().time_since_
epoch().count();
        std::shuffle(deck.begin(), deck.end(), std::default_random_
engine(seed));
        player1 = {deck.begin(), deck.begin() + 13};
player2 = {deck.begin() + 13, deck.begin() + 26};
player3 = {deck.begin() + 26, deck.begin() + 39};
player4 = {deck.begin() + 39, deck.end()};
    }
```

4. Let's write the core logic to play one round. To avoid duplicating the code, we will write a utility function that will compare two players' hands and remove both cards if required:

```cpp
bool compareAndRemove(std::vector<card>& p1, std::vector<card>& p2)
{
    if(p1.back().number == p2.back().number)
    {
        p1.pop_back();
        p2.pop_back();
```

```
        return true;
    }
    return false;
}


void playOneRound()
{
        if(compareAndRemove(player1, player2))
        {
            compareAndRemove(player3, player4);
            return;
        }
        else if(compareAndRemove(player1, player3))
        {
            compareAndRemove(player2, player4);
            return;
        }
        else if(compareAndRemove(player1, player4))
        {
            compareAndRemove(player2, player3);
            return;
        }
        else if(compareAndRemove(player2, player3))
        {
            return;
        }
        else if(compareAndRemove(player2, player4))
        {
            return;
        }
        else if(compareAndRemove(player3, player4))
        {
return;
        }
        unsigned seed = std::chrono::system_clock::now().time_since_
epoch().count();
        std::shuffle(player1.begin(), player1.end(), std::default_random_
engine(seed));
        std::shuffle(player2.begin(), player2.end(), std::default_random_
engine(seed));
```

```
            std::shuffle(player3.begin(), player3.end(), std::default_random_
    engine(seed));
            std::shuffle(player4.begin(), player4.end(), std::default_random_
    engine(seed));
    }
```

5. Now, let's write the main logic to find out who's the winner. We'll call the preceding function in a loop until one of the players can get rid of all their cards. To make the code more readable, we will write another utility function to check whether the game has been completed:

```
bool isGameComplete() const
{
    return player1.empty() || player2.empty() || player3.empty() ||
player4.empty();
}

void playGame()
{
        while(not isGameComplete())
        {
            playOneRound();
        }
}
```

6. To find out who's the winner, let's write a utility function before starting the **main** function:

```
int getWinner() const
{
    if(player1.empty())
        return 1;
    if(player2.empty())
        return 2;
    if(player3.empty())
        return 3;
    if(player4.empty())
        return 4;
}
};
```

7. Finally, let's write the **main** function to execute the game:

```
int main()
{
    game newGame;
    newGame.buildDeck();
    newGame.dealCards();
    newGame.playGame();
    auto winner = newGame.getWinner();
    std::cout << "Player " << winner << " won the game." << std::endl;
}
```

8. One of the possible outputs could be as follows:

```
Player 4 won the game.
```

> **Note**
>
> The winner could be any player from 1 to 4. Since the game is based on random-
> ness seeded by the time during execution, any of the players can win. Running the
> code multiple times may yield a different output every time.

Activity 3: Simulating a Queue for a Shared Printer in an Office

In this activity, we shall implement a queue for handling print requests to a shared printer in an office. Follow these steps to complete the activity:

1. Let's include the required headers:

```
#include <iostream>
#include <queue>
```

2. Let's implement a **Job** class:

```
class Job
{
    int id;
    std::string user;
    int time;
    static int count;
public:
    Job(const std::string& u, int t) : user(u), time(t), id(++count)
    {}
```

```
        friend std::ostream& operator<<(std::ostream& os, const Job& j)
        {
        os << "id: " << id << ", user: " << user << ", time: " << time << "
    seconds" << std::endl;
        return os;
        }
    };
    int Job::count = 0;
```

3. Now, let's implement the **Printer** class. We'll use **std::queue** to have a first come, first served policy for **jobs**. We'll keep the class templated based on the maximum number of jobs it can store in memory:

```
template <size_t N>
class Printer
{
    std::queue<Job> jobs;
public:
    bool addNewJob(const Job& job)
    {
        if(jobs.size() == N)
            return false;
        std::cout << "Added job in the queue: " << job;
        jobs.push(job);
        return true;
    }
```

4. Now, let's implement another major functionality – printing jobs:

```
    void startPrinting()
    {
        while(not jobs.empty())
        {
            std::cout << "Processing job: " << jobs.front();
            jobs.pop();
        }
    }
};
```

5. Now, let's use these classes to simulate the scenario:

```
int main()
{
    Printer<5> printer;
```

```
Job j1("John", 10);
Job j2("Jerry", 4);
Job j3("Jimmy", 5);
Job j4("George", 7);
Job j5("Bill", 8);
Job j6("Kenny", 10);
printer.addNewJob(j1);
printer.addNewJob(j2);
printer.addNewJob(j3);
printer.addNewJob(j4);
printer.addNewJob(j5);

if(not printer.addNewJob(j6))  // Can't add as queue is full.
{
    std::cout << "Couldn't add 6th job" << std::endl;
}

printer.startPrinting();

printer.addNewJob(j6);  // Can add now, as queue got emptied
printer.startPrinting();
}
```

6. Here is the output of the preceding code:

```
Added job in the queue: id: 1, user: John, time: 10 seconds
Added job in the queue: id: 2, user: Jerry, time: 4 seconds
Added job in the queue: id: 3, user: Jimmy, time: 5 seconds
Added job in the queue: id: 4, user: George, time: 7 seconds
Added job in the queue: id: 5, user: Bill, time: 8 seconds
Couldn't add 6th job
Processing job: id: 1, user: John, time: 10 seconds
Processing job: id: 2, user: Jerry, time: 4 seconds
Processing job: id: 3, user: Jimmy, time: 5 seconds
Processing job: id: 4, user: George, time: 7 seconds
Processing job: id: 5, user: Bill, time: 8 seconds
Added job in the queue: id: 6, user: Kenny, time: 10 seconds
Processing job: id: 6, user: Kenny, time: 10 seconds
```

Chapter 2: Trees, Heaps, and Graphs

Activity 4: Create a Data Structure for a Filesystem

In this activity, we will create a data structure using N-ary tree for a file system. Follow these steps to complete the activity:

1. First, let's include the required headers:

    ```
    #include <iostream>
    #include <vector>
    #include <algorithm>
    ```

2. Now, let's write a node to store the data of a directory/file:

    ```
    struct n_ary_node
    {
        std::string name;
        bool is_dir;

        std::vector<n_ary_node*> children;
    };
    ```

3. Now, let's wrap this node in a tree structure for a good interface, and also add a static member so that we can store the current directory:

    ```
    struct file_system
    {
        using node = n_ary_node;
        using node_ptr = node*;
    private:
        node_ptr root;
        node_ptr cwd;
    ```

4. Now, let's add a constructor so that we can create a tree with a root directory:

    ```
    public:
        file_system()
        {
            root = new node{"/", true, {}};
            cwd = root;  // We'll keep the current directory as root in the
    beginning
        }
    ```

5. Now, let's add a function to find the directory/file:

```cpp
node_ptr find(const std::string& path)
{
    if(path[0] == '/')  // Absolute path
    {
        return find_impl(root, path.substr(1));
    }
    else
    {
        return find_impl(cwd, path);
    }
}

private:
node_ptr find_impl(node_ptr directory, const std::string& path)
{
    if(path.empty())
        return directory;
    auto sep = path.find('/');
    std::string current_path = sep == std::string::npos ? path : path.substr(0, sep);
    std::string rest_path = sep == std::string::npos ? "" : path.substr(sep + 1);
    auto found = std::find_if(directory->children.begin(), directory->children.end(), [&](const node_ptr child)
    {
        return child->name == current_path;
    });
        if(found != directory->children.end())
        {
            return find_impl(*found, rest_path);
        }
        return NULL;
}
```

6. Now, let's add a function to add a directory:

```cpp
public:
bool add(const std::string& path, bool is_dir)
{
    if(path[0] == '/')
    {
```

```
            return add_impl(root, path.substr(1), is_dir);
        }
        else
        {
            return add_impl(cwd, path, is_dir);
        }
    }

private:
bool add_impl(node_ptr directory, const std::string& path, bool is_dir)
{
    if(not directory->is_dir)
    {
        std::cout << directory->name << " is a file." << std::endl;
        return false;
    }

auto sep = path.find('/');

// This is the last part of the path for adding directory. It's a base
condition of the recursion
    if(sep == std::string::npos)
    {
        auto found = std::find_if(directory->children.begin(), directory->children.end(), [&](const node_ptr child)
{
    return child->name == path;
});
if(found != directory->children.end())
{
    std::cout << "There's already a file/directory named " << path << " inside " << directory->name << "." << std::endl;
    return false;
}

directory->children.push_back(new node{path, is_dir, {}});
return true;
    }

    // If the next segment of the path is still a directory
    std::string next_dir = path.substr(0, sep);
    auto found = std::find_if(directory->children.begin(), directory-
```

```
>children.end(), [&](const node_ptr child)
{
    return child->name == next_dir && child->is_dir;
});
        if(found != directory->children.end())
        {
            return add_impl(*found, path.substr(sep + 1), is_dir);
        }

std::cout << "There's no directory named " << next_dir << " inside " <<
directory->name << "." << std::endl;
    return false;
}
```

7. Now, let's add a function to change the current directory. This will be very simple since we already have a function to find the path:

```
public:
bool change_dir(const std::string& path)
{
    auto found = find(path);
    if(found && found->is_dir)
    {
        cwd = found;
        std::cout << "Current working directory changed to " << cwd->name
<< "." << std::endl;
        return true;
    }

    std::cout << "Path not found." << std::endl;
    return false;
}
```

8. Now, let's add a function to print a directory or a file. For a file, we'll just print the name of the file. For a directory, we'll print all of its children's names, just like the ls command in Linux:

```
public:
void show_path(const std::string& path)
{
    auto found = find(path);
    if(not found)
    {
        std::cout << "No such path: " << path << "." << std::endl;
```

```
            return;
        }

        if(found->is_dir)
        {
            for(auto child: found->children)
            {
    std::cout << (child->is_dir ? "d " : "- ") << child->name << std::endl;
    }
        }
        else
        {
            std::cout << "- " << found->name << std::endl;
        }
    }
};
```

9. Let's write a main function so that we can use the aforementioned functions:

```
int main()
{
    file_system fs;
    fs.add("usr", true);  // Add directory usr in "/"
    fs.add("etc", true);  // Add directory etc in "/"
    fs.add("var", true);  // Add directory var in "/"
    fs.add("tmp_file", false);  // Add file tmp_file in "/"

    std::cout << "Files/Directories under \"/\"" << std::endl;
    fs.show_path("/");  // List files/directories in "/"

    std::cout << std::endl;
    fs.change_dir("usr");
    fs.add("Packt", true);
    fs.add("Packt/Downloads", true);
    fs.add("Packt/Downloads/newFile.cpp", false);

    std::cout << "Let's see the contents of dir usr: " << std::endl;
    fs.show_path("usr");  // This will not print the path successfully,
since we're already inside the dir usr. And there's no directory named usr
inside it.
```

```
std::cout << "Let's see the contents of \"/usr\"" << std::endl;
fs.show_path("/usr");

std::cout << "Let's see the contents of \"/usr/Packt/Downloads\"" <<
std::endl;
fs.show_path("/usr/Packt/Downloads");

}
```

The output of the preceding code is as follows:

```
Files/Directories under "/"
d usr
d etc
d var
- tmp_file
Current working directory changed to usr.
Let's try to print the contents of usr:
No such path: usr.
Let's see the contents of "/usr"
d Packt
Contents of "/usr/Packt/Downloads"
- newFile.cpp
```

Activity 5: K-Way Merge Using Heaps

In this activity, we will merge multiple sorted arrays into a single sorted array. These steps will help you complete the activity:

1. Start with the required headers:

    ```
    #include <iostream>
    #include <algorithm>
    #include <vector>
    ```

2. Now, implement the main algorithm for merging. It will take a vector of a vector of **int** as input and will contain the vector of all the sorted vectors. Then, it will return the merged vector of **int**. First, let's build the heap node:

    ```
    struct node
    {
        int data;
        int listPosition;
    ```

```
        int dataPosition;
    };

    std::vector<int> merge(const std::vector<std::vector<int>>& input)
    {
        auto comparator = [] (const node& left, const node& right)
            {
                if(left.data == right.data)
                    return left.listPosition > right.listPosition;
                return left.data > right.data;
            };
```

As we can see, the heap node will contain three things – data, the position of the list in the input, and the position of the data item inside that list.

3. Let's build the heap. The idea is to have a min heap with the smallest element from all the lists. So, when we pop from the heap, we are guaranteed to get the smallest element. After removing that element, we need to insert the next element from the same list, if it's available:

```
    std::vector<node> heap;
    for(int i = 0; i < input.size(); i++)
    {
        heap.push_back({input[i][0], i, 0});
        std::push_heap(heap.begin(), heap.end(), comparator);
    }
```

4. Now, we'll build the resultant vector. We'll simply remove the elements from the heap until it is empty and replace it with the next element from the same list it belongs to, if available:

```
    std::vector<int> result;
    while(!heap.empty())
    {
        std::pop_heap(heap.begin(), heap.end(), comparator);
        auto min = heap.back();
        heap.pop_back();

        result.push_back(min.data);
        int nextIndex = min.dataPosition + 1;
        if(nextIndex < input[min.listPosition].size())
        {
            heap.push_back({input[min.listPosition][nextIndex], min.
listPosition, nextIndex});
```

```
            std::push_heap(heap.begin(), heap.end(), comparator);
        }
    }

    return result;
}
```

5. Let's write a **main** function so that we can use the preceding function:

```
int main()
{
    std::vector<int> v1 = {1, 3, 8, 15, 105};
    std::vector<int> v2 = {2, 3, 10, 11, 16, 20, 25};
    std::vector<int> v3 = {-2, 100, 1000};
    std::vector<int> v4 = {-1, 0, 14, 18};
    auto result = merge({v1, v2, v3, v4});
    for(auto i: result)
    std::cout << i << ' ';
    return 0;
}
```

You should see the following output:

```
-2 -1 0 1 2 3 3 8 10 11 14 15 16 18 20 25 100 105 1000
```

Chapter 3: Hash Tables and Bloom Filters

Activity 6: Mapping Long URLs to Short URLs

In this activity, we will create a program to map shorter URLs to corresponding longer URLs. Follow these steps to complete the activity:

1. Let's include the required headers:

    ```
    #include <iostream>
    #include <unordered_map>
    ```

2. Let's write a struct called **URLService** that will provide the interface for the required services:

    ```
    struct URLService
    {
        using ActualURL = std::string;
        using TinyURL = std::string;

    private:
        std::unordered_map<TinyURL, ActualURL> data;
    ```

    As we can see, we've created a map from the small URL to the original URL. This is because we use the small URL for the lookup. We want to convert it into the original URL. As we saw earlier, a map can do fast lookups based on a key. So, we have kept the smaller URL as the key of the map and the original URL as the value of the map. We have created aliases to avoid confusion regarding which string we are talking about.

3. Let's add a **lookup** function:

    ```
    public:

        std::pair<bool, ActualURL> lookup(const TinyURL& url) const
        {
            auto it = data.find(url);
            if(it == data.end())  // If small URL is not registered.
            {
                return std::make_pair(false, std::string());
            }
            else
            {
                return std::make_pair(true, it->second);
            }
        }
    ```

4. Now, let's write a function to register the smaller URL for the given actual URL:

```
bool registerURL(const ActualURL& actualURL, const TinyURL& tinyURL)
{
    auto found = lookup(tinyURL).first;
    if(found)
    {
        return false;
    }

    data[tinyURL] = actualURL;
    return true;
}
```

The **registerURL** function returns if there is already an existing entry in the data. If so, it will not touch the entry. Otherwise, it will register the entry and return **true** to indicate that.

5. Now, let's write a function to delete the entry:

```
bool deregisterURL(const TinyURL& tinyURL)
{
    auto found = lookup(tinyURL).first;
    if(found)
    {
        data.erase(tinyURL);
        return true;
    }

    return false;
}
```

As we can see, we are using the **lookup** function instead of rewriting the find logic again. This function is much more readable now.

6. Now, let's write a function to print all the mappings for logging:

```cpp
void printURLs() const
{
    for(const auto& entry: data)
    {
        std::cout << entry.first << " -> " << entry.second << std::endl;

    }
    std::cout << std::endl;
}
};
```

7. Now, write the **main** function so that we can use this service:

```cpp
int main()
{
    URLService service;

    if(service.registerURL("https://www.packtpub.com/eu/big-data-and-
    business-intelligence/machine-learning-r-third-edition", "https://ml-r-
    v3"))
    {
        std::cout << "Registered https://ml-r-v3" << std::endl;
    }
    else
    {
        std::cout << "Couldn't register https://ml-r-v3" << std::endl;
    }

    if(service.registerURL("https://www.packtpub.com/eu/virtualization-
    and-cloud/hands-aws-penetration-testing-kali-linux", "https://aws-test-
    kali"))
    {
        std::cout << "Registered https://aws-test-kali" << std::endl;
    }
    else
    {
        std::cout << "Couldn't register https://aws-test-kali" <<
    std::endl;
```

```
    }

    if(service.registerURL("https://www.packtpub.com/eu/application-
development/hands-qt-python-developers", "https://qt-python"))
    {
        std::cout << "Registered https://qt-python" << std::endl;
    }
    else
    {
        std::cout << "Couldn't register https://qt-python" << std::endl;
    }


    auto findMLBook = service.lookup("https://ml-r-v3");
    if(findMLBook.first)
    {
        std::cout << "Actual URL: " << findMLBook.second << std::endl;
    }
    else
    {
        std::cout << "Couldn't find URL for book for ML." << std::endl;
    }

    auto findReactBook = service.lookup("https://react-cookbook");
    if(findReactBook.first)
    {
        std::cout << "Actual URL: " << findReactBook.second << std::endl;
    }
    else
    {
        std::cout << "Couldn't find URL for book for React." << std::endl;
    }

    if(service.deregisterURL("https://qt-python"))
    {
        std::cout << "Deregistered qt python link" << std::endl;
    }
```

```
    else
    {
        std::cout << "Couldn't deregister qt python link" << std::endl;
    }

    auto findQtBook = service.lookup("https://qt-python");
    if(findQtBook.first)
    {
        std::cout << "Actual URL: " << findQtBook.second << std::endl;
    }
    else
    {
        std::cout << "Couldn't find Qt Python book" << std::endl;
    }

    std::cout << "List of registered URLs: " << std::endl;
    service.printURLs();

}
```

8. Let's look at the output of the preceding code:

```
Registered https://ml-r-v3
Registered https://aws-test-kali
Registered https://qt-python
Actual URL: https://www.packtpub.com/eu/big-data-and-business-
intelligence/machine-learning-r-third-edition
Couldn't find URL for book for React.
Deregistered qt python link
Couldn't find Qt Python book
List of registered URLs:
https://ml-r-v3 -> https://www.packtpub.com/eu/big-data-and-business-
intelligence/machine-learning-r-third-edition
https://aws-test-kali -> https://www.packtpub.com/eu/virtualization-and-
cloud/hands-aws-penetration-testing-kali-linux
```

As we can see, we are getting both the valid URLs at the end, and not the one we deregistered successfully.

Activity 7: Email Address Validator

In this activity, we will create a validator to check if an email address requested by a user is already taken. Complete the activity using these steps:

1. Let's include the required headers:

```
#include <iostream>
#include <vector>

#include <openssl/md5.h>
```

2. Let's add a class for the Bloom filter:

```
class BloomFilter
{
    int nHashes;
    std::vector<bool> bits;

    static constexpr int hashSize = 128/8;

    unsigned char hashValue[hashSize];
```

3. Let's add a constructor for this:

```
BloomFilter(int size, int hashes) : bits(size), nHashes(hashes)
{
    if(nHashes > hashSize)
    {
        throw ("Number of hash functions too high");
    }
    if(size > 255)
    {
        throw ("Size of bloom filter can't be >255");
    }
}
```

Since we're going to use each byte in the hash value buffer as a different hash function value, and the size of the hash value buffer is 16 bytes (128 bits), we can't have more hash functions than that. Since each hash value is just 1 byte, its possible values are 0 to 255. So, the size of the Bloom filter can't exceed 255. Hence, we're throwing an error in the constructor itself.

4. Now, let's write a hash function. It simply uses the MD5 function to calculate the hash:

```
void hash(const std::string& key)
{
    MD5(reinterpret_cast<const unsigned char*>(key.data()), key.length(),
hashValue);
}
```

5. Let's add the function so that we can insert an email:

```
void add(const std::string& key)
{
    hash(key);
    for(auto it = &hashValue[0]; it < &hashValue[nHashes]; it++)
    {
        bits[*it] = true;
    }
    std::cout << key << " added in bloom filter." << std::endl;

}
```

As we can see, we are iterating from the the bytes **0** to **nHashes** in the hash value buffer and setting each bit to **1**.

6. Similarly, let's add a function to find an email address:

```
bool mayContain(const std::string &key)
    {
        hash(key);
        for (auto it = &hashValue[0]; it < &hashValue[nHashes]; it++)
        {
            if (!bits[*it])
            {
                std::cout << key << " email can by used." << std::endl;
                return false;
            }
        }

        std::cout << key << " email is used by someone else." <<
std::endl;
        return true;
    }
};
```

7. Let's add the **main** function:

```
int main()
{
    BloomFilter bloom(10, 15);

    bloom.add("abc@packt.com");
    bloom.add("xyz@packt.com");

    bloom.mayContain("abc");
    bloom.mayContain("xyz@packt.com");
    bloom.mayContain("xyz");

    bloom.add("abcd@packt.com");
    bloom.add("ab@packt.com");

    bloom.mayContain("abc");
    bloom.mayContain("ab@packt.com");
}
```

The following is one of the possible outputs of the preceding code:

```
abc@packt.com added in bloom filter.
xyz@packt.com added in bloom filter.
abc email can by used.
xyz@packt.com email is used by someone else.
xyz email can by used.
abcd@packt.com added in bloom filter.
ab@packt.com added in bloom filter.
abcd email can by used.
ab@packt.com email is used by someone else.
```

This is one of the possible outputs because MD5 is a randomized algorithm. If we choose the number of functions and the size of the Bloom filter in a thoughtful way, we should get really good accuracy with the MD5 algorithm.

Chapter 4: Divide and Conquer

Activity 8: Vaccinations

In this activity, we will store and lookup the vaccination status of students to determine if they need to be vaccinated. These steps should help you complete the activity:

1. Begin by including the following headers:

```
#include <iostream>
#include <vector>
#include <chrono>
#include <random>
#include <algorithm>
#include <numeric>
```

2. Define the **Student** class as follows:

```
class Student
{
private:
    std::pair<int, int> name;
    bool vaccinated;

public:
    // Constructor
    Student(std::pair<int, int> n, bool v) :
        name(n), vaccinated(v)
    {}

    // Getters
    auto get_name() { return name; }
    auto is_vaccinated() { return vaccinated; }

    // Two people are same if they have the same name
    bool operator ==(const Student& p) const
    {
        return this->name == p.name;
    }

    // The ordering of a set of people is defined by their name
    bool operator< (const Student& p) const
    {
        return this->name < p.name;
```

```
        }

        bool operator> (const Student& p) const
        {
            return this->name > p.name;
        }
    };
```

3. The following function lets us generate a student from random data:

```
auto generate_random_Student(int max)
{
    std::random_device rd;
    std::mt19937 rand(rd());

    // the IDs of Student should be in range [1, max]
    std::uniform_int_distribution<std::mt19937::result_type> uniform_
dist(1, max);

    // Generate random credentials
    auto random_name = std::make_pair(uniform_dist(rand), uniform_
dist(rand));
    bool is_vaccinated = uniform_dist(rand) % 2 ? true : false;

    return Student(random_name, is_vaccinated);
}
```

4. The following code is used to run and test the output of our implementation:

```
void search_test(int size, Student p)
{
    std::vector<Student> people;

    // Create a list of random people
    for (auto i = 0; i < size; i++)
        people.push_back(generate_random_Student(size));

    std::sort(people.begin(), people.end());

    // To measure the time taken, start the clock
    std::chrono::steady_clock::time_point begin = std::chrono::steady_
clock::now();
```

```
    bool search_result = needs_vaccination(p, people);

    // Stop the clock
    std::chrono::steady_clock::time_point end = std::chrono::steady_
clock::now();

    std::cout << "Time taken to search = " <<
        std::chrono::duration_cast<std::chrono::microseconds>
        (end - begin).count() << " microseconds" << std::endl;

    if (search_result)
        std::cout << "Student (" << p.get_name().first
<< " " << p.get_name().second << ") "
            << "needs vaccination." << std::endl;
    else
        std::cout << "Student (" << p.get_name().first
<< " " << p.get_name().second << ") "
            << "does not need vaccination." << std::endl;
}
```

5. The following function implements our logic for whether a vaccination is needed:

```
bool needs_vaccination(Student P, std::vector<Student>& people)
{
    auto first = people.begin();
    auto last = people.end();

    while (true)
    {
        auto range_length = std::distance(first, last);
        auto mid_element_index = std::floor(range_length / 2);
        auto mid_element = *(first + mid_element_index);

        // Return true if the Student is found in the sequence and
// he/she's not vaccinated
        if (mid_element == P && mid_element.is_vaccinated() == false)
            return true;
```

```
        else if (mid_element == P && mid_element.is_vaccinated() == true)
            return false;
        else if (mid_element > P)
            std::advance(last, -mid_element_index);
        if (mid_element < P)
            std::advance(first, mid_element_index);

        // Student not found in the sequence and therefore should be
    vaccinated
        if (range_length == 1)
            return true;
    }
}
```

6. Finally, the driver code is implemented as follows:

```
int main()
{
    // Generate a Student to search
    auto p = generate_random_Student(1000);

    search_test(1000, p);
    search_test(10000, p);
    search_test(100000, p);

    return 0;
}
```

Note

Since we are randomizing values in *step 3*, your output may vary from the expected output shown for this activity.

Activity 9: Partial Sorting

The partial quicksort is only a slight modification of the original quicksort algorithm that was demonstrated in *Exercise 20, Quicksort*. Compared to that exercise, only *step 4* is different. The following is a reference implementation:

1. Add the following header files:

```
#include <iostream>
#include <vector>
#include <chrono>
#include <random>
#include <algorithm>
```

2. Next, we shall implement the partition operation, as follows:

```
template <typename T>
auto partition(typename std::vector<T>::iterator begin,
    typename std::vector<T>::iterator end)
{
    auto pivot_val = *begin;
    auto left_iter = begin + 1;
    auto right_iter = end;

    while (true)
    {
        // Starting from the first element of vector,
        // find an element that is greater than pivot.
        while (*left_iter <= pivot_val && std::distance(left_iter, right_
iter) > 0)
            left_iter++;

        // Starting from the end of vector moving to the beginning,
        // find an element that is lesser than the pivot.
        while (*right_iter > pivot_val && std::distance(left_iter, right_
iter) > 0)
            right_iter--;

        // If left and right iterators meet, there are no elements left to
swap.
        // Else, swap the elements pointed to by the left and right
iterators
```

```
        if (left_iter == right_iter)
            break;
        else
            std::iter_swap(left_iter, right_iter);
    }
    if (pivot_val > *right_iter)
        std::iter_swap(begin, right_iter);

    return right_iter;
}
```

3. Since the desired output also needs an implementation of the quicksort algorithm, we'll implement one as follows:

```
template <typename T>
void quick_sort(typename std::vector<T>::iterator begin,
    typename std::vector<T>::iterator last)
{
    // If there are more than 1 elements in the vector
    if (std::distance(begin, last) >= 1)
    {
        // Apply the partition operation
        auto partition_iter = partition<T>(begin, last);

        // Recursively sort the vectors created by the partition operation
        quick_sort<T>(begin, partition_iter-1);
        quick_sort<T>(partition_iter, last);
    }
}
```

4. Implement the partial quicksort function as follows:

```
template <typename T>
void partial_quick_sort(typename std::vector<T>::iterator begin,
    typename std::vector<T>::iterator last,
    size_t k)
{
    // If there are more than 1 elements in the vector
    if (std::distance(begin, last) >= 1)
    {
        // Apply the partition operation
```

```
        auto partition_iter = partition<T>(begin, last);

        // Recursively sort the vectors created by the partition operation
        partial_quick_sort<T>(begin, partition_iter-1, k);

        // Sort the right subvector only if the final position of pivot < k
        if(std::distance(begin, partition_iter) < k)
            partial_quick_sort<T>(partition_iter, last, k);
    }
}
```

5. The following helper functions can be then used to print the contents of a vector
    and to generate a random vector:

```
 template <typename T>
void print_vector(std::vector<T> arr)
{
    for (auto i : arr)
        std::cout << i << " ";

    std::cout << std::endl;
}

// Generates random vector of a given size with integers [1, size]
template <typename T>
auto generate_random_vector(T size)
{
    std::vector<T> V;
    V.reserve(size);

    std::random_device rd;
    std::mt19937 rand(rd());

    // the IDs of Student should be in range [1, max]
    std::uniform_int_distribution<std::mt19937::result_type> uniform_
dist(1, size);

    for (T i = 0; i < size; i++)
        V.push_back(uniform_dist(rand));

    return std::move(V);
}
```

6. The following function implements the testing logic for our sorting functions:

```
// Sort the first K elements of a random vector of a given 'size'
template <typename T>
void test_partial_quicksort(size_t size, size_t k)
{
        // Create two copies of a random vector to use for the two
algorithms
        auto random_vec = generate_random_vector<T>(size);
        auto random_vec_copy(random_vec);

        std::cout << "Original vector: "<<std::endl;
        print_vector<T>(random_vec);

        // Measure the time taken by partial quick sort
        std::chrono::steady_clock::time_point
begin_qsort = std::chrono::steady_clock::now();
        partial_quick_sort<T>(random_vec.begin(), random_vec.end()-1, k);
        std::chrono::steady_clock::time_point
end_qsort = std::chrono::steady_clock::now();

        std::cout << std::endl << "Time taken by partial quick sort = "
            << 'std::chrono::duration_cast<std::chrono::microseconds>
            (end_qsort - begin_qsort).count()
            << " microseconds" << std::endl;

        std::cout << "Partially sorted vector (only first "<< k <<"
elements):";
        print_vector<T>(random_vec);

        // Measure the time taken by partial quick sort
        begin_qsort = std::chrono::steady_clock::now();
        quick_sort<T>(random_vec_copy.begin(), random_vec_copy.end()-1);
        end_qsort = std::chrono::steady_clock::now();

        std::cout << std::endl <<"Time taken by full quick sort = "
            << std::chrono::duration_cast<std::chrono::microseconds>
            (end_qsort - begin_qsort).count()
            << " microseconds" << std::endl;
```

```
        std::cout << "Fully sorted vector: ";
        print_vector<T>(random_vec_copy);
    }
```

7. Finally, add the driver code, as follows:

```
    int main()
    {
        test_partial_quicksort<unsigned>(100, 10);
        return 0;
    }
```

Activity 10: Implementing WordCount in MapReduce

In this activity, we will implement the MapReduce model to solve the WordCount problem. The following is the solution to this activity:

1. Implement the map task as follows:

```
    struct map_task : public mapreduce::map_task<
        std::string,                            // MapKey (filename)
        std::pair<char const*, std::uintmax_t>> // MapValue (memory mapped
    file contents)
    {
        template<typename Runtime>
        void operator()(Runtime& runtime, key_type const& key, value_type&
    value) const
        {
            bool in_word = false;
            char const* ptr = value.first;
            char const* end = ptr + value.second;
            char const* word = ptr;
            // Iterate over the contents of the file, extract words and emit a
    <word,1> pair.
            for (; ptr != end; ++ptr)
            {
                // Convert the character to upper case.
                char const ch = std::toupper(*ptr, std::locale::classic());
                if (in_word)
                {
                    if ((ch < 'A' || ch > 'Z') && ch != '\'')
                    {
    runtime.emit_intermediate(std::pair<char const*,
                std::uintmax_t> (word, ptr - word), 1);
```

```
                        in_word = false;
                }
            }
            else if (ch >= 'A' && ch <= 'Z')
            {
                word = ptr;
                in_word = true;
            }
        }

        // Handle the last word.
        if (in_word)
        {
            assert(ptr > word);
            runtime.emit_intermediate(std::pair<char const*,
                        std::uintmax_t>(word, ptr - word), 1);
        }
    }
};
```

The preceding map function is applied separately to each file in the input directory. The contents of the input file are accepted as the * character in **value**. The inner loop then iterates over the contents of the file, extracting different words and emitting < *key, value* > pairs, where *key* is a word and *value* is set to 1.

2. Implement the reduce task as follows:

```
template<typename KeyType>
struct reduce_task : public mapreduce::reduce_task<KeyType, unsigned>
{
    using typename mapreduce::reduce_task<KeyType, unsigned>::key_type;

    template<typename Runtime, typename It>
    void operator()(Runtime& runtime, key_type const& key, It it, It const
ite) const
    {
        runtime.emit(key, std::accumulate(it, ite, 0));
    }
};
```

The reduce operation can then be applied to all < key, value > pairs that are emitted by the map function. Since the value was set to **1** in the previous step, we can now use **std::accumulate()** to get the total number of times a key appears among the input pairs of the reduce operation.

Chapter 5: Greedy Algorithms

Activity 11: The Interval Scheduling Problem

In this activity, we will find the optimal scheduling of tasks to maximize the number of tasks that can be completed. Follow these steps to complete the activity:

1. Add the required header files and define the **Task** struct as follows:

```
#include <list>
#include <algorithm>
#include <iostream>
#include <random>

// Every task is represented as a pair <start_time, end_time>
struct Task
{
    unsigned ID;
    unsigned start_time;
    unsigned end_time;
};
```

2. The following function can be used to generate a list of N tasks with random data:

```
auto initialize_tasks(size_t num_tasks)
{
    std::random_device rd;
    std::mt19937 rand(rd());
    std::uniform_int_distribution<std::mt19937::result_type>
uniform_dist(1, num_tasks);

    // Create and initialize a set of tasks
    std::list<Task> tasks;

    for (unsigned i = 1; i <= num_tasks; i++)
    {
        auto start_time = uniform_dist(rand);
        auto duration = uniform_dist(rand);

        tasks.push_back({i, start_time, start_time + duration });
    }

    return tasks;
}
```

3. Implement the scheduling algorithm as follows:

```cpp
auto schedule(std::list<Task> tasks)
{
    // Sort the list of tasks by their end times
    tasks.sort([](const auto& lhs, const auto& rhs)
        { return lhs.end_time < rhs.end_time; });

    // Remove the tasks that interfere with one another
    for (auto curr_task = tasks.begin(); curr_task != tasks.end(); curr_task++)
    {
        // Point to the next task
        auto next_task = std::next(curr_task, 1);

        // While subsequent tasks interfere with the current task in iter
        while (next_task != tasks.end() &&
            next_task->start_time < curr_task->end_time)
        {
            next_task = tasks.erase(next_task);
        }
    }

    return tasks;
}
```

4. The following utility functions are used to print the list of tasks, test our implementation, and include the driver code for the program:

```cpp
void print(std::list<Task>& tasks)
{
    std::cout << "Task ID \t Starting Time \t End time" << std::endl;

    for (auto t : tasks)
        std::cout << t.ID << "\t\t" << t.start_time << "\t\t" << t.end_time << std::endl;
}

void test_interval_scheduling(unsigned num_tasks)
{
    auto tasks = initialize_tasks(num_tasks);

    std::cout << "Original list of tasks: " << std::endl;
```

```
        print(tasks);

        std::cout << "Scheduled tasks: " << std::endl;
        auto scheduled_tasks = schedule(tasks);
        print(scheduled_tasks);
}

int main()
{
        test_interval_scheduling(20);
        return 0;
}
```

Activity 12: The Welsh-Powell Algorithm

We will implement the Welsh-Powell algorithm on the graph in this activity. A reference implementation is given here:

1. Add the required header files and declare the graph that will be implemented later:

```
#include <unordered_map>
#include <set>
#include <map>
#include <string>
#include <vector>
#include <algorithm>
#include <iostream>

template <typename T> class Graph;
```

2. Implement the struct, representing edges like so:

```
template<typename T>
struct Edge
{
        size_t src;
        size_t dest;
        T weight;

        // To compare edges, only compare their weights,
        // and not the source/destination vertices
        inline bool operator< (const Edge<T>& e) const
        {
                return this->weight < e.weight;
```

```
        }

        inline bool operator> (const Edge<T>& e) const
        {
            return this->weight > e.weight;
        }
    };
```

3. The following function allows us to serialize and print graphs by overloading the << operator for the graph datatype:

```
template <typename T>
std::ostream& operator<<(std::ostream& os, const Graph<T>& G)
{
    for (auto i = 1; i < G.vertices(); i++)
    {
        os << i << ":\t";

        auto edges = G.outgoing_edges(i);
        for (auto& e : edges)
            os << "{" << e.dest << ": " << e.weight << "}, ";

        os << std::endl;
    }

    return os;
}
```

4. Implement the graph with the edge list representation, as shown here:

```
template<typename T>
class Graph
{
public:
    // Initialize the graph with N vertices
    Graph(size_t N) : V(N)
    {}

    // Return number of vertices in the graph
    auto vertices() const
    {
        return V;
    }
```

```cpp
    // Return all edges in the graph
    auto& edges() const
    {
        return edge_list;
    }

    void add_edge(Edge<T>&& e)
    {
        // Check if the source and destination vertices are within range
        if (e.src >= 1 && e.src <= V &&
            e.dest >= 1 && e.dest <= V)
            edge_list.emplace_back(e);
        else
            std::cerr << "Vertex out of bounds" << std::endl;
    }

    // Returns all outgoing edges from vertex v
    auto outgoing_edges(size_t v) const
    {
        std::vector<Edge<T>> edges_from_v;
        for (auto& e : edge_list)
        {
            if (e.src == v)
                edges_from_v.emplace_back(e);
        }
        return edges_from_v;
    }

    // Overloads the << operator so a graph be written directly to a
stream
    // Can be used as std::cout << obj << std::endl;
    template <typename T>
    friend std::ostream& operator<< <>(std::ostream& os, const Graph<T>&
G);

private:
    size_t V;        // Stores number of vertices in graph
    std::vector<Edge<T>> edge_list;
};
```

5. Initialize the set of colors that we will use in our implementation of the Welsh-Powell algorithm. Let this number of colors be **6**, as implemented in the following **unordered_map**:

```cpp
// Initialize the colors that will be used to color the vertices
std::unordered_map<size_t, std::string> color_map = {
    {1, "Red"},
    {2, "Blue"},
    {3, "Green"},
    {4, "Yellow"},
    {5, "Black"},
    {6, "White"}
};
```

6. Implement the Welsh-Powell graph coloring algorithm like so:

```cpp
template<typename T>
auto welsh_powell_coloring(const Graph<T>& G)
{
    auto size = G.vertices();
    std::vector<std::pair<size_t, size_t>> degrees;

    // Collect the degrees of vertices as <vertex_ID, degree> pairs
    for (auto i = 1; i < size; i++)
        degrees.push_back(std::make_pair(i, G.outgoing_edges(i).size()));

    // Sort the vertices in decreasing order of degree
    std::sort(degrees.begin(),
        degrees.end(),
        [](const auto& a, const auto& b)
        { return a.second > b.second; });

    std::cout << "The vertices will be colored in the following order: "
 << std::endl;
    std::cout << "Vertex ID \t Degree" << std::endl;
    for (auto const i : degrees)
        std::cout << i.first << "\t\t" << i.second << std::endl;

    std::vector<size_t> assigned_colors(size);
    auto color_to_be_assigned = 1;

    while (true)
    {
```

```
                for (auto const i : degrees)
                {
                    if (assigned_colors[i.first] != 0)
                        continue;

                    auto outgoing_edges = G.outgoing_edges(i.first);
                    std::set<size_t> neighbour_colors;

                    // We assume that the graph is bidirectional
                    for (auto e : outgoing_edges)
                    {
                        auto dest_color = assigned_colors[e.dest];
                        neighbour_colors.insert(dest_color);
                    }

            if (neighbour_colors.find(color_to_be_assigned) == neighbour_colors.end())
                        assigned_colors[i.first] = color_to_be_assigned;
                }

                color_to_be_assigned++;

                // If there are no uncolored vertices left, exit
                if (std::find(assigned_colors.begin() + 1, assigned_colors.end(),
        0) ==
                    assigned_colors.end())
                    break;
            }

            return assigned_colors;
        }
```

7. The following function outputs the vector of colors:

```
    void print_colors(std::vector<size_t>& colors)
    {
        for (auto i = 1; i < colors.size(); i++)
        {
            std::cout << i << ": " << color_map[colors[i]] << std::endl;
        }
    }
```

8. Finally, the following driver code creates the required graph, runs the vertex coloring algorithm, and outputs the results:

```cpp
int main()
{
    using T = unsigned;

    Graph<T> G(9);

    std::map<unsigned, std::vector<std::pair<size_t, T>>> edges;
    edges[1] = { {2, 2}, {5, 3} };
    edges[2] = { {1, 2}, {5, 5}, {4, 1} };
    edges[3] = { {4, 2}, {7, 3} };
    edges[4] = { {2, 1}, {3, 2}, {5, 2}, {6, 4}, {8, 5} };
    edges[5] = { {1, 3}, {2, 5}, {4, 2}, {8, 3} };
    edges[6] = { {4, 4}, {7, 4}, {8, 1} };
    edges[7] = { {3, 3}, {6, 4} };
    edges[8] = { {4, 5}, {5, 3}, {6, 1} };

    for (auto& i : edges)
        for (auto& j : i.second)
            G.add_edge(Edge<T>{ i.first, j.first, j.second });
    std::cout << "Original Graph" << std::endl;
    std::cout << G;

    auto colors = welsh_powell_coloring<T>(G);
    std::cout << "Vertex Colors: " << std::endl;
    print_colors(colors);
    return 0;
}
```

Chapter 6: Graph Algorithms I

Activity 13: Finding out Whether a Graph is Bipartite Using DFS

In this activity, we will check whether a graph is bipartite using depth-first search traversal. Follow these steps to complete the activity:

1. Add the required header files and declare the graph to be used:

```
#include <string>
#include <vector>
#include <iostream>
#include <set>
#include <map>
#include <stack>

template<typename T> class Graph;
```

2. Write the following struct to define an edge in our graph:

```
template<typename T>
struct Edge
{
    size_t src;
    size_t dest;
    T weight;

    // To compare edges, only compare their weights,
    // and not the source/destination vertices
    inline bool operator< (const Edge<T>& e) const
    {
        return this->weight < e.weight;
    }

    inline bool operator> (const Edge<T>& e) const
    {
        return this->weight > e.weight;
    }
};
```

3. Use the following function to overload the **<<** operator for the graph so that it can be written to standard output:

```cpp
template <typename T>
std::ostream& operator<<(std::ostream& os, const Graph<T>& G)
{
    for (auto i = 1; i < G.vertices(); i++)
    {
        os << i << ":\t";

        auto edges = G.outgoing_edges(i);
        for (auto& e : edges)
            os << "{" << e.dest << ": " << e.weight << "}, ";

        os << std::endl;
    }

    return os;
}
```

4. Implement the edge list graph as follows:

```cpp
template<typename T>
class Graph
{
public:
    // Initialize the graph with N vertices
    Graph(size_t N) : V(N)
    {}

    // Return number of vertices in the graph
    auto vertices() const
    {
        return V;
    }
```

```cpp
    // Return all edges in the graph
    auto& edges() const
    {
        return edge_list;
    }

    void add_edge(Edge<T>&& e)
    {
        // Check if the source and destination vertices are within range
        if (e.src >= 1 && e.src <= V &&
            e.dest >= 1 && e.dest <= V)
            edge_list.emplace_back(e);
        else
            std::cerr << "Vertex out of bounds" << std::endl;
    }

    // Returns all outgoing edges from vertex v
    auto outgoing_edges(size_t v) const
    {
        std::vector<Edge<T>> edges_from_v;
        for (auto& e : edge_list)
        {
            if (e.src == v)
                edges_from_v.emplace_back(e);
        }
        return edges_from_v;
    }

    // Overloads the << operator so a graph be written directly to a
stream
    // Can be used as std::cout << obj << std::endl;
    template <typename T>
    friend std::ostream& operator<< <>(std::ostream& os, const Graph<T>&
G);

private:
    size_t V;         // Stores number of vertices in graph
    std::vector<Edge<T>> edge_list;
};
```

5. Create the graph shown in *figure* 6.17, as shown here:

```
template <typename T>
auto create_bipartite_reference_graph()
{
    Graph<T> G(10);

    std::map<unsigned, std::vector<std::pair<size_t, T>>> edges;
    edges[1] = { {2, 0} };
    edges[2] = { {1, 0}, {3, 0} , {8, 0} };
    edges[3] = { {2, 0}, {4, 0} };
    edges[4] = { {3, 0}, {6, 0} };
    edges[5] = { {7, 0}, {9, 0} };
    edges[6] = { {1, 0}, {4, 0} };
    edges[7] = { {5, 0} };
    edges[8] = { {2,0}, {9, 0} };
    edges[9] = { {5, 0} };


    for (auto& i : edges)
        for (auto& j : i.second)
            G.add_edge(Edge<T>{ i.first, j.first, j.second });

    return G;
}
```

6. Now, we need a function so that we can implement our algorithm and check whether the graph is bipartite. Write the function like so:

```
template <typename T>
auto bipartite_check(const Graph<T>& G)
{
    std::stack<size_t> stack;
    std::set<size_t> visited;
    stack.push(1); // Assume that BFS always starts from vertex ID 1

    enum class colors {NONE, RED, BLUE};
    colors current_color{colors::BLUE}; // This variable tracks the color
to be assigned to the next vertex that is visited.
    std::vector<colors> vertex_colors(G.vertices(), colors::NONE);
```

```cpp
    while (!stack.empty())
    {
        auto current_vertex = stack.top();
        stack.pop();

        // If the current vertex hasn't been visited in the past
        if (visited.find(current_vertex) == visited.end())
        {
            visited.insert(current_vertex);
            vertex_colors[current_vertex] = current_color;
            if (current_color == colors::RED)
            {
std::cout << "Coloring vertex "
<< current_vertex << " RED" << std::endl;
                current_color = colors::BLUE;
            }
            else
            {
                std::cout << "Coloring vertex "
<< current_vertex << " BLUE" << std::endl;
                current_color = colors::RED;
            }

            // Add unvisited adjacent vertices to the stack.
            for (auto e : G.outgoing_edges(current_vertex))
                if (visited.find(e.dest) == visited.end())
                    stack.push(e.dest);
        }
        // If the found vertex is already colored and
        // has a color same as its parent's color, the graph is not
bipartite
        else if (visited.find(current_vertex) != visited.end() &&
            ((vertex_colors[current_vertex] == colors::BLUE &&
                current_color == colors::RED) ||
            (vertex_colors[current_vertex] == colors::RED &&
                current_color == colors::BLUE)))
            return false;
    }

    // If all vertices have been colored, the graph is bipartite
    return true;
}
```

7. Use the following functions to implement the test and driver code that tests our implementation of the bipartite checking algorithm:

```
template <typename T>
void test_bipartite()
{
    // Create an instance of and print the graph
    auto BG = create_bipartite_reference_graph<T>();
    std::cout << BG << std::endl;

    if (bipartite_check<T>(BG))
        std::cout << "The graph is bipartite" << std::endl;
    else
        std::cout << "The graph is not bipartite" << std::endl;
}

int main()
{
    using T = unsigned;
    test_bipartite<T>();

    return 0;
}
```

8. Run the program. You should see the following output:

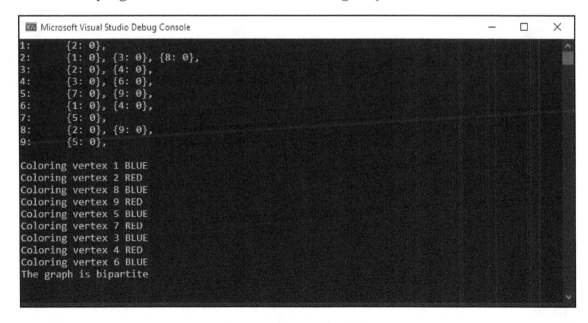

Figure 6.34: Output of Activity 13

Activity 14: Shortest Path in New York

In this activity, we will use the graph of various locations in New York City and find the shortest distance between the two given vertices. Follow these steps to complete the activity:

1. Add the required header files and declare the graph, as shown here:

```
#include <string>
#include <vector>
#include <iostream>
#include <set>
#include <map>
#include <limits>
#include <queue>
#include <fstream>
#include <sstream>

template<typename T> class Graph;
```

2. Implement the weighted edge that will be used in the graph:

```
template<typename T>
struct Edge
{
    size_t src;
    size_t dest;
    T weight;

    // To compare edges, only compare their weights,
    // and not the source/destination vertices
    inline bool operator< (const Edge<T>& e) const
    {
        return this->weight < e.weight;
    }

    inline bool operator> (const Edge<T>& e) const
    {
        return this->weight > e.weight;
    }
};
```

3. Overload the **<<** operator for the **Graph** class so that it can be output to the C++ streams:

```
template <typename T>
std::ostream& operator<<(std::ostream& os, const Graph<T>& G)
{
    for (auto i = 1; i < G.vertices(); i++)
    {
        os << i << ":\t";

        auto edges = G.outgoing_edges(i);
        for (auto& e : edges)
            os << "{" << e.dest << ": " << e.weight << "}, ";

        os << std::endl;
    }

    return os;
}
```

4. Implement an edge list graph, as shown here:

```
template<typename T>
class Graph
{
public:
    // Initialize the graph with N vertices
    Graph(size_t N) : V(N)
    {}

    // Return number of vertices in the graph
    auto vertices() const
    {
        return V;
    }

    // Return all edges in the graph
    auto& edges() const
    {
        return edge_list;
    }

    void add_edge(Edge<T>&& e)
```

```
    {
        // Check if the source and destination vertices are within range
        if (e.src >= 1 && e.src <= V &&
            e.dest >= 1 && e.dest <= V)
            edge_list.emplace_back(e);
        else
            std::cerr << "Vertex out of bounds" << std::endl;
    }

    // Returns all outgoing edges from vertex v
    auto outgoing_edges(size_t v) const
    {
        std::vector<Edge<T>> edges_from_v;
        for (auto& e : edge_list)
        {
            if (e.src == v)
                edges_from_v.emplace_back(e);
        }
        return edges_from_v;
    }

    // Overloads the << operator so a graph be written directly to a
stream
    // Can be used as std::cout << obj << std::endl;
    template <typename T>
    friend std::ostream& operator<< <>(std::ostream& os, const Graph<T>&
G);

private:
    size_t V;          // Stores number of vertices in graph
    std::vector<Edge<T>> edge_list;
};
```

5. Write the following function so that you can parse the graph file and prepare the
   graph:

```
template <typename T>
auto read_graph_from_file()
{
    std::ifstream infile("USA-road-d.NY.gr");
    size_t num_vertices, num_edges;
```

```cpp
    std::string line;

    // Read the problem description line that starts with 'p' and looks
like:
    // p <num_vertices> <num_edges>
    while (std::getline(infile, line))
    {
        if (line[0] == 'p')
        {
            std::istringstream iss(line);
            char p;
            std::string sp;
            iss >> p >>sp >> num_vertices >> num_edges;
            std::cout << "Num vertices: " << num_vertices
<< " Num edges: " << num_edges <<std::endl;
            break;
        }
    }

    Graph<T> G(num_vertices + 1);

    // Read the edges and edge weights, which look like:
    // a <source_vertex> <destination_vertex> <weight>
    while (std::getline(infile, line))
    {
        if (line[0] == 'a')
        {
            std::istringstream iss(line);
            char p;
            size_t source_vertex, dest_vertex;
            T weight;
            iss >> p >> source_vertex >> dest_vertex >> weight;

            G.add_edge(Edge<T>{source_vertex, dest_vertex, weight});
        }
    }

    infile.close();
    return G;
}
```

6. Now, we need a struct that implements a **Label** struct that will be assigned to each vertex as Dijkstra's algorithm runs. Implement it as follows:

```cpp
template<typename T>
struct Label
{
    size_t vertex_ID;
    T distance_from_source;

    Label(size_t _id, T _distance) :
        vertex_ID(_id),
        distance_from_source(_distance)
    {}

    // To compare labels, only compare their distances from source
    inline bool operator< (const Label<T>& l) const
    {
        return this->distance_from_source < l.distance_from_source;
    }

    inline bool operator> (const Label<T>& l) const
    {
        return this->distance_from_source > l.distance_from_source;
    }

    inline bool operator() (const Label<T>& l) const
    {
        return this > l;
    }
};
```

7. Dijkstra's algorithm can be implemented as follows:

```cpp
template <typename T>
auto dijkstra_shortest_path(const Graph<T>& G, size_t src, size_t dest)
{
    std::priority_queue<Label<T>, std::vector<Label<T>>,
std::greater<Label<T>>> heap;
    std::set<int> visited;
    std::vector<size_t> parent(G.vertices());
    std::vector<T> distance(G.vertices(), std::numeric_limits<T>::max());
    std::vector<size_t> shortest_path;
```

```cpp
        heap.emplace(src, 0);
        parent[src] = src;

        // Search for the destination vertex in the graph
        while (!heap.empty()) {
            auto current_vertex = heap.top();
            heap.pop();

            // If the search has reached the destination vertex
            if (current_vertex.vertex_ID == dest) {
                std::cout << "Destination " <<
current_vertex.vertex_ID << " reached." << std::endl;
                break;
            }
            if (visited.find(current_vertex.vertex_ID) == visited.end()) {
                std::cout << "Settling vertex " <<
current_vertex.vertex_ID << std::endl;
                // For each outgoing edge from the current vertex,
                // create a label for the destination vertex and add it to the
heap
                for (auto e : G.outgoing_edges(current_vertex.vertex_ID)) {
                    auto neighbor_vertex_ID = e.dest;
                    auto new_distance_to_dest=current_vertex.distance_from_
source
+ e.weight;

                    // Check if the new path to the destination vertex
// has a lower cost than any previous paths found to it, if // yes, then
this path should be preferred
                    if (new_distance_to_dest < distance[neighbor_vertex_ID]) {
                        heap.emplace(neighbor_vertex_ID, new_distance_to_
dest);
                        parent[e.dest] = current_vertex.vertex_ID;
                        distance[e.dest] = new_distance_to_dest;
                    }
                }
                visited.insert(current_vertex.vertex_ID);
            }
        }
        // Construct the path from source to the destination by backtracking
        // using the parent indexes
        auto current_vertex = dest;
```

```
        while (current_vertex != src) {
            shortest_path.push_back(current_vertex);
            current_vertex = parent[current_vertex];
        }
        shortest_path.push_back(src);
        std::reverse(shortest_path.begin(), shortest_path.end());
        return shortest_path;
    }
```

8. Finally, implement the test and driver code, as shown here:

```
template<typename T>
void test_dijkstra()
{
    auto G = read_graph_from_file<T>();
    //std::cout << G << std::endl;
    auto shortest_path = dijkstra_shortest_path<T>(G, 913, 542);

    std::cout << "The shortest path between 913 and 542 is:" << std::endl;
    for (auto v : shortest_path)
        std::cout << v << " ";
    std::cout << std::endl;
}

int main()
{
    using T = unsigned;
    test_dijkstra<T>();

    return 0;
}
```

9. Run the program. Your output should look as follows:

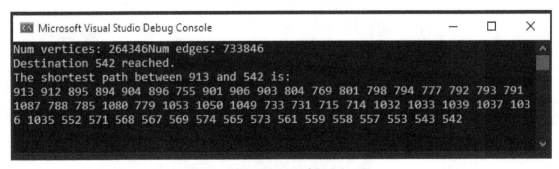

Figure 6.35: Output of Activity 14

Chapter 7: Graph Algorithms II

Activity 15: Greedy Robot

We can solve this activity using the exact algorithm from *Exercise 33, Implementing the Bellman-Ford Algorithm (Part II)*. The potential pitfalls here are related to correctly interpreting the required task and representing the graph within the context of the problem you are actually trying to solve. Let's get started:

1. The first step will be identical to the exercise. We will include the same headers and define an **Edge** struct and an **UNKNOWN** constant:

```cpp
#include <iostream>
#include <vector>
#include <climits>

using namespace std;

struct Edge
{
        int start;
        int end;
        int weight;

        Edge(int s, int e, int w) : start(s), end(e), weight(w) {}
};

const int UNKNOWN = INT_MAX;
vector<Edge*> edges;
```

2. In **main()**, we will declare an integer, **N**, which determines the height/width of the grid. We will then iterate from 0 to N * N - 1 in a **for** loop and read the adjacency data given in the input:

```cpp
int main()
{
    int N;
    cin >> N;

    for(int i = 0; i < N * N - 1; i++)
    {
        string directions;
        int power;
```

```
        cin >> directions >> power;


        ......

    }
    return 0;
}
```

3. Now, we must face the first potential problem – accurately representing the adjacencies. Typically, we would be inclined to think of a grid in two dimensions, and while it would certainly be possible to solve the problem this way, it would not be the optimal approach for this particular problem. To reinterpret the grid and adjacencies in one dimension, we must simply observe the following relationships between the one-dimensional index, **i**, and the corresponding two-dimensional grid coordinates:

```
CURRENT CELL: (x, y) -> i
NORTH: (x, y - 1) -> i - N
SOUTH: (x, y + 1) -> i + N
EAST: (x + 1, y) -> i + 1
WEST: (x - 1, y) -> i - 1
```

4. We can handle these relationships by iterating through the characters of **directions** and containing the logic within a **switch** statement:

```
for(int i = 0; i < N * N - 1; i++)
{
    string directions;
    int power;
    cin >> directions >> power;

    int next;

    for(auto d : directions)
    {
        switch(d)
        {
            case 'N': next = i - N; break;
            case 'S': next = i + N; break;
            case 'E': next = i + 1; break;
            case 'W': next = i - 1; break;
        }
        ......
    }
}
```

5. This leads to the second problematic aspect of this activity; that is, the interpretation of the **power** values. These, of course, will be the values that define the edge weights between adjacent cells, but within the context of this problem, the inputs can be rather misleading. According to the problem's description, we want to find the path that reaches the end with the maximum amount of energy compared to the baseline. A careless reading of the problem statement may lead us to conclude that the **power** values correspond exactly to the edge weights, but this would actually produce the opposite of what we intend to achieve. "Maximizing energy" can be viewed as the equivalent to "minimizing energy loss," and since the negative values actually represent the energy expenditure for each cell and the positive values represent energy gained, we must reverse the sign of each **power** value:

```cpp
for(auto d : directions)
{
    switch(d)
    {
        ......
    }
    // Add edge with power variable's sign reversed
    edges.push_back(new Edge(i, next, -power));
}
```

6. Now, we can implement **BellmanFord()**. This time, our function will take **N** and **edges** as arguments and return an integer equal to the maximum relative energy. To simplify our code, we will pass **N** as the total number of cells in the grid (that is, **N * N**):

```cpp
int BellmanFord(int N, vector<Edge*> edges)
{
    vector<int> distance(N, UNKNOWN);

    // Starting node is always index 0
    distance[0] = 0;

    for(int i = 0; i < N - 1; i++)
    {
        for(auto edge : edges)
        {
            if(distance[edge->start] == UNKNOWN)
            {
                continue;
```

```
                }

                if(distance[edge->start] + edge->weight < distance[edge->end])
                {
                    distance[edge->end] = distance[edge->start] + edge-
>weight;
                }
            }
        }
        ......
    }
```

7. As per the standard implementation, we will also perform a check for negative cycles to handle the condition related to the robot's greedy energy consumption. In the case that a negative cycle is found, we will return **UNKNOWN**:

```
// Check for negative cycles
for(auto edge : edges)
{
    if(distance[edge->start] == UNKNOWN)
    {
        continue;
    }
    if(distance[edge->start] + edge->weight < distance[edge->end])
    {
        return UNKNOWN;
    }
}
return distance[N];
```

8. Now, we can perform a call to **BellmanFord()** in **main()** and handle the output accordingly:

```
int result = BellmanFord(N * N, edges);

(result == UNKNOWN) ? cout << "ABORT TRAVERSAL" << endl
                : cout << -1 * result << endl;

return 0;
```

Activity 16: Randomized Graph Statistics

In this activity, we will generate randomized graphs for interview tests as described in the activity brief. Follow these steps to complete the activity:

1. Begin by including the following headers, as well as defining the **UNKNOWN** constant and the **Edge** struct:

```
#include <iostream>
#include <vector>
#include <iomanip>
#include <algorithm>
#include <queue>
#include <utility>

using namespace std;

const int UNKNOWN = 1e9;

struct Edge
{
    int u;
    int v;
    int w;

    Edge(int u, int v, int w)
        : u(u), v(v), w(w) {}
};
```

2. Our first task is to handle the generation of each graph. For this activity, we will encapsulate our graph data within a struct:

```
struct Graph
{
    int V, E;
    int maxWeight = -1e9;

    vector<Edge> edges;
    vector<vector<int>> adj;
    vector<vector<int>> weight;
```

```
            Graph(int v, int e) : V(v), E(e)
            {
                ...
            }
    };
```

3. To make sure that the generated edges and the resulting graph are valid, we will create an adjacency matrix and check it during every attempt to create another edge. If an edge between the same two nodes already exists, we will begin another iteration. To make sure that every node has at least one incoming or outgoing edge, we will also set the diagonal cells in the matrix to true for each node that is part of an edge. If any of the diagonal cells are false after **E** edges are created, the graph will be invalid. We can indicate a graph as invalid by setting **V** to **-1**:

```
Graph(int v, int e) : V(v), E(e)
{
    vector<vector<bool>> used(V, vector<bool>(V, false));

    adj.resize(V);
    weight.resize(V, vector<int>(V, UNKNOWN));

    while(e)
    {
        // Generate edge values
        int u = rand() % V;
        int v = rand() % V;
        int w = rand() % 100;

        if(rand() % 3 == 0)
        {
            w = -w;
        }

        // Check if the edge is valid
        if(u == v || used[u][v])
        {
            continue;
        }

        // Add to edges and mark as used
        edges.push_back(Edge(u, v, w));
        adj[u].push_back(v);
```

```
            weight[u][v] = w;
            maxWeight = max(maxWeight, w);

            used[u][u] = used[v][v] = used[u][v] = used[v][u] = true;
            e--;
        }
        for(int i = 0; i < V; i++)
        {
            // Set V to -1 to indicate the graph is invalid
            if(!used[i][i])
            {
                V = -1;
                break;
            }
        }
    }
```

4. Let's also define an enum called **RESULT** with the corresponding values for each type of graph we need to consider:

```
enum RESULT
{
    VALID,
    INVALID,
    INTERESTING
};
```

5. In **main()**, we will receive the input, as well as declare the counters for each type of graph. We will then loop through the given number of iterations, create a new graph, and call a **TestGraph()** function that takes a **Graph** object as input and returns **RESULT**. Depending on the value that's returned, we will increment each counter accordingly:

```
int main()
{
    unsigned int seed;
    int iterations, V, E;

    cin >> seed;
    cin >> iterations;
    cin >> V >> E;

    int invalid = 0;
    int valid = 0;
```

```
    int interesting = 0;

    srand(seed);

    while(iterations--)
    {
        Graph G(V, E);

        switch(TestGraph(G))
        {
            case INVALID: invalid++; break;
            case VALID: valid++; break;
            case INTERESTING:
            {
                valid++;
                interesting++;
                break;
            }
        }
    }

    return 0;
}
```

6. **TestGraph()** will first check whether the value of **V** for each graph is equal to **-1** and return **INVALID** if so. Otherwise, it will perform Johnson's algorithm to retrieve the shortest distances. The first step will be to retrieve the reweighting array using the Bellman-Ford algorithm:

```
RESULT TestGraph(Graph G)
{
    if(G.V == -1)
    {
        return INVALID;
    }

    vector<int> distance = BellmanFord(G);

    ......
}
```

7. The implementation of Bellman-Ford that's used in this solution corresponds exactly to the one from the exercise, except that it receives a single **Graph** structure as an argument:

```
vector<int> BellmanFord(Graph G)
{
    vector<int> distance(G.V + 1, UNKNOWN);

    int s = G.V;

    for(int i = 0; i < G.V; i++)
    {
        G.edges.push_back(Edge(s, i, 0));
    }

    distance[s] = 0;

    for(int i = 0; i < G.V; i++)
    {
        for(auto edge : G.edges)
        {
            if(distance[edge.u] == UNKNOWN)
            {
                continue;
            }

            if(distance[edge.u] + edge.w < distance[edge.v])
            {
                distance[edge.v] = distance[edge.u] + edge.w;
            }
        }
    }

    for(auto edge : G.edges)
    {
        if(distance[edge.u] == UNKNOWN)
        {
```

```
                continue;
        }

        if(distance[edge.u] + edge.w < distance[edge.v])
        {
            return {};
        }
    }
    return distance;
}
```

8. As we did in the exercise, we will check whether the vector that's returned by **BellmanFord()** is empty. If so, we return **VALID** (the graph is valid but uninteresting). Otherwise, we will follow through with the rest of Johnson's algorithm by reweighting the edges and performing a call to Dijkstra's algorithm for each vertex:

```
RESULT TestGraph(Graph G)
{
    if(G.V == -1)
    {
        return INVALID;
    }

    vector<int> distance = BellmanFord(G);

    if(distance.empty())
    {
        return VALID;
    }

    for(auto edge : G.edges)
    {
        G.weight[edge.u][edge.v] += (distance[edge.u] - distance[edge.v]);
    }

    double result = 0;

    for(int i = 0; i < G.V; i++)
    {
```

```
            vector<int> shortest = Dijkstra(i, G);



    }
}
```

9. For this solution, let's use a more efficient form of Dijkstra's algorithm, which uses a min-priority queue to determine traversal order. To do this, each value that's added to the queue must consist of two values: the node's index and its distance value. We will do this using **std::pair<int, int>**, which has been redefined here as **State**. When pushing elements to the queue, the first value must correspond to the distance since this is going to be the first value that's considered by the priority queue's internal ordering logic. All of this can be handled by **std::priority_queue**, but we will need to provide three template parameters corresponding to the data type, container, and comparison predicate, respectively:

```
vector<int> Dijkstra(int source, Graph G)
{
    typedef pair<int, int> State;

    priority_queue<State, vector<State>, greater<State>> Q;
    vector<bool> visited(G.V, false);
    vector<int> distance(G.V, UNKNOWN);

    Q.push({0, source});
    distance[source] = 0;

    while(!Q.empty())
    {
        State top = Q.top();
        Q.pop();

        int node = top.second;
        int dist = top.first;

        visited[node] = true;

        for(auto next : G.adj[node])
        {
            if(visited[next])
            {
```

```
                continue;
            }

            if(dist != UNKNOWN && distance[next] > dist + G.weight[node]
    [next])
            {
                distance[next] = distance[node] + G.weight[node][next];

                Q.push({distance[next], next});
            }

        }
    }
    return distance;
}
```

10. Now, we will calculate the averages in **TestGraph()** for each set of paths. We do this by iterating through the array returned by **Dijkstra()** and keeping a sum of distances for which the index is not equal to the starting node's index. The corresponding value is not equal to **UNKNOWN**. Every time a valid distance is found, a counter is also incremented so that we can get the final average by dividing the sum by the count. Each one of these averages is then added to the total result, which is divided by the total number of vertices in the graph. Remember that we must reweight the distances again to get the correct values:

```
double result = 0;

for(int i = 0; i < G.V; i++)
{
    vector<int> shortest = Dijkstra(i, G);

    double average = 0;
    int count = 0;

    for(int j = 0; j < G.V; j++)
    {
        if(i == j || shortest[j] == UNKNOWN)
        {
```

```
            continue;
        }
        shortest[j] += (distance[j] - distance[i]);
        average += shortest[j];
        count++;
    }
    average = average / count;
    result += average;
}
result = result / G.V;
```

11. The last step is to calculate the ratio between the result and the maximum weight in the graph. If the value is less than **0.5**, we return **INTERESTING**; otherwise, we return **VALID**:

```
double ratio = result / G.maxWeight;

return (ratio < 0.5) ? INTERESTING : VALID;
```

12. We can now return to **main()** and print the output. The first line will be equal to the value of **invalid**. The second line will be equal to **interesting / valid**, multiplied by **100**, so that it will be displayed as a percentage. Depending on how you do this, you may have to cast your variables as floating points to prevent the value from being rounded to an integer. When printing the output, you can easily make sure it is rounded to two decimal places by using **cout << fixed << setprecision(2)**:

```
double percentInteresting = (double)interesting / valid * 100;

cout << "INVALID GRAPHS: " << invalid << endl;
cout << "PERCENT INTERESTING: " << fixed << setprecision(2) <<
percentInteresting << endl;

return 0;
```

Activity 17: Maze-Teleportation Game

The entire activity conforms fairly closely to the standard implementations of the algorithms we've discussed in this chapter, but with a few slight modifications.

The terms that were used in the problem description, that is, *maze*, *rooms*, *teleporters*, and *points* could, of course, just as easily have been called *graph*, *vertices*, *edges*, and *edge weights*. The condition in which a player is able to infinitely reduce their score can be redefined as a *negative weight cycle*. Follow these steps to complete the activity:

1. Let's begin by including the necessary headers and setting up the variables and input for the activity:

```cpp
#include <iostream>
#include <vector>
#include <stack>
#include <climits>

struct Edge
{
    int start;
    int end;
    int weight;

    Edge(int s, int e, int w) : start(s), end(e), weight(w) {}
}

const int UNKNOWN = INT_MAX;
vector<Edge*> edges; // Collection of edge pointers
```

2. We will receive input in the same form as our original Bellman-Ford implementation, but we will also build an adjacency list for our graph (represented here as a vector of integer vectors, **adj**):

```cpp
int main()
{
    int V, E;
    cin >> V >> E;

    vector<Edge*> edges;
    vector<vector<int>> adj(V + 1);

    for(int i = 0; i < E; i++)
    {
        int u, v, w;
```

```
        cin >> u >> v >> w;

        edges.push_back(new Edge(u, v, w));
        adj[u].push_back(v);
    }

    vector<int> results;
```

3. The first portion of the problem can be solved by using Bellman-Ford in an identical fashion to what was outlined in *Exercise 32, Implementing the Bellman-Ford Algorithm (Part I)*. However, instead of printing all the values in the distance array, we will set its return type to **int** and include a few extra lines of code so that it returns only the shortest distance from the source vertex (or **UNKNOWN** if a negative cycle is detected):

```
int BellmanFord(int V, int start, vector<Edge*> edges)
{
    // Standard Bellman-Ford implementation

    vector<int> distance(V, UNKNOWN);

    distance[start] = 0;

    for(int i = 0; i < V - 1; i++)
    {
        for(auto edge : edges)
        {
            if(distance[edge->start] == UNKNOWN)
            {
                continue;
            }
            if(distance[edge->start] + edge->weight < distance[edge->end])
            {
                distance[edge->end] = distance[edge->start] + edge->weight;
            }
        }
    }

    // Return UNKNOWN if a negative cycle is found

    if(HasNegativeCycle(distance, edges))
    {
```

```
            return UNKNOWN;
        }

        int result = UNKNOWN;

        for(int i = 0; i < V; i++)
        {
            if(i == start) continue;

            result = min(result, distance[i]);
        }
        return result;
    }
```

4. We can now call this function in **main()** and populate a results vector for output. If **BellmanFord()** happens to return **UNKNOWN**, we output **INVALID MAZE** and terminate the program (as per the first condition). If a certain starting node has no outgoing edges, we can skip the call to **BellmanFord** entirely and simply append **UNKNOWN** to the vector. If we make it through every vertex, we can output the values in the results (or **DEAD END** if the value is **UNKNOWN**):

```
vector<int> results;

for(int i = 0; i < V; i++)
{
    if(adj[i].empty())
    {
        results.push_back(UNKNOWN);
        continue;
    }
    int shortest = BellmanFord(V, i, edges);

    if(shortest == UNKNOWN)
    {
        cout << "INVALID MAZE" << endl;
        return 0;
    }
    results.push_back(shortest);
}
```

```
for(int i = 0; i < V; i++)
{
    cout << i << ": ";

    (results[i] == INVALID) ? cout << "DEAD END" << endl : cout <<
results[i] << endl;
}
```

5. Now, we've come to the final condition – finding rooms in which players can get "stuck." Considering this case in terms of graph connectivity, we can redefine it as follows: find the strongly connected components that have no outgoing edges to other components. There are many simple ways to do this once all the strongly connected components have been acquired, but let's try to maximize our program's efficiency and add the necessary logic directly into our existing Kosaraju implementation.

To accomplish this, we will declare two new vectors: one of type **bool**, named **isStuck** and another of type **int**, named **inComponent**. **inComponent** will store the index of the component each node belongs to, while **isStuck** will tell us whether or not the component with index **i** is cut off from the rest of the graph.

For the sake of simplicity, let's declare the new variables globally:

```
vector<bool> isStuck;
vector<int> inComponent;
int componentIndex;
```

Here, we can really begin to appreciate the benefits of encapsulation and object-oriented implementations of graph structures. Having to pass such a large amount of data between our functions is not only difficult to keep track of mentally, but it greatly complicates any kind of modifications we may want to make in the future (to say nothing about the headache-inducing appearance of a function call such as **GetComponent(node, adj, visited, component, isStuck, inComponent, componentIndex)**. For the sake of example and readability, we opt to declare this data globally, but this sort of approach is highly recommended against within the context of an actual full-scale application.

6. Within our **Kosaraju** function, we initialize the new data as follows:

```
isStuck.resize(V, true);
inComponent.resize(V, UNKNOWN);
componentIndex = 0;
```

7. Now, we will begin our **while** loop, incrementing **componentIndex** by following each DFS traversal that's performed on the stack:

```
while(!stack.empty())
{
    int node = stack.top();
    stack.pop();

    if(!visited[node])
    {
        vector<int> component;

        GetComponent(node, transpose, visited, component);

        components.push_back(component);
        componentIndex++;
    }
}
```

8. Now, we can write the logic in **GetComponent()**, which will handle this case. We will begin by setting the value of each node's index in **inComponent** to **componentIndex**. Now, as we iterate through each node's neighbors, we will include another condition that occurs when the nodes have already been visited:

```
component.push_back(node);
visited[node] = true;

inComponent[node] = componentIndex;

for(auto next : adj[node])
{
    if(!visited[next])
    {
        GetComponent(next, visited, adj, component);
    }
    else if(inComponent[node] != inComponent[next])
    {
        isStuck[inComponent[next]] = false;
    }
}
```

Essentially, we are checking to see whether each previously visited neighbor's component matches the current node's component. If their respective component IDs are different, we can conclude that the neighbor's component has a path that extends to other parts of the graph.

You may be wondering why, in a directed graph, the existence of an edge from the current node indicates that the neighboring node has an outgoing path outside of its own component. The reason this logic seems 'backward' is because it is. Remember that we are traversing the transform of the original graph, so the directions between adjacencies are all reversed!

9. Upon finishing the DFS traversals, we can now return the **components** vector and print the results:

```
auto components = Kosaraju(V, adj);

for(int i = 0; i < components.size(); i++)
{
    if(isStuck[i])
    {
        for(auto node : components[i])
        {
            cout << node << " ";
        }
        cout << endl;
    }
}

return 0;
```

Chapter 8: Dynamic Programming I

Activity 18: Travel Itinerary

Let's begin by considering the base case and recurrence relation for this problem. Unlike some of the other examples we have discussed in this chapter, this particular problem has just one base case – the point at which the destination has been reached. The intermediate states are also quite simple: given a location at index **i** that has a distance limit of **x**, we can travel to any location between indices **i + 1** and **i + x** (inclusive). For example, let's consider the following two cities:

- City 1: `distance[1] = 2`

- City 2: `distance[2] = 1`

Let's say we wanted to calculate the number of ways to reach the city at index **3**. Because we can reach *city* 3 from both *city* 1 and *city* 2, the number of ways to reach *city* 3 is equivalent to the sum of the number of ways to reach city 1 and the number of ways to reach *city* 2. This recurrence is quite similar to the Fibonacci series, except that the number of previous states from which the current state's substructure is formed is variable according to the values of **distance**.

So, let's say we have the following four cities:

```
[1]: distance = 5
[2]: distance = 3
[3]: distance = 1
[4]: distance = 2
```

From this, we want to calculate the number of ways to travel to city 5. To do this, we can formulate the substructure as follows:

```
Cities reachable from index [1] -> { 2 3 4 5 6 }
Cities reachable from index [2] -> { 3 4 5 }
Cities reachable from index [3] -> { 4 }
Cities reachable from index [4] -> { 5 6 }
```

We can now invert this logic to find the cities *from* which we can travel through to reach a given location:

```
Cities that connect to index [1] -> START
Cities that connect to index [2] -> { 1 }
Cities that connect to index [3] -> { 1 2 }
Cities that connect to index [4] -> { 1 2 3 }
Cities that connect to index [5] -> { 1 2 }
```

Taking this a step further, we can now devise an outline of the state logic:

```
Ways to reach City 1 = 1 (START)

Ways to reach City 2 = 1
     1 " 2

Ways to reach City 3 = 2
     1 " 2 " 3
     1 " 3

Ways to reach City 4 = 4
     1 " 2 " 3 " 4
     1 " 2 " 4
     1 " 3 " 4
     1 " 4

Ways to reach City 5 = 6
     1 " 2 " 3 " 4 " 5
     1 " 2 " 4 " 5
     1 " 2 " 5
     1 " 3 " 4 " 5
     1 " 4 " 5
     1 " 5
```

Thus, we can define the recurrence as follows:

- Base case:

  F(1) = 1 (We have reached the destination)

- Recurrence:

$$\sum_{i=1}^{n} F(i) = \sum_{j=1}^{i-1} F(j) \ \ if \ j + distance(j) \geq i$$

Figure 8.22: Formula for defining recurrence

In other words, the number of ways to reach a given location is equal to the sum of the number of ways to reach each location that connects to it. Using this logic, a recursive function for solving this problem might look like this:

```
F(n) -> number of ways to reach n'th location


F(i) =
    if i = N:
            return 1


        Otherwise:
            result = 0


            for j = 1 to distance[i]:
                result = result + F(i + j)
            return result
```

Now that we have a functional definition of the problem's states, let's begin implementing it in code.

1. For this problem, we will include the following headers and the **std** namespace:

   ```
   #include <iostream>
   #include <vector>
   #include <algorithm>
   using namespace std;
   ```

2. Because the outputs of this problem require the computation of numbers that exceed 32 bits, we will use **long long int** for the result. To avoid having to write this repeatedly, we will use a **typedef** statement to abbreviate it:

   ```
   typedef long long LL;
   ```

3. Finally, we will define the modulus value for outputting the results:

   ```
   const LL MOD = 1000000007;
   ```

Handling the input and output in this problem can be implemented very simply:

```cpp
int main()
{
    int n;
    cin >> n;

    vector<int> distance(n);

    for(int i = 0; i < n; i++)
    {
        cin >> distance[i];
    }

    LL result = TravelItinerary(n, distance);

    cout << result << endl;

    return 0;
}
```

4. We will now define a function called **TravelItinerary()** that takes **n** and **distance** as arguments and returns a long integer:

```cpp
LL TravelItinerary(int n, vector<int> distance)
{
    ...
}
```

5. Now, we must convert the recursive algorithm we presented earlier into a bottom-up approach. In pseudocode, this might appear as follows:

```
DP -> Array of size N + 1

DP[0] = 1 (There is one way to reach the starting location)

for i = 0 to N-1:

    for j = 1 to distance[i]:

        DP[i + j] += DP[i]

return DP[N]
```

6. To code this in C++, we will first declare a one-dimensional DP table of size **n +
   1** and initialize all of its elements to **0**. Then, we will set its first element to **1** to
   represent the base case:

```cpp
vector<LL> DP(n + 1, 0);

DP[0] = 1;
```

7. To implement the recurrence we described previously, we will first reverse the
   distance array so that we are essentially beginning our calculations from the
   destination index. There are several reasons for this, but the primary reason is so
   that our algorithm processes the current state by combining the results of earlier
   states, as opposed to calculating future states from the results of the current state.
   Though the logic described in the pseudocode will produce the correct result, it is
   generally preferable to formulate bottom-up logic in terms of how the solutions of
   the previous states form the result of the immediate state:

```cpp
reverse(distance.begin(), distance.end());

DP[0] = 1;

for(int i = 1; i <= n; i++)
{
    int dist = distance[i-1];

    for(int j = 1; j <= dist; j++)
    {
        DP[i] = (DP[i] + DP[i - j]) % MOD;
    }
}
return DP[n];
```

This is certainly a viable solution to the problem that will be completely
satisfactory in the vast majority of cases. However, since dynamic programming
is first and foremost an optimization technique, we should still ask ourselves if a
better approach exists.

Handling the Extra Credit Test Case

As both **n** and the maximum **distance** value increase, even the preceding algorithm will eventually prove to be rather inefficient. If **n** = **10000000** and the distance values can vary between 1 and 10000, then the inner **for** loop would have to perform nearly 100000000000 iterations in the worst case. Thankfully, there is a very simple technique that will allow us to completely remove the inner loop, which means we will have to perform exactly **n** iterations for any input.

To handle this reduction, we will create a **prefix sum array**, which will allow us to calculate the range sums we previously handled by the inner loop in constant time. If you are unfamiliar with this technique, the basic concept is as follows:

- Create an array called **sums** that has a length equal to the total number of values to sum plus one, with all the elements initialized to **0**.

- For each index **i** from **0** to **n**, use **sum[i + 1]** = **sum[i]** + **distance[i]**.

- After the sums have been calculated, the sum of all elements in any range **[L, R]** will be equal to **sum[R+1]** - **sum[L]**.

Take a look at the following example:

```
        0 1  2  3  4
A   =   { 3 1 10  2  5 }


          0 1 2  3  4  5
sums  =  { 0 3 4 14 16 21 }


range(1, 3) = A[1] + A[2] + A[3]
            = 1 + 10 + 2
            = 13
```

```
sums[4]  - sums[1] = 13
```

```
range(3, 4) = A[3] + A[4]
            = 2 + 5
            = 7
```

```
sums[5] - sums[3] = 7
```

8. We can implement this approach in our function as follows:

```
LL TravelItinerary(int n, vector<int> distance)
{
    vector<LL> DP(n + 1, 0);
    vector<LL> sums(n + 2, 0);

    DP[0] = sums[1] = 1;

    reverse(distance.begin(), distance.end());

    for(int i = 1; i <= n; i++)
    {
        int dist = distance[i-1];
        LL sum = sums[i] - sums[i - dist];

        DP[i] = (DP[i] + sum) % MOD;
        sums[i + 1] = (sums[i] + DP[i]) % MOD;
    }
    return DP[n];
}
```

9. Now, there is still one more problem that you are likely to encounter, and that is that the result returned by the preceding function will be negative. This is due to the fact that the modulo operations are causing higher-indexed values in **sums** to be less than lower-indexed values, which leads to a negative result when subtracting. This sort of issue can be very common in problems requiring frequent modulo operations on very large numbers, but can be easily fixed by modifying the return statement slightly:

```
return (DP[n] < 0) ? DP[n] + MOD : DP[n];
```

With these slight modifications, we now have an elegant and efficient solution to the problem that can handle massive input arrays in a fraction of a second!

Activity 19: Finding the Longest Common Subsequence by Using Memoization

1. As we did with the subset sum problem, we will include each new approach within the same code file so that we can compare their relative performance. To that end, let's define our **GetTime()** function in the same way as before:

```
vector<string> types =
{
    "BRUTE FORCE",
    "MEMOIZATION",
    "TABULATION"
};

const int UNKNOWN = INT_MAX;

void GetTime(clock_t &timer, string type)
{
    timer = clock() - timer;

    cout << "TIME TAKEN USING " << type << ": " << fixed << setprecision(5)
<< (float)timer / CLOCKS_PER_SEC << " SECONDS" << endl;

    timer = clock();
}
```

2. Now, let's define our new function, **LCS_Memoization()**, which will take the same arguments as **LCS_BruteForce()**, except that **subsequence** will instead be replaced by a reference to a two-dimensional integer vector, **memo**:

```
int LCS_Memoization(string A, string B, int i, int j, vector<vector<int>>
&memo)
{
    ......
}
```

3. Our code for this function will also be quite similar to **LCS_BruteForce()**, except we will invert the logic by recursively traversing the prefixes of the two strings (beginning with the complete strings) and storing the results in our memo table at each step:

```
// Base case - LCS is always zero for empty strings
if(i == 0 || j == 0)
{
    return 0;
}

// Have we found a result for the prefixes of the two strings?
if(memo[i - 1][j - 1] != UNKNOWN)
{
    // If so, return it
    return memo[i - 1][j - 1];
}

// Are the last characters of A's prefix and B's prefix equal?
if(A[i-1] == B[j-1])
{
    // LCS for this state is equal to 1 plus the LCS of the prefixes of A
and B, both reduced by one character
    memo[i-1][j-1] = 1 + LCS_Memoization(A, B, i-1, j-1, memo);

    // Return the cached result
    return memo[i-1][j-1];
}

// If the last characters are not equal, LCS for this state is equal to
the maximum LCS of A's prefix reduced by one character and B's prefix, and
B's prefix reduced by one character and A's prefix

memo[i-1][j-1] = max(LCS_Memoization(A, B, i-1, j, memo),
                     LCS_Memoization(A, B, i, j-1, memo));

return memo[i-1][j-1];
```

4. Now, let's redefine our **main()** function to perform both approaches and display the time taken by each:

```cpp
int main()
{
    string A, B;
    cin >> A >> B;

    int tests = 2;

    clock_t timer = clock();

    for(int i = 0; i < tests; i++)
    {
        int LCS;

        switch(i)
        {
            case 0:
            {
                LCS = LCS_BruteForce(A, B, 0, 0, {});

                #if DEBUG
                    PrintSubsequences(A, B);
                #endif
                break;
            }
            case 1:
            {
                vector<vector<int>> memo(A.size(), vector<int>(B.size(),
UNKNOWN));

                LCS = LCS_Memoization(A, B, A.size(), B.size(), memo);
                break;
            }

        }
        cout << "Length of the longest common subsequence of " << A << "
and " << B << " is: " << LCS << ends;
```

```
        GetTime(timer, types[i]);

        cout << endl;
    }
    return 0;
}
```

5. Now, let's try performing our two algorithms on two new strings, **ABCABDBEFBA** and **ABCBEFBEAB**. Your program's output should be similar to the following:

```
SIZE = 3
    ABC_____ ABC_____
SIZE = 4
    ABC_B_____ ABCB_____
    ABC_B_____ ABC___B___
    ABC_B_____ ABC_____B
    ABC___B____ ABC_____B
    ABC____E___ ABC____E__
    ABC_____B_ ABC___B___
    ABC_____B_ ABC_____B
    ABC_____A ABC_____A_
SIZE = 5
    ABCAB_____ ABC_____AB
    ABC_B_B____ ABCB_____B
    ABC_B__E___ ABCB___E__
    ABC_B____B_ ABCB__B___
    ABC_B____B_ ABCB_____B
    ABC_B_____A ABCB____A_
    ABC_B_B____ ABC___B__B
    ABC_B__E___ ABC___BE__
    ABC_B____B_ ABC___B__B
    ABC_B_____A ABC___B_A_
    ABC___BE___ ABC___BE__
    ABC____E_B_ ABC____E_B
    ABC____E__A ABC____EA_
    ABC_____FB_ ABC__FB___
    ABC_____BA ABC___B_A_
SIZE = 6
    ABC_B_BE___ ABCB__BE__
```

```
      ABC_B__E_B_ ABCB___E_B
      ABC_B__E__A ABCB___EA_
      ABC_B___FB_ ABCB_FB___
      ABC_B____BA ABCB__B_A_
      ABC_B__E_B_ ABC___BE_B
      ABC_B__E__A ABC___BEA_
      ABC___BE_B_ ABC___BE_B
      ABC___BE__A ABC___BEA_
      ABC____EFB_ ABC_EFB___
      ABC_____FBA ABC__FB_A_
   SIZE = 7
      ABC_B_BE_B_ ABCB__BE_B
      ABC_B_BE__A ABCB__BEA_
      ABC_B__EFB_ ABCBEFB___
      ABC_B___FBA ABCB_FB_A_
      ABC____EFBA ABC_EFB_A_
   SIZE = 8
      ABC_B__EFBA ABCBEFB_A_
Length of the longest common subsequence of ABCABDBEFBA and ABCBEFBEAB is:
8
TIME TAKEN USING BRUTE FORCE: 0.00242 SECONDS

Length of the longest common subsequence of ABCABDBEFBA and ABCBEFBEAB is:
8
TIME TAKEN USING MEMOIZATION: 0.00003 SECONDS
```

6. Of course, the time taken by the brute-force approach is going to be affected by the additional step of printing out the subsequences. By running our code again after setting the **DEBUG** constant to **0**, the output is now as follows:

```
Length of the longest common subsequence of ABCABDBEFBA and ABCBEFBEAB is:
8
TIME TAKEN USING BRUTE FORCE: 0.00055 SECONDS

Length of the longest common subsequence of ABCABDBEFBA and ABCBEFBEAB is:
8
TIME TAKEN USING MEMOIZATION: 0.00002 SECONDS
```

7. Now, let's try pushing the limits of our algorithm using two much larger strings, **ABZCYDABAZADAEA** and **YABAZADBBEAAECYACAZ**. You should get an output something like this:

```
Length of the longest common subsequence of ABZCYDABAZADAEA and
YABAZADBBEAAECYACAZ is: 10
TIME TAKEN USING BRUTE FORCE: 8.47842 SECONDS

Length of the longest common subsequence of ABZCYDABAZADAEA and
YABAZADBBEAAECYACAZ is: 10
TIME TAKEN USING MEMOIZATION: 0.00008 SECONDS
```

> **Note**
>
> The actual values for the time taken will vary depending on your system. Please note the difference in the values.

As we can clearly see, the gains in performance provided by memoization are quite significant!

Activity 20: Finding the Longest Common Subsequence Using Tabulation

As we did previously, we will add a new function, `LCS_Tabulation()`, to the same code file that contains our brute-force and memoized solutions.

1. Our `LCS_Tabulation()` function receives two arguments– strings **A** and **B** – and returns a string:

```
string LCS_Tabulation(string A, string B)
{
    ......
}
```

2. Our first step is to define our DP table, which we will represent as a two-dimensional vector of integers, with the first dimension's size equal to one greater than the size of string **A**, and the second dimension's size equal to one greater than the size of string **B**:

```
vector<vector<int>> DP(A.size() + 1, vector<int>(B.size() + 1));
```

3. Like the subset sum problem, all of our algorithm's logic can be contained within two nested loops, with the first one iterating from **0** to the size of **A**, and the second iterating from **0** to the size of **B**:

```
for(int i = 0; i <= A.size(); i++)
{
    for(int j = 0; j <= B.size(); j++)
    {
        ......
    }
}
```

4. Unlike the subset sum problem, our base case will not be handled prior to the execution of the loops, but rather at the beginning of each loop. This is because our base case will occur any time the prefix of **A** or **B** is empty (that is, **i** = **0** or **j** = **0**). This is represented in our code as follows:

```
if(i == 0 || j == 0)
{
    DP[i][j] = 0;
}
```

5. Now, we must handle the case where the characters at the end of A's prefix and B's prefix are equal. Remember that the LCS value for this state is always equal to **1**, plus the LCS value of the state where both prefixes are one character smaller than they are currently. This can be represented as follows:

```
else if(A[i-1] == B[j-1])
{
    DP[i][j] = DP[i-1][j-1] + 1;
}
```

6. For the final case, the end characters are *not* equal. For this state, we know that the LCS is equal to the maximum of the LCS of A's previous prefix and B's current prefix, and the LCS of B's previous prefix and A's current prefix. In terms of our table's structure, this is equivalent to saying that the LCS is equal to the maximum of the value contained in the same column and previous row of the table, and the value contained in the same row and previous column:

```
else
{
    DP[i][j] = max(DP[i-1][j], DP[i][j-1]);
}
```

7. When we are done, the length of the longest common subsequence will be contained in **DP[A.size()][B.size()]** – the value of the LCS when the prefixes of both **A** and **B** are equal to the entire strings. Therefore, our complete DP logic is written as follows:

```
string LCS_Tabulation(string A, string B)
{
    vector<vector<int>> DP(A.size() + 1, vector<int>(B.size() + 1));

    for(int i = 0; i <= A.size(); i++)
    {
        for(int j = 0; j <= B.size(); j++)
        {
            if(i == 0 || j == 0)
            {
                DP[i][j] = 0;
            }
            else if(A[i-1] == B[j-1])
            {
                DP[i][j] = DP[i-1][j-1] + 1;
            }
            else
            {
                DP[i][j] = max(DP[i-1][j], DP[i][j-1]);
            }
        }
    }

    int length = DP[A.size()][B.size()];
    ......
}
```

At this point, we have discussed several ways to find the length of the longest common subsequence, but what if we also want to output its actual characters? Of course, our brute-force solution does this, but very inefficiently; however, using the results contained in the preceding DP table, we can use backtracking to reconstruct the LCS quite easily. Let's highlight the path we would need to follow in the table to accomplish this:

	""	A	B	C	B	E	F	B	E	A	B
""	0	0	0	0	0	0	0	0	0	0	0
A	0	1	1	1	1	1	1	1	1	1	1
B	0	1	2	2	2	2	2	2	2	2	2
C	0	1	2	3	3	3	3	3	3	3	3
A	0	1	2	3	3	3	3	3	3	4	4
B	0	1	2	3	4	4	4	4	4	4	5
D	0	1	2	3	4	4	4	4	4	4	5
B	0	1	2	3	4	4	4	5	5	5	5
E	0	1	2	3	4	5	5	5	6	6	6
F	0	1	2	3	4	5	6	6	6	6	6
B	0	1	2	3	4	5	6	7	7	7	7
A	0	1	2	3	4	5	6	7	7	8	8

Figure 8.23: Activity 20 DP table

By collecting the characters associated with each column in the path where the value increases, we get the LCS **ABCBEFBA**.

8. Let's define a function called **ReconstructLCS()** that takes **A**, **B**, **i**, **j**, and **DP** as arguments. Our backtracking logic can be defined as follows:

```
if i = 0 or j = 0:
    Return an empty string

If the characters at the end of A's prefix and B's prefix are equal:
    Return the LCS of the next smaller prefix of both A and B, plus the
equal character

Otherwise:
    If the value of DP(i - 1, j) is greater than the value of DP(i, j -
1):
        - Return the LCS of A's next smaller prefix with B's current prefix
        - Otherwise:
            Return the LCS of B's next smaller prefix with A's current prefix
```

In C++, this can be coded as follows:

```cpp
string ReconstructLCS(vector<vector<int>> &DP, string &A, string &B, int
i, int j)
{
    if(i == 0 || j == 0)
    {
        return "";
    }

    if(A[i-1] == B[j-1])
    {
        return ReconstructLCS(DP, A, B, i-1, j-1) + A[i-1];
    }
    else if(DP[i-1][j] > DP[i][j-1])
    {
        return ReconstructLCS(DP, A, B, i-1, j);
    }
    else
    {
        return ReconstructLCS(DP, A, B, i, j-1);
    }
}
```

9. Now, we can return the result of **ReconstructLCS()** in the final line of **LCS_Tabulation()**:

```cpp
string LCS_Tabulation(string A, string B)
{
    ......

    string lcs = ReconstructLCS(DP, A, B, A.size(), B.size());

    return lcs;
}
```

10. Our code in **main()** should now be modified to accommodate the addition of **LCS_Tabulation()**:

```cpp
int main()
{
    string A, B;
    cin >> A >> B;
```

```
    int tests = 3;

    clock_t timer = clock();

    for(int i = 0; i < tests; i++)
    {
        int LCS;

        switch(i)
        {
            ......

            case 2:
            {
                string lcs = LCS_Tabulation(A, B);

                LCS = lcs.size();

                cout << "The longest common subsequence of " << A << " and
" << B << " is: " << lcs << endl;

                break;
            }
        }
        cout << "Length of the longest common subsequence of " << A << "
and " << B << " is: " << LCS << endl;

        GetTime(timer, types[i]);
    }
    return 0;
}
```

11. Using the strings **ABCABDBEFBA** and **ABCBEFBEAB**, your program's output should be similar to this:

```
Length of the longest common subsequence of ABCABDBEFBA and ABCBEFBEAB is:
8
TIME TAKEN USING BRUTE FORCE: 0.00060 SECONDS

Length of the longest common subsequence of ABCABDBEFBA and ABCBEFBEAB is:
8
TIME TAKEN USING MEMOIZATION: 0.00005 SECONDS
```

```
The longest common subsequence of ABCABDBEFBA and ABCBEFBEAB is: ABCBEFBA
Length of the longest common subsequence of ABCABDBEFBA and ABCBEFBEAB is:
8
TIME TAKEN USING TABULATION: 0.00009 SECONDS
```

Note

The actual values for the time taken will vary depending on your system. Please note the difference in the values.

Now, we have looked at another detailed example of how the same logic can be applied to the same problem using different techniques and the corresponding effect this has on the execution time of the algorithm.

Activity 21: Melodic Permutations

The first question to ask ourselves is: what constitutes a single state in this problem?

Base case --> Empty set:

1. Consider each note in the melody.
2. For each subset of notes that was previously encountered, either append the current note or do nothing.
3. If the subset matches the target, add it to the solutions.

Given that our options are to either append a note to a previous subset or leave it as-is, we could restate the logic as follows:

For a given note in the melody, the count of subsets of size | n | containing the note is equal to the total count of all subsets of size | n - 1 | that did not contain the note.

So, each state can be expressed in two dimensions:

- **Dimension 1**: The length of the melody considered so far.
- **Dimension 2**: The resulting subset formed by taking a previously found subset and either appending the note located at index `[length - 1]` of the melody to it or doing nothing.

In pseudocode, the logic could be expressed as follows:

```
for i = 1 to length of melody (inclusive):

        for each subset previously found:
        DP(i, subset) = DP(i, subset) + DP(i - 1, subset)
        DP(i, subset U melody[i - 1]) = DP(i, subset U melody[i - 1]) + DP(i -
1, subset)
```

So, the primary question now is, how can we represent these states?

Remember that for an n-element collection, there are a total of 2^n subsets comprising it – for example, a set of 4 elements can be divided into a total of 2^4 (or 16) subsets:

```
S = { A, B, C, D }


{ }                 ->          { _ _ _ _ }


{ A }               ->          { # _ _ _ }
{ B }               ->          { _ # _ _ }
{ C }               ->          { _ _ #_  }
{ D }               ->          { _ _ _ # }


{ A, B }            ->          { # # _ _ }
{ A, C }            ->          { # _ #_  }
{ A, D }            ->          { # _ _ # }
{ B, C }            ->          { _ # #_  }
{ B, D }            ->          { _ # _ # }
{ C, D }            ->          { _ _ # # }


{ A, B, C }         ->          { # # # _ }
{ A, B, D }         ->          { # # _ # }
{ A, C, D }         ->          { # _ # # }
{ B, C, D }         ->          { _ # # # }


{ A, B, C, D } ->               { # # # # }
```

If we iterate from 0 to (2^4 - 1) inclusive in binary, we get the following numbers:

```
0     ->    0000    ->    { _ _ _ _ }
1     ->    0001    ->    { # _ _ _ }
2     ->    0010    ->    { _ # _ _ }
3     ->    0011    ->    { # # _ _ }
4     ->    0100    ->    { _ _ # _ }
5     ->    0101    ->    { # _ # _ }
6     ->    0110    ->    { _ # # _ }
7     ->    0111    ->    { # # # _ }
8     ->    1000    ->    { _ _ _ # }
9     ->    1001    ->    { # _ _ # }
10    ->    1010    ->    { _ # _ # }
11    ->    1011    ->    { # # _ # }
12    ->    1100    ->    { _ _ # # }
13    ->    1101    ->    { # _ # # }
14    ->    1110    ->    { _ # # # }
15    ->    1111    ->    { # # # # }
```

As we can see, the digits of each binary number from 0 to 2^n correspond exactly to the indices of one possible subset of n elements. Since there are 12 notes in the scale, this means there is a total of 2^{12} (or 4,096) possible subsets of notes. By mapping each note in the scale to a power of 2, we can use bitwise arithmetic to represent the subsets encountered across each state.

The following are the steps to solve this activity:

1. Moving on to the code, we should begin by including the following headers:

```cpp
#include <iostream>
#include <vector>
#include <string>
#include <map>

using namespace std;
```

2. Let's start by handling the input in our **main()** function:

```
int main()
{
    int melodyLength;
    int setLength;

    cin >> melodyLength;

    vector<string> melody(melodyLength);

    for(int i = 0; i < melodyLength; i++)
    {
        cin >> melody[i];
    }

    cin >> setLength;

    vector<string> set(setLength);

    for(int i = 0; i < setLength; i++)
    {
        cin >> set[i];
    }

    ......

}
```

3. Now, let's write a function called **ConvertNotes()**,that receives a vector of note strings as input and returns a vector of their corresponding integer values. Each of the 12 total notes in the scale will need to be mapped to a particular bit (beginning with **A**), with enharmonically equivalent notes assigned to identical values. We will use **std::map** to handle the conversions:

```
vector<int> ConvertNotes(vector<string> notes)
{
    map<string, int> M =
    {
        { "A",  0 },
        { "A#", 1 },
        { "Bb", 1 },
        { "B",  2 },
        { "Cb", 2 },
```

```
        { "B#", 3 },
        { "C",  3 },
        { "C#", 4 },
        { "Db", 4 },
        { "D",  5 },
        { "D#", 6 },
        { "Eb", 6 },
        { "E",  7 },
        { "Fb", 7 },
        { "E#", 8 },
        { "F",  8 },
        { "F#", 9 },
        { "Gb", 9 },
        { "G",  10 },
        { "G#", 11 },
        { "Ab", 11 }
    };

    vector<int> converted;

    for(auto note : notes)
    {
        // Map to powers of 2
        converted.push_back(1 << M[note]);
    }
    return converted;
}
```

4. Now, we will define a function called **CountMelodicPermutations()** that takes two integer vectors, **melody** and **set**, as arguments and returns an integer:

```
int CountMelodicPermutations(vector<int> melody, vector<int> set)
{
    ......
}
```

5. Our first step is to define our target subset. We will do this using the bitwise or operator:

```
unsigned int target = 0;

for(auto note : set)
{
    target |= note;
}
```

6. As an example, if our target set is **{ C, F#, A }**, the mapping would look like this:

```
C  = 3
F# = 9
A  = 0

converted = { 23, 29, 20 } = { 8, 512, 1 }

target = (8 | 512 | 1) = 521

  0000001000
+ 0000000001
+ 1000000000
= 1000001001
```

7. We will now define a two-dimensional DP table, with the first dimension initialized to **melodyLength + 1**, and the second dimension initialized to one greater than the maximum subset value (that is, **111111111111 = 2^{12} - 1**, so the second dimension will contain 2^{12}, or 4,096, elements):

```
vector<vector<int>> DP(melody.size() + 1, vector<int>(4096, 0));
```

8. Our DP formula can be defined as follows:

```
Base case:

    DP(0, 0) -> 1

Recurrence:

    DP(i, subset) -> DP(i, subset) + DP(i - 1, subset)
    DP(i, subset ∪ note[i-1]) -> DP(i, subset ∪ note[i]) + DP(i - 1,
    subset)
```

Here, **i** ranges from **1** to the length of the melody. We can write the preceding logic in C++ like this:

```cpp
// Base case -> empty set
DP[0][0] = 1;

for(int i = 1; i <= melody.size(); i++)
{
    for(unsigned int subset = 0; subset < 4096; subset++)
    {
        // Keep results for previous values of i
        DP[i][subset] += DP[i-1][subset];

        // Add results for union of subset with melody[i-1]
        DP[i][subset | melody[i-1]] += DP[i-1][subset];
    }
}

// Solution
return DP[melody.size()][target];
```

9. Now, we can finish our **main()** function by calling **CountMelodicPermutations** and outputting the result:

```cpp
int count = CountMelodicPermutations(ConvertNotes(melody),
ConvertNotes(set));

cout << count << endl;
```

Chapter 9: Dynamic Programming II

Activity 22: Maximizing Profit

In this activity, we will optimize our inventory for sale to maximize our profits. Follow these steps to complete the activity:

1. Let's begin by including the following headers:

    ```
    #include <iostream>
    #include <vector>
    using namespace std;
    ```

2. First, we will define a structure, **Product**, that encapsulates the data associated with each item:

    ```
    struct Product
    {
        int quantity;
        int price;
        int value;

        Product(int q, int p, int v)
            : quantity(q), price(p), value(v) {}
    };
    ```

3. Next, we will handle the input in the **main()** function and populate an array of the **Product** type:

    ```
    int main()
    {
        int N, budget, capacity;
        cin >> N >> budget >> capacity;

        vector<Product> products;

        for(int i = 0; i < N; i++)
        {
            int quantity, cost, value;
            cin >> quantity >> cost >> value;
    ```

```
            products.push_back(Product(quantity, cost, value));
        }
    ...

    return 0;
    }
```

4. As with any DP algorithm, we must now define the states and base cases. We know that the subset of items that form the final result must match the following criteria:

   - The sum of the **cost** of all the products in the subset must not exceed **budget**.

   - The sum of the **quantity** of all the products in the subset must not exceed **capacity**.

   - The sum of the **value** of all the products in the subset must be maximized.

   Given these criteria, we can see that each state can be defined by the following parameters:

   - The current item being considered

   - The number of units previously purchased

   - The total cost of the purchased items

   - The total profit gained after selling the products at retail value

   We can also conclude that a search will terminate when:

   - All the items have been considered

   - The total cost exceeds the budget

   - The total number of units exceeds the capacity

   Like the traditional 0-1 knapsack problem, we will consider each item from **0** to **N-1** linearly. For each item at index **i**, our states can transition in one of two ways: by either including the current item or leaving it. Writing the recursive logic in pseudocode may look like this:

   ```
   F(i, count, cost, total):


   I          -> The index of the current item
   Cost       -> The total money spent
   count      -> The number of units purchased
   total      -> The total profit value of the chosen items
   ```

Base cases:

```
if i = N: return total
if cost > budget: return 0
if count > capacity: return 0
```

Recurrence:

```
F(i, count, cost, total) = maximum of:

F(i + 1, count + quantity[i], cost + price[i],
      total + value[i]) - Include the item

    AND

    F(i + 1, count, cost, total) - Leave as-is
```

As shown in the preceding code, the recurrence relation is defined according to the values of **i**, **count**, **cost**, and **total**. Converting this logic from top down to bottom up can be done like so:

Base case:

```
DP(0, 0, 0) = 0 [Nothing has been chosen yet]
```

For i = 1 to N:

```
Product -> quantity, price, value

For cost = 0 to budget:

    For count = 0 to capacity:

        If price is greater than cost OR
        quantity is greater than count:

            DP(i, cost, count) = DP(i-1, cost, count)

        Otherwise:
```

```
DP(i, cost, count) = maximum of:

    DP(i-1, cost, count)
            AND
    DP(i-1, cost - price, count - quantity) + value
```

In other words, each state is described according to the current index, total cost, and total count. For each pair of valid **cost** and **count** values, the current result for an item at index **i** will be equal either to the maximum subset sum that was found for the same values of **cost** and **count** at index **i** - 1 (that is, **DP[i - 1][cost] [count]**) or the sum of the current item's **value** with the maximum sum at index **i** - 1 with **cost** and **count** equal to what they would have been prior to including the item (that is, **DP[i - 1][cost - price][count - quantity] + value**).

5. We can code the preceding logic as follows:

```
vector<vector<vector<int>>> DP(N + 1, vector<vector<int>>(budget + 1,
vector<int>(capacity + 1, 0)));

for(int i = 1; i <= N; i++)
{
    Product product = products[i-1];

for(int cost = 0; cost <= budget; cost++)
{
        for(int count = 0; count <= capacity; count++)
        {
            if(cost < product.price || count < product.quantity)
            {
                DP[i][cost][count] = DP[i-1][cost][count];
            }
            else
            {
                DP[i][cost][count] = max
                (
                    DP[i-1][cost][count],
                    DP[i-1][cost - product.price][count - product.
quantity] + product.value
                );
            }
```

```
            }
        }
        cout << DP[N][budget][capacity] << endl;
    }
```

As you can see, the implementation is equivalent to the 0-1 knapsack solution with an additional dimension.

Activity 23: Residential Roads

This activity has quite a few potential pitfalls if you do not approach it with some forethought. The most difficult aspect of it is the fact that it requires a number of distinct steps, and a careless mistake at any point can cause the entire program to fail. Therefore, it is recommended to approach the implementation step by step. The primary steps that are required are as follows:

1. Handling the input

2. Building the graph (finding adjacencies and weight values)

3. Finding the shortest distances between graph nodes

4. Reconstructing the edges in the shortest paths

5. Redrawing the input grid

Since this is considerably lengthier than the other activities in this chapter, let's attack each of these steps individually.

Step 0: Preliminary Setup

Before we write any code related to input, we should decide how we want to represent our data in advance. The input we will receive is as follows:

- Two integers, H and W, representing the height and width of the grid.

- An integer, N, representing the number of houses contained on the property.

- H strings of width W representing the map of the property. We can store this data as an H-element vector of strings.

- H rows of W integers representing the ruggedness of the terrain. We can store these values in an integer matrix.

- N lines containing two integers, x and y, representing the coordinates of each house. For this, we can create a simple structure called **Point** containing two integers, x and y.

Now, let's look at the implementation:

1. Include the required headers and define some global constants and variables that we will need later in this problem. We will declare most of our data globally for the sake of convenience, but it is worth reiterating the point that this is generally considered bad practice within the context of a full-scale application:

```cpp
#include <iostream>
#include <vector>
using namespace std;

const int UNKNOWN = 1e9;
const char EMPTY_SPACE = '.';
const string roads = "-|/\\";

struct Point
{
    int x;
    int y;

    Point(){}
    Point(int x, int y) : x(x), y(y) {}
};

int N;
int H, W;

vector<string> grid;
vector<vector<int>> terrain;
vector<vector<int>> cost;
vector<Point> houses;
```

Step 1: Handling the Input

2. Since there is a fair amount of input required for this problem, let's contain it all in its own function, **Input()**, which will return void:

```cpp
void Input()
{
    cin >> H >> W;
    cin >> N;

    grid.resize(H);
    houses.resize(N);
```

```
        terrain.resize(H, vector<int>(W, UNKNOWN));    cost.resize(H,
    vector<int>(W, UNKNOWN));

        // Map of property
        for(auto &row : grid) cin >> row;

        // Terrain ruggedness
        for(int I = 0; i < H; i++)
        {
            for(int j = 0; j < W; j++)
            {
                cin >> terrain[i][j];
            }
        }

        // House coordinates
        for(int i = 0; i < N; i++)
        {
            cin >> houses[i].x >> house[i].y;

            // Set house labels in grid
            grid[houses[i].y][houses[i].x] = char(i + 'A');
        }
    }
```

Step 2: Building the Graph

The problem description states the following:

- A road can be built between two houses if and only if there is a direct horizontal, vertical, or diagonal path between them.

- Roads may not be built across bodies of water, mountains, forests, and so on.

- The cost of building a road between two houses is equal to the sum of ruggedness values on the path between them.

To test the first condition, we simply need to compare the coordinates of two points and determine whether any of the following three conditions are true:

- $A.x = B.x$ (there is a horizontal line between them)

- $A.y = B.y$ (there is a vertical line between them)

- $| A.x - B.x | = | A.y - B.y |$ (there is a diagonal line between them)

Now, let's get back to our code.

3. To do this, let's write a function **DirectLine()**, that takes two points, **a** and **b**, as arguments and returns a Boolean:

```
bool DirectLine(Point a, Point b)
{
    return a.x == b.x || a.y == b.y || abs(a.x - b.x) == abs(a.y - b.y);
}
```

4. To handle the second and third cases, we can simply perform a linear traversal from point **a** to point **b** in the grid. As we consider each point in the grid, we can accumulate the sum of values contained in the terrain matrix. As we do this, we can simultaneously check the character in **grid[a.y][a.x]**, terminating it as soon as we encounter a character that is not equal to **EMPTY_SPACE** (that is, '.'). If at the end of the traversal point **a** is equal to point **b**, we will store the sum we acquired in the **cost** matrix; otherwise, we have determined that there is no adjacency between **a** and **b**, in which case we return **UNKNOWN**. We can do this using the **GetCost()** function, which takes two integers, **start** and **end**, as arguments. These represent the indices of **a** and **b**, respectively, and return an integer:

```
int GetCost(int start, int end)
{
    Point a = houses[start];
    Point b = houses[end];

    // The values by which the coordinates change on each iteration
    int x_dir = 0;
    int y_dir = 0;

    if(a.x != b.x)
    {
        x_dir = (a.x < b.x) ? 1 : -1;
    }
    if(a.y != b.y)
    {
        y_dir = (a.y < b.y) ? 1 : -1;
    }
    int cost = 0;
```

```
        do
        {
            a.x += x_dir;
            a.y += y_dir;

            cost += terrain[a.y][a.x];
        }
        while(grid[a.y][a.x] == '.');

        return (a != b) ? UNKNOWN : res;
    }
```

5. The final line requires that we define **operator !=** in our **Point** struct:

```
    struct Point
    {
        . . . . . .

        bool operator !=(const Point &other) const { return x != other.x || y
    != other.y; }
    }
```

6. Now, let's create the following **GetAdjacencies()** function:

```
    void GetAdjacencies()
    {
        for(int i = 0; i < N; i++)
        {
            for(int j = 0; j < N; j++)
            {
                if(DirectLine(houses[i], houses[j])
                {
                    cost[i][j] = cost[j][i] = GetCost(i, j);
                }
            }
        }
    }
```

Step 3: Finding the Shortest Distances between Nodes

The problem states that two houses should be connected by a road that is on the path that minimizes the cost of reaching the exit point. For this implementation, we will use the Floyd-Warshall algorithm. Let's get back to our code:

7. Let's define a function, **GetShortestPaths()**, that will handle both the implementation of Floyd-Warshall as well as the path's reconstruction. To handle the latter case, we will maintain a N x N integer matrix called **next** that will store the index of the next point on the shortest path from nodes **a** and **b**. Initially, its values will be set to the existing edges in the graph:

```
void GetShortestPaths()
{
    vector<vector<int>> dist(N, vector<int>(N, UNKNOWN));
    vector<vector<int>> next(N, vector<int>(N, UNKNOWN));

    for(int i = 0; i < N; i++)
    {
        for(int j = 0; j < N; j++)
        {
            dist[i][j] = cost[i][j]

            if(dist[i][j] != UNKNOWN)
            {
                next[i][j] = j;
            }
        }
        dist[i][j] = 0;
        next[i][i] = i;
    }
    ...
}
```

8. We will then perform the standard implementation of Floyd-Warshall, with one additional line in the innermost loop setting **next[start][end]** to **next[start][mid]** every time we find a shorter distance between **start** and **end**:

```
for(int mid = 0; mid < N; mid++)
{
    for(int start = 0; start < N; start++)
    {
        for(int end = 0; end < N; end++)
        {
```

```
            if(dist[start][end] > dist[start][mid] + dist[mid][end])
            {
                dist[start][end] = dist[start][mid] + dist[mid][end];
                next[start][end] = next[start][mid];
            }
        }
    }
}
```

Step 4: Reconstructing the Path

With the data that we obtained in the **next** matrix, we can easily reconstruct the points on each path in a similar way to the reconstruction approaches for the LCS or 0-1 Knapsack problems. For this purpose, we will define another function, **GetPath()**, that has three parameters–two integers, **start** and **end**, and a reference to the **next** matrix – and returns an integer vector containing the node indices of the path:

```
vector<int> GetPath(int start, int end, vector<vector<int>> &next)
{
    vector<int> path = { start };

    do
    {
        start = next[start][end];

        path.push_back(start);
    }
    while(next[start][end] != end);

    return path;
}
```

9. Returning to **GetShortestPaths()**, we will now add a loop underneath our implementation of Floyd-Warshall that calls **GetPath()** and then draws lines in the grid corresponding to each pair of points in the path:

```
for(int i = 0; i < N; i++)
{
    auto path = GetPath(i, N - 1, next);

    int curr = i;

    for(auto neighbor : path)
    {
        DrawPath(curr, neighbor);
```

```
                curr = neighbor;
        }
    }
```

Step 5: Redrawing the Grid

10. Now, we must draw the roads in the grid. We will do this in another function, **Draw-Path()**, which has the **start** and **end** parameters:

```
void DrawPath(int start, int end)
{
    Point a = houses[start];
    Point b = houses[end];

    int x_dir = 0;
    int y_dir = 0;

    if(a.x != b.x)
    {
        x_dir = (a.x < b.x) 1 : -1;
    }
    if(a.y != b.y)
    {
        y_dir = (a.y < b.y) 1 : -1;
    }

    ......
}
```

11. We will need to choose the correct character corresponding to the orientation of each road. To do this, we will define a function, **GetDirection()**, that returns an integer corresponding to an index in the **roads** string we defined at the beginning ("-|/\"):

```
int GetDirection(int x_dir, int y_dir)
{
    if(y_dir == 0) return 0;
    if(x_dir == 0) return 1;
    if(x_dir == -1)
    {
        return (y_dir == 1) ? 2 : 3;
    }
}
```

```
        return (y_dir == 1) ? 3 : 2;
    }


    void DrawPath(int start, int end)
    {
        ......

        int direction = GetDirection(x_dir, y_dir);

        char mark = roads[direction];


            ......
    }
```

12. We can now perform a linear traversal from **a** to **b**, setting each cell in the grid to **mark** if its value is **EMPTY_SPACE**. Otherwise, we must check to see whether the character in the cell is a road character of a different orientation, in which case we set it to **+**:

```
    do
    {
        a.x += x_dir;
        a.y += y_dir;

        if(grid[a.y][a.x] == EMPTY_SPACE)
        {
            grid[a.y][a.x] = mark;
        }
        else if(!isalpha(grid[a.y][a.x]))
        {
                // If two roads of differing orientations intersect, replace
    symbol with '+'

                grid[a.y][a.x] = (mark != grid[a.y][a.x]) ? '+' : mark;
        }
    }
    while(a != b);
```

13. All that is left is to call our functions in **main()** and print the output:

```
int main()
{
        Input();
        BuildGraph();
        GetShortestPaths();

        for(auto it : grid)
        {
            cout << it << endl;
        }
        return 0;
}
```

Index

About

All major keywords used in this book are captured alphabetically in this section. Each one is accompanied by the page number of where they appear.

A

abstract: 80, 345-346, 350
accessor:13
accessors: 11, 35
ackermann:227
activity: 24, 39, 44-45,
  52-53, 80, 88, 133,
  139-140, 152-154,
  166-167, 184, 189-190,
  192, 207-209, 236,
  238-239, 266-267, 270,
  290-291, 304, 307-311,
  322, 324-325, 335,
  337-340, 342-344, 385,
  388-389, 403-404,
  406-408, 412, 444,
  446-447, 468, 470-472
address: 3, 7, 11, 43,
  46, 118, 139-140
adjacency: 90-91, 94, 98,
  280, 330-332, 334,
  344-345, 455, 457, 462
algorithm: 12, 20, 34, 51,
  85, 88, 94, 109, 127,
  133, 139-140, 143-148,
  152-153, 155-157, 159,
  161-162, 164, 167-168,
  170, 172-173, 176, 178,
  180, 189, 193, 195-196,
  198, 203, 210-214,
  216-217, 219-220, 225,
  227, 229, 232-233,
  235-236, 240, 243-245,
  249, 252, 257-259,
  263, 267-271, 273, 277,
  279-283, 287-291,
  293-298, 300-301, 304,
  311-312, 314, 316-320,
  323, 329-330, 332-334,
  344-345, 350, 361, 364,
  366, 370, 373, 377, 386,
  389, 398, 404-405,
  423-424, 426, 428,
  431, 434, 438-439, 441,
  443, 448-451, 455, 457,
  460-462, 464, 467
algorithms: 2, 51, 98, 102,
  133, 143-145, 154-156,
  160, 166-168, 176, 178,
  193, 195, 197, 210, 240,
  243-246, 265-266,
  270, 280, 293-294, 311,
  345-346, 349, 413, 415,
  418, 422, 424, 447-448,
  451, 460, 470, 473
allocate: 20, 23, 46, 235
allocated: 3-4, 20
allocation: 7, 19, 23-24
allocator: 23-24, 40, 48
allocators: 23, 48
allotted: 355, 444
allowance:441
all-pairs: 322, 451, 460
amortized:118
appending: 113, 359, 379
applicable: 145, 197,
  240, 244, 294
applicants:322
approaches: 101, 108, 145,
  195, 197, 344, 346, 350,
  356, 360, 372, 377-378,
  385, 392, 403, 415-416
arbitrary: 79, 162, 167,
  235, 258, 297
archetypal:413
argument: 7-8, 21, 182,
  298, 381, 456
arguments: 17, 22, 315,
  317-318, 330-332,
  361, 398, 462
arithmetic: 10, 31
array-like: 12, 24
arrays: 3-4, 6-9, 11, 18-19,
  24, 31, 46, 57, 88,
  127, 146, 151, 155-156,
  158-159, 162, 165, 167,
  317, 344, 350, 369,
  373-374, 378, 426
ascending:76
assign: 89, 228, 236,
  259, 267, 463
assigned: 11, 232-233,
  236, 238, 252, 267-269,
  277, 355, 418
assignment: 11, 48,
  56, 416, 442
associated: 178, 210,
  244, 270, 280, 328,
  335-336, 425, 447, 460
asymptotic: 4, 166,
  176, 296, 330
automata:245
automate:322
average: 20, 23, 48, 51,
  113, 197-199, 323, 373
aviation:90

B

backtrack:304
backward: 24, 31, 40,
  43-44, 53, 56
balanced: 71, 76,
  78-79, 336
banknotes: 357-358
benchmark: 130, 148, 345
benchmarks: 52, 148, 151
bilateral:89
billion:103
billions: 102, 139
binary: 29-30, 59, 63,
  66-69, 71, 77, 79,
  145-155, 280, 290,
  393, 418, 422
biomedical:88